EVERYDAY ANTIRACISM

EVERYDAY ANTIRACISM

Getting Real About Race in School

EDITED BY MICA POLLOCK

THE NEW PRESS

NEW YORK
LONDON

Requests for permission to reproduce selections from this book should be mailed to:
Permissions Department, The New Press, 120 Wall Street, 31st floor, New York, NY 10005

Published in the United States by The New Press, New York, 2008
Distributed by Two Rivers Distribution

ISBN 978-1-59558-567-7 (e-book)

LIBRARY OF CONGRESS CATALOGING-IN-PUBLICATION DATA

Everyday antiracism : getting real about race in school/ edited by Mica Pollock.
p. cm.
Includes bibliographical references and index.
ISBN 978-1-59558-054-2 (pbk.)
1. Racism in education—United States. 2. Educational equalization—United
States.   I. Pollock, Mica.
LC212.2.E94 2008
371.82900973—dc22   2008000843

The New Press publishes books that promote and enrich public discussion and understanding of the issues vital to our democracy and to a more equitable world. These books
are made possible by the enthusiasm of our readers; the support of a committed group of
donors, large and small; the collaboration of our many partners in the independent media
and the not-for-profit sector; booksellers, who often hand-sell New Press books; librarians;
and above all by our authors.

www.thenewpress.com

Book design by Westchester Book Group
Composition by Westchester Book Group
This book was set in 10/13 New Caledonia Roman

Printed in the United States of America

19 18

Contents

Acknowledgments   xi
Suggestions for Using This Book   xiii
Introduction: Defining Everyday Antiracism   xvii

SECTION A

RACE CATEGORIES: WE ARE ALL THE SAME,
BUT OUR LIVES ARE DIFFERENT   1

Part I: Remember That Racial Categories Are
         Not Biological Realities   3

1. *Exposing Race as an Obsolete Biological Concept*
   Alan H. Goodman   4
2. *No Brain Is Racial*
   Mica Pollock   9
3. *Getting Rid of the Word "Caucasian"*
   Carol C. Mukhopadhyay   12

Part II: Get Ready to Talk about a Racialized Society   17

4. *Beginning Courageous Conversations about Race*
   Glenn E. Singleton and Cyndie Hays   18
5. *Talking Precisely about Equal Opportunity*
   Mica Pollock   24
6. *Nice Is Not Enough: Defining Caring for Students of Color*
   Sonia Nieto   28

Part III: Remember That People Do Not Fit Neatly and
           Easily into Racial Groups   33

7. *Following Children's Leads in Conversations about Race*
   Kimberly Chang and Rachel Conrad   34
8. *Observing Students Sharing Language*
   Ben Rampton   39

Part IV: Remember That People Are Treated as Racial Group
          Members and Need to Examine That Experience   43

9. *Strengthening Student Identity in School Programs*
   Patricia Gándara   44

10. *Uncovering Internalized Oppression*
    Angela Valenzuela   50
11. *Helping Students See Each Other's Humanity*
    L. Janelle Dance   56

Part V: Emphasize Individuality   61

12. *Constructing Colorblind Classrooms*
    Samuel R. Lucas   62
13. *Knowing Students as Individuals*
    Joshua Aronson   67
14. *Showing Students Who You Are*
    Heather M. Pleasants   70

SECTION B

HOW OPPORTUNITIES ARE PROVIDED
AND DENIED INSIDE SCHOOLS

                                                                 75

Part VI: Remember That Students Experience Racially
         Unequal Expectations about Their Brainpower   77

15. *Helping Students of Color Meet High Standards*
    Ronald F. Ferguson   78
16. *Providing Supportive Feedback*
    Geoffrey L. Cohen   82

Part VII: Counter Racially Patterned Skill Gaps   85

17. *Teaching and Transcending Basic Skills*
    Amanda Taylor   86
18. *Grouping in Detracked Classrooms*
    Beth C. Rubin   90

Part VIII: Help Students Gain Fluency in "Standard"
           Behaviors While Honoring the "Nonstandard"
           Behaviors They Already Have   97

19. *Standards vs. "Standard" Knowledge*
    Edmund T. Hamann   98
20. *Valuing Nonstandard English*
    John Baugh   102
21. *Teaching Students Fluency in Multiple Cultural Codes*
    Prudence Carter   107

Part IX: Defy Racially Based Notions of Potential
          Careers and Contributions   113

22. *Challenging Cultural Stereotypes of "Scientific Ability"*
    Maria Ong   114
23. *Finding Role Models in the Community*
    Meira Levinson   120

Part X: Analyze Racial Disparities in Opportunities to Learn   125

24. *Providing Equal Access to "Gifted" Education*
    Karolyn Tyson   126
25. *What Discipline Is For: Connecting Students to the
    Benefits of Learning*
    Pedro A. Noguera   132

SECTION C
CURRICULUM THAT ASKS CRUCIAL
QUESTIONS ABOUT RACE

139

Part XI: Create Curriculum That Invites Students to
          Explore Complex Identities *and* Consider
          Racial Group Experiences   141

26. *Using Photography to Explore Racial Identity*
    Alexandra Lightfoot   142
27. *Exploring Racial Identity Through Writing*
    Jennifer A. Mott-Smith   146
28. *Involving Students in Selecting Reading Materials*
    Christine E. Sleeter   150

Part XII: Create Curriculum That Analyzes
           Opportunity Denial   155

29. *Teaching Critical Analysis of Racial Oppression*
    Jeff Duncan-Andrade   156
30. *Using Critical Hip-Hop in the Curriculum*
    Ernest Morrell   161
31. *Engaging Youth in Participatory Inquiry for Social Justice*
    María Elena Torre and Michelle Fine   165

Part XIII: Create Curriculum That Represents a
            Diverse Range of People Thoroughly and Complexly 173

32. *Arab Visibility and Invisibility*
Thea Abu El-Haj   174

33. *Evaluating Images of Groups in Your Curriculum*
Teresa L. McCarty   180

34. *Teaching Representations of Cultural Difference Through Film*
Sanjay Sharma   186

35. *What Is on Your Classroom Wall? Problematic Posters*
Donna Deyhle   191

36. *Teaching Racially Sensitive Literature*
Jocelyn Chadwick   195

Part XIV: Create Curriculum That Discusses History
             Accurately and Thoroughly   199

37. *Making Race Relevant in All-White Classrooms:*
Using Local History
Mara Tieken   200

38. *Teaching Facts, Not Myths, about Native Americans*
Paul Ongtooguk and Claudia S. Dybdahl   204

SECTION D

RACE AND THE SCHOOL EXPERIENCE:
THE NEED FOR INQUIRY   209

Part XV: Investigate Learning Experiences in Your Classroom   211

39. *Inviting Students to Analyze Their Learning Experience*
Makeba Jones and Susan Yonezawa   212

40. *Interrogating Students' Silences*
Katherine Schultz   217

41. *Questioning "Cultural" Explanations of Classroom Behaviors*
Doug Foley   222

42. *Creating Safe Spaces in Predominantly White Classrooms*
Pamela Perry   226

43. *On Spotlighting and Ignoring Racial Group Members*
in the Classroom
Dorinda J. Carter   230

Part XVI: Spearhead Conversations with Students about
              Racism in Their Lives and Yours   235

44. *Racial Incidents as Teachable Moments*
Lawrence Blum   236

45. *Debating Racially Charged Topics*
    Ian F. Haney López   242
46. *Developing Antiracist School Policy*
    David Gillborn   246

Part XVII: Talk Thoroughly with Colleagues
            about Race and Achievement   253

47. *Focusing on Student Learning*
    John B. Diamond   254
48. *Moving Beyond Quick "Cultural" Explanations*
    Vivian Louie   257
49. *Naming the Racial Hierarchies That Arise During School Reforms*
    Rosemary Henze   262
50. *Spearheading School-wide Reform*
    Willis D. Hawley   267

Part XVIII: Analyze, with Colleagues and Students, How
             Your Race Affects Your Teaching   273

51. *Responding to the "N-Word"*
    Wendy Luttrell   274
52. *Engaging Diverse Groups of Colleagues in Conversation*
    Alice McIntyre   279
53. *Locating Yourself for Your Students*
    Priya Parmar and Shirley Steinberg   283
54. *Expanding Definitions of "Good Teaching"*
    Lee Anne Bell   287

SECTION E
ENGAGING COMMUNITIES FOR REAL   291

Part XIX: Inquire Fully about Home Communities   293

55. *Valuing Students' Home Worlds*
    Eugene E. García   294
56. *Getting to Know Students' Communities*
    Leisy Wyman and Grant Kashatok   299
57. *Helping Students Research Their Communities*
    Kathleen Cushman   305

Part XX: Discuss Parents' Experiences of Racially Unequal
          Opportunity   309

58. *Cultivating the Trust of Black Parents*
    Beverly Daniel Tatum   310
59. *Helping Parents Fight Stereotypes about Their Children*
    Janie Victoria Ward   314
60. *Informing Parents about Available Opportunities*
    Roslyn Arlin Mickelson and Linwood H. Cousins   318

                    SECTION F
                 KEEPING IT GOING   325

Part XXI: Struggle to Change a System That Is Unequal,
           While Working Within It   327

61. *Resisting the "Lone Hero" Stance*
    Audrey Thompson   328
62. *Recognizing the Likelihood of Reproducing Racism*
    Eduardo Bonilla-Silva and David G. Embrick   334
63. *Staying Hopeful*
    Ronald David Glass   337
64. *What Is Next?*
    Mica Pollock   341

    Complete List of Everyday Antiracist Strategies   343
    Notes   349
    Reference List   361
    Index   381

Acknowledgments

This book thrived on the patience and good spirit of its authors. I also relied upon the commitment of dozens of graduate students at the Harvard Graduate School of Education, most teachers themselves, who read and discussed these essays in their many drafts. Doctoral students in the "Everyday Antiracism Working Group" in 2006 and 2007 included coordinators Susan Klimczak and Amanda Taylor, and the following additional readers, commentators, and collaborators: Liz Blair, Trish Braga, Connie Chung, Sherry Deckman, Deidra Suwanee Dees, Charlene Desir, Marit Dewhurst, Shari Dickstein, Jennifer Dorsey, Sarah Fiarman, Amy Fowler, Erica Frankenberg, Cynthia Gordon, Pam Gordon, Ann Ishimaru, Zenub Kakli, Jo Louie, Meredith Mira, Elaine Mo, Jennifer Mott-Smith, Marielle Palumbo, Debby Saintil, Carla Shalaby, Gayle Simidian, Diane Smith, Steve Song, Mara Tieken, Anita Wadhwa, Dyan Watson, and Jennie Weiner. The preservice teachers who took the "Everyday Antiracism for Educators" course I taught in spring 2007 at the Harvard Graduate School of Education also made countless insightful suggestions as to how to make these pieces, and the book as a whole, work better for educators. I am indebted to all these readers for their insistent and thoughtful ideas. I also thank the Radcliffe Institute for Advanced Study for supporting me as a Mary I. Bunting Fellow during the year I conceptualized this book project. Thanks to the Milton Fund at Harvard University, the Achievement Gap Initiative at Harvard, and the Third Millennium Fund for providing some financial support for this editing effort, and to the Dean's Dissemination Fund at HGSE for supporting the book's publicity.

This project would have remained just a crazy idea were it not for the energy and enthusiasm of Ellen Reeves, Education Editor at the New Press. Her excitement about this book encouraged me to actually create it, and to keep honing it for educator use. Grey Osterud helped me find extra words to cut when I thought I could find no more. Alicia Redemske, my staff assistant at HGSE and a teacher herself, made huge efforts to help me actually get the book into production. Jennifer Rappaport, at the New Press, answered thousands of final questions. I am deeply grateful to all four people.

Finally, I thank my sweet small children, Elea and Jonah, and my husband, Joe, for their patience and support as this book consumed my days.

I hope that all of us, together, have produced something of great use to the field.

—Mica Pollock

Suggestions for Using This Book

Every day, educators trying to deal with race in school encounter a classic American quandary. If we want schools to be vehicles for countering racial inequality, when and how should we be "colorblind," and when and how should we be "race conscious"?

For this book, I asked over sixty researchers to get real about this basic question. At the same time, I asked each author to propose a single action an educator could take on an everyday basis to help counteract racial inequality and racism in schools and society.

In my own work with educators, I have found that these essays work best if you test and apply these tools and ideas in discussions of real-life incidents and dilemmas in your own practice. You can have these discussions in formal professional development settings, use these essays in inquiry groups or team meetings, or share these essays with your colleagues to start conversations. You can share them with your students as well.

We hope this book will assist you in developing an **everyday race consciousness** about the relevance of race in school. To counteract racial inequality and racism on a daily basis, educators need to *keep inquiring* in daily life:

Am I seeing, understanding, and addressing the ways the world treats me and my students as race group members?

Am I seeing, understanding, and addressing communities and individuals in their full complexity?

Am I seeing, understanding, and addressing the ways opportunities to learn or thrive are unequally distributed to racial groups?

What actions offer necessary opportunities to students in such a world?

To answer the fourth question regarding any particular action, you might draw a simple number line:

less educational opportunity ⟵⟶ more educational opportunity

Looking at the number line, you can ask yourself and your colleagues:

Do we think this action is moving students closer to a necessary educational opportunity, or farther away from it? Why? What is our evidence?

Finally, I suggest doing three things to make your conversations about these essays most productive.

1. **Pull out the gold nuggets.** This book prompts conversations about some of the most complicated issues American society has to offer. I suggest that you allow your conversation partners to ramble at times, to state ideas that aren't necessarily clear, and to get as emotional as they need to. But I also suggest that as you talk, you pull out "gold nuggets" from your conversation. By "gold nuggets," I mean moments of wisdom: clear, useful, and compelling ideas. So keep asking yourself as you talk with colleagues:

What's the most useful tool for thinking or acting to pull out of this essay, or out of our conversation?

Finding the "gold nugget" means *naming* some clear ideas and tactics to carry with you for daily use, rather than leaving a conversation with your head spinning.

2. **Think on three levels as you read and discuss these pieces.** I suggest you never end an essay or conversation before pinpointing something useful to you at each of three levels: (1) a **core principle** about what "antiracism" entails; (2) a **general strategy** an educator might want to use in various situations; and (3) a specific solution for your specific classroom and school (what I call "**try tomorrows**").

As you read or discuss, you can keep a list, like this:

- PRINCIPLE:
- STRATEGY:
- TRY TOMORROW:

Discussion questions at the end of each essay are designed to help prompt inquiry on all three levels. But as you read and discuss, you can ask yourself:

*What big ideas (**core principles**) about antiracist teaching and the pursuit of equal opportunity does the essay or conversation spark in my head?*

(In a group, see if you can come to consensus on one or more principles.)

*What general actions suggested by the author (**strategies**) do I find compelling or not compelling?*

(In a group or on your own, consider how an educator might utilize the essay's proposed strategy or strategies. What do you think of the author's proposals? Discuss how to start tailoring the strategies for a given subject or grade level.)

*What actions (specific solutions) could I actually imagine **trying tomorrow** in my own classroom or school, and what minefields might I encounter if I did?*

(This step tailors the strategy for your local setting. You can debate specific solutions to try tomorrow, depending on the dynamics of your classroom and school. Role playing situations can be extremely helpful.)

3. **Consider and share related resources.** Rather than provide explicit lesson plans in these essays, authors presented ideas that teachers of any subject could take in their own direction. There are extra resources at the end of each essay, in a resource list. A full research bibliography appears at the end of the book, in a reference list.

I hope you will take advantage of this chance to think deeply with your colleagues about issues we often discuss simplistically—if at all.

Introduction:
Defining Everyday Antiracism

Everyday things represent the most overlooked knowledge.
—Don DeLillo, 1997

To see what is in front of one's nose needs a constant struggle.
—George Orwell, 1946

For this book, I invited over sixty researchers, many of whom are former teachers, to boil down their school-based research into knowledge usable for K–12 classroom practice. I wanted each author to suggest a school-based action educators could take, every day, to help counteract racial inequality and racism in schools and society. We call these actions *everyday antiracism*.

This book is not designed to convince you that you intentionally harm children. Instead, it is designed to get you thinking about how everyday actions can harm children unintentionally. It is not designed to get you to ask, "Am I a bad person?" Instead, it is designed to get you to ask, "Do my everyday acts help promote a more equitable society?"

We collectively define "racism" as any act that, even unwittingly, tolerates, accepts, or reinforces racially unequal opportunities for children to learn and thrive; allows racial inequalities in opportunity as if they are normal and acceptable; or treats people of color as less worthy or less complex than "white" people. Many such acts taken in educational settings harm children of color, or privilege and value some children or communities over others in racial terms, without educators meaning to do this at all. That is why this book zooms in on ordinary acts taken by educators on a daily basis, and focuses proactively on suggestions for everyday *anti*racism. We not only show what acts inside schools and classrooms perpetuate racial inequalities, but we suggest alternative acts that can help to dismantle such inequalities instead.

Educational policies and "outside" realities of health care, housing, and family employment have huge effects on the opportunities the children in our schools need and receive. Stereotypes and inaccuracies about "race groups" circulate in society at large. But inside schools, everyday acts matter, too. In schools, people interact across racial lines, distribute opportunities moment to moment, react to "outside" opportunity structures, and shape how future generations think about difference and equality. Interactions in educational settings help build or dismantle racial "achievement gaps." To a student, one action can change everything. Everyday acts explored in this book include how we talk with our students and discipline them; the activities we set up for them to do; the ways we frame and discuss communities in our curriculum; and the ways we assign students to groups, grade their papers, interact with their parents, and envision their futures. Few of the contributors to this book see such actions as "small potatoes" efforts. Rather, we propose that such antiracist work helps remake social structure one bit at a time.

I acknowledge that the word "antiracism" can have a negative cast, for it implies that the educator is constantly fighting against and reacting to racial inequality, rather than struggling more positively and proactively to equalize opportunity and create an egalitarian society. It also can be heard as suggesting that some *people* are "racist" and others are not. Yet this book frames dismantling racial inequality and pursuing racial equality as two sides of the same collaborative undertaking. It also sets forth to counteract racial inequality and racism in society, not just inside "bad people." The word "everyday" is also crucial: it suggests that educators can, and must, help counter racial inequality and racism in society at routine moments of the schooling experience.

Pursuing racially equal opportunity and counteracting racism on a daily basis in our classrooms and schools requires more than being a great teacher of a subject; it requires particularly hard thinking about our choices in complex situations. In a society where racism and racial inequality already exist, it is often hard to figure out which of our everyday activities are harmful to students or others and which are helpful to them. Blanket advice to "be colorblind" regarding our students, to "celebrate" their or others' diversity, or to "recognize" their "race" and our own is not that helpful in real life. In daily life, sometimes educators' being colorblind is quite harmful to young people, since they live in a world that often treats them racially; sometimes a particular celebration of diversity can be reductive and stereotypic; sometimes seeing a person primarily as a member of a "race" detracts from recognizing our common humanity.

Antiracist educators must constantly negotiate between two antiracist impulses in deciding their everyday behaviors toward students: they must choose between the antiracist impulse to treat all people as human beings rather than racial group members, and the antiracist impulse to recognize people's real experiences as racial group members in order to assist them, understand their situation better, and treat them equitably. I ask the reader to keep a basic question in mind throughout the book. In your practice, when does treating people as racial group members help them, and when does it harm them? This core question ties this book together. Academics who write about racism and antiracism in education often neglect to answer, or even consider, this basic question. But in a world that has been organized for six centuries around bogus biological categories invented in order to justify the unequal distribution of life's necessities, some antiracist activity refuses to categorize people racially. Other antiracist activity recognizes people living as racial group members in order to analyze and transform a racially unequal world.

In countless daily ways, teachers, administrators, and program directors hoping to protect and assist young people must decide which acts counteract racial inequality. This involves deciding whether and how to see, treat, or talk about students, parents, colleagues, or others in racial terms. Some ways of recognizing students as "black" buoy them up with confidence; others trap them in reductive or stigmatizing notions of what being "black" means. Many colleagues may not consider it relevant that they or their students are "white"; yet ignoring their lived experience as "white" people can miss a major dimension of their reality. Some ways of framing students as "Latino" make Latino students feel welcome and safe; others make them feel excluded or likely to fail. Some framings in curriculum of parents as "Asian" or a community as "Indian" can be deeply inaccurate, yet ignoring people's experiences as "Asians" and "Indians" can prevent recognition of their struggles and joys. Specific ways of highlighting or downplaying our own racial-ethnic experiences or identities in conversations with students or colleagues can be dangerous or useful.

Really, everyday antiracism requires both addressing people's experiences in the world as racial group members and refusing to distort people's experiences, thoughts, or abilities by seeing them only or falsely through a racial lens. This applies when educators interact with students in classrooms, design and discuss curriculum, interact with students' families, or even think about ourselves and our colleagues. Educators must analyze, concretely, *when, where,* and *how* it helps to treat people as racial group members, and when, where, and how it harms. Above all, educators must keep analyzing which of our everyday actions counteract racial inequality and which do not.

All of us, then, suggest specific, concrete ways educators can help equalize students' academic and social opportunities to learn and thrive in K–12 educational settings, and more generally combat racism and racial inequality from within schools and classrooms. We differ in the methods we suggest to move in that direction. Some of the authors here measure "helping" as getting students to achieve higher test scores; others measure "helping" as getting students to believe in their own potential to become scientists. Some measure "harming" as actions that cause students to doubt their abilities, to lower their career aspirations, or even to despise themselves or others. Some authors analyze the treatment of students of color in particular; many essays' recommendations can apply to schools and classrooms of any demographic composition. Educators with a range of personal styles, in a variety of school situations, will find different suggestions useful and compelling.

These essays focus on things to do in our schools and classrooms, rather than just on ways to think differently about ourselves or others. Antiracist

practice requires the intermingling of actions and ideas. The contributors recognize that being effective at countering racism and racial inequality requires
us to develop skills as well as commitment. Many educators say they enter the
field seeking to improve opportunities for all children but end up either frustrated or failing at this task because they cannot figure out how to navigate
race issues while doing this. So, each essay in the book asks educators to rethink their ordinary activities and to try doing something differently in everyday life. I asked each author to boil her or his recommendation down to one
sentence that I have used in the introduction to each section, forcing us all to
pinpoint strategies and principles of everyday antiracism.

We assume that readers are committed to helping children to learn and
thrive. We do not assume that readers will accept or agree with our analyses
of how the everyday acts discussed here might help equalize opportunity for
children, or combat racism and racial inequality in society. I asked each author
to support each of his or her claims with research and personal experience. I
also asked each author to clarify claims about "race" and "racism." Finally, and
perhaps most importantly, I asked each author to walk the educator through
the minefields or pitfalls educators might encounter if they take his or her advice. Educators work in a world of ever-changing complexity; we expect that
readers will modify and rework these ideas for their own purposes and contexts.

In "Suggestions for Using This Book," I suggest that as you read and discuss these essays, you seek to name antiracist *principles*: core ideas about how
to pursue racially equal opportunity and counteract racism from within
schools and classrooms. To get us started, let me propose four foundational
principles. Everyday antiracism in education involves

> Rejecting false notions of human difference;
>
> Acknowledging lived experiences shaped along racial lines;
>
> Learning from diverse forms of knowledge and experience; and
>
> Challenging systems of racial inequality.

First, everyday antiracism in education involves rejecting false notions of
human difference and actively treating people as equally worthy, complicated,
and capable. In educational settings, antiracism entails actively affirming that
no racially defined group is more or less intelligent than any other. We can tell
students that racial categories have no valid genetic basis. Through our curriculum and in our everyday interactions, we can challenge oversimplified notions about racial-ethnic identities or group behaviors. We can remember that
any "race" group is composed of individuals who have complicated identities
and lives.

Second, everyday antiracism in education involves acknowledging and engaging lived experiences that do vary along racial lines. Genetically bogus racial categories like "white," "black," and "Asian" were built upon genetically insignificant physical differences (hair, noses, and bone structures). Racialized categories like "Latino," "Native American," and "Arab" lump together people from countless regions and, in some cases, people who speak totally different languages. Still, over six centuries of American history and even now, people have been lumped into ranked "races" by others and forged solidarity along racial-ethnic lines themselves as a means of social empowerment. The Irish "became white" in the nineteenth century, and Jews "became white" in the twentieth, to gain opportunity in a system that already favored "whites" of European descent. Lumped together as a "race" to be enslaved by "whites," Africans and their descendants in America simultaneously forged deep solidarity as "black" people. People from a variety of Asian origins made alliances as "Asian Americans" starting in the 1960s. "Latinos" converged at that time as well, voicing the plurality of their origins and the unity of their agendas. Distinct tribes of Native Americans recognized common experiences of displacement and forced assimilation. "Arabs" have shared many U.S.-based experiences, particularly in recent years. All such "racial" groups in the United States today bring different historic and contemporary experiences to the table, and after several centuries of opportunities being distributed differentially along racial lines, racial group members still have differential access to educational resources and opportunities for success. Everyday antiracism entails engaging our own and one another's experiences *as* racial group members— particularly of this differential treatment, whether we have benefited from it or been sabotaged by it.

Third, everyday antiracism in education involves learning from diversity in human experience, and valuing equally the knowledge and activity shared within various "groups." As Cornel West wrote, for example, being "black" today can involve both experiencing stigmatization, particularly from "whites," and enjoying a community that has bonded through expressive practices and political resistance in the midst of oppression.[1] Respecting such shared experiences and knowledge also involves appreciating the critical lenses that members of groups can offer—even as we highlight the diversity within groups and emphasize each person's individuality.

Fourth, everyday antiracism in education involves equipping ourselves and others to challenge racial inequalities of opportunity and outcome, rather than accepting racial disparities as normal. We can clarify the ways in which educational and life opportunities are still unequal along racial lines; we can help equip students, parents, ourselves, and our colleagues to analyze and demand the opportunities each child needs and deserves. We can ensure that within our own schools and classrooms, necessary opportunities to learn and thrive are provided, and distributed equitably; every day, we can try to help level the playing field of opportunity. Children and youth need to come to understand that they are disadvantaged or privileged by a social system that they, like educators, can help make more equitable.

These four principles are not self-contradictory. Rejecting false notions of human difference, engaging lived experiences shaped along racial lines, learning from diversity in human experience, and challenging systems of racial inequality can all happen simultaneously, and each can be emphasized in particular situations. Antiracism requires not treating people as racial group members when that is harmful, and recognizing them as racial group members when that helps people to analyze life experiences and equalize opportunity. Deciding which move to take and when requires thinking hard about everyday life in educational settings. These choices are complex, anxiety-ridden, and deeply consequential. That is why we wanted to prompt analysis of everyday actions in schools, to help educators consider how their own actions might help dismantle racial inequality.

We urge readers to hone our proposed strategies for use in their own schools, to critique these strategies, and to brainstorm and experiment with new strategies along with students, parents, and colleagues. We hope you will make the most of this chance to "zoom in" and think deeply about the potential consequences of your daily practice.

Note: Hundreds of thinkers contributed to the ideas proposed in this book; their work is gathered in the reference list. Three authors in particular helped shape this book's specific concept of "everday antiracism" in education. Philomena Essed first framed "everyday racism" as the re-creation of "structures of racial and ethnic inequality through situated practices" normalized in everyday life (see 2002, 18). Michèle Lamont first adopted the phrase "everyday antiracism," for her work on the ideas people in different countries employ to challenge racist notions about the relative worth of various groups (and what makes these groups unequal) (2000a and 2000b). In my work, I share the phrase to refer to everyday actions challenging racism and racial inequality in the educational domain. See also Jane Mansbridge (e.g., Mansbridge and Flaster 2007), who coined the analogous term "everyday feminism."

EVERYDAY ANTIRACISM

SECTION A

Race Categories: We Are All the Same, But Our Lives Are Different

Part I

Remember That Racial Categories Are Not Biological Realities

The essays in this part share a core principle of everyday antiracism: *race categories are not biological or genetic realities. They are categories that humans made up.*

What strategies can educators use to deal with this situation?

1. Teach students why race is an obsolete biological concept.

   Alan Goodman suggests that educators should tell students directly that race categories are not genetic or "biological" realities. Rather, they are social categories made up by people.

2. Resist the programmed assumption that different racial groups have different intellectual abilities.

   Mica Pollock proposes that educators must struggle consciously against a longstanding lie: we must remind ourselves routinely that "race groups" are not unequally intelligent.

3. Try not using the word "Caucasian."

   Carol C. Mukhopadhyay suggests discontinuing the word "Caucasian," as it suggests falsely that "races" are biologically "real."

1

Exposing Race as an Obsolete Biological Concept

Alan H. Goodman

In November 1999, a cover story on "new ideas about race" appeared in the *Valley Advocate*, a free weekly newspaper covering western Massachusetts. I was quoted extensively and, to my surprise, I received many requests from K–12 teachers to help teach their students about the invalidity of racial categories from a biological standpoint. One of the most successful collaborations involved a group of about eighty-five eighth-grade students at Amherst Regional Middle School (ARMS), who were team-taught by four teachers sharing four subjects: English, Math, Social Studies, and Science. Madeline Hunter, the English teacher and primary developer of the curriculum, told me that the team's goal in combining disciplines was to go beyond presenting current knowledge to inspire their students to consider how knowledge is gained and to ask "How do I know what is true?"

The key scientific point I taught in a lesson opening the curriculum was this: while humans have come to live our social lives through racial categories, these categories simply are not useful for classifying human genetic diversity. At this point, differences in wealth, health, or educational attainment between groups we call "races" are the products of history and social life, not biologically determined. For example, racial differences in infant mortality exist because of disparities in health care and nutrition, not genetics.

In a single lesson, we found, students can come to understand that human biological variation is too broad to be classified into "races." The take-home point all students should be taught is that despite common understandings, "race" as a biological category should be put on the scrap heap of outmoded scientific ideas. In learning about the biology of human variation, students learn important lessons about the development and dismantling of racist ideologies in science. Educators in all subjects can also challenge scientifically an incorrect notion about biological difference that is particularly damaging in schools: that intelligence is genetically unequally distributed among different racial groups. This lesson can be quite effective in middle and high schools and may be targeted to younger students.

In the Amherst middle school classroom, I began a lesson on these ideas by asking the students some big questions: "What is race?" "Is it biological?" Before my visit to the school, Jennifer Welborn, the science teacher, had students read two articles on race and science (see Begley 1995, Goodman 1997, in Resource list). So I was surprised to discover that the students were still equally divided between those who said that race was biological and those who countered that race was a social construct.

As I launched into my lesson, I made four points:

- Racial categories are an idea that developed historically.
- The idea of racial categories has real social effects on people's lives.
- Human biological variation is real, in the sense that humans are not genetically identical.
- It was once thought that human biological variation fit into racial categories, but it does not.

I gave students the basic history. When European scientists such as Linnaeus first tried to explain human variation in the seventeenth and eighteenth centuries, they divided humans into a discrete set of racial types. However, this attempt to understand and categorize human differences was a failure: human diversity does not fit into any set of "races." Genetically, scientists later confirmed, individuals in the species *homo sapiens* are about 99.9 percent alike. Racial categories are not biological realities, but social constructions. By the time of Linnaeus, the idea of "race" categories, with some categories superior to others, was an integral part of the dominant European worldview. This idea fit wealthy Europeans' belief in their own essential superiority to other peoples around the globe. It stuck because ideologies about racial superiority and inferiority supported their policies of taking away land (in the Americas) and wealth (in Asia) and rationalized the enslavement of Africans.

Scientists now know that biologically, human diversity does not fit into the racial categories that we have created. To consider racial categories useful biological containers or, worse, an explanation for social differences among us is bad science. Yet even now, I told the students, few people realize this.

I then offered five reasons why the notion of race as biological is wrong and harmful.

First, ideas such as unchanging racial "types" of humans are completely incompatible with evolutionary theory. We now know that living beings change over time; they are not classifiable into unchanging "types" like "races."

Second, there is no clear marker to designate where one "race" begins and another ends. Skin color, the physical characteristic that Americans most often use to falsely distinguish racial groups, itself cannot be classified into clear-cut "types" of "colors." We just imagine that it can!

Third, skin color is correlated with a few other traits, such as hair and eye color (such that many people with dark hair and skin have brown eyes), but not with most of the traits a baby inherits. It is a truism that "race is only skin deep."

Fourth, genetic variation within so-called racial groups is much greater than the variation between them. Contrary to commonly held assumptions, there is actually little genetic variation between the groups we have come to call races. Two individuals who identify as "white" might well be far more genetically different from one another than from someone self-identified as "black." In biological perspective, rather than seeing Europeans and Asians as "races," we may regard them as different-looking subsets of Africans, since the entire human population is descended from ancestors who originated on that continent. Given these genetic realities, the genetic variation among us simply does not fit into "race" categories.

Fifth, human beings cannot be consistently classified by "race." Social classifications based on skin color, the trait we have most often used to imagine where one race starts and another begins, differ over time and place. A person who is considered "white" in Brazil can be considered "black" in the United States; someone who lives as "white" in the United States today might have been considered "Mexican" a generation earlier. Racial groups are impossible to define in a stable and universal way, so no scientific generalizations can be made about them.

In discussion after I presented these ideas, a student who had previously thought that racial categories were biological gave a nice example of why these categories are social. What really made these ideas concrete was a discussion of the label on the back of a TUMS bottle. I brought some calcium products with me, including TUMS, most of which had identical health advisories suggesting that these products would be beneficial specifically to "Asian" and "Caucasian" females. Knowing now that groups like "Asian" and "Caucasian" are not biological realities (indeed, the label "Caucasian" describes no clear-cut population at all; see Mukhopadhyay, Chapter 3), the students took it upon themselves to write the maker of TUMS to find out why certain groups were listed specifically as benefiting from TUMS, while others were not. The students asked to see the biological data that the TUMS manufacturers had used to support the decision that populations were biologically distinct enough to respond to TUMS differently. Dissatisfied with the responses they received, they petitioned the FDA to change the race-specific language on the back of the TUMS bottle. The students recognized the crudeness of recommending a supplement based on racial categories that were biologically suspect, and were challenged to consider how bad science enters public policy. This awareness is part of becoming effective citizens. Around 2003, I noticed that racial labeling on TUMS and many other products was greatly reduced. Although I cannot claim any credit for this accomplishment, it suggests that what students do can make a difference.

I have not always been as successful in teaching this material as I was this first time. However, students often say that the basic information I presented on the lack of a biological basis for racial categories was important and even transformative for them.

For this type of lesson to be successful in another environment, some key conditions need to exist. First, a school system must provide space for deep questioning of taken-for-granted ideas. A lesson like this interweaves science with social issues. We discussed how science is social and political. The students appreciated that science is not merely objective, but a human enterprise. While the content of this lesson is unlikely to appear on standardized tests, the biological critique of racial categories can easily be incorporated into standardized lessons. The science curriculum involves understanding experimental design, and an investigation of whether racial groups really do respond differently to calcium can be used as a concrete example. This basic information can be presented to students in any subject.

Second, success requires enthusiastic and energetic teachers. Their excitement about learning this new information encouraged their students to become engaged as well. Finally, the teachers had confidence in their students and validated students' knowledge and opinions. Along the way, students were given tools to unpack a core concept that affects all of our lives. Students were then able to channel their energy and enthusiasm toward a formidable challenge: telling others about the biological invalidity of "race."

RESOURCES

American Anthropological Association Statement on Race: www.aaanet.org/stmts/
    racepp.htm.
Sharon Begley. 1995. "Three Is Not Enough." *Newsweek*, February 13, 67–69.
Alan H. Goodman. 1997. Bred in the Bone?" *The Sciences*, March/April, 20–25.
Race: Are We So Different? www.understandingrace.org/home.html.
Race: The Power of an Illusion. Three-part documentary, from California Newsreel:
    www.newsreel.org; also www.pbs.org/race.
Race: A Teacher's Guide: www.understandingrace.org/resources/for_teachers.html.

DISCUSSION QUESTIONS

1. **Principle:** Have you thought, in the past, that "race" categories are biological realities? What might your students believe?
2. **Strategy:** How might you incorporate this lesson or its ideas into your curriculum? How could you prepare to lead this discussion yourself?
3. **Try tomorrow:** What minefields can you imagine encountering if you taught this information in your classroom? How could you prepare for these?

Alan Goodman is the president of the American Anthropological Association (2005–2007) and professor of biological anthropology at Hampshire College. He focuses on the interactions among power, ideologies, ecologies, and human biologies, such as how ideas such as "race" have consequences for our understanding of human biology.

2

No Brain Is Racial

Mica Pollock

Look inside yourself and ask: have you ever thought that different racial groups have different intellectual abilities? You might immediately say "no." But the assumption is more ingrained than most Americans would like to admit. Indeed, after almost 600 years of programming, it would be surprising if you did not have this scientifically false notion somewhere in your head. (You can take a test online to examine your unconscious bias; see Resources.)[1]

Over several centuries, social and natural scientists constructed the myth that "white" people were smarter than non-"white" people. They did so to justify Europeans' enslavement of Africans, and worldwide European colonial conquest begun in the 1400s. In a cruel cycle, the notion that intellectual ability was distributed differently among so-called races was developed by white scientists through the eighteenth, nineteenth, and twentieth centuries to explain and justify a system of economic, social, and political inequality organized along racial lines.

For example, to rationalize slavery and its treatment of Africans as inherently less worthy than Europeans, natural scientists classified people descended from northern Europeans as the "race" with superior reason and the people descended from Africans as an inferior "race" fit only for labor and subordination.[2] Even after the abolition of slavery, scientists tried to justify the racial hierarchy that was reconstructed as Jim Crow segregation by arguing that "the races" differed in intellect. Indeed, that effort was inextricably intertwined with the development of intelligence tests and the very idea of the "intelligence quotient," or IQ.[3] People classified as "black" or "Negro" bore the brunt of these ascriptions of inferior ability, but they affected other "nonwhite" groups as well. Mexican Americans working as low-paid field laborers for white landowners after the U.S. conquest of the Southwest were deemed mentally inferior and shunted by whites into classes and schools for the "retarded."[4] Italians, at the bottom of the labor pool at the turn of the twentieth century and widely regarded by U.S.-born "whites" at the time as not quite white, were pronounced disproportionately "retarded" on the new intelligence tests. So were Jews, who, as Eastern European immigrants and non-Christians to boot, ranked low in the national status hierarchy.[5] Repeatedly, experts designing "intelligence" tests tweaked these instruments until they showed what they were meant to show: that lower-status populations were less intelligent than higher-status ones. These notions persist today. In *The Bell Curve*, published in 1994, Richard J. Hernstein and Charles Murray suggested that people of color were less successful educationally and economically because they were less intelligent.

The active effort to prove a lie—that the "races" differ in intellectual ability—has taken its toll on every one of us, regardless of the racial category through which we live our lives. In contemporary America, it is difficult to think about racial groups without thinking about them as unequally intelligent. Being brought up white typically involves learning to believe that we are smarter than those who are not white; being brought up nonwhite often means battling the fear that perhaps we will be judged less intelligent than those who are white.[6] In a more recent variation on this pattern, being brought up Asian American entails contending with racialized presumptions of our superior ability in math and science, which can sometimes prompt achievement and sometimes stunt it.[7]

At first glance, after six centuries of programming, "races" can seem to be easily identifiable and fundamentally different types of humans. Some of us are lighter skinned, some darker; some of us have straight hair, some curly; our bone structures vary. Yet we have fallen for the misconception that internal differences, including intellectual ones, accompany these visible differences.[8] American educators reactivate this cruel programming every time we imagine, even for a fleeting second, that students' physical appearance signals anything at all about their brain power. Since assumptions of racially distributed intelligence are in the air we breathe, antiracist practice requires actively resisting this notion. When we say that we have "high expectations for all students," we should think more specifically about what it is we are saying. What we really mean is that we are struggling against the expectations we have been programmed to have, that some "race groups" are smarter than others.

RESOURCES

American Anthropological Association's Statement on Race and Intelligence: http://www.aaanet.org/stmts/race.htm.
Stephen Jay Gould. 1996. *The Mismeasure of Man.* New York: W.W. Norton.
Harvard Implicit Project: To take a test of your unconscious or "implicit" racial bias, see https://implicit.harvard.edu/implicit/.

DISCUSSION QUESTIONS

1. **Principle:** How common is the view that "the races" are unequally intelligent?

2. **Strategy:** How, if at all, might it make a difference for your students if you reminded yourself routinely that the notion of racially based intelligence was a lie?

3. **Try tomorrow:** In your own classroom, how can you imagine conveying the truth that one's skin color, nose shape, hair type, or language has nothing to do with one's intelligence?

Mica Pollock is associate professor at the Harvard Graduate School of Education. An anthropologist of education, she studies how people in educational settings struggle daily over fundamental questions of racial inequality and diversity.

3

Getting Rid of the Word "Caucasian"

Carol C. Mukhopadhyay

Racial labels and categories, like all terms and concepts, are human-made classifying devices that we learn, internalize, and then use to interpret the everyday world in which we live. But conventional American racial categories are rooted in colonialism, slavery, and an elaborate ideology developed to justify a system of racial inequality. Given racial categories' sociohistorical rather than biological roots, the notion that "races" describe human biological variation has been officially rejected by the American Anthropological Association. (See the Association's statement, in Resource list.) As we critique outmoded systems of racial classification, we must also question the labels we use for "races."

The Civil Rights Movement dismantled the most explicit forms of racism, including many biological-sounding racial labels. Terms like "Negroid," the "Red Man," and the "Yellow Race" were replaced—often by group members themselves—with words like "Black" or "African American," "Native American," and "Asian," which indicate that these groups are political, not biological, realities. Today, terms like "Oriental" would immediately mark the user as seriously out of touch with current understandings. Yet there is one striking exception in our modern racial vocabulary: the term "Caucasian." Despite being a remnant of a discredited theory of racial classification, the term has persisted into the twenty-first century, within as well as outside of the educational community.

It is high time we got rid of the word Caucasian. Some might protest that it is "only a label." But language is one of the most systematic, subtle, and significant vehicles for transmitting racial ideology. Terms that describe imagined groups, such as Caucasian, encapsulate those beliefs. Every time we use them and uncritically expose students to them, we are reinforcing rather than dismantling the old racialized worldview. Using the word Caucasian invokes scientific racism, the false idea that races are naturally occurring, biologically ranked subdivisions of the human species and that Caucasians are the superior race. Beyond this, the label Caucasian can even convey messages about which groups have culture and are entitled to recognition as Americans.

The term Caucasian originated in the eighteenth century as part of the developing European science of racial classification.[1] After visiting the region of the Caucasus Mountains, between the Caspian and Black seas, German anatomist Johann Blumenbach declared its inhabitants the most beautiful in the world, the ideal type of humans created in "God's image," and deemed this area the likely site where humans originated. (Humans actually originated in Africa.) He decided that all light-skinned peoples from this region, along with Europeans, belonged to the same race, which he labeled Caucasian.

Blumenbach named four other races that he considered physically and morally "degenerate" forms of "God's original creation." He classified Africans (excepting lighter-skinned North Africans) as "Ethiopians" or "black." He split non-Caucasian Asians into two separate races: the "Mongolian" or "yellow" race of China and Japan, and the "Malayan" or "brown" race, including Aboriginal Australians and Pacific Islanders. Native Americans were the "red" race.

Blumenbach's system of racial classification was adopted in the United States. American scientists tried to prove that Caucasians had larger brains and were smarter than people of other races.[2] Racial science dovetailed with nineteenth-century evolutionary theories, which ranked races from more "primitive" "savages" to more "advanced" or "civilized," with Caucasians on top. Racial hierarchies were used to justify slavery and other forms of racial discrimination.

The U.S. legal system drew on Blumenbach's definitions to decide who was eligible to become a naturalized citizen, a privilege the 1790 Naturalization Act restricted to "whites." This schema created dilemmas. Blumenbach's Caucasians included such groups as Armenians, Persians (Iranians), North Indians, Arabs, and some North Africans. In 1923, however, the U.S. Supreme Court rejected the naturalization petition of an immigrant from North India, saying he was Caucasian but not white and citing, among other things, his skin color.

The constant tweaking of categories like "Caucasian" to include or exclude newcomers provides evidence of these categories' social rather than biological basis. By the 1920s, eugenicists (who were concerned with the improvement of the species through the reproduction of the "superior" race) had divided Caucasians into four ranked sub-races: Nordic, Alpine, Mediterranean, and Jew (Semitic), and designated Nordics intellectually and morally superior. These subdivisions were used to justify discriminatory immigration laws that preserved the ethnic dominance of northern and western Europeans. Not until after World War II, when theories of "Aryan" racial superiority were thoroughly discredited by their association with the Nazis, did these distinctions begin to dissolve and European Americans become fully homogenized into the category "white." The status of groups like Armenians, Iranians, and South Asians remained ambiguous, demonstrating that "white," like "Caucasian," was a category that could easily be bent to exclude those deemed unworthy.

The North American system of racial classification continues to shift in response to historical, economic, and political events. Yet the basic conceptual framework imagining biologically distinct racial categories remains surprisingly stable. The word Caucasian is still used in many forms of data collection, medical circles, and popular discourse. Most other labels have changed. New terms more accurately reflect geographic locations or ancestral origins, broadly defined. In contrast, the more biological-sounding word Caucasian stubbornly persists. I suggest that each time we, as educators, use or subject our students uncritically to the term Caucasian, we are subtly re-inscribing key elements of the racist world view.

Caucasian has more explicitly biological connotations than other contemporary racial terms. To most of us, the Caucasus does not signify a geographical area. Virtually none of our students and probably very few of us could locate the Caucasus on a map or specify what countries or regional groups it includes today (answer: Georgia, Armenia, Azerbaijan, parts of north Iran, and central southern Russia). So what does it mean to designate someone Caucasian? It does not, at least in the twenty-first century United States, suggest anything cultural—that is, a shared set of behaviors and beliefs. U.S. Caucasians do not speak Caucasian. Since it does not connote location or language, it implies something more "natural" than cultural—a profoundly dangerous assumption.

Of course, categories such as Asian, African, and Native American are human-made classifications, too. These labels also falsely imply that clear dividing lines exist between geographically defined "races." For example, the category Asian is internally diverse and has shifting boundaries. It includes Chinese, Japanese, Korean, and Vietnamese people, but what about the peoples of the Indian subcontinent, the Indonesian archipelago, or the Pacific islands? Still, students can identify specific languages and countries in Asia or Africa. Unlike Caucasian, labels like African, Asian, and Native American, while oversimplified, connote culture-bearing historical and political entities.

Anthropologists have long struggled to convince the public that races are not discrete, bounded, biologically based categories but artificial inventions, arbitrary divisions in a continuum of human diversity. Using the label Caucasian masks the equally arbitrary and invented character of this racial category. It renders invisible the diverse ethnic, linguistic, religious, and political groups that make up Europe, which constituted the significant identities of most European Americans until the past half century. The term Caucasian implies that people of European descent form a coherent, stable, homogeneous, biological entity, reinforcing obsolete biological notions of "race."

Using the word Caucasian also tends to imply that whites (the two terms are often used interchangeably) differ from other major racial groupings in the United States in being just plain Americans whose immigrant origins remain unmarked. Yet European Americans originally arrived as immigrants and refugees and were often unwanted by those who had preceded them. Today, they are no more authentically American than any other group. Compared to Native Americans, all European Americans are recent immigrants. Most African Americans' ancestors were brought to these shores before the ancestors of most European Americans arrived. Yet the term Caucasian, because it now lacks any geographic connotation, masks this group's foreign ancestry while other labels, such as Asian American or African American, highlight those groups' foreign roots.

The word Caucasian also reinforces the tendency to equate "American" with people of European descent because, as a one-word designation, Caucasian reinforces the "hyphenated" status of other American groups. Linguistically, adding a modifier to a generic term—for example, adding Asian or African to American—generally signifies that the modified form is less "normal." The more fundamental, typical, "normal" form is left unmarked. (For example, we add the gender modifier "male" to mark the unusual, abnormal category of "male" nurses. "Nurse" refers to the typical, taken-for-granted, "normal" nurse, who is female.) Most standard U.S. racial labels today other than Caucasian add a specific modifier to American. These modifiers, unless used for all racial-ethnic groups, subtly marginalize the "marked" groups, implying they are not fully American. Some groups remain framed eternally as immigrants, regardless of how many generations they have been in the United States.

Finally, for those designated Caucasian, the term subtly erases their ethnicity, their own ancestry, cultural traditions, and experiences. Ironically, we are starting to talk as if ethnicity and culture are attributes of only some groups, especially marginalized groups. My university has an umbrella organization for the diverse cultural groups on campus, but it does not include any European American ethnocultural groups. But of course, what is Caucasian culture? The category is empty.

Being more specific about origins allows European American students the opportunity to explore their ethnic identities and ancestries. Linking histories or cultural practices to specific cultural or linguistic regions by calling them English, German, Italian, Polish, and so forth, situates them as one among many cultural traditions brought to the United States by immigrants.

European American is a more precise substitute for Caucasian than white—at least as long as we feel the need to classify U.S. residents into a few large groupings. If we wish to describe lived experiences of privilege and the distribution of opportunities based upon ancestry, both "European American" and "white" can be useful. The label European American (or "Euro") may sound bulky or strange at first, but so did African American!

We can also challenge the notion of "pure races" by substituting a more accurate term, "multiracial," for "of mixed race." The terminology of mixture draws upon the old notion of distinct races. In fact, the history of our species is one of constant interaction and mating between populations; that is why humans have remained one species. Moreover, in the process of "mixing," one element gets "diluted." The term "multiracial" connotes the possibility of multiple cultural traditions, multiple identities, and a richer, rather than diluted, cultural legacy.

What can we do beyond using language that reinforces the ideas we want to convey? We can encourage our students to think about everyday, popular language, its roots, and the subtle meanings it conveys. We can invite them to alter their own everyday talk.

RESOURCES

Carol C. Mukhopadhyay, Rosemary Henze, and Yolanda T. Moses. 2007. *How Real Is Race? A Sourcebook on Race, Culture, and Biology*. Lanham, MD: Rowman & Littlefield. A sourcebook of conceptual background material, activities, and lesson plans for teachers regarding race categories.

DISCUSSION QUESTIONS

1. **Principle:** How can we use racial labels like "white," "black," or "Asian" without suggesting biological differences that do not really exist? On the other hand, what would be lost if we deleted all racial terms from our language?
2. **Strategy:** Mukhopadhyay suggests replacing the word "Caucasian" not with "white" but with "European American." What do you think of this substitution? Does it mask the social experience of living as "white" in the United States?
3. **Try tomorrow:** What might you say the next time a student or colleague refers to someone as "Caucasian"? Role-play the interaction.

Carol Chapnick Mukhopadhyay has forty years of teaching, research, publishing, and consulting experience on education-cultural diversity issues related to ethnicity and gender in the United States and India. She is a professor of anthropology at San Jose State University (California) and a Key Advisor for the American Anthropological Association's RACE project.

Part II

Get Ready to Talk about a Racialized Society

So race categories are not real, biologically. But socially, they are. We live lives as racial group members. And schools are particular places where race still matters.

The essays in this part share a core principle of everyday antiracism: *teachers need to discuss the relevance of race in school with students, parents, and each other.*

What strategies can educators use to get started in discussing the relevance of race in school?

1. Start developing the will, skill, and capacity to engage in courageous conversations about race.

   Glenn Singleton and Cyndie Hays suggest that educators agree to a few key commitments, such as "speak your truth" and "stay engaged," before talking with colleagues or students about race issues.

2. Start talking precisely about moving students to opportunity.

   Mica Pollock suggests that educators strive to talk more specifically about which of their actions actually provide the opportunities students need.

3. Start thinking critically about what it means to "care" for students.

   Sonia Nieto suggests that educators discuss which actions are most "caring" for students of color in particular in a racially unequal society.

4

Beginning Courageous Conversations about Race

Glenn E. Singleton and Cyndie Hays

As Cornel West wrote in *Race Matters*:[1]

> Race is the most explosive issue in American life precisely because it forces us to confront the tragic facts of poverty and paranoia, despair and distrust. In short, a candid examination of race matters takes us to the core of American democracy. And the degree to which race matters in the plight and predicament of fellow citizens is a crucial measure of whether we can keep alive the best of this democratic experiment we call America.

A "candid examination" of race is not easy for educators. We discovered long ago from our work in K–12 districts and universities across the country that students are usually far better at engaging in interracial conversations about race than the educators leading them. More often than not, students from kindergarten through graduate school find exploring race edgy, provocative, and nourishing. Sometimes a conscious or precocious student does not wait for our permission to engage the taboo topic, and she will make a comment about race that launches an orderly classroom into conflict, controversy, or deafening silence.

This essay offers educators guidelines for more successful interracial dialogue about crucial issues with both students and colleagues. We call these guidelines the "Four Agreements of Courageous Conversation," which help create the conditions for safe exploration and profound learning for all. Courageous conversation is a strategy for breaking down racial tensions and raising racism as a topic of discussion that allows those who possess knowledge on particular topics to have the opportunity to share it, and those who do not have the knowledge to learn and grow from the experience.

Educators should keep in mind that interracial conversations about race are always a bit dangerous, as they unleash emotions that we have all learned to bury. What is most courageous about interracial conversations about race is mustering the strength to facilitate them. Opening up these dialogues when it appears that certain things are much better left unsaid or unspoken is frightening. We want to acknowledge that fear and encourage educators to find the courage to risk moving beyond it. To get ready for courageous conversations about race with their students, educators might first learn to engage with their colleagues. After developing proficiency in applying the guidelines, they can assist students to examine racial issues in a variety of subjects. As educators gain familiarity with courageous conversations' ebbs and flow, they can steer their students toward safe harbors rather than allowing them to wander into frighteningly familiar stormy waters.

Educators can tackle topics that relate to their own personal experiences. High school teachers might discuss racial achievement gaps; teachers of younger students might explore students' tension-provoking uses of racial slurs on the playground. The discussion leader must have thought through these issues from multiple angles in order to steer the conversation in a positive direction. As Cornel West suggests, "How we set up the terms for discussing racial issues shapes our perception and response to these issues."[2] Educators experience extraordinary pressure, both implicit and explicit, not to talk about race.[3] To get started, educators must introduce a new set of agreements that defy and perhaps even contradict the tightly held cultural norms relating to race talk. They must stay engaged, expect to experience discomfort, speak their truth, and expect and accept a lack of closure.

Stay Engaged

First and foremost, stay engaged. On day one and each time, until it becomes a part of the culture of dialogue, discussion leaders must explicitly invite participants into a dialogue about race. Giving peers permission to engage in dialogue about race and holding a lofty expectation that they will stay engaged in these conversations throughout the semester or year is the first of the four agreements for courageous conversation. While initially, some participants may be eager to enter into these conversations, our experience indicates that the more personal and thus risky these topics get, the more difficult it is for participants to stay committed and engaged.

Participants may notice patterns in the behavior and perspectives of white participants that differ from those of participants of color. Falling into silence is one example. Although silence does not always mean disengagement (see Schultz, Chapter 40), it is often predictable which participants will become silent, and when, and why. White participants often resort to silence in fear that their comments will be misconstrued as evidence of racist thinking, while participants of color may feel it is unsafe or futile to give voice to their inner thoughts. The facilitator should draw attention to these patterns by acknowledging that a silence is occurring and inviting participants to reflect upon, write about, and share the thoughts and feelings giving rise to the silence. In these moments, participants may develop an awareness of patterns that can be harmful to the progress of the dialogue.

Expect to Experience Discomfort

Second, expect to experience discomfort. When most people experience personal or collective discomfort in conversations, they are prone to disengage. It is important to inform colleagues right away that a hallmark of examining race is feeling uncomfortable with what we discover about our own and others' perspectives. Those who engage in courageous conversations about race must admit that they may not know all they have claimed to know or honestly believed they knew. Since we are—individually and collectively—constantly being socialized into racialized points of view, it is likely that we will discover places of intense disagreement and experience new levels of cognitive dissonance as we unpack the perspectives we have absorbed. We must not retreat from the conversation when our opinions do not align with those of others or those we previously held. Through normalizing the presence of multiple perspectives, we can avoid a situation in which one dominant way of understanding race invalidates all other experiences and different points of view. We discover just how racialized our own identities and viewpoints have been. Participants should encourage one another to engage in self-examination of their racial identities and personal racial histories. We have found that full engagement and successful management of these intense emotions eventually give way to feelings of liberation.

Singleton's former professor at Stanford University once described this phenomenon: "like a flying trapeze artist, he must eventually let go of the rope he is holding onto in order to reach out and grab the next rope swinging before him. In a moment he is suspended between the two ropes, wondering if he will survive the transition or fall to the nets below." Each of us must let go of the racial understandings that we have been holding onto in order to move forward. One of the most common themes educators have defined as a part of the racist tapes that play constantly in their heads is the habit of focusing on factors external to the school, or solely blaming the students themselves when explaining low achievement, rather than examining instructional and school-wide practices as well. A courageous conversation requires that we grow accustomed to the discomfort of abandoning old habits.

Speak Your Truth

Third, speak your truth. A courageous conversation requires that participants be honest about their thoughts, feelings, and opinions. Too often participants are afraid of offending, appearing angry, or sounding ignorant in conversations about race and fall silent, allowing their beliefs and opinions to be misinterpreted or misunderstood. Many beliefs concerning race are based on misconceptions. It is precisely through the sharing of honest and heartfelt sentiments—regardless of whether the participant believes them to be embraced by the discussion leader, their peers, or people of other races—that participants can begin to transform themselves. The discussion leader must help participants open up and share their perspectives regardless of how unusual or unpopular they fear those views might be.

At times, because of the pervasive silence that cloaks or smothers racial discourse in schools, participants do not actually know what they feel about racial issues. As people try to formulate opinions on the spot, they may rely on the problematic, unexamined perspectives of friends and family. They may sit quietly in agonizing uncertainty. It is crucial that we not mistake this silence for resistance to engage in the conversation, or quickly deem any perspective to be an indication of a participant's fixed racist ideology. In these situations, the discussion facilitator can engage more deeply with the participant using reflective questions:

- Can you tell me what you mean when you say . . . ?
- Is it possible for you to say more about . . . ?
- Have the thoughts you shared been shaped by others, or is this your own personal perspective?
- Why do you think others might want to challenge your perspective?

Questions like these prompt reflection and grant participants an opportunity to reconsider the opinions they expressed.

Expect and Accept a Lack of Closure

Fourth, expect and accept a lack of closure. As much as participants appreciate definitive answers, conversations about race usually provide no resolution. Just as teachers help their students to recognize that the classroom cannot provide closure for a topic that is not closed in the real world, participants should accept that their courageous conversations will be ongoing.

Conclusion

Discussion facilitators cannot leave the flow and direction of race conversations to chance. The Four Agreements of Courageous Conversation—stay engaged, expect to experience discomfort, speak your truth, and expect and accept a lack of closure—provide a roadmap for negotiating interracial conflict.

Racial topics in the United States tend to be "hot button" issues that cause people of color to become vocally angry and white people to become silent, defiant, or disconnected. Although the vast majority of Americans accept this interracial disengagement, we must engage one another in courageous conversations about the racial issues we face. Using these strategies to facilitate a deeper dialogue about race over the past fifteen years, we have witnessed lively, gut-wrenchingly positive conversations with educators, as well as with students from kindergarten through graduate school. Every one of these transforming interactions has enhanced our confidence in our peers' and students' ability to create a more compassionate and socially just world.

RESOURCES

Glenn Singleton and Curtis Linton. 2006. *Courageous Conversations about Race: A Field Guide for Achieving Equity in Schools*. Thousand Oaks, CA: Corwin Press.
Beverly Daniel Tatum. 1997. *Why Are All the Black Kids Sitting Together in the Cafeteria? And Other Conversations about Race*. New York: Basic Books.

DISCUSSION QUESTIONS

1. **Principle:** Why might educators find talking about race particularly difficult?
2. **Strategy:** If you have had—or tried to have—conversations about race with your colleagues, or with your students, what happened? If you have not, describe a time you wish you had, and what stopped you from initiating or participating fully in the conversation.
3. **Try tomorrow:** If you were to start a conversation about some race issue with your colleagues, what issue would you like it to be?

Glenn E. Singleton is the founder and president of Pacific Educational Group, Inc. of San Francisco, California. He is an award-winning author, professional developer, and keynote speaker on issues of equity, race, and systemic transformation. Singleton is also an adjunct professor of educational leadership at San Jose State University.

Cynthia A. Hays, Ed.D., is the director of Leadership, Organizational Development and Strategic Planning for Pacific Educational Group. She has nearly thirty years of experience in urban and suburban schools. She is a licensed superintendent, high school principal, K–12 Spanish teacher, and K-8 bilingual-bicultural education teacher and has taught at the University of Minnesota.

5

Talking Precisely about Equal Opportunity

Mica Pollock

In a world that is unequal across both race and class lines—and in which student populations are increasingly diverse—educators must strive to talk more precisely about which acts help equalize opportunity for whom. Educators must particularly strive to talk more precisely about which acts help equalize opportunity for various students of color, because educators are often inundated with particularly vague proposals of ways to treat students of color "equally" in schools: "celebrate diversity!" "pursue equity!" "don't be colorblind!" However well-intentioned, these suggestions never pinpoint which everyday actions inside schools actually help provide necessary opportunities for which students, and why. I offer three suggestions for making everyday talk about equal opportunity more precise.

Ask Whether Specific Actions Move Students Closer to Opportunity

Educators need to keep asking a basic question: which of our everyday acts move specific students or student populations toward educational opportunity, and which acts move them farther away from it? When considering any given action (e.g., a particular disciplinary practice), educators can draw a simple number line (as illustrated below) and literally ask one another: do we think this act is moving the students in question closer to educational opportunity, or farther away from it? Why? What is our evidence?

less educational opportunity ← → more educational opportunity

Talk in Detail about Which Students Need Which Opportunities

Second, educators can also talk more precisely about specific subpopulations in their school, and their needs. People trying to describe students of color often use words like "urban," "inner city," "disadvantaged," or "at-risk" that gloss over the actual local needs of specific children and subgroups, such as racial groups (in some cases) or English language learners.[1] Generic phrases like "low-income minority" can also mask differences in financial circumstance, like whether students are living in stable housing or rotating foster care or whether they have health insurance. These differences affect what assistance students need from educators and other opportunity providers to have an equal opportunity to succeed in school.

Individual students have individual academic needs, and educators must analyze these needs. (And of course, students' strengths must always be analyzed alongside their needs.) But different subgroups, including racial subgroups in a school or locality, sometimes share some needs that educators can respond to, too. One school's Latino families on average might start kindergarten without having attended preschool; educators can respond by beefing up early literacy experiences for those students (or by pushing state and city legislators to fund universal preschool).[2] Conversely, some claims about large subgroups' needs should be broken down further in order to pinpoint even smaller groups' needs. A school's Salvadoran students might need particular psychological supports from school counselors and teachers after migrating to escape political violence; talk of "Latinos'" needs sometimes misses such important distinctions.[3] Similarly, talk of "Asian immigrants" can forget that one school's Chinese students, migrating from cities, may be better equipped in mathematics than are the school's Hmong students, coming from rural villages. On the other hand, some experiences may be shared by many "Asian immigrants," such as families split through the immigration process or working multiple jobs. In order to serve students more effectively, educators need to discuss, in detail, which students need which opportunities in each local situation.

When discussing student needs, educators can draw another "number line" (as illustrated below) on the board and ask the following questions about their ongoing conversation. Which needs are shared by subgroups, larger groups, or all of our students? Where on this spectrum does our current talk about the needs of students fall? Are we describing student needs precisely enough?

individual students ← → subgroups ← → larger groups ← → all students

Talk More Precisely about the Causes of Racial Disparities

Third, educators can talk more precisely about the causes of racial disparities, and about which students need which opportunities if disparities are to be eliminated. Refusing to talk about racial disparities at all, which is one aspect of what I call "colormuteness" in schools,[4] can have harmful consequences.

But we often "explain" racial disparities reductively and with insufficient information, and fail to pinpoint which opportunities students need. So just talking more about disparities is not necessarily helpful; we need to talk more precisely about causes and solutions.

For example, the high school teachers I taught with in California (and wrote about in my book *Colormute*) often remarked privately on a troubling racial disparity they never mentioned in public: the students wandering in the hallways during classes were disproportionately black. In public, they talked only of "the kids wandering in the halls," and the overrepresentation of black students was left to stand for years. But privately, the same teachers often explained this racial disparity reductively, by blaming black students alone for it. They also offered quick assumptions as facts, contending that black students had negative attitudes, or that their parents did not value educational attainment enough. Less frequently, they would blame the administrators or security guards who allowed black students to wander. But in this partial and imprecise analysis, they failed to pinpoint how they themselves were disproportionately ejecting black students from their classrooms into the hallways, as I saw repeatedly in classroom observations. They also failed to ask whether black students might be disproportionately disengaged from particular teachers' classes and therefore cutting class; this was something many black students revealed when I talked to them. The educators thus missed the chance to fully investigate the pattern's complex causes, to talk to black students about their interactions with teachers and administrators, and to investigate whether black students were being sufficiently encouraged and supported to stay in class and learn.

Imprecise analysis of the cause of any racial pattern misses drawing players into the solution. Whenever talking about racial disparities, educators can ask: Are we considering and including all the actors who contribute to producing these disparities? Do we really have evidence for the contributions we are naming? Who else needs to be pulled in to help dismantle these disparities, and to provide specific opportunities to students? How might students and others join forces in solving the disparity?

To avoid an unproductive "blame game" during such conversations, facilitators should point out that the goal is not to figure out which people to blame, but rather to analyze precisely how various actors might help undo the disparity. I call this pursuing "an urgent language of communal responsibility." When analyzing how to undo a pattern, educators must take great care to consider whether their own actions offer students optimal opportunity. Understandably, the typical tendency is to delete oneself from the analysis. (See also John Diamond, Chapter 47).

The goal of such "precise" talk about assisting students is to prompt precise analysis of what offering "equal" opportunity inside a school actually entails. When we talk imprecisely about this goal, we pursue it imprecisely as well.

RESOURCES

Mica Pollock. 2004. *Colormute: Race Talk Dilemmas in an American School*. Princeton, NJ: Princeton University Press.
Mica Pollock. 2008. *Because of Race: How Americans Debate Harm and Opportunity in Our Schools*. Princeton, NJ: Princeton University Press.

DISCUSSION QUESTIONS

1. **Principle:** Why might educators talk generally about assisting students, rather than about the precise needs of particular children or subgroups?
2. **Strategy:** How can educators talk more precisely about who needs to provide which opportunities inside schools to help dismantle racial disparities, without raising the defenses of colleagues who feel "blamed" by the analysis? What if some educators feel the "real cause" of a disparity lies outside the school?
3. **Try tomorrow:** Try using Pollock's first number line. Think of a particular action or institutional situation you fear moves a specific population of students farther from educational opportunity rather than closer to it. How could you start a conversation with a colleague about your concerns? Try role-playing a situation with a colleague.

Mica Pollock is associate professor at the Harvard Graduate School of Education. An anthropologist of education, she studies how people in educational settings struggle daily over fundamental questions of racial inequality and diversity.

6

Nice Is Not Enough: Defining Caring for Students of Color

Sonia Nieto

"But I'm a nice guy," the young man sitting across from me said plaintively, attempting to explain why all the talk about racism in education in our class was so unsettling to him. He would soon begin his teaching career, no doubt in an urban school, and he believed that being "nice" would see him through the challenges of teaching young people with whom he had had very little experience or connection until then.

This scene took place fifteen years ago, but it was not the first time, and it certainly would not be the last, that a student had come into my office to try to shed the guilt he was feeling about being white and to reaffirm his sense of being a nice person who was trying to help students of color. In my thirty years of teaching teachers and prospective teachers, this scene has been repeated countless times, sometimes accompanied by hand-wringing, sometimes by tears, often by frustration or remorse. Usually the feelings students describe are brought on by readings and discussions in my classes in multicultural education, which convey a message that is hard for some of them to hear: that, regardless of our individual personalities, we are all situated within a racially unequal structure that we often unwittingly perpetuate. When confronting stark realities they have never thought about, or have chosen not to see, many white students experience palpable pain and disconcerting disequilibrium. My greatest challenge as a teacher educator has been to help white students and students of color understand that racism is not simply a personal attitude or individual disposition and that feeling guilty or "being nice" are not enough to combat racism. Racism involves the systemic failure of people and institutions to care for students of color on an ongoing basis. Although most of my students who experience guilt and frustration about their role in an unequally caring structure are white, I include student teachers of color in my analysis. Being a person of color does not insulate us from biased perceptions and actions toward those whose backgrounds are unlike our own. Latinos may harbor biased views of African Americans, African Americans may have prejudiced views of Cambodians, and so on. People can even harbor biased views about their own group (see Valenzuela, Chapter 10).

Caring within a structure plagued by inequality takes multiple forms, and at some moments when we think we are caring for students of color we actually are harming them because we are failing to counter a social structure that treats them unequally. Mary Ginley, a gifted white teacher, articulated this idea beautifully in a journal entry for one of my classes:

> School is a foreign land to most kids (where else in the world would you spend time circling answers and filling in the blanks?), but the more distant a child's culture and language are from the culture and language of school, the more at risk that child is. A warm, friendly, helpful teacher is nice but it isn't enough. We have plenty of warm friendly teachers who tell the kids nicely to forget their Spanish and ask mommy and daddy to speak to them in English at home; who give them easier tasks so they won't feel badly when the work becomes difficult; who never learn about what life is like at home or what they eat or what music they like or what stories they have been told or what their history is. Instead, we smile and give them a hug and tell them to eat our food and listen to our stories and dance to our music. We teach them to read with our words and wonder why it's so hard for them. We ask them to sit quietly and we tell them what's important and what they must know to "get ready for the next grade." And we never ask them who they are and where they want to go.[1]

As this reflection makes clear, teachers can participate in practices of racism—that is, practices that deny students of color equal opportunities along racial lines—even when they think they are individually being "nice." In the examples Ginley provides, "nice" educators sometimes convey, even unwittingly, a deep disdain and disrespect for families by suggesting that home cultural values have no place in school. I have seen numerous cases in which "nice" teachers expected less of their students of color, believing that by refusing to place the same rigorous demands on their students of color as they do on white students, they were making accommodations for the students' difficult home life, poverty, or lack of English-language proficiency. Such "accommodations" may unintentionally give students the message that teachers believe these students are incapable of learning (see also Taylor, Chapter 17).

Even as we purport to care about all students equally, we also often tolerate policies in our districts and schools that harm students of color, especially those who are poor and those for whom English is a second language: unequal resources, punitive high-stakes testing, and rigid ability-group tracking are some key examples.[2] Racism in these forms involves failing to ensure that institutions care for students. The late Meyer Weinberg, a historian who studied school desegregation, defined racism as a system of privilege and penalty.[3] According to this definition, a student is rewarded or punished in education (as in housing, employment, health, and so on) by the simple fact of belonging to a particular racialized group, regardless of his or her individual merits or faults. Within such an unequal system, even "nice" people can accept and even distribute these unfair rewards and punishments. This idea is difficult, even wrenching, for many people to accept.

I have utilized several strategies to get preservice teachers to consider and debate how, despite their best intentions, they might actually participate in various institutional practices of not caring for students. To ensure that their institutions *are* caring for students, educators can begin to ask one another, in so many words, what it *means* to "care" for their student body. Participants should make this discussion of caring safe, but not necessarily personally comfortable; participants will need to struggle with hard ideas about themselves and about institutions.

To help teachers explore particularly critically what sort of caring assists students of color struggling within unequal systems, I ask them to do an in-depth case study of a student (for guidelines, see Nieto and Bode 2008, Resource list). Looking carefully at an individual member of a group dispels stereotypes about the needs of all people from particular backgrounds, while at the same time gives teachers a more complete understanding of how group membership affects the contexts in which students live. I also have them read "coming of age" stories of young people from various backgrounds (see Nieto and Bode 2008) so that they understand the specific challenges of encountering racism and start thinking about what students of color might need from their teachers. These activities are followed by dialogue, reflection, and analysis designed to get teachers discussing how they and their students are members of structurally positioned groups. Teachers come to see that caring for students within unequal structures requires going beyond "niceness" to challenge institutional inequality.

I then ask teachers to think deeply about and debate what it means to demonstrate care in a classroom. Teachers may think of caring as unconditional praise, or as quickly incorporating cultural components into the curriculum, or even as lowering standards. On the contrary, others have argued, an "ethic of care"[4] means a combination of respect, admiration, and rigorous standards. What is needed, as described by researcher Rosalie Rolón-Dow,[5] is *critical care* that responds to students' actual personal lives and to the institutional barriers they encounter as members of racialized groups. Teachers must understand individual students within their concrete sociopolitical contexts and devise specific pedagogical and curricular strategies to help them navigate those contexts successfully. This work begins when we ask what it means to "care."

RESOURCES

Sonia Nieto and Patty Bode. 2008. *Affirming Diversity: The Sociopolitical Context of Multicultural Education*. 5th ed. Boston: Allyn & Bacon. Companion website: http://wps.ablongman.com/ab_nieto_diversity_5.

Rethinking Schools: www.rethinkingschools.org. Rethinking Schools is a nonprofit independent newspaper advocating the reform of elementary and secondary public schools, with an emphasis on urban schools and issues of equity and social justice.

DISCUSSION QUESTIONS

1. **Principle:** What distinguishes "critical care" from less "critical" "caring" for students?
2. **Strategy:** How might you discover and respond to your own students' needs—both their individual needs and their needs as members of groups in American society?
3. **Try tomorrow:** Describe a time you feel that you "cared" for a student successfully. After reading Nieto's definition of "care," how do you feel you have "cared" for your students? Describe an experience when you fear that you did not do so.

Sonia Nieto is professor emerita of language, literacy, and culture at the University of Massachusetts–Amherst. She has taught at all levels from elementary grades through graduate school. Her areas of research are multicultural education, teacher education, and the education of students of culturally and linguistically diverse backgrounds.

Part III

Remember That People Do Not Fit Neatly and Easily into Racial Groups

Your "race" shapes your experience in society and in schools, but no one fits a standard template as a racial group member. Some of us test the boundaries of racial categories all the time. The essays in this part share a core principle of everyday antiracism: *people do not fit easily and neatly into racial groups, even though they often experience the world as racial group members.*

What strategies can educators use to observe people's important struggles with racial categories?

1. Try to follow children's leads in conversations about race.

   Kimberly Chang and Rachel Conrad suggest that teachers engage in dialogue with students who ask them hard questions about racial categories.

2. Observe the complex ways that students interact informally.

   Ben Rampton proposes that educators observe how young people test and transcend the boundaries of race categories with one another.

7

Following Children's Leads in Conversations about Race

Kimberly Chang and Rachel Conrad

Too often, adults feel that they possess greater understanding of race than children, and that antiracist education involves adults imparting their knowledge. Whether they choose to emphasize racial identities or to highlight human similarities, adults set the terms of discussions about race and position children as the recipients of adult ideas. They discount how children use and understand race in their own social interactions.[1]

Children's attempts to make sense of racial categories are often revealed through spontaneous questions and remarks that emerge in the contexts of everyday conversations and activities. A three-year-old's question, "why do white people have vaginas?"[2] a five-year-old's query, "what's a kike?"[3] and a ten-year-old's assertion that her father's "asking about whether people are Asian American or African American or white is racist,"[4] are examples of children's attempts to grapple with racial meanings in conversation with adults. Adults are often caught off guard by these questions; children's direct use of racial terms unsettles adults' assumptions about what children can and should know about race. Yet these questions provide crucial opportunities for adults and children to grapple together with the ambiguities and complexities of racial terms and racial categories. As Ayers writes, children's questions "ask us to reconsider the world, to confront our own gaps and ignorance, to rethink the taken-for-granted, the habitual, our insistent common sense."[5]

We suggest that children's questions can be important entry points into conversations between adults and children about race and racism. These conversations are possible only if adults do not shut them down by shushing or lecturing children. Adults must be prepared and willing to follow children's leads by listening to children, using their terminology, building on children's ideas, and trying to understand children's statements in the contexts of their experiences. Paradoxically, in order to follow a child's lead, adults must also bring their own viewpoints and concerns about racism into the discussion as ideas to discuss rather than as right answers. Only in this way can these conversations evolve into dialogues that examine the ideas of both children and adults and challenge racism.

For the last six years, we have team-taught a college course called "Children and Their Cultural Worlds" that focuses on young children's experiences and understandings of race and culture. Our students work with children at an elementary after-school program and contribute to the development of its multicultural and antiracist curriculum. We have spent many hours with our students developing age-appropriate activities and carefully crafting questions that directly engage children in discussing issues of race and racism. Yet some of the most profound learning moments have come from the provocative questions and remarks that children have posed to our students. These moments challenged our students' assumptions about children and race and led us to think about how adults and children both struggle with racial meanings in their conversations and interactions.

In the two examples that follow, which are adapted from our students' papers, a child initiates a conversation with an adult. In the first example, a child questions one of our students about her racial identity and she struggles to respond. In the second example, a child's hostile words and actions about a racial group lead one of our students to try to follow the child's meaning. By examining the ways in which our students respond, we explore what prevents and enables dialogue about race and racism between children and adults.

One afternoon on the playground at the after-school program, Michelle, one of our students, was asked by seven-year-old Steven, "Are you black or white?" Michelle hesitated and then replied: "I'm white." After a moment, Steven said, "I'm white too." When Michelle did not respond, Steven added, "My skin is dark, but I'm white." In her written reflections on this conversation, Michelle said that Steven's remarks confused and unsettled her. From her perspective, she could "clearly see this boy was not white." She wondered how she should have responded: "Was I supposed to ask him why he thought he was white? He was only seven; I had no idea how much he was capable of understanding." She felt pressured to respond but was frozen by her failure to think of something "enlightening" to say. Suddenly Patti, a twelve-year-old girl who, according to Michelle, "happened to have dark skin," cut in to say sharply to Steven: "What did you say? You're not white! Why did you say that?" "I'm just kidding around," Steven said. "You don't do that," Patti replied. "You're black, you know that." The conversation came to an abrupt halt and Michelle stood there, in her words, "looking like a silent idiot."

Like so many of the questions about race that children posed to our students, Steven's query about Michelle's racial group membership came "out of nowhere," as Michelle put it, and caught her off guard. But she quickly regained her composure and, not wanting to "avoid" talking about race and feeling she had it "all figured out and all under control," she confidently answered his question. In just giving Steven the answer about her race, Michelle missed a critical opportunity to enter into dialogue with Steven and explore what he may have meant by "black" and "white." She could have interpreted his question as an invitation to suspend certainty that there are clear answers about race and enter into a more open-ended and mutual exploration of racial categories. For example, she could have elicited Steven's opinion about her own "race" by asking "what do *you* think?" She could have called attention to the potential discrepancy between the way she identifies herself and the way he identifies her by responding with a comment designed to elicit further discussion, e.g., "*I* think I'm white, what do *you* think?" Alternatively, Michelle could have prompted a dialogue by asking what "black" and "white" refer to, e.g., "do you think my skin *really* looks black or white?"

Steven's subsequent remarks—"I'm white too" and "my skin is dark, but I'm white"—suggest a more complicated understanding of racial categories than Michelle initially believed he possessed. His later admission that he was "just kidding around" suggests that his opening question was a playful invitation to explore the ambiguity of the terms "black" and "white" and to test the boundaries of racial group membership. Yet Michelle could not see his remarks as an invitation for dialogue in part because she attributed them to what she viewed as his limited understanding. She herself was confused, yet rather than admit this to Steven by asking, "can you be white if your skin is dark?" she fell into the trap of feeling that as an adult she had to respond definitively, as if she had a clear understanding of these categories herself. In the end, she missed the opportunity to engage in a rich dialogue with Steven that would perhaps have furthered both of their understandings.

Patti's role in this conversation also deserves comment. We can never know what Patti meant by the charged way in which she chided Steven—"You don't do that. You're black, you know that"—because Michelle did not take this opportunity to learn from her. Michelle could have questioned Patti's admonition by asking "why not?" Yet Michelle remained silent, feeling that she "had no business going there and thrusting my opinions onto these kids who were already figuring out the world for themselves." Michelle felt that if she could not be the all-knowing adult, she had no place in these conversations with children about race, so she missed a key opportunity to engage these children.

In another example, Sarah, a college student, found herself in a private conversation with seven-year-old Malik. Malik constructed a doll from a cotton ball and feather and proclaimed, "Look, it's an Indian!" He then cut the feather into pieces and remarked, "Ha, ha, ha, now he's gone." In her written reflection, Sarah noted that she felt Malik was trying to provoke a response from her, yet she remained "calm" in order to "question Malik while keeping the conversation open." "What would make you want to do that to an Indian?" she asked him. "They're mean," Malik replied. Sarah continued to follow his lead by repeating his words, asking, "Why do you think they're mean?" "No, my friend thinks they're mean." "Well, why does your friend think they're mean?" Sarah responded. Malik answered, "This guy is mean to my stepdad and he [this guy] is Indian." Sarah then asked, "Do you think all Indians are that way or just that particular Indian was mean?" After a brief silence, Malik responded, "I need the glue."

In contrast to Michelle, Sarah saw Malik's remark as an entry point into his ideas, and she made a deliberate decision to take up his provocative invitation to talk about "Indians." Sarah recognized that what mattered in this exchange was the meaning of the term "Indian" for Malik and how he used it to make sense of his world.

Sarah's initial response—"What would make you want to do that to an Indian?"—acknowledged her alarm over Malik's use of the term "Indian" in the context of his hostile action. Yet she did not respond in a reproachful manner, by asking "Why did you do that?!" which might have produced a defensive reaction and closed down further conversation. When Malik claimed that his friend was the one who thought "Indians" were "mean," Sarah followed this lead and inquired about the friend's beliefs rather than "reprimand [Malik]." When Malik subsequently revealed his personal experience involving his stepfather, Sarah considered this a "success" in terms of her ability to help Malik "figure out what race means to him and how it applies to his own life." Equally important was Sarah's ability to bring in her own concerns about racism without allowing them to dominate the conversation.

With her final question, "Do you think all Indians are that way or just that particular Indian was mean?" Sarah started to more explicitly instruct Malik about the dangers of stereotyping "all Indians." A question at this point could elicit a useful discussion about stereotyping. In this case it did not, in part because the forced-choice question, unlike her more open-ended questions, carried a thinly veiled attempt to get him to choose the "right" answer. More importantly, by asking about "all Indians" rather than about what happened to Malik's stepfather, Sarah moved the conversation toward a more abstract level removed from Malik's everyday experience. No wonder Malik declared at that moment that he needed the glue!

These examples illustrate contrasting ways of responding to children's spontaneous remarks and questions about race. In the first example, Michelle was paralyzed by her need to play the role of all-knowing adult. She could not bring her own questions and confusions about race into the conversation and was unable to engage in a dialogue about race with the children. In the second example, Sarah intentionally adopted a less authoritative role in which she wanted to talk *with* rather than *to* the child. Sarah did not assume that her role was "to convey what [she] knew about race," but rather to facilitate an "equal dialogue that allows for the child to understand race in [his or her] own way." Yet even for Sarah, dialogue was difficult to sustain. While conversations about stereotyping are important, they must be framed in terms that stay close to the child's experience. It is important for adults to bring their own agendas and uncertainties alongside children's in these conversations, but it is equally important that they do so in a way that does not override children's language and experience.

First and foremost, adults must listen to the questions children ask about race, for these questions, if we can follow them, "may become occasions for the ethical to emerge."[6] In following children's leads, adults must be willing to use children's terminology, build on children's ideas, and try to understand their racial statements in the contexts of children's experiences. Only then can the terms of antiracist practice—whether to emphasize racial identities or to highlight human similarities—be jointly determined by adults and children.

RESOURCES

Mary Cowhey. 2006. *Black Ants and Buddhists: Thinking Critically and Teaching Differently in the Primary Grades.* Portland, ME: Stenhouse.

DISCUSSION QUESTIONS

1. **Principle:** What facilitates or hinders dialogue about race between adults and children?
2. **Strategy:** As educators seek to follow children's leads in conversations about race, when, if ever, should educators simply tell students that their ideas about race are wrong?
3. **Try tomorrow:** Can you think of an example in your teaching when a student asked you a question or made a comment about race? How did you respond, and where did the conversation go? How might you have responded differently using the child-centered guidelines suggested by the authors?

Kimberly Chang is associate professor of cultural psychology at Hampshire College, where she teaches about the psychology of globalization and the dilemmas of identity and belonging for people whose lives span national borders and cultural worlds.

Rachel Conrad is associate professor of psychology and childhood studies at Hampshire College, where she teaches about children's social lives and conceptions and representations of childhood in psychology and other disciplines.

8

Observing Students Sharing Language

Ben Rampton

Educators should seek to understand students' everyday "race relations." One way to do so is to listen carefully to how students interact informally across racial lines. Educators should not listen only for moments when students explicitly discuss race and ethnicity; important interactions also take place in conversations about other things.

In my research, I have examined how young people informally, moment to moment, take on the language habits of other groups. I observed ethnically mixed friendship groups in an English neighborhood, and examined moments when youngsters of African Caribbean and Anglo descent used Punjabi language, youngsters of Punjabi and Anglo descent used Caribbean Creole, and all three groups used a form of stylized South Asian English. I collected evidence on the ways in which youngsters used the tiny details of talk to work their ways through group difference and division. I focused on two issues: language "crossing," or students using languages from other groups, and "stylization," or students doing exaggerated performances of different speech styles.

Readers may like to consider how often their own students "cross" in their informal interactions. While some such interactions harm, many interactions that might seem "racist" to the educator can also be important moments of cross-group alliance.

Here is one example of fifteen-year-olds making spontaneous use of one another's ethnic languages. This example comes from a discussion of Punjabi *bhangra* music, a musical form blending traditional and contemporary Indian and British sounds. Sally (fifteen, female, Anglo descent) has joined Gurmit (fifteen, female, Indian descent) and some of her friends including Winnona (female, Anglo) who are listening to some *bhangra* tapes outside. Sally has been told that the cassette they are listening to belongs to Lorraine (fifteen, female, Anglo), who is nearby. A complex and prestigious cultural movement was developing around *bhangra*, with Punjabi youngsters acting as the inheritors and interpreters of adult Punjabi tradition and a number of non-Punjabis, mainly white girls, accepting the status of novice learner of *bhangra*. Sally had developed an enthusiasm for *bhangra* through Imran, her boyfriend. Her friend Winnona cited the Punjabi song lyrics ("kenoo minoo" and "holle holle") enthusiastically as well.

SALLY (CALLING OUT): OH LORRAINE EH LORRAINE HAS IT GOT KENOO MINOO on it?

GIRL: You want the other side

WINNONA: It's got (SINGING) holle holle

SALLY (SINGS): O kennoo mennoo I love—

GURMIT: Oh that

Similarly, youth of various groups regularly used black speech features noted in South London, such as "dat's sad, man." Many adolescents aspired to use Creole-sounding terms in their ordinary speech because Creole was seen as central to youth culture; one informant referred to it as "future language." In the United States, many nonblack children intersperse African American Vernacular English terms into their ordinary informal speech (on AAVE, see Baugh, Chapter 20).

Sometimes, on the other hand, black, white, and Punjabi youngsters used a kind of stylized Indian English in overtly racist taunts directed at youngsters with Bangladeshi roots, minority group who had arrived most recently. Youngsters hardly ever directed this kind of critical Indian English toward Punjabi friends, because all sensed they would sound racist if they did. In games, however, stylized Indian English could feature in praise and encouragement, such as an Indian-accented "very good shot!"

How do we connect the practice of language crossing with group relations? With the important exception of Indian English used to taunt Bangladeshi youngsters for appearing to be inept outsiders, moments of ethnolinguistic crossing and stylization (like the Sally and friends example) challenged "ethnic absolutism"[1] and were important moments of antiracism. "Ethnic absolutism" assumes that a person's racial-ethnic identity is fixed, and that racial-ethnic identity is the most important aspect of a person's identity, overshadowing or erasing gender, class, region, and occupation. In contrast, youth language crossing like Sally's and Winnona's indicated solidarities and allegiances based on shared identities of neighborhood, class, gender, age, institutional role, and recreational interest. For many adolescents, ethnolinguistic crossing symbolized a multiethnic youth culture. Students offered examples of language crossing when trying to illustrate the ways in which friends with different ethnic backgrounds might be "one of us," "in our sort of community."

But language crossing did not mean that racial-ethnic identity was meaningless. Inherited racial-ethnic identity still played quite a significant role in the formation of friendship groups, and its unfair influence on employment opportunities, education, housing, and wealth was well recognized by students. Language crossing seemed to involve a subtle combination of both respect and disregard for racial-ethnic differences. Students showed respect for ethnic boundaries by not crossing in certain contexts. Black and white adolescents seldom used Asian English to make fun of Punjabi friends, and most whites and Asians either avoided or made little use of Creole in the company of black peers. Crossing generally only occurred in moments, activities, and relationships when the constraints of ordinary social order were relaxed, like games, joking abuse, and performance.[2] Because they generally crossed only at special moments like these, a white youth using Creole or a black youth using Punjabi never claimed that they were really black or Asian. They did not assume that they could move unproblematically in and out of their friends' heritage language at random. Adolescents normally only tested out the language of others at moments when it could be safely understood that they were not making any claims to real, equal, and enduring membership of an ethnic out-group.

It would be foolish to call all forms of ethnolinguistic crossing and stylization acts of everyday antiracism in this book's terms. The interactions I have described were situated in long-term friendship and neighborhood co-residence. Commercial marketing gives rise to very different dynamics of language-sharing among youth, in which youth "try on" others' languages, often from a great distance.[3] In many such cases, racism is the most striking feature of language crossing.[4] Even so, there are good grounds for seeing small acts of crossing as significant contributions to the emergence of "new ethnicities" founded in "a new cultural politics which engages rather than suppresses difference."[5] They also show that aggression and hostility are not the only ways children and adolescents respond to racial and ethnic difference when left to their own devices. The jokes, nonsense, gossip, rowdiness, games, and fashions that youngsters enjoy can also sustain antiracism. Educators should pay attention to these everyday moments of "crossing."

RESOURCES

Gautam Malkani. 2005. *Londonstani.* London: HarperCollins.
Ben Rampton. 1996. Language Crossing, New Ethnicities and School. *English in Education* 30(2): 14–26.

DISCUSSION QUESTIONS

1. **Principle:** When does sharing someone else's language (or dress, or movement) respect difference? When does it mock difference?

2. **Strategy:** What examples of language crossing (or "crossing" in dress or behavior) have you seen in your school, or in other informal spaces your students frequent? What do you think is a useful educator reaction to such "crossing"?

3. **Try tomorrow:** How might you discuss, with students, which of their play with racial-ethnic language styles is antiracist and which racist?

Ben Rampton works at the Centre for Language Discourse & Communication at King's College London. His work involves ethnography and interactional discourse analysis, and his interests cover urban multilingualism, ethnicity, class, youth, and education.

Part IV

Remember That People Are Treated as Racial Group Members and Need to Examine That Experience

Even as we test the boundaries of racial categories and group norms, others still treat us as members of race groups. The essays in this part share a core principle of everyday antiracism: *students (and teachers) need to process their experiences in the world as racial group members.*

How can educators assist students in this "processing"?

1. Create cocoons for strengthening identities.

   Patricia Gándara suggests that students of color in particular can benefit from some time voluntarily "cocooned" with students from the same racial group, in order to process their schooling and life experiences *as* group members and build healthy identities as such.

2. Be aware that students of color may need to heal from internalized oppression.

   Angela Valenzuela reminds us that racism can involve people hating themselves, not just "others," and that students need to be assisted to analyze how such self-hatred comes about.

3. Urge students to see and treat one another as equally worthy.

   Lory J. Dance suggests that students need concrete opportunities to learn to value each other equally across racial lines.

9

Strengthening Student Identity
in School Programs

Patricia Gándara

Ignoring students' race is often perceived as being antiracist by teachers, counselors, and administrators who have little sense of the fundamental importance and far-reaching consequences of racial-group experiences for people of color, as well as for Anglos. Official policy in recent years has promoted this "colorblind" attitude in education. On the heels of the passage of Proposition 209, the anti-affirmative action ballot initiative in California, schools were told that they could not consider race for selection or programming purposes in college access programs. Since then, many schools have been reluctant to group students by race or ethnicity for any purpose.

I contend that to help students of color who feel especially vulnerable as visible minorities in school settings to succeed in school and to go on to college, it may, instead, be antiracist to cluster students occasionally and temporarily by racial-ethnic background for academic, social, and counseling purposes. Sometimes it also makes sense to match them with adult mentors who share the same background. These practices counter students' marginalization in the majority environment and their vulnerability when asked to share their views and experiences, which have been shaped in environments very different from their Anglo classmates'.

I call this occasional and temporary separation from the majority group into a cluster of same-ethnicity peers "cocooning," because the strategy provides some protection for the young person to form her identity in a healthy and supportive environment and to develop the strength and skills necessary to confront marginalizing experiences. The well-meaning teacher who remarks when looking at his classroom, "I don't see color, I see children," is missing some critically important information about his students' needs, such as how membership in a racial group shapes experience, access to social and cultural capital, and perspectives.

For more than a decade, my students and I have been investigating how low-income students of color can successfully navigate the tortuous path through high school and into higher education. The data show that most do not succeed in reaching this goal, but we have surveyed, interviewed, and observed both those who do and those who do not. We have studied programs that purport to provide students with the assistance they need to succeed in high school, which are variously known as "early intervention programs," "college access programs," and "outreach programs." All attempt to support low-income students, usually students of color, who would be the first in the family to make it into college.

We have learned a great deal about what makes these programs effective, as well as the kinds of limitations that are inherent in them. One successful strategy is assigning a full-time person to monitor individual students across classes and grade levels, who gets to know them on a personal level. Since close and careful monitoring of students is labor intensive, it is expensive to operate programs this way, and budgetary constraints mean that most programs severely limit the numbers of students they serve.

While studying these programs, we have heard a deafening silence on one vital question: is it sometimes advisable to subdivide students by racial-ethnic group to increase their chances of success? Conversely, do programs that serve all racial-ethnic groups together in a "colorblind" manner have equal success with all groups? Most people we interview lack a vocabulary to talk about this issue of racial-group programming. Many find the topic uncomfortable, or even anathema to the perspectives on race they share with their funders. We often act as though even thinking about the implications of a student's race and ethnicity for how she or he navigates the difficult path to higher education is "racist" in itself. I have become convinced that our discomfort about engaging race and ethnicity is undermining some of our best efforts to expand academic opportunity.

As an antiracist move, I suggest providing students with "cocoons," grouping them by racial-ethnic identity in order to enable them to analyze their situations in a protected environment and, if possible, with mentors who belong to their racial-ethnic group. When "cocooning" students, educators can provide these protected learning environments for students for part of the day or part of the year, occasionally or routinely, and at various moments in students' development. Educators must decide who will be placed in these "cocooned" environments, what the curriculum of these environments will entail, and who will run them. Here I briefly describe just one effective program to illustrate the types of cocooning experiences that can be provided for students.

The High School Puente program in California focuses on Latino students, meets for one hour of each school day, and emphasizes rigorous instruction in writing and Chicano literature, mentoring provided by an academically successful Chicano/Latino member of the community, and intensive college preparatory counseling, sometimes provided by a Chicano/Latino counselor.[1] Through field trips, the Puente program encourages participants to spend time outside the classroom together, supporting one another's identities and academic goals. Curriculum in the Puente English classroom includes community-based folklore and assignments that incorporate parents and other family members in research. One typical classroom activity focuses on *dichos* (proverbs). In Latino culture, *dichos* serve as guidelines for appropriate behavior and demonstrate life lessons. They can also be used to motivate and guide students toward success in school, and they provide the opportunity for students to analyze both language and culture. Many Latino parents are familiar with *dichos* and most enjoy contributing their favorites to the class. For example, one popular *dicho* is "Dime con quien andas, y te diré quien eres" ("Tell me who you hang out with and I will tell you who you are.") An examination of this *dicho* brings complex issues to light, such as how students choose their friends and are chosen by them; how their parents feel about these friends; what constitutes a good friend or friendship (e.g., friendship with a high-achieving student or with a loyal friend who is failing in school); and what consequences these choices entail.

In the aftermath of the passage of Proposition 209, the Puente program was threatened with a lawsuit if it continued to recruit only Latino students. In response, the program opened its doors to all students, but remained firmly committed to its focus on Chicano culture and on curricular and counseling strategies that had proved effective for Latino students. Counseling strategies included guiding students in critical analysis of the factors that impede Latino students from going to college and holding Spanish-language information sessions for their parents.

A guiding principle of the Puente program is that it is crucial for young Latinos to analyze their own educational situation as Latinos. Without a critical perspective, students run the risk of internalizing and acting out the racist stereotypes they see all around them about Latinos who are failing in school, holding only low-level jobs, and are prone to criminal (male) or seductive (female) behavior. Another key principle is that adults must deeply understand and, to the extent possible, have experienced the same racially and ethnically specific circumstances as their students. The program matches highly qualified adults with students from the same community, though not all program staff members are Latino.

Racially and ethnically homogeneous peer groupings are important because students from the same background share specific experiences and family practices that allow them to empathize with one another and to discuss sensitive issues surrounding their challenges in school. Early in our evaluation of the program,[2] we noted the deep sense of safety that Latino students felt in the Puente classroom, as they revealed to each other the difficult circumstances of their migration to the United States, the problems of living here without legal documentation, the challenges inherent in growing up in a family in which parents had only a few years of formal education, or of dealing with the trauma of siblings involved in gangs—many things that would be embarrassing to admit in front of others who did not share such experiences.

These issues impinged on their ability to succeed in high school and enter-tain the thought of going to college. Adolescents, who value, above all, being accepted by their peers, are generally very protective about what they reveal to others.

These safe places were created in classrooms by talented and sensitive Anglo teachers as well as skilled teachers of color. It is likely that these stu-dents would never have divulged such personal information in a classroom of more heterogeneous peers, however. It may be possible to achieve the same sense of safety in a heterogeneous classroom, or one that incorporates students from similar circumstances who belong to different racial-ethnic groups. But my own experience is that few adults have the talent and skills required to achieve this goal. By reducing its variability, the complexity of the task is reduced.

How do these programs reconcile racial and ethnic grouping with the equally important need for students to learn to move with ease and confi-dence in the broader society and among peers and adults of different racial-ethnic backgrounds? Does the structure of the program actually impede this learning? In order to gauge students' comfort in interacting with adults and students across racial and ethnic lines, we surveyed and interviewed them about their thoughts concerning appropriate mentors and asked students about the ethnic backgrounds of their best friends to see whether they pre-ferred interacting with peers from the same racial-ethnic group.

On the first point, surprisingly, a slight majority felt that racial or ethnic background made no difference in an adult's ability to connect with and support them. However, they felt it was important that the teachers, coun-selors, and mentors who interacted with their parents be able to speak the same language and understand their parents' circumstances and attitudes. As we reviewed the features of college access programs that were particularly successful,[3] we observed that programs with mostly African American staff often had better outcomes for African American students, and those with mostly Latino staff seemed to have an advantage in working with Latino stu-dents. Some programs with strong male staff also appeared to be more success-ful in attracting and retaining males. Students may have been more likely to take seriously the advice and counseling they received from these same-ethnicity, same-sex adults.

Students had similarly complex reactions regarding the importance of in-teracting with Latino peers. While the safety net and support structure of the program was predicated on involving peers from the same background, students also expressed a desire to interact with others who were not from the same background. Some students even refused to answer the question about the ethnicity of their best friend, saying "it's nobody's business." In focus groups, students often stated that race and ethnicity "didn't matter" in their choice of friends, though survey results showed that the overwhelming majority of students of all racial-ethnic groups tended to choose best friends from the same background. Like adults in the society in which they live, high school students are deeply ambivalent about discussing or even acknowledging racial differences. The students' survey responses suggested that race was an important factor in their social and educational lives and they valued interacting with peers and adults from the same racial-ethnic background, but they were not comfortable discussing this question.

Powerful evidence demonstrates that students need to have safe places to address many of the issues that have held them back educationally: lack of support from family and friends, racist actions by their teachers and counselors, and ugly stereotypes that caused them to question their own abilities. To succeed academically and interact with people across racial and ethnic boundaries, students need to develop strong identities as members of a racial-ethnic group that is often marginalized or vilified in the dominant society. An effective way to support the development of a healthy identity is through contact with adult members of their community who have successfully addressed that challenge. At the same time, low-income students and students of color who are most successful educationally are comfortable moving back and forth between their home culture and mainstream culture and between homogeneous and heterogeneous groups (see also P. Carter, Chapter 21).[4] Educators should simultaneously offer students opportunities for the strengthening provided by cocooning and the broadening offered by boundary crossing. Because students are often tracked into racially segregated classes and engage in different social activities according to race, many heterogeneous schools do not provide real opportunities for border crossing. Just as with cocooning, programs designed to promote border crossing must be skillfully structured.

Sometimes the most effective antiracist strategy for helping students of color to navigate high school and move on to college is to give them opportunities to be "cocooned" for some period of time in contexts that allow them to analyze in a safe environment what it means to be a racial-ethnic group member in and out of school and to draw inspiration and support from those who have traveled the same road before them. The opportunity for safe exploration is appropriate to the key developmental years of early to mid-adolescence, when young people are "trying on" possible identities.[5] This strategy allows students to enter the mainstream culture with the self-confidence required to succeed, while feeling pride and comfort in their own racial-ethnic background.

RESOURCES

Martha Montero-Sieburth and Francisco Villarruel. 2000. *Making Invisible Latino Adolescents Visible.* New York: Falmer. This book includes a number of chapters on various aspects of the culture of Latino youth.

Tom Musica and Ramon Menendez. 1988. *Stand and Deliver* [Motion Picture].
Warner Brothers. Looks at Latino students in a math classroom and the personal
and cultural challenges they face together.
The Puente program: www.ucop.edu/puente/.

DISCUSSION QUESTIONS

1. **Principle:** When does placing students in racially and ethnically homogeneous environments assist them, and when does it harm them? Have
   you seen successful and unsuccessful examples of this strategy?
2. **Strategy:** In racially and ethnically homogeneous groupings, what
   types of activities or curricular material might prompt students to analyze their shared experiences?
3. **Try tomorrow:** What specific professional development or learning experiences might you need if you were leading a cocoon for students
   who did not belong to your own racial-ethnic group? How might you
   prepare if you did belong to the same group?

*Patricia Gándara is professor of education at UCLA, Co-Director of the Civil
Rights Project/El Proyecto de CRP, and associate director of the University of
California Linguistic Minority Research Institute. Professor Gándara's research explores the education of English Learners and issues of access and equity in education.*

10

Uncovering Internalized Oppression

Angela Valenzuela

I begin by sharing a personal story that has great significance for U.S. Mexican and other children of color. Borrowing from Pizarro (see Resources), I suggest that teachers too rarely notice the "soul wounds" that students of color inflict upon one another. These wounds can result in internalized oppression, meaning that minority group members subscribe to the dominant group's negative stereotypes of their group.[1] Even well-meaning teachers routinely fail to help children and youth of color heal from the soul wounds that they experience at the hands of white students and adults; they often fail even to notice the ways that children and youth of color wound one another. In order to help students begin to heal from these wounds, educators need to learn from stories like this one.

I suppressed this memory for years. I finally wrote this account on July 1, 2003, after visiting with a childhood friend Norma, who still resides in San Angelo, Texas, my hometown. This painful memory from my seventh-grade year fills me with a deep sense of guilt and remorse, but it also reveals a larger problem of self-hatred and internalized oppression that originates within powerful societal institutions like schools, a primary site where young people internalize dominant ideologies that nonwhite selves are inferior.[2]

I was in the seventh grade at Robert E. Lee Junior High School, where Mexican-origin and African American youth comprised about a third of a school population that was otherwise Anglo. I remember being small and scared. I was especially afraid of getting beaten up by a group of African American girls who would bully the smaller students for their lunch money. I recall my seventh-grade year being a continuous dodging experience and a series of narrow escapes from these threatening bullies. Consequently, I felt the need to show toughness and hang out with students who were tough. I befriended Norma, who was tougher and more physically mature than I. Whenever I was around her, I felt protected. Norma was not only attractive, but she strutted about with an attitude, wearing her stylish threads. Though from a poor family, she always dressed fashionably, primarily because she made all of her clothing herself. All of us girls admired her for her looks, and in my case, how they combined with her tough *chola* (wannabe gangster) demeanor.

Norma had a problem with another female student that I had trouble understanding. Although her name was Jovita, she pronounced her name "Joe-vita," an Anglicized version of her name (in Spanish, the j sounds like an h). Unlike Norma, myself, and the majority of Mexican-origin youth, who were Mexican American, she was an immigrant girl who spoke more Spanish than we did and wore a lot of makeup together with clothes that Norma derisively referred to as "K-Mart specials." Norma routinely ridiculed all of these things. Norma had so much power over me that I felt embarrassed and became secretive about the fact that my mother purchased my clothes from K-Mart whenever she did not make them herself. Hypocritically, I recall occasionally chiming in when Norma commented on Jovita's clothing. I drew warped, teenage pleasure in making Jovita the object of our ridicule. It seemed harmless enough in the beginning, especially since the two of us did not know her anyway.

As time wore on, Norma's antipathy toward Jovita deepened. Jovita seemed to symbolize all that Norma wanted to expunge from her own sense of self. While Mexican Americans like Norma and me also spoke Spanish at home and English at school, we regularly distinguished between ourselves, as Mexican Americans, and Mexican immigrants. Norma reserved her strongest West Texas twang for times when she would talk or joke about "those Mexicans from the other side" or "those Mexicans from 'ol Mexico.'" Despite our shared origins, we tended to view the less Anglicized immigrants among us as inferior distant cousins or to ignore their existence altogether. Unfortunately, I was not sophisticated enough to recognize these behaviors as manifestations of internalized oppression. I now understand that in disparaging all poor Mexican immigrants, Norma disparaged herself.

My need to be Norma's friend kept me from sharing a lot of my own Mexican-ness with her, including the fact that my mother's parents were from Mexico. I felt pressured to be Mexican American, with the emphasis on American—somehow better, superior, and "richer" than "those Mexicans" like Jovita. My relationship with Norma provided the support I needed in order to be tough. The use of profanity, especially in Spanish, became a personal strategy for securing both Norma's esteem and my survival in middle school. Thinking, acting, and feeling tough just like Norma would carry me through, I thought.

The pecking order among the Mexican girls was established in gym class. Norma would make a nasty comment at Jovita, and Jovita would snap back. They carried on this way until one day, one of them challenged the other to a fight after school. Word spread like wildfire throughout the school: Norma and Jovita were going to fight. I remember how my heart of darkness—a toxic mixture of internalized racism and teenage cruelty—desired to witness the fight. But I was unable to come up with an excuse for my mother, so she picked me up from school that day as she customarily did. I would like to think that my own sense of integrity kept me from going, but I know that had I had the opportunity, I would have gone.

The next day, the school was abuzz about the knock-down, drag-out fight that had unfolded in a secluded lot nearby. I heard from friends that the fight got really wild and crazy, with Norma giving Jovita a black eye, and how Norma peeled off Jovita's shirt and how she fought in her bra. The details of the punches, scratches, and kicking before a jeering crowd horrified me. In my adolescent mind, I agonized over the implications. What had Jovita done to deserve this? I thought to myself. What crime was it to be Mexican and poor? Were we not all only just a notch above her, if even that much? Why did Norma hate Jovita so intensely? I wish that back then I had a language for internalized oppression. I can now say with confidence that Norma's punishing of Jovita was a punishing of her own Mexican self. The hatred that many students of color today hold toward members of their own ethnic group signifies a hidden injury resulting from our country's sordid racial history. Messages about the inferiority of non-"whites," particularly immigrants, continue to circulate openly today.

Jovita missed several days of school. Not many days remained. When she finally did return, I remember seeing her black, blue, and dark-green eye. I observed her as she walked with great poise, silently, through the crowd. She held her head up high and looked straight ahead as faces turned to catch a glimpse of the damage. Gossip and whispers filled the air as she walked through the school's main hallway, momentarily transformed into a gauntlet that perpetuated the spectacle. I remember looking at Jovita and feeling sorry for her and feeling deeply ashamed, as if I had done something wrong. I took exceptional comfort in knowing that I had not witnessed the fight, but wondered whether she knew that. I feared that the more likely case was that she saw me as a perpetrator, little different from the throng that gathered on that fateful day.

Looking back, I realize that Norma, Jovita, and all the school's Mexican Americans had to walk a tightrope of holding onto our childhood tongue and identity in a schooling context that was indifferent, even hostile, to it. Although Spanish was my first language, English assumed dominance during elementary school even as Spanish became a resource central to middle school peer-group survival. We Mexican Americans and Mexican immigrants were subjected to English-only school policies and practices premised on cultural erasure. Texas history was particularly degrading. The way it was taught reminded us Mexicans that we were losers and that Anglos were militarily and culturally superior. Never mind that Anglos fought this war in order to defend their right to own slaves or that Texas Mexicans also fought and died at the Alamo.

I can now see that this experience, coupled with hearing my parents' and grandparents' stories of racism, classism, and sexism, marked a turning point in the development of my social and political consciousness. I remember vividly how I resented feeling at once vulnerable and dependent on her. Thankfully, by the eighth grade, the bullies were gone and I no longer needed Norma for protection. While I remained friends with her, our friendship continued more on my own terms. As for Jovita, I never saw her again. Did she move to another school? Had she dropped out of school before her eighth-grade year? Did Jovita pay the price of soul wounds inflicted by internalized racism, with Norma and me acting as its unwitting agents? Given the severe humiliation she had endured, I inferred the worst and have felt guilty about it ever since. As if in silent agreement, Norma and I never spoke of the incident again. Perhaps she, too, felt guilty.

I suppressed the whole incident from my memory. My memory resurfaced just recently upon visiting Norma, whom I had seen only twice in the last twenty-four years. She spoke negatively and in a scornful tone about "Mexican people" and how "they" are often not very supportive of one another. Her own self-hatred jolted me that evening, reminding me of the sentiments that fueled her animosity against Jovita. She sounded little different from bigoted Anglos who make blanket judgments about all Mexicans, constructing a dehumanizing "we/they" dichotomy that expresses their power and sense of superiority over them.

I hope that in writing this story, I can finally put this incident to rest. Experiences like Jovita's are not in vain if we as educators use these stories, first to educate ourselves about internalized racism, and then to afford children of color the chance to speak and write of their own experiences of denigrating others or being denigrated as racial and ethnic minorities in a racist, sexist, and classist society.

Even educators who have not experienced internalized oppression themselves have been affected by the pejorative meanings that are assigned to racial and ethnic groups in the United States. By reflecting with students on how these ideas circulate inside schools or in the media, educators can help students dissect the multiple ways that such societal institutions condition all people to hold harmful stereotypes and blanket judgments and condition many to take the oppressor role against members of their own group.

To get started, educators might discuss with students what media images of their group look like, and how such images affect students' sense of themselves, as well as others. For example, they might analyze the effects that political campaigns promoting English-only policies and anti-immigrant sentiments have on nonimmigrants' notions about immigrants—or on immigrants' (or children of immigrants') thoughts and feelings about themselves.[3]

Educators can ask students to consider how similar dynamics of berating particular groups play out in their school. In my book, *Subtractive Schooling* (1999), I show how Mexican immigrant and Mexican American students struggle daily in schools with what to make of their "Mexican" traits in an "American" context—even in a segregated, virtually all-Mexican-origin school.[4] I show the

damage done to self when a student of Mexican descent seeks in a school context to expunge those allegedly socially objectionable traits that are often associated with their *Mexicanidad* (Mexicanness). By this term, I do not suggest
that a unitary "Mexican" identity does or should exist. Rather, U.S. Mexicans
occupy a borderlands space characterized by constant negotiation around
meanings of their hybrid and frequently conflicted identities.[5]

Students from all minority groups must struggle constantly with whether
and how to keep or discard the group traits they see in themselves, which are
so often disparaged by others that they come to disparage them themselves.
My research points to schools as a key site for this struggle. Students can engage in discussions of whether and how young people are pushed to fit themselves into categories of racial difference; for example, they can consider
whether in their school, as in my own junior high, youth are expected to
choose between being Mexican or American in an either/or, rather than in a
both/and fashion. They can discuss how it affects them personally if the cultures, languages, and histories—including women's histories—of their own
groups are excluded or ignored in the curriculum. They can then start the
complex process of discussing how some students, or they themselves, might
come to condemn the cultural and linguistic traits that reside within their own
peer networks and neighborhood community.

Long before ever setting forth to engage students compassionately in an
analysis of how disparaging treatments of self can arise, educators must start
becoming aware of the soul wounds inflicted by young group members on
themselves. Educators' basic awareness of such dynamics promises not only
to help students like Norma and Jovita but also to humanize and enrich the
classroom and schooling experience for all.

RESOURCES

Marcos Pizarro. 2005. *Chicanas and Chicanos in School: Racial Profiling, Identity
    Battles, and Empowerment*. Austin: University of Texas Press.

RECOMMENDED FILMS

National Latino Communications Center. 1996. *Chicano! The History of the Mexican
    American Civil Rights Movement*. Galán Productions Inc., NLCC Educational
    Media: www.albany.edu/jmmh/vol3/chicano/chicano.html.
Edward James Olmos. 2006. *Walk Out* [Motion Picture]. HBO, Olmos Production,
    Esparza/Katz Productions. Based on the East L.A. student protests of 1968: www
    .hbo.com/films/walkout/.
Lee Mun Wah. 1994. *The Color of Fear* [Motion Picture]. Berkeley, CA: Stirfry
    Films: www.stirfryseminars.com/pages/coloroffear.htm.

RECOMMENDED WEBSITES

Colorín Colorado: www.colorincolorado.org/webcasts/assessment.
Educational Equity, Politics & Policy in Texas: texasedequity.blogspot.com.
Facing History and Ourselves: facinghistory.org/campus/reslib.nsf.
James Forman Jr.'s blog on Education, Race, Kids and Justice:
    extracredit.wordpress.com.
Latinitas: On-Line Magazine for Teens: www.latinitasmagazine.org.
La Politiquera: http://www.lapolitiquera.com.
Rumbo en Internet: www.rumbonet.com/rumbo/portada.asp.
Third World Traveler: www.thirdworldtraveler.com.

DISCUSSION QUESTIONS

1. **Principle:** How can educators help students heal from damaging images about their "group"? To what extent can anyone fully heal from these soul wounds?

2. **Strategy:** Valenzuela argues that hearing or telling stories like this one can promote healing. How can an educator help students emerge stronger rather than weaker from discussions about such incidents? How can an educator from a different "group" get equipped to help?

3. **Try tomorrow:** How might you, with your own students, begin analyzing denigrating images of "groups"? How could you encourage this inquiry without forcing students?

Angela Valenzuela is a professor in educational administration and the Department of Curriculum & Instruction at the University of Texas–Austin. She also directs the Texas Center for Education Policy. Her research and teaching interests are in educational policy, sociology of education, urban education, and Latino immigration.

11

Helping Students See
Each Other's Humanity

L. Janelle Dance

We are people of the Mighty . . . Mighty people of the Sun!
In our heart lies all the answers to the truth you can't run from!
—Earth, Wind, and Fire

The words of this song have always touched, moved, and inspired me. I first became aware of these lyrics during the 1970s, when I lived in a Black, working-class community in the South. Although I was just a child, I had already experienced the horrors of dehumanization at the hands of White children and adults. I had already been treated like a "thing" that deserved to be hated, yelled at, and abused both physically and emotionally, instead of a person with feelings, dignity, and dreams.

I did not experience the life-threatening horrors of dehumanization like those my parents, grandparents, great-grandparents, and enslaved ancestors had suffered from the Middle Passage until the Civil Rights Movement, but other experiences threatened my self-worth. By the age of ten, I had been treated as if I were inferior by whites who had convinced themselves that they were not prejudiced, but being polite and civil when they called me a "negra" or "one of *those* children." I had been assaulted by two White children who, though only a little older than myself, had already learned to mistreat Black children. During a summertime visit to Niagara Falls, New York, two White children stopped me as I rode a bicycle through a white neighborhood. I thought they wanted to play, but they attacked me and called me *"Nigger!"* The boy held me down while the girl hit me and scolded me repeatedly: "Don't you get your black on me!" Although a fighter and a tomboy, I did not fight back because I was taken by surprise. I had hoped the Civil Rights Movement had ended all that, at least in the North.

That day, my physical bruises were insignificant, but the wounds to my self-esteem were more substantial. This was not the first time, nor would it be the last, that I was seen as a less-than-human "thing" worthy of degradation. Even then, I realized how dehumanization wounded those who experienced it and twisted those who perpetrated it. Throughout my childhood, my mother told me that "God don't like ugly!" This proverb was my mother's way of metaphor-ically holding up a mirror, getting me to reflect on the impression I was making on others. My mother helped me to realize that there is no moral excuse for robbing another person of his or her dignity and sense of self-worth.

Even more useful are the words of Mahatma Gandhi: "You must be the change you wish to see in the world." The antiracist move I propose for edu-cators is that we exemplify change by working actively and personally with our students against the dehumanization of other human beings.

Educators can first do this work on a personal level. If we want to prompt young people never to treat others as inferior, we must first reflect upon moments when our own humanity was insulted, bruised, battered, or robbed, or when we may have insulted, bruised, battered, or robbed the hu-manity of another person. We can consider how we ourselves did or did not heal from such events, and prepare to offer better healing experiences to our students.

"We are people of the Mighty . . . Mighty people of the Sun!" Those sooth-ing, soulful lyrics by Earth, Wind, and Fire helped to heal my wounds by de-claring that Black was beautiful. Before the Civil Rights and Black Power movements, African Americans suffered relentless spiritual assaults by con-stantly being cast by the dominant culture as abnormal and inferior: we were too "African," too "Black," our lips were too big, our hair too kinky. We were told that White was the beauty standard and we were the antithesis. By the 1970s, Black Americans claimed our "Black" skin, thick lips, and kinky hair. "In our heart lies all the answers to the truth you can't run from!" reminded us that our ancestors came from Africa, the continent of the sun. This truth was a reason for pride rather than shame. Educators can consider what texts, affir-mations, and ideas help students heal from similar experiences with being treated as lesser-than.

My own healing did not entail just affirming myself, however: I had to seek out positive role models and spend time with friends and family mem-bers who affirmed my self-worth, but without insulting or robbing the humanity of others. Having been at the receiving end of racism, I did not want to live in a new age where "Black" was valued and "White" was deemed evil and ugly. The truth I would not run from was that all so-called races are "Mighty Mighty people of the sun." According to social scientific evidence, we are all distant cousins who share ancestral grandparents originating from Africa. Instrumental to my healing was recognizing that we are one human race. This is now the core message I seek to convey to young people: we must embrace every group's humanity.

Educators and students can take specific actions to convey this message, particularly when addressing incidents when students dehumanize others be-cause of their racial-ethnic group membership. As an educator, I use incidents I have witnessed as teaching tools to show students what dehumanization looks like in everyday life. I also tell them how I personally have intervened against this dehumanization. For example, I describe how I have stopped fights between African American and Haitian immigrant teens and between teenagers in Sweden from different immigrant backgrounds. I have mediated disputes between Asian American and Black American students. I mentored a Black male teenager from a poor neighborhood who was attacked by members of a White racist gang. I tell my students that learning to mediate such conflicts and resolve intergroup differences is always a work in progress, and I propose some starting points.

For example, those intervening can address the specific interpersonal event, but ask questions about the larger patterns of social relations that caused the incident. Ordinary dehumanizing moments are a part of larger societal processes through which children are socialized to respect people who belong to certain categories and to disrespect people who belong to other categories. After breaking up a fight or mediating disputes, I ask students how we got wrapped up in this ugly, distorting behavior. No one is born disfigured by racism, I say; we are taught to be racist, anti-Semitic, anti-immigrant, and so on. How, I ask students, are we socialized into dehumanizing others? How have we learned to treat others as lesser human beings?

I also work with young people to create a safe space or shelter for healing. Students at the receiving end of dehumanization need meaningful opportunities to vent, reassess, and reflect upon their encounters with racism. Because healing is a process, children, teens, and college students need a safe space to which they can return to debrief (for examples of how to create such spaces within educational environments, see Adams et al., Resource list). Students need a shelter or sanctuary-like space in their school, neighborhood, youth center, mentoring program, or organization where they can embrace their own self-worth without dehumanizing those who dehumanized them. I have seen teachers create such spaces in the backs of classrooms, in spaces that were formerly teacher's offices or lounges, and in recreation areas. Teachers and youth workers decorate, announce, and enforce these spaces as "hate-free" zones. All students are welcome, both wounded and wounders, as long as they seek to learn to treat others with respect.

Finally, I work with young people to create opportunities for students to interact with members of other racial-ethnic groups as equals. I give assignments that ask students to walk in their classmates' shoes. For example, during a class meeting, two African American male students stated that people seemed afraid to sit beside them on buses, subway trains, and other forms of public transportation. I turned these students' experiences into a research project during which the entire class of twenty students—which included young women and men, Asians, Blacks, and Whites—rode the D.C. Metro to see if subway riders were more or less likely to sit beside them based upon their racial appearance and gender. The project was too small for the results to be statistically significant, but it had an enormous impact upon members of the class. The Black male students felt vindicated, yet learned that one of the Asian male students shared their fate. Students described the experience as "eye-opening" and said it generated compassion.

Above all, learning to see others as equally worthy human beings requires students to build relationships and friendships with members of racial-ethnic groups different from their own, and to really talk.[1] Tensions and conflicts are a normal part of the process. But the goal is dialogue, not debate. During a debate the goal is to win an argument; during a dialogue the goal is communication. During a debate you attack what the other person says; during a dialogue you respect what another is saying, even if you eventually agree to disagree. Students need more time, opportunities, and support for building close relationships with members of other racial-ethnic groups. Human history is full of intolerance, hatred, racism, and social conflict. It may take a lifetime to build meaningful relationships with those whom we have been socialized to see as "other."

As we address the causes of group conflict, create safe spaces, and facilitate friendships across group differences, we must be aware of potential minefields to avoid. Educators cannot place ourselves above or outside the intergroup conflicts that we seek to resolve. Students resent the lofty vantage points from which educators become god-like, infallible, and inaccessible instead of acknowledging and addressing their own limitations. Educators should prepare students and their parents for innovative activities that directly address issues and experiences of dehumanization; students should always have the option of not participating. Finally, educators should realize that we cannot undo the effects of dehumanization all by ourselves; we need to seek support from colleagues, parents, and students themselves. If a conflict does result, educators should endeavor to turn the incident into a learning experience. Educators can be mindful of such minefields without being paralyzed by fear, remembering that countless of us are limping, walking, or running toward a truth about human commonality: "We are people of the Mighty . . . Mighty people of the Sun! In our heart lies all the answers to the truth you can't run from!"

RESOURCES

Maurianne Adams, Lee Anne Bell, and Pat Griffin, eds. 1997. *Teaching for Diversity and Social Justice: A Sourcebook*. London: Routledge.

Maurianne Adams, Warren J. Blumenfeld, Rosie Castaneda, and Heather W. Hackman, eds. 2000. *Readings for Diversity and Social Justice: An Anthology on Racism, Sexism, Anti-Semitism, Heterosexism, Classism, and Ableism*. London: Routledge.

Facing History and Ourselves: www.facinghistory.org/campus/reslib.nsf.

DISCUSSION QUESTIONS

1. **Principle:** Name a time you experienced the sorts of dehumanization Dance describes, or saw others experience it. At your school, are any "types" of people treated as inferior?
2. **Strategy:** How could you invite students to a "healing space" in your own educational setting? How would your own racial-ethnic experiences influence your role in that space?
3. **Try tomorrow:** What specific activities can you think of that would build equal, humanizing relationships between students of different racial-ethnic groups at your school? What sorts of activities might prod a more homogeneous student population to engage the same issues of dehumanization?

Lory J. Dance is an associate professor of sociology at the University of Nebraska–Lincoln. Dance's areas of interest include the sociology of education, ethnic relations, intersectional theory, and qualitative methods. Her recent research projects have been conducted in Sweden.

Part V

Emphasize Individuality

We treat one another as racial group members, but we are also complex individuals. We must remember that individuality as an essential part of everyday antiracism. The essays in this part share a core principle of everyday antiracism: *we must get to know one another as individuals, not just as "racial group" members.*

How can educators emphasize students' individuality and their own, while not ignoring people's experiences in the world as racial group members?

1. Refuse to see individuals as automatic representatives of "achievement gaps."

   Sam Lucas proposes that teachers be "colorblind" in a particular way: they must remember that any individual in front of them, regardless of their "race," could have any level of achievement.

2. Cultivate a mindset of curiosity about your students as individuals.

   Josh Aronson suggests that educators actively refuse stereotypes by seeking information about students as complex individuals.

3. Cultivate individualized points of personal connection with your students.

   Heather Pleasants suggests that educators share their own interests, passions, and skills with students.

12

Constructing Colorblind Classrooms

Samuel R. Lucas

Race has no place in the classroom. Orienting to the race of the students, the race of the teacher, and the racial similarity or dissimilarity of teacher and students endangers students' learning, nurturance, and growth.

Is this claim, coming from a black scholar who studies the sociology of education and social stratification and inequality, a betrayal of disadvantaged students of color? Is this statement a sign that the call for colorblind policies is irresistible at the turn of the twenty-first century even in such bastions of putative multicultural sensitivity as Berkeley, California? I leave those assessments to others; I ask simply to be given a chance to make the case. My point is not that race cannot be discussed in class; my point is that abstract notions about a student's race should not be used to determine how he or she will be treated, neither to confer presumed advantage nor to inflict disadvantage.

Race has played an important role in the development of educational systems, first slowing the emergence of public education in the South[1] and then defining dual systems with vast disparities in resources.[2] The slow dismantling of *de jure* (legally enforced) segregation that followed *Brown* did not usher in an era of equal access to resources regardless of race. Instead, less than twenty years later, in *San Antonio v. Rodriguez* (1973), the Supreme Court ruled large interdistrict funding inequalities constitutional, and in *Milliken v. Bradley* (1974) it bounded the geographic scope of remedies for segregation, disallowing urban-suburban desegregation as a remedy and signaling a federal retreat from enforcing a right to equal access to education.

Race continues to play a role in educational policy, affecting students through the retreat from desegregation and affirmative action, in the advance of high-stakes testing policies such as No Child Left Behind, and in school financing.[3] The claim that race is irrelevant to education is patently false. Nowhere is race more visible with respect to education than in observed racial inequality in achievement and attainment.

Many facts about racial disparities in academic achievement are well known: the average measured achievement of black and Latino/a students lags behind that of white and Asian students. A great deal of scholarly research has focused on understanding these inequalities. Jencks and Phillips edited an entire volume titled *The Black-White Test Score Gap*[4] containing more than a dozen analyses of the problem. While most analysts rightly reject explanations that point to "racial" differences in innate intelligence,[5] the debate over why the gap exists remains contentious. Analysts have considered whether lower black achievement is caused by teachers,[6] black students' culture of resistance,[7] and various other factors and actors.[8] Still other researchers contend that standardized tests are constructed using procedures that enact a self-fulfilling prophecy[9] and are culturally biased.[10] Others maintain that grades are poor indicators of achievement by race, owing to the possibility of teacher bias in grading and punishment.[11]

Bias is possible not only because a few teachers may be prejudiced,[12] but also because most teachers are aware of racial inequalities in achievement.[13] It may be difficult for any teacher to maintain high expectations for black and Latino/a students in the face of data showing failure. The scholarly literature, with its laser-like focus on average inequality in achievement by race, does not make it any easier.

Average achievement outcomes are not the entire story, however. I recently graphed the math and reading achievement distributions for the nation's cohort of eighth graders in one recent year, for example (to access this graph, see Resource list). Black, white, Asian, and Latino/a students are spread through approximately 98 percent of the distribution. Although black and Latino/a students are less likely to be represented among students achieving above the 75th percentile on each test than are white and Asian students, some black and Latino/a students do score at or above that level. Focusing on the group average obscures a deeper, important reality: any black, white, Asian, or Latino/a student standing in front of us might have any level of achievement. This observation may seem trivial; we all know that achievement varies. But this fact is momentous because it means that, regardless of the average level of achievement for students of a given racial group, knowing the race of a specific child offers no information whatsoever about that child's current or potential achievement.

Sociologists, economists, and public policy analysts, by focusing constantly on the averages, almost guarantee that educators who interact with individual students will lose sight of the full range of outcomes and act toward a student according to the average achievement of the child's ascribed racial group. The focus on average achievement of groups likely leads teachers to engage in statistical discrimination,[14] which occurs when we use the average performance of a group—such as black children or boys—in order to determine how we should offer opportunity to the specific person—black child, or boy—we encounter. This kind of discrimination, which is akin to racial profiling, is illegal. Furthermore, race does not tell us what a child's interests, motivations, experiences, strengths, and weaknesses are. Statistical discrimination may easily occur in school in the provision of opportunities to learn, as teachers assign students to courses based on their race. Such abstract racial thinking is unwise and potentially damaging when considering any given student.

Individual students of color (like any student) given opportunities for which they are not ready will likely fail. This kind of paternalistic racism may plant lasting, insidious doubt about their capabilities as well as distrust about whether institutions will protect them and their interests. Peers may observe the failure, undercutting their belief in the capabilities of black and Latino/a students. At the same time, students of color denied opportunities for which they are ready—a type of racial profiling evident in the presumption that "They wouldn't be interested in advanced algebra, the chess club, the Shakespeare production"—will fail to obtain the experiences to which they have earned access. Peers may observe this denial of opportunity, undercutting their belief in the value of black and Latino/a students and the fairness of the school and society.

Racialized readings of students' potential achievement will teach all students that individual intellectual achievement is not the principle that determines opportunity in school, eroding the legitimacy of the institution in the eyes of students. Focusing on individual achievement rather than group membership must also mean ending the ability of white or well-off parents to have their children placed in advanced classes and obtain other learning opportunities the students have not earned. Research suggests this kind of inequity is widespread and consequential.[15]

A teacher may act to rectify this situation in his or her classroom by ignoring race and focusing on getting to know students as individuals. In doing so, we may find that factors such as the student's culture—their actual practices and lived experiences—and the student's relationship to power—their actual experiences with power brokers—make a difference in the student's performance in school. Culture includes the student's experience of power in society, the student's meaning-making activity, the student's own language, and more. In order to employ information about these factors, the teacher must interact with the student in an exploratory manner, learning the student's own understanding of his or her culture. The teacher cannot use easily observable aspects that may be correlated with some of the larger communities in the United States to label the student's culture and then, using the label as a guide, act toward the student as if the student shares the culture identified by the label. Two students with the same ostensible cultural label may orient to that label so differently that for one the cultural label may be useful, while for the other it may be misleading or even inapplicable. There is no shortcut to coming to know the student as an individual. The teacher must interact with the child and his or her family to gain the information needed to tailor the provision of learning opportunities for the student.

My contention that lived culture and power are key aspects requiring teachers' attention differentiates my position from that espoused by some other advocates of "colorblind" policies. I am not calling for colorblind policies but for ignoring abstract notions about race when we look at our students as individual learners. This call for colorblind classrooms is not a call for ignorant classrooms. We can no more teach U.S. history without reference to race than we can teach it without reference to the quest for religious freedom, or teach mathematics without reference to the concept of quantity. If we want to teach students about contemporary life, we must talk about race. Every student should be exposed to world literature, including European, African, and Asian texts. Every student should be examined on their knowledge of world history, encompassing the peoples of Africa, Asia, and the Americas, as well as Europe. The race of the student is irrelevant to his need to learn about the world we inhabit, as well as to his ability to learn about that world.

Classrooms must be places of unbounded opportunity. Many teachers committed to providing opportunity meet each child where he or she is, point toward the next door, open it, and encourage the child to walk through on his or her own. In those quintessential moments of teaching and learning, race means nothing. In contrast, biography, culture, and relations of power may mean everything. We will be unable to see the importance of lived experience, culture, and power if we are blinded by our assumptions of what a child's biography might be given the visible markings of what is called race.

In conclusion, I contend that teachers, principals, and their allies outside the schoolhouse door should attend to lived culture and power and leave the abstract concept of race to the abstract realm of social science and policy. Although state-level policy making and its handmaiden, social science, may need to use abstract concepts that are rooted in a history of oppression in order to grab hold of the complex patterns of inequality that are evident in datasets encompassing tens of thousands or even millions of persons, abstract concepts such as race are of no use for the teacher who stands in front of a living, breathing, human child.

When a child enters the classroom for the first time adults must proceed as if all things are possible. The adult can quickly lose that moment by acting as if the possibilities are limited, especially when those imposed limitations flow from a limiting view of persons. The possibilities are, in truth, limited only by the limits of our imagination.

To preserve that moment for pedagogic action, the teacher need ask such questions as: What is the child's biography? What is the child's culture, as he or she lives it? What has meaning for the child? What is the child's and the child's caretakers' relation to power? Answering these questions will help the teacher target instruction and provide opportunities in a nurturing, supportive way. None of these questions is effectively answered by knowing the child's race.

RESOURCES

To see graphs showing individual students scattered across an achievement distribution, see http://sociology.berkeley.edu/faculty/lucas/everydayantiracismfigures.pdf.

DISCUSSION QUESTIONS

1. **Principle:** How is considering students' concrete, lived experiences in the world different from thinking generically or "abstractly" about students as racial group members?
2. **Strategy:** Do you think that keeping your school's racial achievement averages in mind can *ever* serve students?
3. **Try tomorrow:** How might you actually interact with one of your students differently if you tried to discard generic racial notions about his or her potential achievement or academic interests?

Samuel R. Lucas studies tracking in the United States, the role of social class in high school completion and college entry, and the effects of race and sex discrimination on children and adults. He is an associate professor of sociology at the University of California–Berkeley.

13

Knowing Students as Individuals

Joshua Aronson

How can teachers mitigate the mistrust that students of color often feel in schools as social institutions? Over the past decade, research has shown that negative, stereotypic assumptions engender a range of academic problems. When students of color take standardized tests, they are often aware of the racist assumption that non-"white" groups have inferior intelligence, which increases their anxiety and impairs their performance.[1] When they expect to be treated with prejudice, students of color experience discomfort, perform poorly, and have difficulty maintaining their motivation in the face of teachers' criticisms.[2] In order to understand and remedy these problems, we must form and maintain trusting relationships, seeing and treating one another as individuals, rather than reducing one another to the social categories to which we belong. It would be absurd for teachers to pretend not to see a student's race or ethnicity. But as teachers, we must learn to see beyond these categories and avoid letting our stereotyped assumptions—and we all have them—obscure our views of students as individuals.

A recent study supports this argument. The researcher, Thomas Dee,[3] found that students tended to get higher test scores when assigned to a same-race teacher: black students performed more poorly when assigned to white teachers, just as white students performed more poorly when assigned to black teachers. But this happened only when the classes were large. If students were assigned to small classes where students and teachers had more opportunities to get to know and trust one another as individuals, the race of the teacher made no difference at all.

The experience of not being seen as an individual in the classroom engenders a deep sense of mistrust, separateness, and exclusion. My own efforts as a teacher and mentor have benefited most from one insight: my students want to be known and appreciated as unique individuals and not by a group stereotype—not as the short Latino guy, the blonde girl with braces, the quiet Asian, or the black guy in back third row.

The everyday antiracist "move" I rely upon is to cultivate a mindset of insatiable curiosity about my students as individuals: who they are, the experiences they have had, what they think about things, and how they think. Curiosity is the diametrical opposite of stereotyping and prejudice, the assumption that you know who a person is, what they think, or how they will act simply because you know what category they belong to. Stereotypes are a lazy mind's best friend, a mental shortcut to save us the trouble of asking and listening. I try to do the opposite by getting curious. During class discussion, for example, I internally adopt the mindset that the bored-looking guy with the baseball cap on backward, slumped in his seat like the stereotypical frat-boy jock, may actually turn out to be the most interesting and intelligent person in the class if I can find out who he really is. Or I ask myself whether the "angry-looking" black woman in the third row might be concentrating hard, rather than feeling angry. More often than not, when I refrain from jumping to conclusions based on first impressions and seek constantly to get to know students as individuals, I end up learning that my stereotypic assumptions were wrong and that the individual is indeed a lot more interesting—and interested—than I would have assumed.

Curiosity, I have learned, tends to be contagious; when I model it to my students by asking them questions about themselves as individuals and their individual opinions in class discussions, they become more curious about one another, more respectful, more open. True curiosity is not a tactic; it is a mindset that cannot be faked. But I have found certain questions particularly helpful if I want to support their learning: "What do you think about the work we are doing?" "What motivates you?" "What can I do to help?" I have found no better words for inviting individual expression than these: "That's interesting." "Tell me more." "Help me understand." And often, the question that best cuts through the fog of stereotyping is this: "What are you going through?"

RESOURCES

E. Aronson. 2000. *Nobody Left to Hate: Teaching Compassion after Columbine*. New York: W.H. Freeman.

Joshua Aronson. 2004. "The Threat of Stereotype." *Educational Leadership* 62(3): 14–19.

Vivian G. Paley. 1979. *White Teacher.* Cambridge, MA: Harvard University Press.

DISCUSSION QUESTIONS

1. **Principle:** The suggestion to get to know students as individuals seems common sense. But how do we often fail to get to know our students individually?

2. **Strategy:** What pitfalls should educators remain mindful of as we "cultivate curiosity" about our students' individual ideas and experiences?

3. **Try tomorrow:** How might you start to get to know a particular student you do not yet really know at all?

Joshua Aronson is an associate professor of psychology and education at New York University. His research focuses on the social psychological influences on academic achievement, and he is internationally known for his research on how stereotypes affect performance.

14

Showing Students Who You Are

Heather M. Pleasants

Consider this question: in your experience, what opportunities exist for teachers and students to understand one another beyond their school-defined identities? Schools offer few occasions for teachers and students to connect as complex individuals outside their prescribed roles. While conceptions of culturally relevant teaching and learning[1] emphasize the need for teachers to increase their knowledge of students' multifaceted identities, space for this kind of knowledge-building is often limited. Occasions for teachers to present themselves to their students as whole people are also limited.

In an antiracist classroom, just as teachers must strive to get to know their students as individuals, students should have opportunities to know their teachers. After a decade of teaching multicultural education to preservice and in-service teachers, I do not believe that we can practice antiracism while hiding behind a one-way pedagogical mirror, expecting students to open themselves personally while remaining closed about our personal lives and experiences. Revealing our own complexities to students is an important aspect of antiracist teaching because racism is partially about viewing others through a reductive lens, treating people as if they were defined by their racial-ethnic group membership. My proposed antiracist move involves sharing teachers' individual out-of-school identities with students, which facilitates the formation of authentic relationships between teachers and students in which both parties see each other as complex and rich human beings. The aspects of ourselves that we expose to students do not have to be explicitly related to race, though antiracist practices can be facilitated through the inclusion of these experiences in the curriculum. I call this process "growing our own points of connection" with students.

This suggestion is not without obvious dangers. As teachers, we often keep our out-of-school identities hidden. There are valid reasons to refrain from divulging those aspects of our lives not related to our roles as teachers. While students relish opportunities to see educators as real people, teachers are mindful of the fact that bringing our interests into day-to-day classroom interactions can be unproductive, detracting from students' interest in the material and potentially distracting them from important topics and ideas. Concerns about how much personal information we divulge and how to integrate it into the curriculum are important. Yet, how can we expect students to take teachers' interests in their lives seriously if teachers do not reveal to their students what is central to their own lives?

I encourage my students who teach to find productive and creative ways to share their interests and passions with their students. My language development class encourages preservice teachers to think through two interrelated questions:

- Outside of school, what are you passionate about?
- How can you draw from these passions to create authentic points of human connection with students in your classroom?

To illustrate how connections might be made successfully, I present two examples drawn from the work of teachers in the class.

Ann is white and married, and was born and raised in New Jersey in a middle-class Italian American family. Ann is a poet as well as a middle school language arts teacher, and she has kept a journal since she was ten years old. Ann's identity as a writer contributes directly to her love of figurative language and her ability to teach her students how to identify and utilize figurative language as they write from different perspectives. Last year Ann asked the children to keep notebooks to record all of the instances of figurative language they heard during the day, as well as the context within which it was used. She began by sharing some of her own writing with students and referred to the figurative language that had been used in the classroom that morning. Students tuned in to the assignment immediately. They mentioned popular music and television programs, parents' conversations and, to the bemused dismay of her colleagues, discussions in other classes. So Ann decided to pursue the creation of "figurative language journals" that she could share with other teachers. Ann's students have used their journals to grow as readers and writers, and Ann has used their journals to construct more nuanced understandings of the students' interests and perspectives.

Stacey is a white, single twenty-two-year-old, originally from an upper-middle class family that still lives in a small town in Ohio. As a teenager, she was a member of a puppet theater company that performed at her church and local schools. She kept two of her favorite puppets in shadowboxes in her apartment. Stacey is also a novice second-grade teacher in an inner-city charter school; most of her students are from low-income families, and many are students of color. Although she has picked up some elements of African American Vernacular English (AAVE), to which her students have responded favorably, she often senses that her students and their parents lack respect for her as a newcomer to the community and are skeptical about what she is trying to do in the classroom. Stacey has identified three girls in her class who regularly engage in behavior and conversations that undermine her instructional goals. Three weeks into the new school year, one of the girls in the group called her a "bitch." Initially, Stacey tried to connect with her students by being "sweet," but after a miserable first year of teaching, she tried something unconventional. She made three sock puppets and brought them into her classroom to complement her science and math instruction, the two curriculum areas in which she and her students struggled the most. Stacey introduced the puppets to the class at the same time that she shared her previous puppeteering experience. She had them speak in AAVE. Over time, the puppets have become an alter ego for Stacey in the classroom. She has used the puppets' AAVE to engage playfully in conversations about her lack of knowledge of her students' social and cultural worlds, and her students have begun to feel more comfortable in bringing their experiences into classroom activities.

The point of these examples is not the specifics of what these teachers did; doing a figurative language lesson and making puppets and learning to speak in AAVE draw on these particular teachers' individual skills and interests. The point is that these two teachers' selective inclusion of their out-of-school lives served as a point of departure for them to connect with their students as complex and authentic human beings, and for their students to connect with their teachers as people with interests and passions that go well beyond their formal interactions during the school day. Crucial to these teachers' experiments was continual reflection concerning how what they did in the classroom could open up their own thinking and their students' thinking about one another as complex individuals with varying interests and perspectives. We discussed such questions as:

- How might we, as teachers and learners, make a space to include our out-of-school lives in the curriculum, and to analyze if and how that inclusion is serving the learning process?
- What creative strategies might we need to employ to do this kind of pedagogical work and still accomplish mandated goals?

For some teachers, answers to these questions led them to apply for grants for supplies and release time.

The growth of connections and opportunities for dialogue between teachers and students is a fundamental aspect of everyday antiracism. By bringing what is meaningful to us in our out-of-school lives into the classroom and finding appropriate ways to include our interests in our instruction, we can grow our own spaces for connection to students who may feel that their own out-of-school lives are irrelevant to formal learning activities. By integrating what excites you beyond your work as a teacher into your pedagogy, questions concerning race and culture can be framed by "What can I do to help the kids better understand me?" as well as "What can I do to understand these kids?"

RESOURCES

P.A. Connor-Greene, C. Mobley, C.E. Paul, J.A. Waldvogel, L. Wright, and A. Young, eds. 2006. *Teaching and Learning Creatively: Inspirations and Reflections.* West Lafayette, IN: Parlor Press.

The Creative Teaching Site: www.creativeteachingsite.com.

P. McKay, and K. Gaves, eds. 2006. *Planning and Teaching Creatively within Required Curriculum for School-age Learners.* Alexandria, VA: Teachers of English to Speakers of Other Languages, Inc.

DISCUSSION QUESTIONS

1. **Principle:** Why might it be "antiracist" to use some of your individual passions to help build personal connections with your students?
2. **Strategy:** How might "growing your own" points of connection to students help you pursue standardized or mandated goals?
3. **Try tomorrow:** What specific skill or interest of yours would you like to bring in to your classroom?

Heather M. Pleasants is an assistant professor of qualitative research at the University of Alabama. Dr. Pleasants's research explores links between voice, identity, multimodal literacy, and social justice. Through this work, she is dedicated to promoting public discourse that actively challenges traditional distinctions between teaching, research, and service.

SECTION B

How Opportunities Are Provided and Denied Inside Schools

Part VI

Remember That Students Experience Racially Unequal Expectations about Their Brainpower

No brain is racial, but people treat one another as if brains are racially unequal. The essays in this part share a core principle of everyday antiracism: *educators must remember that students may have experienced unequal expectations based on their race. Educators need to counter student anxiety about unequal intelligence or potential.*

How can educators counter unequal expectations students may have already experienced?

1. To promote persistent achievement among students of color, be a perfectionist, but help students meet high standards.

   Ron Ferguson suggests that educators hold students of color to standards of "perfection" while offering explicit and ongoing assistance to reach that goal.

2. When giving feedback to students of color, emphasize high standards and assert your belief in their ability to reach them.

   Geoff Cohen proposes that an educator give thorough, critical feedback to students of color (like all students) on assignments, while explicitly emphasizing that he or she trusts that the student can reach high standards.

15

Helping Students of Color
Meet High Standards

Ronald F. Ferguson

Some teachers cultivate classroom environments that are highly effective in helping students do their best work consistently. This essay discusses research in elementary schools with a wide range of racial compositions, representing both urban and suburban locations in northeastern and midwestern states. Student and teacher surveys were conducted as part of the Tripod Project for School Improvement, which I founded several years ago.[1] The evidence suggests that students invest more effort under two instructional conditions I call "high help" (i.e., when the teacher communicates convincingly that she likes it when they ask questions and loves to help them when they get confused or make mistakes) and "high perfectionism" (i.e., when the teacher continually presses students to strive not only for understanding but also for accuracy as they complete their assignments).

The combined effect of these two conditions appeared to be especially significant in classrooms where African American and Latino students were the majority. Most such classrooms in this research were predominantly African American, with some Latinos, and included Native American, Pacific Islander, Arab, and multiracial students. Teaching styles characterized by *high help with high perfectionism* correlated with good behavior, positive peer supports for achievement, and persistent effort. High help environments, especially when accompanied by high perfectionism, elicited better behavior and greater academic engagement in classrooms of all racial compositions, but appeared substantially more important for classrooms where three-quarters or more of the students were students of color. Hence, combining cheerful helpfulness with pressure for producing correct answers is an antiracist strategy for raising achievement and narrowing achievement gaps.

When white students were the majority, the most common classroom type found in this study was *high help, low perfectionism*. Teachers seemed very happy to provide assistance but did not press much for correct answers. For whites, this combination appeared to produce the best behavior and only slightly less persistent effort than high help, high perfectionism. Conversely, the most common classroom type when students of color were the vast majority was the opposite, *low help with high perfectionism*, a combination that produced much worse behavior and substantially lower effort. The final type of classroom, *low help with low perfectionism*, was the worst by any measure.

In classrooms where students of color were more than 75 percent of the student body, any condition other than high help with high perfectionism was associated with a particularly large decline in student effort and persistence by the spring. Conversely, in classrooms where teachers practiced high help with high perfectionism, students showed sustained persistence in effort from fall to spring. In high help, high perfectionism classrooms, 77 percent affirmed in the spring that they had done their best all year.

What are *high help, high perfectionism* pedagogies? Compared to teachers in other classrooms, teachers in high help and high perfectionism classrooms reported significantly greater agreement with the first five statements below:

1. I have several ways of explaining the things that students find difficult to understand.
2. I welcome questions, even if it slows the class down.
3. I try to pay special attention to students who seem sad or upset.
4. I talk to students about their lives outside of school.
5. I talk about the joy of learning.

More than other teachers, these teachers' survey responses indicated that they also applied these pedagogic strategies:

1. When planning lessons, they thought about whether students would enjoy them.
2. They tried to call on low achievers as much as on high achievers.
3. They often waited for students to answer when called on, even if it took a long time.
4. They encouraged low achievers to ask questions and did not fear that this would slow the class down too much.
5. They felt equally effective at teaching students from various racial backgrounds.

When examined together, teacher and student survey responses suggested that the most powerful helping practices were welcoming questions from low achievers and waiting for low achievers to respond when called upon.

It is important to note that insistence on correct answers (perfectionism) can be problematic in the absence of assistance. While a teacher might believe she is serving students of color well by having high expectations, if she does not help her students sufficiently to meet her goals she can do them a disservice, since students of color are particularly at risk for believing that they may be unable to succeed with difficult work (see Cohen, Chapter 16).

Students' responses offered insights into what high perfectionism classrooms entail in the absence of high help. Compared to students in high help, high perfectionism classrooms, students in low help, high perfectionism classrooms (the most common for students of color) reported more often that:

1. High achievers get called on much more than low achievers.
2. The teacher tells individual students when peers outperform them.
3. Students are made to feel that doing poorly on an assignment is a bad thing, even if they tried their best.
4. Struggling students are allowed to give up when the work gets hard.
5. Mistakes are strongly frowned upon, even if students are learning.
6. When students do poorly on assignments, they are seldom given opportunities to redo the work to improve it.

These conditions also impaired peer support. Students in low help, high perfectionism classrooms agreed more that "In our class, some kids tease you if you make a mistake" and "In our class, kids tell you when they do better than you." Peers and teachers seemed less supportive.

If students are pressed to achieve correct answers on challenging work without adequate assistance, some may come to believe that success is impossible, resulting in anxiety and disengagement from academic tasks. An excessive emphasis on correct answers can detract from the joy of learning and encourage a focus on extrinsic instead of intrinsic sources of satisfaction.

To avoid high perfectionism, low help conditions, teachers should:

1. Avoid calling disproportionately on high achievers.
2. Avoid interpersonal comparisons of student performance that reflect negatively on some students, such as telling students when peers outperformed them.
3. Help students understand that making mistakes is okay if they tried their best.
4. Push students to persist, but also give appropriate assistance, when assignments seem too difficult.
5. Emphasize that the major goal is thorough understanding, not simply right answers; making mistakes is okay as long as students are learning.
6. Give students periodic opportunities to redo assignments on which they do poorly.

Many of the most valuable assignments aim to help students develop higher-order thinking and reasoning skills and may have no single correct response.

In such cases, an emphasis on correct answers is misguided; the focus should be on careful reasoning.

Persistent effort throughout the school year tended to be highest for all racial groups and all classroom racial compositions when both help and perfectionism were high. Failure to combine ample assistance with high expectations appeared to have the greatest detrimental consequences where students of color were the majority of the class.

Every teacher should seek ways to communicate, "I truly love to answer your questions, but I also insist that you concentrate in order to complete your work accurately." A consistent and compassionate effort to transmit this message, especially to students of color, is an antiracist strategy for improving behavior, increasing persistence, raising performance levels, and narrowing achievement gaps within and among elementary school classrooms.

RESOURCES

Tripod Project: Content, Pedagogy, Relationships: http://www.tripodproject.org.

DISCUSSION QUESTIONS

1. **Principle:** What do you make of Ferguson's finding that "high help, high perfectionism" teaching was particularly successful in classrooms serving many children of color, but was less common than "low help, high perfectionism" in classrooms of such demographics?
2. **Strategy:** Think of a teacher you know whose pedagogy seems to fit the "high help, high perfectionism" model. What sorts of interactions and activities occur in his or her classroom?
3. **Try tomorrow:** What's one specific way you could convey a stance of high help, high perfectionism to your students?

Dr. Ronald Ferguson has taught at Harvard University's John F. Kennedy School of Government since 1983. In the past decade, his research and writing have focused on racial achievement gaps and appeared in publications of the National Research Council, the Brookings Institution, and the U.S. Department of Education.

16

Providing Supportive Feedback

Geoffrey L. Cohen

Negatively stereotyped students, such as African Americans and Latinos, are more likely than other students to perceive that they are being treated unfairly by their teachers. This perception, which can occur regardless of the actual level of bias that exists in the classroom, reinforces disparities in performance between different racial-ethnic groups. My colleagues and I call this subjective inequality. Group members' perceptions that they are being treated unequally can reinforce objective inequalities between those groups.

Trust is key in the subjective experience of classroom settings. Aware of the reality of prejudice, members of negatively stereotyped groups may mistrust feedback on academic work that they receive from teachers and mentors.[1] They may worry that critical feedback issues from the teacher's belief in a negative stereotype about their group as less intellectually able. This concern can arise even in interactions with teachers who share students' racial-ethnic group membership, if these teachers are perceived as having advanced in the academic system by downplaying their group membership and identifying with the majority group.[2]

In one series of studies we conducted, African American and European American college students received critical feedback on essays that they wrote.[3] As part of the experiment, each student attached a photograph of himself or herself to the essay. Participants were thus made aware that anyone who subsequently evaluated their essay would be able to identify them racially. One week later, students returned to the laboratory and received two pages of critical feedback on their essay, ostensibly from a European American, white professor. This feedback pointed out areas of weakness in the essay and suggested strategies for improvement. Although the feedback that the two racial groups received was standardized, African American students mistrusted the feedback more than did European American students. They rated the evaluator as more biased and were less likely than European American students to take the feedback at face value.

This trust gap translated into subsequent differences in motivation. African American students expressed less interest in revising their essays than did European American students. Our later research found that, upon receiving critical feedback from a professor on a research presentation, members of another negatively stereotyped group, female science and engineering students, performed worse on a revision of their presentation than did their non-stereotyped peers.[4]

These results challenge a "colorblind" and "gender-blind" approach to pedagogy. Students do not necessarily experience interactions with educators as non-racialized or non-gendered. Objectively equal treatment, in the form of equivalent feedback, did not translate into subjectively equal experience for members of different groups. Members of negatively stereotyped racial and gender groups had grounds to wonder about the intentions motivating the critical feedback they had received. This uncertainty made the students experience the feedback as potentially critical not just of their specific performance but also of their academic ability and overall intelligence. These differences in subjective experience can have important academic consequences.[5]

How can teachers and mentors bridge racial divides in perception and generate trust? Good intentions alone do not necessarily lead to positive outcomes. For example, previous research suggests that some teachers and evaluators over-praise African American and Latino American students in an effort to be encouraging and establish rapport.[6] They may do so even when presented with a mediocre performance on the part of the student. Excessive praise can backfire. Minority students may detect it and believe that they are being held to lower expectations, undermining their motivation.[7] Being over-praised can lead students to doubt the sincerity of their teachers, blunting the impact of positive feedback that is merited. Consistently positive feedback— if unmerited— also provides little information about how to improve.

One effective intervention is to continue to provide critical feedback but to accompany it with an explicit, two-step message: a reference to high performance standards and a personal assurance of students' capacity to reach those standards. In our research, we found that African American college students trusted critical feedback as much as their European American peers when that feedback was accompanied by (1) an explicit statement on the part of the teacher that the critical nature of the feedback was motivated by high performance standards (e.g., "The essay itself is okay—you've followed the instructions and produced an articulate paper. On the other hand, judged by a higher standard, the one that really counts, I have serious reservations. . . ."); and by (2) an equally explicit statement that the student in question has the capacity to reach those standards (e.g., "Remember, I wouldn't go to the trouble of giving you this critical feedback if I didn't think, based on what I read in your essay, that you are capable of meeting the higher standard I mentioned").[8] When given critical feedback in this manner, African American students were even slightly more motivated to revise their essays than were European American students.

The intervention proposed here may prove ineffective or even counterproductive (1) if an assurance of faith in the student's ability is provided when the student requires no such assurance (this might convey that the student in question is perceived as needing encouragement);[9] (2) if the same message of high standards and assurance were provided in a rote, repetitive, or unpersuasive manner (its sincerity might be doubted); or (3) if the intervention is unaccompanied by the resources (for example, instructional materials) needed to support and sustain positive student outcomes.

Reducing the racial achievement gap in the United States will require expenditures of resources to improve the objective conditions of racial-ethnic minority groups both in school and in society. However, even when objective conditions are equalized, a subjective gap in perception of everyday treatment may persist for students from different groups.[10] Decades of psychological research suggest that human motivation is fragile.[11] Seemingly small moves that we make in the classroom can thus produce large effects for our students, both for good and for ill.[12]

RESOURCES

J. Aronson, ed. 2002. *Improving Academic Achievement: Impact of Psychological Factors on Education.* San Diego: Academic Press.

DISCUSSION QUESTIONS

1. **Principle:** Why might the moment of giving feedback on an assignment be a key antiracist moment?
2. **Strategy:** How have your students responded to your feedback on their assignments? Do you have any indication that your students' racial group membership or your own might play a role in their level of trust as Cohen suggests might occur?
3. **Try tomorrow:** Imagine putting Cohen's suggestions about critical feedback into action as you turn back your next assignment. In your own words, how might you emphasize high standards and assert your belief in students' ability to reach them?

Geoffrey Cohen is an associate professor of psychology at the University of Colorado–Boulder. He is an experimental social psychologist, and conducts research in the areas of stereotyping and stigma, identity and intervention, and social conflict and attitude change.

Part VII

Counter Racially Patterned Skill Gaps

In schools, racial achievement patterns take shape over time, as students advance or fall behind based on skills they are offered or denied. The essays in this part share a core principle of everyday antiracism: *educators must give students skills they have previously been denied or failed to acquire.*

What tactics can educators employ to ensure that optimal skill development occurs for students from all racial groups?

1. Never confuse teaching academic skills with holding low expectations for student achievement.

   Amanda Taylor suggests that educators must guide students in high-level work, but simultaneously offer students basic skills if they have not yet mastered those skills.

2. Think carefully about how you use groups in detracked classrooms.

   Beth Rubin proposes that teachers in detracked settings ensure that group work helps to overcome prior skill and status inequalities.

17

Teaching and Transcending Basic Skills

Amanda Taylor

Maybe I thought I would be Michelle Pfeifer, who played the butt-kicking and life-changing white teacher in the movie *Dangerous Minds*. Maybe I wanted to be like that guy in *Stand and Deliver*. It was not an accident that brought me to the front steps of "American" High School. I was almost charmed by the graffiti on the concrete walls, the broken metal detectors, and the windowless classrooms. I was twenty-three, white, and from the middle-class suburbs of Virginia. My students were seventeen and eighteen, black and Latino, and most had never left their low-income and high-crime neighborhoods in the San Francisco Bay area. But no matter: armed with my newly minted teaching certificate and a pair of rose-colored glasses, I knew that all it would take was the right combination of high expectations and creative lesson plans to motivate my students to achieve academically.

A few weeks later, in the midst of an activity designed to help students learn to critique mainstream media messages, I found myself standing on my desk during my fifth-period English class of fifty-two students, screaming and sweating. They were just not getting it. Though my carefully planned pedagogy was exciting and did seem to be developing students' critical thinking skills, many students had not mastered the basic reading and writing skills these lessons required. We had rich, high-level discussions and an energetic classroom environment, but when it came to writing a paper or taking a test, students continued to flounder, frustrated with themselves and with me for not helping them develop the tools they needed to express their knowledge in academic form.

I wondered what I was supposed to do. Teach basic grammar to seventeen-year-olds? Even though I knew that my students would need to master these skills in order to enter college or the white-collar workforce, I was terrified that changing the focus of my lessons from higher-order thinking skills toward more basic literacy skills would be akin to lowering my expectations. If I had learned anything from my teacher education program, it was that holding high expectations was the key to ensuring the success of students of color. Research demonstrated that teachers, especially white teachers, are more likely to hold low expectations for students of color and low-income students.[1] But I believed in the academic potential of my students; that was why I was working in an inner-city school.

I felt trapped: both teaching and not teaching basic skills to my students of color felt like potentially racist acts. For one, if I did not teach my students the basic academic skills they had not mastered, I was being professionally irresponsible. It was my job to provide my students with the skills they would need in the business and academic world beyond American High; not doing so would make me complicit in limiting their future options. This problematic situation felt particularly charged for me as a white teacher. I knew that my students lived in a world that automatically privileged people who looked like me, not like them. I was acutely aware that to counter this process of social advantaging and disadvantaging, it was even more vital that my students master basic academic skills.

In other ways, however, teaching such elementary skills to high school seniors of color seemed racist. I knew that many teachers limit the level of instruction they provide to students of color, continually reiterating basic skills rather than moving to the next cognitive level. Although my students had not yet mastered these basic skills, I feared that teaching them might suggest that I harbored deep-seated assumptions about the intellectual inferiority of black and Latino/a students. I was afraid that I would be inadvertently signaling to my students that I thought they were unable to handle the more challenging work that white, suburban, more economically privileged students enjoyed during their senior year.

In the end, I realized I had to do both: I had to embed necessary work on the fundamentals in substantive academic content that would challenge students to grow as analytical and critical thinkers.[2]

Many teachers confuse, like I did, teaching low-level skills to students of color who have not yet mastered them with holding low expectations for student achievement. White, middle-class teachers may be particularly vulnerable to this dilemma. But teaching basic skills if students lack them is quite different from holding low estimations of students' academic potential. Antiracist teachers must understand this distinction and recognize that teaching basic academic skills, if students still need them and if they are taught in conjunction with higher-order critical thinking skills, does not mean lowering expectations. On the contrary, teachers must do whatever they can to ensure that students of color learn the skills necessary for academic success.

Teachers should recognize the difference between our expectations about students' current academic performance and our expectations about students' academic potential. Research on teacher expectations demonstrates that there is a "self-fulfilling prophecy" in education: when teachers believe something to be true about a student, even if it is not true, the student tends to perform to meet the teacher's expectation level, whether high or low.[3] What particularly concerns parents and advocates is that many teachers underestimate the academic potential of students of color. Often, though, this issue is not distinguished in the research literature or in teacher training from the task of assessing students' current academic performance in order to pinpoint and provide the skills students still actually need.[4]

At American High, I worried that I would be lowering my expectations if I admitted that some of my students' skills were below the level expected of twelfth-graders. But I was simply assessing my students' previous and current academic achievement. If I had thought that my students had no realistic chance of attending college so I might as well not teach them these basic skills, that would have reflected a low estimation of my students' potential, both as individuals and as racial group members. Since I held high expectations for my students' academic potential despite their currently low academic skill levels, I thought, "these students do not currently have the academic writing skills that they need to successfully demonstrate their academic ability. I need to teach those skills right away, so we can work to reach their full potential." Although teachers of students of color need to be careful never to place limits on their students' academic potential, they must assess the limitations of their students' current academic performance in order to know how to help students reach their potential.

White teachers from middle-class backgrounds may have a particularly hard time making this distinction. Many of us focus exclusively on higher-order skills that we feel will convey our high expectations to our students. We might feel that we are enabling students to demonstrate their intellectual ability without highlighting their basic skill deficiencies. However, we must be ready to identify and address our students' current skill levels, no matter how uncomfortable it makes us. The teaching of basic skills becomes a problem when we incorrectly frame students' limitations as permanent, genetic, or inevitable. Ironically, if teachers fail to teach students the academic skills they need to succeed,[5] their students may actually perceive that their teachers have low expectations for them.

Teachers must be mindful not to abandon higher-order thinking skills when addressing basic skills. Basic skill work should be seen as a necessary but temporary endeavor.

RESOURCES

Deborah Stern. 1994. *Teaching English So It Matters: Creating Curriculum for and with High School Students*. New York: Corwin. Lesson plan ideas co-constructed with students that address both fundamental skill development and critical thinking skills in the high school English classroom.

DISCUSSION QUESTIONS

1. **Principle:** How might an educator struggling with the issue of teaching "basic skills" also be struggling with tough issues of racial inequality?
2. **Strategy:** How do your assignments and assessments allow you to pinpoint and address students' fundamental skill needs while also cultivating "higher-order thinking skills"?
3. **Try tomorrow:** How might you organize your curriculum to treat basic skill work as a "necessary but temporary endeavor"?

Amanda Taylor is currently a doctoral student at the Harvard Graduate School of Education. Her research interests include the ways in which race, class, and power are negotiated in urban schools and communities. She has taught in urban, rural, and international schools and has worked as a university admissions director.

18

Grouping in Detracked Classrooms

Beth C. Rubin

It is the middle of the first semester in a detracked ninth-grade English class in a racially integrated urban high school with an equal mix of Asian American, African American, and White students. As the students file into the classroom, they look for their names, written in black marker on sheets of paper taped to each grouping of four desks. Christie, who is African American, finds her name posted in a group with two White boys and two empty desks. As she swings her backpack onto one of the empty desks and sits down, she exclaims loudly, "You trying to get all the Black kids away from each other, before we cause a nuclear holocaust!" She punctuates this statement with a loud handclap.

Group work is frequently advocated as a best practice for teaching in detracked classrooms.[1] Detracking is a reform intended to counter the effects of separating students into different academic classes based on perceived ability, which in many integrated schools relegates low-income, African American, and Latino students to low-skill classes while their White peers enjoy high-skill environments.[2] In detracked settings, educators intentionally group students heterogeneously, balancing groups in terms of race, gender, and academic ability. If the point of detracking is to break down social barriers and allow students to benefit from one another academically, then putting students in balanced groups seems a logical remedy.

The reality, however, is more complex.[3] Detracking is a response to tracking, and in any detracked environment, tracking has already had serious consequences for students both socially and academically. Researchers argue that students in lower tracks, often low-income students and students of color, are denied well-taught, challenging college preparatory curricula, while students in the higher tracks, who often are mainly White and middle class, take part in a rigorous curriculum taught by more experienced and skilled teachers.[4] When classes are detracked, diverse students are brought together in an attempt to remedy the inequalities caused by tracking. However, students can bring damaging ideas about one another from broader societal contexts, as well as differences in academic preparation resulting from years of difference in instructional quality. In this setting, group work, which puts students into intimate and interdependent relationships, can become a complicated endeavor fraught with race-related pitfalls.

When teachers construct balanced groups for cooperative learning activities, race is woven into the issues that arise. These difficulties can develop in any classroom in which teachers are attempting to racially balance students in group work activities. The problem is amplified in detracked classrooms in which previously separated students come together or in which teachers rely on balanced groups to assist instruction for formerly low-track students. While many teachers and researchers advocate detracking as an equity move, they are often uncomfortable with directly addressing the ways that prior tracking continues to affect detracked classrooms. I briefly examine three of these minefields, using real scenes I have observed in detracked classrooms as illustrations.

Notice students' interpretations of their placement in balanced groups. Christie interprets her placement in a group with two White boys as indicating that the teacher thought it was dangerous to group African American students together. While this was not the teacher's intention, Christie's passionate comment demonstrates how aware some students are of race and its implications. Group placement can bring these tensions to the fore.

Students of color can interpret teachers' group placement decisions as motivated by a desire to distribute students with lower academic abilities and feel negatively marked by this placement. Conversely, placements may compound the privileged position of their White peers, since White students are often subtly made to feel as though they possess higher academic abilities and are distributed among groups in order to help their peers of color. While students in any classroom may feel marked by group placement, in detracked settings balancing can mean both racial and skill balancing, putting some students in awkward positions. In this setting, the teacher's rationale for balancing students within small groups was sometimes obvious to students and led to situations in which students of color negatively interpreted their placement as an attempt to distribute "problem" students. Teachers can work to prevent this interpretation by making group placements flexible, so that no one feels repeatedly "distributed" in racial terms.

A few minutes after Christie took her seat in her assigned group, her friend Tiffany, who is also African American, entered the room. Tiffany found her name in a group of four high-achieving White students, but no seat was available. "There ain't no chair!" she complained angrily to the teacher who, in the middle of explaining the assignment, did not answer her right away. Then, pausing to help Tiffany get situated, the teacher moved a White boy out of Tiffany's assigned group and into an empty seat in Christie's group, saying "I see an imbalance. Dan, can you move over here?" As Dan moved, Christie commented, "I don't see why Tiffany can't sit here." The obvious interpretation was that Tiffany and Christie were put

into separate groups because of their race and perhaps their ability levels:
there was, after all, a free seat available in Christie's group. Again, teachers
can work around this minefield by varying group composition and being flexible about it, so they do not falsely make it seem imperative that students of
various racial groups are separated. They can avoid always placing higher-
achieving students in groups with lower-achieving students, as if this were
the only way to develop the skills of students who were underserved through
tracking.

Avoid inhospitable learning environments for students of color. Cooperative group assignments require close collaboration. Students' preconceptions and stereotypes about each other's abilities, talents, and motivations
can come into play in these situations. In Tiffany's group, for example, the
group leader, a White boy, assumed that Tiffany had not done the homework
assignment and had not brought her book to class. When he asked group
members to lend him a book so they could complete their group quiz on the
Lord of the Flies, he asked each of the other group members, all of whom
were White, and did not ask Tiffany—who, as it turns out, did have the
book. The group leader failed to assign Tiffany a role for the group assignment as recorder, artist, reporter, or researcher, and he did not include her
in the conversation. The consequences for Tiffany's academic confidence
became clear toward the end of class when she asked the teacher to go out
into the hall with her, where she told him: "They don't want me in their
group. They don't think I'm smart." In schools where the low tracks have
been populated by students of color and the high tracks have been the domain of White students, White students often stereotype students of
color when they come together in a detracked setting. White students
can create inhospitable and unproductive group work situations for their
peers. Conversely, formerly lower-tracked students can assume that their
higher-tracked peers are more academically competent and allow them to
complete group tasks rather than engaging with the assignment themselves.
Teachers can navigate this minefield by using smaller groups, a configura-
tion in which interpersonal dynamics are usually less complex and in which
each individual has a greater opportunity to participate. They can also
take a more explicit approach to teaching group skills and organize group
assignments.

Make sure to address the academic needs of formerly low-tracked students.
Educators may feel uncomfortable about taking on the skill deficiencies
brought by students coming from the lower rungs of a racially tracked system.
Reluctant to draw attention to these academic needs and fearful of stigmatizing students, teachers may find the notion of balanced groups an appealingly
discreet way to scaffold instruction so that "high achieving" students teach
their peers the skills they lack. This practice can allow students of color to
continue to suffer unequal opportunities.

Students' opportunities to learn and practice skills in heterogeneous group settings vary depending on which tasks they are asked to engage in. In another group assignment, Frankie, who is African American, was assigned the role of actor. While this was a key role within the group, his group mates, all of whom were White and doing better than Frankie in the class, took on the roles of researchers and writers, garnering more opportunity to build skills traditionally valued in academic settings. If, over the course of the year, the same formerly low-tracked students, who are disproportionately students of color, are consistently assigned roles that offer little opportunity to develop these valued skills, academic disparities can continue to increase. Teachers can steer a safe path through this minefield by organizing group work tasks thoroughly so that each student builds the skills he or she needs and by not leaving students with the sole responsibility for building the academic competencies of their peers.

To counter these difficulties, teachers should approach their grouping decisions with care, creating lesson plans that go beyond putting students in diverse groups. I offer these suggestions for how to implement group work practice.

First, go smaller. Overuse of the same group work format can create cynicism and frustration among students. Vary the size of the groups you use, and consider making groups smaller. Students working in pairs have an opportunity to build relationships outside of the peer dynamics of larger groups; it can be easier to exchange ideas and to divide the work load equitably. Pairs can also be an efficient structure for accomplishing difficult tasks.

Second, vary group composition. Do not assume that a well-balanced group is necessarily equivalent to a racially diverse group, or even that balance of any sort is a necessity. With the proper support, students can learn well in all sorts of groups. Varying the composition of groups over the course of an academic year will keep things interesting for students, help acquaint them with more of their classmates, and counter the sense that students are put in groups for particular racial or academic reasons. Students of color may find time spent in same-race groups to be a source of support and affirmation in a racially integrated setting.

Third, make group work skills an explicit part of your curriculum. Teach students the skills of facilitating, questioning, listening, organizing, and recording. Group tasks and expectations should be less complex and demanding at the beginning than at the end of the school year; create a plan for their gradual and logical development. Pressure on groups to accomplish difficult tasks without appropriate instruction can generate tension among group members. Planning for the development of group work competencies ensures that students build the skills that you hope they acquire through this practice, and that students will be able to do group tasks successfully no matter the composition of the group.

Finally, scaffold group work tasks thoroughly and make sure they build students' academic skills rather than rely on their previous proficiencies. Group work tasks need to be scaffolded through a supportive framework. While the best tasks for group work are complex enough to merit attention from more than one person, students need to be presented with such tasks in a way that allows them to be successful. Do not assume that high-performing students will instruct their peers or carry them through the task; this assumption exacerbates tensions among students and reinforces assumptions about them. A carefully scaffolded approach that breaks down complex tasks and intentionally builds competencies in each student, rather than drawing on skills that only some students have, benefits all students. As students become more proficient with complex tasks over time, this scaffolding can be reduced.

In a detracked classroom in which the teacher varies group size and composition over the course of the year, carefully plans for the development of group work skills, and makes sure that each group work task is thoroughly scaffolded to build academic skills for each student, students like Christie need not experience their group placement as a comment on the intersection of race and academic ability. In such a classroom, group work could be a tool for helping realize detracking's goal of providing better education for all.

RESOURCES

Michelle Fine et al. 1998. *Off Track: Classroom Privilege for All*. [Motion Picture]. New York: Teachers College Press.

Beth Rubin, ed. 2006. "Detracking and Heterogeneous Grouping." *Theory into Practice* 45(1). Ten practice-oriented articles on teaching in detracked and heterogeneous classrooms.

M. Watanabe. *"Heterogenius" Classrooms: Universal Math and Science Acceleration for All*. [Motion Picture]. Contact watanabe@sfsu.edu for details.

DISCUSSION QUESTIONS

1. **Principle:** What should the criteria be for placing students in small groups? When, if ever, should the desire to balance students racially trump other concerns, like skill levels or personalities?

2. **Strategy:** What successes and problems have you experienced in attempts to "balance" students in small groups? Have you ever seen a group work assignment organized so that underskilled students gained skills without feeling like "problems"?

3. **Try tomorrow:** How might you react next time a student responds negatively to her placement in a small group? Try role-playing such a situation.

Beth C. Rubin, assistant professor of education at Rutgers, the State University of New Jersey, conducts ethnographic research on the intersection of classroom life and social inequality. Dr. Rubin's current work focuses on detracking in the classrooms of diverse schools, and students' constructions of civic identity.

Part VIII

Help Students Gain Fluency in "Standard" Behaviors While Honoring the "Nonstandard" Behaviors They Already Have

Certain behaviors, often associated with people who are middle-class and "white," get students ahead in the schools and workforce we have; certain skills are measured on standardized assessments. But they are not the only skills worth praising. The essays in this part share a core principle of everyday antiracism: *educators must help students to be successful on "standard measures"—even as we remember that often, students have and need far more skills than we may be assessing.*

How can educators help students gain fluency in "standard" behaviors as necessary, yet still honor their "nonstandard" skills and behaviors?

1. Teach to standards, but also honor nonstandard knowledge.

    Ted Hamann suggests that educators can reward students for skills, such as the ability to translate, that they have above and beyond "standard" skills measured on typical assessments.

2. Do not disparage the nonstandard varieties of English students speak.

    John Baugh suggests that educators should teach "standard English" without ever denigrating the value of nonstandard English varieties.

3. Do not disparage students' own cultural codes; help them become fluent in multiple cultural codes.

    Prudence Carter proposes that educators should help students gain additional fluency in dominant behaviors, but never assign lesser worth to the "nondominant" behaviors (like dress and speech) that students value.

19

Standards vs. "Standard" Knowledge

Edmund T. Hamann

The standards movement is intrinsically incomplete. All students bring to school personally useful, complex knowledge, but this knowledge is not always recognized or valued. Students of color, bilingual students, and students who are not middle class often have skills, knowledge, and capabilities that should count as intellectual achievements in schools but do not, which puts them at an academic disadvantage. Schools and teachers should value the nonstandard knowledge some students bring.

Students need skills that favorably impress those who are positioned to appraise them: parents and community leaders as well as teachers. These skills broaden their opportunity horizons, support their upward social mobility, and help them develop self-confidence, as well as allow them to participate in family, community, workplace, and social group contexts. However, in defining the skills that standards should require for all students, we often ignore the fact that students negotiate different school and community contexts and that, in order to navigate those contexts successfully, they may need to have skills that rarely show up on typical assessments. Teachers can counter this problem by adopting a "standards-plus" orientation. They can identify and record their students' unique or uncommon but academically relevant skills and review their own teaching practices to see if they ask students to display skills that they subsequently do not credit.

Let me illustrate what I mean by nonstandard, yet important knowledge. Sixteen years ago, I observed two student performances in an urban middle school ESL (English as a Second Language) classroom that I have thought about ever since. This story is not an example of good teaching practice; it illustrates the perpetuation of structural disadvantage for English language learners. The instruction did not even support the class's purported goal, teaching English, as most students were not engaged in that task. An overtaxed monolingual ESL teacher, as seen here, is not atypical.[1] But here I focus on two students' displays of skill in this classroom, even though the skills they displayed did not count as necessary under common standards.

The ESL teacher taught from the front of the room, with the chalkboard behind her and students' desks in rows facing her. She seemed a little overwhelmed, perhaps because she had observers. She directed her instruction primarily at one Latina twelve-year-old, rather than at everyone. After making a point, the teacher would wait as the student translated her comments for her Spanish-speaking classmates. Then the teacher would wait again as a Khmer-speaking student offered a version in Khmer for her classmates who spoke that language. Both interpreters displayed sophisticated linguistic and cultural knowledge. Clearly their teacher thought they were performing these tasks well: she had organized her instruction around using them as intermediaries. As children growing up in a multilingual city, they had developed skills in English, Spanish, and Khmer that were relevant in their lives both inside and outside of the classroom.

Yet these multilingual skills are not expected of all students, so these two students' display of skill did not and would not count on any standards-aligned rubric. Indeed, these displays of skills might have backfired. Because their teacher had converted them into a lifeline through which to communicate with and manage the class, these students were kept in this low level of ESL, and their second-language skills became a trap rather than a recognized accomplishment. These students' demonstration of a highly useful capability as interpreters counted nowhere on their official records; it may even have made them look like slow learners. Researcher Guadalupe Valdés describes a similar dynamic in *Learning and Not Learning English*;[2] some students were held back so monolingual ESL instructors could use students' assistance in orienting new students.

There are two kinds of racism worth considering here. First, we can ask why it was acceptable in this system for Southeast Asian and Latino kids to encounter such poor instruction. Ten years after this observation, when I was involved in an evaluation of this district's bilingual and ESL programs, I found that inadequate teaching in these programs was still common, though not universal. Second, we can ask why we do not have, or do not use, a measurement of interpreting skills that could count and credit displays of linguistic adroitness like these. Being a capable interpreter did not seem to help these students achieve tangible academic recognition.

In *Expanding the Definitions of Giftedness*, Valdés discusses unrecognized displays of linguistic skill by bilingual child interpreters.[3] She asks why successful interpreting is not counted as an alternative qualifying skill for placement in gifted and talented programs, since the interpreters, like other students in gifted and talented programs, bring exceptional talents that schools should accommodate and recognize as an asset. Gifted programs are usually reserved for only a small percentage of a school's enrollment (see Tyson, Chapter 24). More importantly in this context, this solution (gifted placement) cannot resolve the problem that any student can have noteworthy, academically relevant skills that are not part of standards-sanctioned knowledge.

Many of the Yemeni American girls described by Loukia Sarroub in *All American Yemeni Girls: Being Muslim in a Public School* display sophisticated adeptness at reconciling home cultural expectations regarding gender and family roles and the expectations of Michigan high schools.[4] Their bicultural accomplishments were not recognized by educators and administrators; the girls were measured solely against the agreed-upon standards for all. Expecting these girls to meet common academic standards is not problematic, but noting and recording their extra accomplishments would assist them further.

The standards movement's focus on only "what everyone needs to know" privileges those who come from personal circumstances similar to those canonized in the standards. The standards rightly focus on the style of English used in mainstream media, business communication, and middle-class American life. But many students negotiate households, neighborhoods, and cultural networks where this dialect is not used. Not everyone needs to learn African American Vernacular English (AAVE).[5] (See also Baugh, Chapter 20). Yet many students master this dialect, need it for their nonschool lives, and could use it as a pedagogical stepping stone. The mastery and appropriate use of AAVE is a useful intellectual accomplishment requiring a sophisticated linguistic awareness. Mastery merits acknowledgment not because it is useful to all, but because it is vital to some.

How might we recognize academic and social knowledge and accomplishment that not everyone needs? What can teachers do to account for the intrinsic incompleteness of standards? How can teachers credit the exceptional knowledge that individual students and students from particular groups bring to the classroom? Teachers can advocate a "standards-plus" orientation. More concretely, teachers could give credit to students who demonstrate mastery of nonstandard skills, for example by adding written descriptions of a student's particular prowess to academic files. High school teachers who write college recommendations for students do this routinely. More formally, we could create new metrics that measure and give credit for the skills that students need to negotiate bilingual or bicultural terrains. This shift would require pinpointing the skills students need for a multicultural and multilingual existence; students and parents could be involved in crafting these schemas. These new, locally developed metrics would complement or supplement the standards, not displacing them but acknowledging standards' intrinsic incompleteness.

Without a mechanism for recognizing such intellectual skills as mastering two languages or successfully navigating differing home, school, and neighborhood environments, the standards-based movement denies the value of some skills that actually support academic achievement. If we want the standards movement to be part of an equity effort, then we need to also embrace extra skills that fall outside of the standards.

RESOURCES

What Kids Can Do: www.whatkidscando.org.

DISCUSSION QUESTIONS

1. **Principle:** Think back to your time in school. What language skills, or cultural navigation skills, did you or other students have that went unrewarded in that learning environment? Do you think this was inequitable? Were these skills recognized in another context, and if so, how?
2. **Strategy:** In your own classroom or school, how might you learn about, build upon, and credit your students' "extra," nonstandard skills?
3. **Try tomorrow:** Consider a specific skill you have seen exhibited by a student in your classroom that has not been recognized by others in the school. How could you recognize or build upon that skill in a way that would serve the student academically or socially?

Dr. Edmund "Ted" Hamann is an assistant professor in the department of Teaching, Learning, and Teacher Education at the University of Nebraska–Lincoln. He is particularly interested in how education policy for English learners and other newcomers is created and in how school reform efforts can be shaped to assure responsiveness to newcomers.

20

Valuing Nonstandard English

John Baugh

We often overlook the linguistic dimension of racism in our classrooms. White students typically attend K–12 schools without ever having a teacher whose linguistic background differs substantially from their own. Nonwhite students are far more likely to encounter teachers who either disparage their language use or fail to assist them in gaining standard language proficiency.

Teachers working with students from diverse linguistic backgrounds often unwittingly hold negative views about those students' use of nonstandard language varieties: their use of languages other than English, and their use of nonstandard varieties of English. Amid current debates over bilingual education, we tend to talk more about the first issue than the second, so I focus here on nonstandard English.

African American vernacular speech norms are one form of nonstandard English; Spanish-inflected English is another. This essay examines how teachers respond to students' use of African American vernacular. The conclusions can be transferred to any moment when a teacher responds disparagingly to a student's use of any variety of nonstandard English.

First, we must quickly define two key terms that are frequently misused in educational debates, Ebonics and African American Vernacular English (AAVE). Before the mid-1970s, scholars disagreed about how to label African American speech norms. The terms "Nonstandard Negro English," "Black Street English," and "Black English vernacular," among others, were frequently used interchangeably.[1] Recently, African American Vernacular English (AAVE, pronounced like the abbreviation for *avenue*) has emerged as a suitable and serviceable addition to the common nomenclature. As a linguist, I typically use AAVE to refer to nonstandard varieties of English spoken by persons of African origin throughout the United States. AAVE is not a separate language but a variety of English that developed as Africans in the United States interacted with one another and Europeans. An example of speaking AAVE in our classrooms rather than standard English is, "She be done did her homework," instead of "She has already completed her homework."

AAVE is frequently confused with another specific linguistic term, Ebonics. The term Ebonics was originally designed to have a more international use than AAVE, which pertains specifically to the U.S. Black vernacular. Social scientists and educators sought a single, all-inclusive term to describe the wide-ranging linguistic consequences of the African slave trade worldwide. According to Robert Williams, who turned the word into common currency, Ebonics describes "the communicative competence of the West African, Caribbean, and United States slave descendant of African origin. It includes the grammar, various idioms, patois, argots, ideolects, and social dialects of Black people."[2] Ebonics encompasses language practices in Haiti, Brazil, and the Dominican Republic, as well as the United States. Originally, Ebonics was an umbrella term, referring to a complex variety of European, African, and hybrid languages and dialects born of and affected by the slave trade.

Both AAVE and Ebonics are terms for nonstandard varieties resulting originally from the African slave trade: nonstandard English in the case of AAVE, and all the various postcolonial languages spoken by descendants of slaves in the case of Ebonics. But Ebonics is commonly, and mistakenly, equated with AAVE. The discussion of students' use of nonstandard English varieties in U.S. schools suffered a setback when the concept of Ebonics came to national and then global attention in December 1996, when the Oakland, California, school board ignited a political tinderbox and was chastised in the media for suggesting that a majority of Black students in their district spoke Ebonics *rather* than English.[3]

According to the board's argument, since students who speak languages other than English can receive additional funding and special programs to address their lack of English fluency, African American students who speak AAVE should also be eligible. The Oakland school district's African American Educational Task Force proclamation of 1996 called for this provision, stating that, like "Asian-American, Latino-American, Native American and all other language different children," "African-American pupils" should be given bilingual education funds "and ESL programs to specifically address their LEP/NEP needs."[4] Fearing a potential budgetary and political crisis, U.S. Secretary of Education Richard Riley rejected this position, indicating that "the Administration's policy is that Ebonics is a nonstandard form of English and not a foreign language."[5]

As a linguist, I agree that African Americans do not speak a foreign language; many speak an African American variety of English. Yet, politics and semantics aside, the crucial fact remains that, from a linguistic and educational point of view, people who speak AAVE confront substantial barriers in educational and occupational contexts.

Issues of language are intertwined with issues of educational access. Just as African Americans have been denied equal educational resources, the linguistic behavior of the descendants of slaves has always been criticized when compared to the European-based "American" standard. Critiques of Black language usage also abound in schools in Brazil, Canada, Mexico, and the

Caribbean, among other places where the descendants of enslaved Africans have settled. Because so many people, including some Black people themselves, have come to view Black language usage as synonymous with "improper" usage, in our classrooms we often denigrate Black language usage, or even improperly classify black students as "disabled" because of it. Geneva Smitherman describes her own experience as a young African American student whose speech pathology tests indicated "abnormal English development" when, in reality, she had normal language development in her African American community.[6]

In 1979, some harms pertaining to educators' treatment of African American language usage came to the legal fore for the first time. Eleven African American students enrolled in the Martin Luther King School in Ann Arbor, Michigan, had been evaluated using speech pathology diagnostics that indicated they lacked normal linguistic development. Thanks to the research of many scholars,[7] we now know that these antiquated speech pathology diagnostics were developed from the perspective of middle-class white Americans who were native speakers of standard English. The tests regularly evaluated normally developing African American children in inner-city or rural communities as abnormal. The students at the Martin Luther King School in Ann Arbor were placed in remedial special education classes where their academic development decelerated, so their parents brought a class-action lawsuit. Many scholars argued during the trial that AAVE was a coherent, rule-governed linguistic system that resulted from the African slave trade. Because the students had used AAVE rather than standard English in their home setting, it was unreasonable to expect them to obtain standard English fluency without explicit instruction. These arguments ultimately won out. The court ruled that the school board had failed to acknowledge the students' linguistic circumstances. Today, educators must beware of improperly assessing speakers of AAVE as lacking language ability. Instead, educators must offer AAVE speakers explicit instructional attention assisting them to attain standard English fluency.

Teachers should resist the temptation to regard AAVE as a deficient way of speaking, but they must also assist Black students to gain fluency in Standard English. U.S. descendants of African origin float in language policy limbo, neither recognized as needing assistance nor understood when it comes to the kind of assistance they need.[8] As a former director of teacher education, I know that those who teach AAVE speakers often care deeply about them. I offer several modest suggestions for the classroom.

If you teach students who are not native speakers of standard English, I recommend that you reinforce the value of their native vernacular, whatever it may be. Emphasize, in so many words, that people who speak alternative nonstandard varieties of English, or who are English language learners, are no less intelligent and capable than are students who display standard English fluency. Those for whom standard English is not native should never be made to feel ashamed of their linguistic heritage. If you teach students who are native speakers of standard English, they should be taught, and you should remember, that speaking standard English is not a sign of superior intelligence.

How can a teacher embrace a nonstandard English variety without suggesting falsely that students do not need to gain fluency in standard English as well? Educators have made various attempts to address AAVE speakers' academic linguistic needs to learn standard English for school use while not denigrating their use of AAVE. After the 1979 Ann Arbor case, educators assisted AAVE speakers to learn standard English, rather than placing them in special education. In California, several school districts participated in a new program called the Standard English Proficiency Program for Speakers of Black Language.[9] The program provided instructional materials and in-service teacher workshops to help African American students gain greater proficiency in speaking, writing, and reading standard English. Educators in Oakland, California, undertook similar efforts. The problem was that, in arguing for attention to black students' language needs, they overstated just how different black students' language was. The mainstream media's oversimplified and reactionary coverage of the controversy did not foster serious discussion of the subject.

Educators have attempted to address AAVE speakers' linguistic needs by enlisting popular culture to advance academic literacy in the classroom, since popular culture is saturated by AAVE. H. Samy Alim trained high school students from African American, Mexican American, and Pacific Islander backgrounds to become linguistic ethnographers in their home community and to share their findings about local language use with their classmates.[10] He asked students to collect family oral histories that he used as the bases for instruction, to analyze and accentuate respect for family members' different linguistic norms. Each individual's linguistic and cultural heritage was celebrated in the classroom, even as students pursued proficiency in standard English through their academic work.

The essential task at hand is to work toward acceptance, not mere toleration, of people from diverse linguistic backgrounds, while pursuing mastery of academic English as well. Teachers are the indispensable frontline professionals who must help to model and instill values of linguistic acceptance and skills of linguistic fluency.

RESOURCES

H. Samy Alim. 2004. *You Know My Steez: An Ethnographic and Sociolinguistic Study of Styleshifting in a Black American Speech Community*. Publications of the American Dialect Society No. 89. Durham, NC: Duke University Press.

John Baugh. 1999. *Out of the Mouths of Slaves: African American Language and Educational Malpractice*. Austin: University of Texas Press.

DISCUSSION QUESTIONS

1. **Principle:** How have educators responded to students' nonstandard language in the schools and classrooms in which you have worked? Which responses seem to be the most likely to move students toward opportunity?

2. **Strategy:** Baugh suggests building upon nonstandard English varieties in the classroom, while facilitating students' learning of standard English. Can you think of one way you could do this in your curriculum?

3. **Try tomorrow:** How might you respond the next time a student uses nonstandard English in a class discussion, or on an assignment?

John Baugh is the Margaret Bush Wilson Professor in Arts and Sciences at Washington University in St. Louis, where he directs the African and African American Studies Program. He has written extensively on linguistic discrimination and the social stratification of linguistic diversity in advanced industrialized societies.

21

Teaching Students Fluency in Multiple Cultural Codes

Prudence Carter

During the course of an interview in her office at a desegregated school in South Africa where the majority of pupils identify as Black, a White high school principal remarks during a formal interview with me that students' "hair must be neat and tidy. . . . We don't allow dyed and colored hair, dreadlocks, braidings, and all of those things. Those are regarded as fancy hairstyles." I ask why a "fancy" hairstyle is forbidden. The principal responds, "Well, because it's just not normal." Her comment signals her belief that "fancy" styles are not just "abnormal," but not respectable; Black students must adapt to their White principal's aesthetic about hair. I wonder how "ethnic" hairstyles could so easily be described as abnormal and perceived to be untidy, especially since all the students I saw with "fancy" hairstyles were carefully groomed.

Here in the United States, a nation that struggles with the legacies of its own racial apartheid past, a group of African American, Latino, and White students sits in a history class on the first day of school in an urban district. The group includes Alberto, a dark-skinned Dominican youth dressed hip-hop style in an oversized T-shirt and baggy jeans hanging below his waist. As an introductory exercise, the teacher asks the students about their career aspirations and prods them to think about a historical occurrence that could be relevant to the professions to which they aspire. Several White students articulate high ambitions: they want to be archaeologists, astronauts, doctors, fashion designers, and so on. At his turn, Alberto—in speech peppered, unlike his peers', with "yo" and "butters," colloquial expressions that emerged among poor and working-class Black and Latino youth and gained widespread prominence through the dissemination of rap music—mentions that he aspires to practice law and serve on the Supreme Court. He explains that unfair laws and discrimination throughout history have kept people in the ghettos from "getting paid." The middle-class White male teacher smirks as Alberto speaks and responds incredulously, "Well, that's ambitious!" The teacher offers no support for Alberto's ambitions, unlike his affirming response to the White students who voiced their ambitions in standard English. As Alberto told me privately, he sensed that this teacher had low expectations for him. Once the teacher told Alberto that his "gangsta lifestyle" would lead to an early death. When I asked Alberto why his teacher thought he was a gangster, he replied that his appearance and mannerisms, including his tastes for baggy jeans, extra-large sweatshirt, and baseball cap worn askew gave the impression that he was a "thug" who sold drugs. Alberto had felt insulted, even though he said with feigned bravado that he pays "no mind" to White people dismissing his potential when they see him and hear him speak.

The South African principal's comment and Alberto's teacher's remark both reveal the cultural racism that students who display nondominant styles of dress or speech encounter in schools when their teachers and principals treat them as if they signal abnormality and lesser potential. The South African principal's assumption that dreadlocks and braids are "not normal" and Alberto's teacher's assumption that a student who does not conform to middle-class norms of dress and speech is unlikely to succeed—or even survive—express and reinforce prejudices about a group's inferiority by rendering relatively benign cultural practices as deviant, abnormal, and dangerous. My research has shown that teachers often falsely judge racial and ethnic minority students' academic commitments or abilities based on those students' stylistic presentations of self.[1] They make those judgments even when students from groups with disproportionately less social, economic, and political power form the school's numerical majority. K–12 educators assert control over styles and symbols in schools, often forcing conformity to dominant styles in ways that harm students who display nondominant styles. Educators' evaluations of students' commitments and abilities hinge on how teachers react to noncognitive and nonacademic factors such as the student's appearance and everyday speech. When a student's style clashes with what the teacher regards as a signifier of competence, intelligence, and studiousness, the result can be a damaging negative assessment of the student's academic potential.

Over the last decade, students from myriad backgrounds in the United States and South Africa have shared with me their tales of how their teachers perceive their commitments, abilities, and motivations negatively based on their dress, speech, and other cultural expressions. These students feel their teachers develop negative expectations for them based on how their tastes diverge from middle-class White norms. In the United States, youth of color participating in the dress and speech of hip-hop style, especially boys, lament that teachers continually mark them as "gangsters" and "thugs" because of the way they dress. They sense that their teachers doubt that they could be serious students.

Social scientists have demonstrated that some teachers do make judgments about students' capacities based on their self-presentations, particularly when teachers do not share the socioeconomic and/or racial position of their students.[2] We have become so preoccupied with how students present themselves that state lawmakers in Florida, Louisiana, and Virginia have proposed to criminalize some styles, forbidding "do-rags," hooded sweatshirts, and the low-riding pants many urban youth wear.[3] Lawmakers believe that some youth use clothing styles as markers of gang membership, so these policies are supposed to inhibit fighting. Yet the majority of youth who embrace these styles are not gang members. Educators can find more effective ways to ameliorate gang conditions, such as holding town meetings with students to discuss the issues of gang-related activity and symbols, rather than criminalizing the hip-hop styles most kids pick up from popular culture. Ironically, while cultural gatekeepers in schools and other mainstream institutions consider hip-hop cultural styles deviant, the producers of this youth culture have a mainstream enough following to sustain a multibillion-dollar industry.

A racist interpretation of a nondominant style attaches a negative judgment of the style to a presumption of a particular racial group's intellectual, social, economic, and cultural inferiority. This type of judgment perpetuates the notion that styles more typical of White and middle-class people are inherently superior. Many school dress codes and policies are predicated on the idea that "good," "intelligent," and "moral" tastes and styles are those created by and for the White middle and upper classes. Accordingly, the styles and behavior of the poor and nonWhites on the bottom of the social hierarchy are disproportionately sanctioned by school codes and policies as signals of lesser worth.

Such cultural racism has academic, psychological, and social costs for students of color. The entrenchment of a White Anglo aesthetic signals to students of color that their hair, clothes, music, and vernacular tastes are deficient. Students expressing frustration and exasperation at educators who mislabel them based on stereotypical assumptions about their physical presentation often rebel and act out, setting into motion a spiral of poor evaluations and bad marks that lead to school failure.

Some well-meaning educators counter that in our society, students who are not born into what researcher Lisa Delpit describes as a racial "culture of power"[4] must be taught the dominant cultural practices that, coupled with academic achievement, can be converted into access to higher education, good jobs, and higher status. Therefore, this argument goes, educators who allow poor and racial-ethnic minority students to dress, speak, interact, and wear their hair in nondominant ways put these students at a disadvantage in the opportunity structure.

Should educators allow students to present themselves stylistically however they want? Or should educators point out that those self-presentations might deny students opportunity in a society where the gatekeepers judge what is dominant as that which is "normal," "good," and conducive to success?

My research and analyses suggest that K–12 educators need to do both. They should both avoid interpreting students' stylistic self-presentations as symbols of academic, social, or inherent deficiency and help children and adolescents of color become facile at what I refer to as "multicultural navigation"—that is, being fluent in different cultural and stylistic codes and adapting their behavior as the situation demands. The well-meaning liberal educator—including teachers of color—cannot simply celebrate the nondominant stylistic practices of poor and minority students. Educators must also help students learn to ascertain when and where various stylistic currencies are advantageous. Educators should never automatically assign higher value to mainstream White cultural practices, either in their minds or in their communication with students. Some students of color will turn off altogether when they sense that their teachers expect that they must permanently adopt mainstream cultural practices or elevate those practices above their own. Rather, educators can explicitly assist students to tap into dominant cultural practices when and where they are useful, without denigrating the students' own tastes. While most middle-class students have social contacts from whom they acquire dominant cultural preferences and codes, poor and minority students often do not have models from which to learn such behaviors for situational use. Educators should present these dominant cultural practices explicitly, but without denigrating students' own styles.

Educators must learn something about the languages, dialects, and self-presentations that students value. Some might even try those styles on themselves once in a while. Not long ago, a student in South Africa emphatically commented to me, "Miss, if they [Whites] want us to act more like them, then they have to get to know more about us, too. It is a two-way process." This student indicated to me that if White teachers wanted to encourage the development of racial and ethnic minority students' multicultural selves, teachers themselves could try to become multiculturally fluent by learning an African language and increasing their knowledge of the cultures and communities they were teaching. In the United States, for a parallel example, teachers could enrich their knowledge of the history and development of African American vernacular speech, for which numerous volumes and dictionaries exist (see Baugh, Chapter 20). They could investigate the evolution of fashion or interactive styles within the ethnic and immigrant communities they teach. Students, in turn, can teach their teachers. Educators can cultivate their own multicultural navigational skills both to develop empathetic insight into the social, cultural, political, and material realities of nondominant groups and to model for students how people effectively negotiate among cultures.

In sum, teachers can explicitly encourage students to move back and forth across different cultural territories just as cosmopolitan world travellers learn to cross national and language boundaries. They can engage students in explicit conversations about how different cultural currencies—languages and dialects, codes of conduct, mannerisms, and physical presentations of selves—pay off in various communities. Teachers' ability to cultivate their own multicultural navigational skills remains crucial. The main objective is to help Alberto and his peers around the nation acquire multiple cultural competencies, so that if they aspire to high status in any group—their co-ethnic peers, their teachers, or future employers—they can do so successfully. The antiracist multicultural navigator respects students' multiple cultural identities, engaging in pedagogic practices that expand the students' worldviews, increase their cultural capital, and imbue them with pride in their own multidimensional identities.

RESOURCES

Lisa Delpit. 2006. *Other People's Children: Cultural Conflict in the Classroom.* New York: The New Press.

DISCUSSION QUESTIONS

1. **Principle:** How is asking students to become fluent in dominant cultural styles different from asking students to conform and bow to them?
2. **Strategy:** In your own school, how have educators responded to students' "nondominant" cultural styles? In this process, were students moved toward opportunity or further from it?
3. **Try tomorrow:** How might you respond the next time a student displays a nondominant style of dress or speech? How might you help guide the student toward fluency in dominant stylistic practices while not devaluing the student's nondominant style?

Prudence L. Carter is an associate professor at Stanford University's School of Education, with expertise in education, culture, and racial and ethnic relations. Currently, Dr. Carter is conducting a cross-national, comparative study of the interplay between mobility and culture for students in desegregated schools in South Africa and the United States.

Part IX

Defy Racially Based Notions of Potential Careers and Contributions

Schools are supposed to prepare young people for adult life, and the messages students get in schools about their futures are crucial. The essays in this part share a core principle of everyday antiracism: *students may sense that their future careers and contributions are limited to certain "races," and teachers must open up that sense of limited possibility.*

What tactics can educators employ to help all students envision and plan for major contributions to society?

1. Challenge cultural messages of who can and cannot do science.

    Mia Ong suggests that educators explicitly demonstrate to all students that certain careers, especially science and math careers, are not limited to particular "races."

2. Introduce students to "ordinary" role models; then have them practice what they learn.

    Meira Levinson proposes that rather than be restricted to learning about "super" heroes like Martin Luther King, students should also be introduced to local role models who change society for the better.

22

Challenging Cultural Stereotypes of "Scientific Ability"

Maria Ong

More often than not, movies and television portray scientists as middle-aged white men in lab coats. American history texts tend to highlight great scientists who are white men, such as Albert Einstein. The pervasive cultural message students gain, after exposure to thousands of these images,[1] is that the white man is an icon of intellect and scientific competence. Although most young Americans do not pursue science principally because of their weak academic preparation in K–12 science and mathematics,[2] research also reveals that widespread images of both "super" and "ordinary" scientists as white men discourage many talented young females and students of color from exploring science, technology, engineering and mathematics (STEM) as career options.[3] Girls and women of color, who hold dual minority positions within the U.S. stratification system, are at especially high risk of attrition in these fields.[4] Between 1997 and 2003, out of about 1100 Ph.D. physics degrees awarded annually in the United States, on average, fewer than three were awarded to Hispanic women and fewer than three were awarded to African American women.[5] The lack of female scientists of color with doctoral degrees translates into greater lack of diversity in teachers, mentors, and role models for the next generation, not to mention a significant loss of talent and creativity.

Promoting the interest of all students, especially students of color, in STEM must be a central concern of educators in the twenty-first century. As a country, we face a crisis caused by a gap between our increasing need for scientists and engineers and our lagging production of them.[6] Restrictive immigration and foreign policies following September 11, 2001, in addition to the expansion of opportunities elsewhere in the world, have caused a continuing decline in the enrollment of international students who traditionally filled up to a third of U.S. science and engineering graduate programs and jobs. The growing gap points to the neglect of our own young people as potential resources to fill positions in STEM. In 2001, only 9 percent of doctoral degrees and 16 percent of bachelor's degrees in science and engineering were awarded to African Americans, Hispanics, American Indians, and Alaska

Natives, while in 2003, students of color constituted 40 percent of the nation's youth population (ages 0–24) and are projected to reach 47 percent by 2020.[7] Asian Pacific Americans (APAs) who are U.S. citizens and permanent residents can also be considered an underutilized resource. Many people assume that APAs do not need support in STEM because their numbers are mistakenly conflated with larger numbers of international students from Asia. The prevalent "model minority" stereotype contributes to the erroneous idea that APAs as a broad category are doing fine educationally.[8] Representations cloud the reality: while some subgroups, such as Chinese and Koreans, are well represented in STEM education and careers, many others are not, such as Filipinos, Vietnamese, and Native Hawaiians.[9] Asian American women join other women of color in their severe underrepresentation among university faculties in top STEM departments in the country.[10]

Unfortunately, many teachers unwittingly transmit to their students the myth about white men as inherent generators and keepers of scientific knowledge. Teachers reinforce this myth by not exposing students to scientists of color and their many contributions and by their tendency to place students of color, particularly African American and Hispanic students, into lower math tracks.[11] While teachers may argue that such students exhibit poor mathematics skills and therefore deserve to be in lower tracks, research suggests that criteria for determining track placement, such as standardized test results and teachers' judgments, are often racially biased and subjective, so that 50 percent of students are tracked into lower, remedial classes, while 90 percent have the potential to master the material.[12] Placement of students in lower math tracks can have devastating effects on their futures: it can derail them, as early as age eleven, from potential paths in STEM. Only upper-track students enroll in high school calculus courses, which are, in turn, prerequisites for most university mathematics and science courses. Through lack of exposure to scientists of color and restrictive tracking systems, students of color get treated as racial group members who do not have potential in STEM arenas. This treatment harms everyone because it prolongs the loss of talent in STEM education and careers.

Teachers can take antiracist steps in their classrooms to promote more future STEM workers. The first charge of the teacher is to cultivate passion in science and mathematics. Students, regardless of ethnicity or race, must love science and math if they are going to pursue it. Unfortunately, relative to white students, students of color do not receive the same levels of encouragement, inspiration, or exposure to STEM, and they do not have nearly as many role models who look like them. I found in my own research on young physics majors of color that the key to their catching the "science bug" at a very young age was having adult mentors—parents, aunts, uncles, older siblings, neighborhood mentors such as community center directors, or teachers—share the wonder and excitement of exploring the physical world.[13] Passion may be cultivated simply by providing children with time and access to science museums, programs, books, magazines, and hands-on projects and, importantly, by making the information relevant to their lives. Three examples of relevant science and mathematics for elementary school children are collecting and studying wildlife in a nearby pond or forest, determining the contents of the neighborhood drinking water, and planning and constructing a playhouse for the school playground.[14] Exposing students to emergent trends in science and allowing them to participate in research is another effective strategy. Susan Klimczak, a mentor in the "Learn 2 Teach" program based in Roxbury, Massachusetts (see Resources), said, "We want our youth to be the innovators of the future and we believe exposing them to what might be the next great pushes in science might help them navigate strategically toward those fields. For instance, we have been field testing (in Boston Public Schools and a charter school) an 8th grade hydrogen fuel cell technology unit where the youth actually build a hydrogen fuel cell car. One of the projects was to adapt the hydrogen fuel cell car with solar cells (instead of battery) to generate hydrogen from water. This also exposes them to technologies that would address a real problem in Roxbury: sky high rates of asthma caused by the location of the city bus terminal and the presence of idling buses."

Basing scientific inquiry in community-based problems may be a way to engage students of color in STEM, since research suggests that people of color search for ways to connect with their communities through their education and tend to remain active in their home communities longer than whites.[15] While early, frequent, and meaningful exposure to science is valuable for the learning of all students, it is especially critical for the promotion of students of color, since cultivated passion can serve as a steady, driving force that counteracts the discouraging experiences—such as exclusion from study groups, condescending remarks from faculty or peers, or isolation and lack of encouragement—they will be more likely to encounter along their academic and career paths.[16]

Second, teachers must serve as a critical source for cultivating connections to science careers and to actual scientists, preferably scientists of color. Typically, students of color, especially those from lower socioeconomic levels, do not meet their first professional scientist or learn about what scientists do until they reach college. By this time, it may be too late to lay the groundwork of interest and knowledge needed to successfully pursue a STEM major and career. Teachers can help students to forge early connections to science by providing explicit information about what courses to take, out-of-school experiences to pursue, and summer opportunities for meaningful internship work. Teachers can also arrange for people of color at different stages along the STEM path to teach science in their classrooms and to give advice to their students. Contact university science departments and technology or medical research companies and ask to speak with directors of their Diversity Office for names of potential speakers. Advanced college and graduate students of color in physics actively seek ways to "give back" to their communities, and teaching younger kids is especially fun and rewarding. Organizations such as the National Society of Black Engineers (NSBE) and the Society for the Advancement of Chicanos and Native Americans in Science (SACNAS) seek to include high school teachers and students in their activities.

Third, teachers should make explicit to students the pervasive cultural messages about who can, and cannot, do science, so that these messages can be debunked. One white third-grade teacher in a classroom of predominantly white students did this by asking her kids to draw pictures of a scientist. The majority of the students turned in drawings approximating a white, male, wild-haired mad scientist. The teacher displayed the drawings around the room and used them as starting points for a series of conversations to dispel common myths about people who practice science and mathematics. She talked with her students about the sources of their ideas (e.g., television, comics, movies, parents), challenged them to identify counterexamples in media, and introduced real-life counterexamples in the classroom, including a local woman economist who enthusiastically talked to the students about her use of mathematics in her work. By challenging students' and society's assumptions about what a scientist looks like, teachers and students together can deconstruct the cultural conflation of whiteness, maleness, and scientific and mathematical ability. Follow-up activities might include providing examples that counter these damaging messages on an ongoing, everyday basis.

Students might be interested to learn that African sailors once navigated the oceans by the stars[17] and that the first confirmed use of the number zero occurred in India in 896 C.E.[18] (See Resource list.) Students might do research projects on prominent historical and contemporary male and female scientists of color, such as Edward Bouchet, Shirley Ann Jackson, Mae Jemison, Lydia Villa-Komaroff, Luz Martinez-Miranda, Eloy Rodriguez, and C.S. Wu. In my own study, Geordi, a fictional black scientist character in *Star Trek*, served as an early role model for an African American male physicist! To avoid the dangers of focusing only on famous people or "super-scientists," which may suggest that only a few people of color can achieve in science (see Levinson, Chapter 23), educators and students should also focus on more ordinary scientists, such as local STEM students and professionals of color. Conducting oral history interviews with these individuals may provide students with rich insights about the excitement of science and various pathways to majors and careers in STEM. If and when students of color enter university STEM classrooms, it is unlikely that they will encounter underrepresented minority professors;[19] knowledge of scientists who resemble themselves may be crucial in providing role models.

We must incorporate knowledge about scientists of color in a context that supports, rather than marginalizes, minorities. Once I observed a second-grade teacher who singled out the only African American boy in the classroom to read to his classmates about the work of African American inventor George Washington Carver. Later, during Black History Month, the boy was again singled out to read passages about Harriet Beecher Stowe. While the teacher may have meant well, she used the boy as a representative of a racially based group in a harmful way: both the student and the people he read about were framed as essentially token visitors to a Eurocentric curriculum and classroom culture. It would have been more supportive to the young African American student and his classmates if the responsibilities of reading and learning about Carver, Stowe, and others were distributed among many students throughout the year.

In a classroom of any demographic, the conversation about what scientists look like might be part of a larger conversation about the lack of any relationship between intelligence and "race" (see also Pollock, Chapter 2). Teachers can help students unlearn this myth by explaining how science has historically played a key role in constructing this false relationship between intelligence and "race." *The Mismeasure of Man*, by Stephen Jay Gould,[20] is a well-written and accessible book that teachers could use to have this complex conversation with students. Students of color could gain a valuable and sophisticated perspective on how some people, in the name of science, have hurt their communities in the past, but also how, since then, others have used science to refute the race-and-intelligence argument and have used science to establish race as not biologically real but as socially constructed (see Goodman, Chapter 1).

To prepare young students of color for STEM fields, we must provide them with a healthy variety of role models. In a classroom of any demographic, both male and female super and ordinary scientists of color ought to be made visible, first and foremost, as people who have positively contributed to knowledge. Their lives and contributions should be actively studied by everyone, alongside the lives and contributions of white male scientists.

RESOURCES

Maurice Bazin, Modesto Tamez, Exploratorium Teacher Institute. 2002. *Math and Science Across Cultures: Activities and Investigations from the Exploratorium*. New York: The New Press.

Jarita C. Holbrook. 2005. "Astronomy, Africa: Modern, Traditional, and Cultural." In Anthony Appiah and Henry Louis Gates, eds., *Africana: The Encyclopedia of the African and African American Experience*. Oxford, UK: Oxford University Press.

Learn 2 Teach, Teach 2 Learn program: www.tech-center-enlightentcity.tv.

National Society of Black Engineers (NSBE): national.nsbe.org.

David Eugene Smith. 1958. *History of Mathematics*, vol. 2, *Special Topics of Elementary Mathematics*. New York: Dover.
Society for the Advancement of Chicanos and Native Americans in Science (SACNAS): www.sacnas.org.

DISCUSSION QUESTIONS

1. **Principle:** How do children learn messages about who can be a scientist, or who "belongs" in any career? How can students be guided to question these messages?
2. **Strategy:** How can an educator talk simultaneously about successful scientists of color and about their unjust underrepresentation in these professions?
3. **Try tomorrow:** What is one thing you could do to inspire your own students to enter STEM fields, even if STEM is not your field?

Maria (Mia) Ong, Ph.D., is the founder and director of Project SEED (Science and Engineering Equity and Diversity), an initiative of the Civil Rights Project at Harvard University. She is also a project leader at the Center for School Reform at TERC in Cambridge, Massachusetts.

23

Finding Role Models in the Community

Meira Levinson

I have taught low-income students of color in urban middle schools for eight years. Nearly all of the students I have taught could speak eloquently about famous activists such as Martin Luther King Jr. and Rosa Parks and describe the central role they played in fighting injustice in American society. If you were to ask these students what message they drew from King's or Parks's life, they would explain the importance of fighting for what you believe in, standing up for what is right, and similar inspirational platitudes. If you asked these students what concrete things they learned from King and Parks that would enable them to take a stand and make a difference, however, the vast majority would stare at you blankly. Students rarely connect the actions and accomplishments of famous leaders such as King and Parks with their own lives.

This disconnection between what students say they have learned from extraordinary historical role models and what they actually believe and do in their everyday lives has serious consequences. On standard measures, young people in the United States today have fairly low levels of civic and political engagement, compared both to adults and to young people from previous generations. They demonstrate less interest in current events and politics; less knowledge about politics, government, and civil society; less political efficacy, the belief that they can influence government to change society for the better. They take fewer actions, such as voting, protesting, boycotting or buycotting, contacting public officials, running for office, joining a political party, joining a neighborhood association or other community group, or writing a letter or e-mail to the editor.[1] Young people who are nonwhite and low-income have even lower rates of civic and political engagement. Students like those I teach are least likely to be confident, skilled, or practiced at changing society through political action, even though they have the most to gain from social and political reform.

The poorest individuals express an interest in politics and feelings of political efficacy at levels almost a full standard deviation lower than the wealthiest. Latinos also express significantly lower levels of political efficacy than African Americans, who in turn feel significantly less politically efficacious than whites do. Similar disparities appear among Latinos, African Americans, and whites ages fifteen to twenty-five when asked how confident they are that "I can make a difference in solving the problems of my community." These attitudinal differences are strongly associated with people's rates of political and civic participation. In the 2004 presidential election, Latino and Asian voting-age citizens voted at a rate only about two-thirds that of eligible whites, while poor people voted at barely half the rate of middle-class and wealthy people. People who earn over $75,000 annually are politically active at up to six times the rate of those who earn under $15,000, whether measured by working for a campaign, serving on the board of an organization, participating in protests, or contacting public officials.[2]

Educators who teach low-income and nonwhite students can take steps to combat these gaps in political attitudes and civic engagement. First, we can go beyond the typical list of famous activists of color and introduce students to "ordinary" role models, people who share their racial, ethnic, cultural, and/or class-related characteristics, live and/or work locally, may be relatively unknown, and are effectively engaged in civic or political action. We can teach students that the ordinary, everyday acts taken by these people make significant differences to their communities. Finally, we can help students identify and practice the key skills deployed by these "ordinary" role models as a means of becoming efficacious, engaged civic and political actors themselves.

In every community, ordinary people work hard to change society in everyday but extremely significant ways: youth workers, clergy members, city councillors, school board members, nonprofit organization directors, policy makers, and social service providers. These people often live in students' own neighborhoods and are thrilled to share what they do with interested young people. Their work is concrete: students can easily understand what they do and why it matters to those being served. By inviting these "ordinary" role models into the classroom, teachers can help students discover the effectiveness of civic and political engagement by people like themselves.

Teachers need to exercise care both in inviting guests into the classroom and in preparing both guests and students for the visit. Adults who do great things are not necessarily able to convey the excitement of their actions to students. Seek out adults who already work with young people, since they will know how to talk with students. Teachers should explain in advance what the purpose of the visit is, how their visit fits into the curriculum the students are studying, how long they should plan to talk and answer questions, what kinds of materials students might be interested in seeing, and what the classroom climate may be like. Arrangements should be made with any guest to permit the teacher to jump in during a presentation to clarify information or help connect what students are hearing with what they have learned in previous lessons.

Students need to be prepared as well. They should be told in advance who is visiting, how the visit fits into the curriculum, what to expect from the presentation, what they themselves should do during the presentation, when and how to ask questions, and what they will be expected to do with what they have learned afterward. This preparation is time consuming in the beginning, when students are learning how and why to welcome guest speakers into their classroom, but it gets easier with each visit, especially if the ground rules remain the same. I use a "Public Speaker Reflection Sheet" to guide my eighth-grade students' listening and participation. It includes a mix of factual questions and opportunities for reflection: the speaker's occupation, personal characteristics, and main points; what students learned; and how the presentation related to the subject of our inquiry.

After a guest visits, teachers should help students identify the skills and practices that were crucial for helping him or her achieve social or political change. It is important to keep students focused on specific actions rather than allowing them to lapse into generalities. Then students can concretely consider how they themselves could take an effective stand on an issue they care about.

One year we hosted Sam Yoon, who was then working for the Asian Community Development Corporation and running to be Boston's first Asian American city councillor. (He won.) After his presentation, it would have been easy for students to pick out such generic attributes as getting an education, caring about others, and working hard as keys to his success. Instead, we examined the specifics of his efforts for social change: how he tried to use the media's interest in his personal story as the first Asian American candidate for citywide office in order to focus attention on the issues he cared about, such as affordable housing. Students were inspired to learn about how to communicate with the media, present themselves publicly, and use their own personal stories to direct others' attention to issues such as neighborhood violence and lack of job opportunities for youth. They developed valuable communication and presentation skills while incorporating their own backgrounds, interests, and concerns. The fact that students actually met and talked with Yoon—one student saw him in a neighborhood diner a few days later, and another ran into him on the bus—helped keep them energized and fostered their sense that learning these skills might enable them to make a difference.

Emphasizing ordinary people does not mean exposing students only to grassroots activists. Nor does it mean limiting students' experiences to those who resemble them in racial-ethnic and class identification. Although I recommend that teachers take their students' racial-ethnic identities into account when planning speakers, curricula should not be restricted to people who share their background (see also Sleeter, Chapter 28). A curriculum that failed to educate low-income students of color about the broader world beyond their communities would disempower students far more than the curriculum we have now, which includes a few great men and women as representatives of entire racial groups.

Including these "ordinary role models" may be seen by students and visitors as simply another form of tokenism: "Oh, gee, we need to put some local people of color into the curriculum, so let's invite someone for Hispanic Heritage or Black History Month. . . ." Classroom guests and the activities related to their visits should always be closely tied to the curriculum. If students and the teacher cannot explain how a guest speaker's presentation relates to what is being studied, then the presentation will be quickly forgotten and students will be unlikely to adopt the guest as a role model for civic or political engagement.

Despite the risks, the benefits are great. This approach counters the implicit, racist belief that there are only a few great nonwhite people. Elevating such extraordinary figures as Martin Luther King Jr. and Rosa Parks and concentrating on their accomplishments to the exclusion of the foot soldiers who sustained the Civil Rights Movement, for example, implies that only a few people are called to change the world, especially within low-income and/or nonwhite communities, and that everyone else might as well stand aside. This discouraging message is generally not conveyed about whites because efficacious "ordinary" white people are prevalent in curricula, textbooks, and the media. Bringing in ordinary role models from students' own communities and cultures changes this dynamic. Also, rather than merely teaching about others who made a difference, this approach teaches students to make a difference themselves. This connection is especially important in schools that serve predominantly low-income and nonwhite students, since historically their schools have provided only limited opportunities for students to learn and practice skills for political and civic engagement.

Finally, by sparking academic inquiry and social action through discussions with local activists, the ordinary role model approach also collapses the false distinction between real-life knowledge and academic knowledge. School becomes a place where "real life" people share their knowledge and experiences and students can apply new-found skills to issues they care about, whether in or out of school. By helping students learn the civic and political skills generally attributed to extraordinary historical figures, this approach inspires students not simply to venerate great leaders but to act for change themselves.

RESOURCES

Campaign for the Civic Mission of Schools: for curricula, programs, recommendations, and other resources for implementing powerful civic education in classrooms and schools, visit www.civicmissionofschools.org.

Center for Information and Research on Civic Learning and Engagement (CIRCLE): to learn more about young people's civic knowledge, skills, and participation, visit www.civicyouth.org.

DISCUSSION QUESTIONS

1. **Principle:** What are the advantages and risks of incorporating "ordinary" role models into the curriculum?
2. **Strategy:** How might you identify and determine who is a good role model from your school's community? What forms of local work do you think your students should be exposed to? Who else in the community could be asked to help make this decision?
3. **Try tomorrow:** How might you find and invite local role models without overemphasizing their roles as racial group representatives, and rather in a way that emphasizes their expertise? Role-play the invitation.

Meira Levinson, an assistant professor at the Harvard Graduate School of Education, has taught civics, English, American history, and humanities for eight years in the Atlanta and Boston Public Schools. She is currently writing a book on civic and multicultural education in de facto segregated, urban public schools.

Part X

Analyze Racial Disparities in Opportunities to Learn

Many racial inequalities in life opportunity take shape outside of schools. Educators must attend to those as well, but educators must especially address the inequalities and inadequacies in learning opportunity that take shape inside school walls. The essays in this part share a core principle of everyday antiracism: *if certain school practices are denying opportunity to students along racial lines, those practices must be shifted so that children are provided opportunity instead.*

How can educators start to ensure that necessary learning opportunities are equitably distributed to every child?

1. Push for optimal learning opportunities for all children as if they were your own.

   Karolyn Tyson urges that educators offer "gifted" learning opportunities to more children, rather than offering them exclusively to a limited few.

2. Avoid disproportionately disciplining students of color, and always use discipline to reconnect students to the benefits of learning.

   Pedro Noguera asks educators to analyze whether current disciplinary practices are excluding or humiliating students, rather than reconnecting students to learning opportunities.

24

Providing Equal Access to "Gifted" Education

Karolyn Tyson

Many schools across the country have special programs designed for students who are labeled "gifted" that provide enriched instruction for students who are insufficiently challenged by the regular curriculum. In most places, the students invited to participate are overwhelmingly white.[1] The National Research Council reports that, of all racial-ethnic minority groups, African Americans are least likely to be represented in gifted programs. Only 3 percent of black students are served by these programs nationally, compared to nearly 8 percent of white students, roughly 5 percent of American Indian students, and 3.5 percent of Hispanic students. Asian students fare better than all other groups, with 10 percent enrolled in gifted programs.[2] Even in schools where the majority is nonwhite, white students still account for the majority of those in the gifted programs. In research examining student placement in gifted programs in North Carolina, my colleagues and I found that in most of the 250-plus elementary schools we studied, minority students were represented in gifted programs at less than half the rate of their presence in the general student body.[3] The pattern was much starker when we focused on black students in individual schools. For example, at Holt Elementary School (all schools mentioned here are pseudonymous), students in the gifted program were all white, although the school's student body was 70 percent black.

Differences in standardized test scores explain only some of this disparity. While student test performance is a major factor in placement decisions, teachers play a pivotal role. In fact, most schools nationwide use some form of teacher recommendation to screen or place students, and the majority of referrals are made by teachers.

In this essay, I focus on things teachers can do to ensure that all students have equal access to the high-quality, challenging curriculum available in gifted programs and that they all have ample opportunities to master complex material in the regular classroom, which builds the academic self-confidence gifted programs nurture. My research has found that regardless of their level of achievement, students who are identified as gifted are more likely to describe themselves as "smart" or "intelligent" and to enroll in Advanced Placement (AP) and honors courses in high school. Being labeled "gifted" is itself a benefit, and it is enhanced by enriched education. Researchers consistently find that exposure to challenging curricular materials has significant positive effects on academic achievement.[4] Many minority and low-income students miss out on these benefits because of their systemic, disproportionate underrepresentation in "gifted" education programs.

This underrepresentation has social consequences for the entire student body. For example, my colleagues and I have found that animosity between and within groups tends to be more prominent at secondary schools where there are highly visible racial or social class disparities in students' course placement than at schools where academic grouping appears more equitable.[5] We found considerably more resentment toward and ridiculing of higher-tracked students in high-disparity schools, as well as more racial and class-based friction between students.

In secondary schools where the number of racial-ethnic minorities in rigorous courses and programs is noticeably disproportionate to these students' overall presence in the school, a racialized image of achievement develops. In these contexts, where students of color are underrepresented in high-track and "gifted" classes, black students are more likely to perceive achievement as the domain of whites and to accuse peers enrolled in accelerated courses of "acting white." This self-protective accusation shields black students from a painful but common misperception about the cause of black underrepresentation in rigorous courses and programs: the mistaken belief that blacks are less intellectually capable than whites.

How do these glaring disparities in racial representation come about? When making referrals for gifted programs, most teachers do not deliberately sort students by race. Some practices and policies can unintentionally have this effect, however. For example, teachers and counselors often use behavior and language cues as indicators of aptitude or potential. As a counselor at Georgetown Elementary School explained, low-income and minority students, especially black boys, were less likely to be screened or referred to gifted placement than higher-income white students because their behavior was seen as "disruptive" and used as an indicator of low potential. In contrast, at Ivory Elementary School, minority students (Latinos and African Americans combined) were overrepresented in the gifted program because school staff had made a deliberate effort to change the way they viewed and assessed "disruptive" behavior: behaviors described as "overly social" and "showing signs of boredom" and "curiosity" were reframed as indications that a child might need more challenging curricular materials. According to school personnel, many of these students began to thrive academically and their classroom behavior improved after placement in the gifted program.

As an educator, you can bring about change by being mindful both of your own thinking about how "giftedness" looks and sounds and of the school-wide policies and practices that contribute to the disproportionate underrepresentation of black and other minority students in gifted programs. One strategy is to push for doing away with gifted programs and other tracking practices that sort and separate students. Children who are exposed to the challenging curricular materials offered in gifted programs do better academically than children who are not exposed to them, independent of their prior achievement. Ultimately, the goal should be to provide all children access to this kind of education. However, if you are in a situation where this option is not immediately available, you can take other steps to address racial disparities in academic placement, either individually or with your colleagues.

Begin by taking stock of the present situation at your school. Trying to address the disproportionate underrepresentation of minority students in gifted programs by adopting a colorblind strategy is not helpful. In fact, teachers' and administrators' strong reluctance to examine the racial demographics of gifted programs has probably contributed to minority underrepresentation. Initially, then, you must be attentive to the racial composition of your school's most rigorous courses and programs. Find out what the racial composition is and compare it to that of your school's total student population. Consider, for example, the case of Holt Elementary School, where no black students were enrolled in the school's gifted program although blacks accounted for 70 percent of the school population. Remember, the more glaring the disparity, the more likely we are to find animosity between white and minority students and resentment directed toward students in higher-level courses and programs. Rather than simply comparing "white" to "minority," break out each racial group (e.g., black, Hispanic/Latino, Asian, American Indian, white) separately to ensure the most accurate assessment. Depending on your school's demographics, you may want to consider even finer ethnic comparisons; for example, in some schools, Chinese students may be represented proportionately in gifted programs, while Cambodian students may be underrepresented.

If you and your colleagues decide that the level of disparity at your school is not acceptable, the next steps are assessment and mindfulness. Assess your school's procedures and policies for screening and identification. What procedures are used for identifying and referring gifted students? Do some procedures or practices seem to allow for the identification of a more diverse group of students? Do some procedures and practices seem to inhibit the identification of a diverse group? What are the signs or indications of giftedness commonly used at your school? What instruments does your school use to assess giftedness? Conduct research to find out what methods and/or instruments have been demonstrated to identify a broader range of talents and potential. If your school intends to continue the gifted program, it is important that you actively work to find ways to ensure that more than a token number of students from the racial-ethnic minority groups at your school are asked to participate.

Perhaps the most important way you can address minority underrepresentation in gifted programs is to be mindful of your own thinking about ability, aptitude, and potential. Examine the perceptions you hold regarding your students, and then think about how those perceptions affect the day-to-day decisions you make in the classroom. Do you tend to assume that children from black, Latino, or low-income families do not have as much family, community, and peer support for academic endeavors as children from other families and therefore should not be expected to realize high levels of academic achievement? Do you assume that enriched instruction will be of little or no use or value to these children? Many teachers are already practicing mindfulness around issues of gender fairness in the classroom—for example, taking care that they do not act as if girls were less able in mathematics than boys. Similarly, consider how you think about the aptitude and potential of black and Latino students as compared to white or Asian students, or about how you believe that living in poverty, low-income, or single-parent households affects ability or achievement. Even if you conclude that some or all of those factors can or do have some negative consequences for student achievement, do you sometimes think those consequences are inevitable? Are you making potentially false assumptions or judgments about your students' abilities or aptitudes based on these factors, or on their language or behavior? Do you sometimes feel that a student's aptitude is innate and cannot be developed? Consider whether and how your assumptions about aptitude and ability could be influencing which students you are most likely to refer for gifted services and which you are least likely to refer.

One practical step you might take to help improve your mindfulness is to start looking at each child in your classroom as if she or he were your own. If that child were yours, what would you want her school experience to be? What kind of an education would you want for her? How would you want her teachers to see and treat her? Would you allow her to be overlooked for an opportunity to experience a high-quality, challenging curriculum? Would you make sure she has access to the best education available? Would you envision her potential as reaching beyond your own education or family income? If you saw every child in your classroom as your own, you might be more inclined to see their strengths rather than their weaknesses, to imagine their potential rather than highlight their limitations, and to be an advocate for them on every front to ensure that they receive all of the educational services they require and all the opportunities they deserve.

School personnel often complain about parents who demand that their children be placed in the gifted program or advanced classes, or who push for a particular service that is believed to provide educational benefits, even when the children do not meet the official criteria for inclusion. In our studies, teachers and administrators typically described such parents as "white," "wealthy" and "pushy." Understandably, these parents want the best for their children; the difference is that they believe they are entitled to the best and they usually have the means to find ways to obtain it.[6]

Who advocates for children whose parents do not push? Who ensures that they are not overlooked, but have access to optimal learning opportunities? As a teacher, you can. Seeing every child in your classroom as if she were your own may prompt you to refer more students for gifted services. It might also mean that you incorporate more rigorous academic activities into your regular classroom teaching for the benefit of all children. If you saw every child as your own, you might consistently think of aptitude as something to be developed and attempt to develop it in all of your children, not just a select, privileged few.

RESOURCES

The Educational Research Information Center (ERIC): ERIC, available online and at libraries, provides a wide range of information on what methods and instruments have been demonstrated to identify a broader range of talents and potential. See http://www.eric.ed.gov.

Annegret Staiger. 1996. *Learning Difference: Race and Schooling in the Multiracial Metropolis.* Stanford, CA: Stanford University Press.

————. 2004. "Whiteness as Giftedness: Racial Formation at an Urban High School." *Social Problems* 51(2): 161–81.

DISCUSSION QUESTIONS

1. **Principle:** What are the percentages of each racial group in your student population, and what are the percentages of these racial groups in your gifted, advanced, or AP classes? Do you think that the procedures for placing students in these classes are fair?

2. **Strategy:** How realistic is the idea of doing away with exclusive "gifted" programs at your school, and making "gifted" learning opportunities available to all children? Would you support that idea? Why or why not?

3. **Try tomorrow:** What concrete steps could you and your colleagues take to reframe how "gifted" students are identified, or to provide "gifted" learning opportunities to students throughout the school?

Karolyn Tyson is an associate professor in the department of sociology at the University of North Carolina–Chapel Hill. Her research examines the complex interplay between school- and individual-level factors to understand how school practices and policies affect student outcomes, particularly among black students.

25

What Discipline Is For: Connecting Students to the Benefits of Learning

Pedro A. Noguera

Throughout the United States, schools tend disproportionately to punish the students who have the greatest academic, social, economic, and emotional needs.[1] Examination of which students are most likely to be suspended, expelled, or removed from the classroom for punishment reveals that members of racial-ethnic minority groups (especially Blacks and Latinos), males, and low achievers are vastly overrepresented.[2] Close scrutiny of disciplinary practices reveals that a disproportionate number of the students who receive the most severe punishments are students who have learning disabilities, are from single-parent households, are in foster care, are homeless, or qualify for free or reduced-price lunch. In many schools, these students are disproportionately students of color.

Educators must reflect upon the factors that give rise to such imbalances in school discipline. Often students' unmet needs cause misconduct, and schools' inability to address the needs of their most disadvantaged students results in their receiving the lion's share of punishment. I urge educators to ask whether discipline is meted out fairly and responds to students' needs.

Students who are behind academically, who are more likely to be students of color, are also more likely to engage in disruptive behavior, sometimes out of frustration or embarrassment.[3] Children who suffer from abuse or neglect at home or who are harassed and teased by their peers[4] are also more likely to misbehave. Since poverty rates are higher among racial minorities in the United States, students of color are more likely to exhibit behavior problems because of unmet needs. In many schools, it is common for the neediest students to be disciplined and for the needs driving their misbehavior to be ignored. Disturbingly, these disparities in who gets punished and how often do not evoke alarm, or even concern, because these patterns are accepted as normal.

Some of this disproportionate discipline may occur because of educators' racial bias, rather than students' disproportionate "disruption." But educators are unlikely to admit bias even to themselves, so it is more effective to ask educators to examine the disproportionate effects of their actions. Teachers and administrators who seek to reduce the disproportionate discipline of children of color can start by using data to demonstrate that this disproportion exists and then probe to find out why it occurs.

An administrator at a middle school in New Haven, Connecticut, began a professional development activity by writing the reasons teachers gave for sending a student to the office on the blackboard. He then went down the list with the group and asked whether they felt the infractions listed were legitimate reasons for referring a student to the principal's office for punishment. In a public setting with their colleagues present, no one would defend sending a student to the office for chewing gum, wearing a hat, or forgetting to bring a pencil. Yet, these and other minor infractions were the reasons given on the bulk of the referrals. He pointed out that Black and Latino boys received over 80 percent of these referrals; and he engaged the staff in a discussion of the implications of these practices.

Holding educators accountable for racial imbalances in discipline need not result in finger-pointing or recriminations about racist intentions that cannot be proved. However, if educators are going to reduce the disproportionate discipline meted out to poor children of color, they must accept responsibility for racial disparities in discipline patterns. Analyzing their approaches to maintaining order can help educators to identify alternative methods for producing positive learning environments. Alternatives are essential if schools are to stop using discipline as a strategy for weeding out those they deem undesirable or difficult to teach and instead to use discipline to reconnect students to learning.

Educators sometimes discipline students of color for tiny offenses that do not require discipline at all. Even when responding to more egregious acting out, educators typically punish children of color without reflecting on the factors that may be motivating the misbehavior. Instead of asking why a student is disrespectful to a teacher, fighting, or disturbing a classroom, many schools react to the behavior by inflexibly enforcing rules and imposing sanctions. By responding to conduct while ignoring the factors that cause it, schools inadvertently further the educational failure of these students and may ultimately contribute to their marginalization as adults.

The marginalization of students who are frequently punished occurs because schools rely primarily on two strategies to discipline students who misbehave: humiliation and exclusion. Typically, they respond to minor infractions with humiliation, by singling out a misbehaving student for rebuke and ostracism, or placing a student in the back of the room or the hallway. If problems persist, most schools exclude the student from the classroom, starting with referrals to the principal's office and gradually escalating to removal from the school through suspension, or in the most serious cases, expulsion. These strategies effectively deny targeted students access to instruction and the opportunity to learn and do little to enable students to learn from their mistakes and develop a sense of responsibility for their behavior. The fact that many schools frequently punish a small number of students repeatedly[5] suggests that these approaches are ineffective in changing students' behavior and making schools more orderly.

Discipline strategies that rely upon humiliation and exclusion are based on the assumption that by removing disruptive children from the learning environment, others will be allowed to learn in peace. While the logic behind this approach may seem compelling, a closer look at the consequence of these practices reveals obvious flaws. Students who are punished for fairly minor behavior problems when they are young frequently perpetrate more serious offenses as they get older. The almost exclusive reliance on suspension and other forms of exclusion makes little sense, especially since many of the students who are suspended dislike school and there is little evidence that it works as a deterrent to misconduct. In schools where suspension rates are high, sorting out the "bad" students rarely results in a better education for those who remain, because many students are deeply alienated from school, have weak and even antagonistic relationships with the adults who serve them, and believe that very few teachers care about them.[6]

An implicit social contract serves as the basis for maintaining order in schools as it does in society:[7] in exchange for an education, students are expected to obey the rules and norms operative within school and to comply with the authority of the adults in charge. Students are expected to relinquish a certain degree of individual freedom in exchange for receiving the benefits of education. For the vast majority of students, this arrangement elicits a relatively high degree of compliance with school rules and to adult authority. Despite surveys that suggest a growing number of teachers and students fear violence in school, schools in the United States are actually generally safe places.[8] Even though children significantly outnumber adults, they largely conform to adult authority and, through their compliance, make it possible for order to be maintained.

This arrangement tends to be least effective for students who do not receive the benefits promised by the social contract. Students who are behind academically, have not been taught by teachers who have cultivated a love of learning, or have come to regard school as a boring, compulsory chore are more likely to disrupt classrooms and defy authority. Although these students are typically more likely to be disciplined, punishing them is often ineffective because it is not aimed at connecting them to learning. As they come to understand that the rewards of education—admission to college and access to well-paying jobs—are not available to them, students have little incentive to comply with school rules. Students who frequently get into trouble may have so many negative experiences in school that they conclude school is not for them and that the rewards associated with education are beyond their reach. As students develop identities as "troublemakers" and "delinquents," they often internalize the label and, instead of changing their behavior, embrace the stigma.[9] Punishment reinforces undesirable behavior rather than serving as an effective deterrent.

To break the cycle of failure, schools must find ways to reconnect students who have become disaffected through prior disciplinary experiences and academic failure to learning and the goals of education. Students who disrupt the learning environment for others must come to see the benefits of the knowledge and skills that education offers. In order to be motivated to comply with school norms, they must be inspired to believe that education can serve as a means for them to improve their lives and help their families and community.

This task necessarily involves providing these students with access to teachers and other adult role models who can establish supportive, mentoring relationships with youth who have had negative experiences with the school system. In many schools, such mentors are in short supply, both because racial-ethnic and class differences often make it difficult for teachers to provide the "tough love" and moral authority that students need and because adults are often positioned in antagonistic relationships with students. Those who learn to cross racial and class boundaries to forge strong, productive bonds with students are able to use those relationships to motivate students to apply themselves and get them to see that education can serve as a vehicle for self-improvement.[10] Creating these types of relationships requires educators to take time to find out what students are personally interested in or concerned about so the content of the curriculum can be made relevant to students.

While seeking to learn about and meet students' individual needs, educators should also respond to any more structural local factors underlying students' acting out. A program created in Berkeley, California, in 1987 demonstrates such an approach that works. Concerned about a crack trade that relied heavily upon local teenagers to serve as foot soldiers and salesmen on the streets and was contributing to discipline problems and a rising dropout rate, the city funded a novel program aimed at preventing young people from becoming involved in drug dealing. The Real Alternative Program (RAP) recruited middle school students who had committed at least one criminal offense and were regarded by their teachers and parents as at risk of greater delinquency. Students were provided with tutors, recreational opportunities, summer employment, and a caseworker. The city funded the program by hiring an additional officer for parking meter enforcement and earmarking the revenue to the program. An evaluation showed that RAP was extremely successful at reducing delinquency and improving school performance. Delinquency prevention programs in communities and schools throughout the country have proven effective at changing student behavior and reducing the incidence of juvenile delinquency. Yet, even though they are substantially cheaper to fund than more punitive approaches, they have not been adequately supported.

In most cases, what separates teachers who experience frequent behavior problems from those who do not is their ability to keep their students focused on learning. Unless we focus on how to engage students, schools will continue to be revolving doors for students who are bored, restless, behind academically, and unconvinced that schooling will provide benefits for them and who, in consequence, often act out. When we locate discipline problems exclusively in students and ignore the school and local contexts in which problematic behavior occurs, we overlook the most important factors that give rise to misbehavior. Schools that suspend large numbers of students, or suspend small numbers of students frequently, typically become so preoccupied with discipline and control that they have little time to address the conditions that influence teaching and learning.

Finally, schools must focus on the values students should learn when they are disciplined. In his pioneering research on moral development in children, Lawrence Kohlberg argued that teaching students to obey rules in order to avoid punishment was far less effective than helping students to develop the ability to make reasoned ethical judgments about their behavior.[11] Rather than punishing students by sending them home for fighting, educators should teach students how to resolve conflicts peacefully; discipline should always teach a moral lesson. Students who vandalize their building can be required to do community service aimed at cleaning up or improving their school, and students who are disrespectful to teachers can be required to assist that teacher on a project and to write a letter of apology. Over time, students will understand the values that underlie the operation of the school and appreciate that all members are accountable to them, that the social contract holds. Research on school discipline and safety shows that, rather than leading to a more lenient environment that tolerates misbehavior, schools promoting an ethical culture can create an environment where misconduct is less likely.[12]

By relying upon alternative discipline strategies rooted in ethics and a determination to reconnect students to learning, schools can reduce the likelihood that the neediest and most disengaged students, who are frequently children of color, will be targeted for repeated punishment. Some of these alternative strategies are practiced in private and public schools for affluent children, but they are less common in public schools that serve poor children of color. There are some exceptions. Phyl's Academy in Fort Lauderdale, Florida, has been praised for adhering to principal Monica Lewis's admonition to "treat children with kindness." In describing her school, Lewis reports: "We don't have a rigid hand. We show them values. Once you give a child reasons, you get them to follow directions."[13]

Producing safe and orderly schools need not require turning schools into prisons or detention centers. It is possible to create schools where learning and academic achievement is encouraged for all students and where disciplinary problems are responded to in a manner that is consistent with the broader educational goals. We must recognize that the children of the poor and children of color are no less deserving than the children of the affluent to be educated in a nurturing and supportive environment. Perhaps what is needed even more than a shift in disciplinary tactics is recruitment of educators who question the tendency to punish through exclusion and humiliation and see themselves as advocates of children, not as wardens and prison guards. Without this approach, the drive to punish will be difficult to reverse.

RESOURCES

William Ayers, Rick Ayers, and Bernardine Dohrn. 2001. *Zero Tolerance: Resisting the Drive for Punishment*. New York: The New Press.

DISCUSSION QUESTIONS

1. **Principle:** For what sorts of behaviors are students in your school punished? Does discipline in your school often take the form of humiliation or exclusion, as Noguera suggests? Does such discipline disproportionately affect students of color?
2. **Strategy:** What sorts of alternative disciplinary strategies have you seen reconnect students to the benefits of learning?
3. **Try tomorrow:** Think of a student you often discipline, or see disciplined. How might you and other educators at your school reconnect that student to the learning experience?

Pedro Noguera is a professor in the Steinhardt School of Education at New York University. His research focuses on urban school reform, conditions that promote student achievement, youth violence, the potential impact of school choice and vouchers on urban public schools, and race and ethnic relations in American society.

SECTION C

Curriculum That Asks Crucial Questions about Race

Part XI

Create Curriculum That Invites Students to Explore Complex Identities *and* Consider Racial Group Experiences

It is often through curriculum that we can prompt students to think hard about race. Yet we often ask students to think or write about racial identities in reductive ways—that is, in ways that do not acknowledge people's full complexity. The essays in this part share a core principle of everyday antiracism: *racial identities are always in flux and complex, never fixed or simple, and they should be discussed that way in the classroom.*

How can educators help students engage racial identities—their own, and others'—as complex and in flux?

1. Use photography to wrestle with questions of racial identity.

    Alex Lightfoot proposes that teachers use photography to join students in analyzing identities as complicated and multiple.

2. Encourage students to explore racial identities in their writing.

    Jennifer Mott-Smith suggests that students, in this case immigrant students, should be encouraged to explore their own racial identities in their writing, while never being forced to do so.

3. Involve students in selecting reading materials.

    Christine Sleeter proposes that teachers involve students in choosing what to read, guided by the principle that students need chances both to learn about "selves" and to learn about "others."

26

Using Photography to Explore Racial Identity

Alexandra Lightfoot

Questions of racial identity—people's identities as members of racial groups, and the complex ways in which identities are not simple or predictable, at all—arise routinely in classrooms. In this essay, I offer photography as a tool to get educators and students "wrestling" with questions of racial identity.[1]

The "Regarding Race" project, a collaboration between the Center for Documentary Studies at Duke University (where I have an affiliation) and the Teaching Fellows Program at the University of North Carolina–Chapel Hill, engages preservice teachers in an exploration of racial identity through photography and writing, aiming to cultivate "healthy/whole teachers" who have "taken the time, energy, and discipline to examine [themselves] especially in relationship to their own race and racial identity and in relationship to the race and racial identity of their students."[2]

"Regarding Race" grew out of my doctoral research on the collaboration between a white woman artist, Wendy Ewald, and an African American classroom teacher, Robert Hunter, in a photography project called "Black Self/White Self." The project prompted children in a newly integrated Durham, N.C., middle school to examine their own racial identities by asking them to produce, manipulate, and write about photographic images of themselves. "Regarding Race" adapted that approach to teachers. The project challenges participants to make a pair of written and photographic portraits. One self-portrait depicts who they are in a racialized world, or how they see themselves, and the second envisions who they might be as the member of a race other than their own, or how they might involuntarily be seen by others. We use a Polaroid Pro-Pack camera with positive/negative film or a digital camera with software capable of altering images. Both allow participants to change their photographic portraits: they can make alterations directly to the Polaroid film negative, or manipulate the image digitally, enhancing the image and extending their ideas with designs or words written on and around it. Participants write a narrative or poem that is displayed with the visual image. The resulting self-portraits, both visual and written, reveal that the participants hold quite complicated notions of their own racial identities, as well as about how their identities are perceived by others.

Typically, these self-portraits prompt class discussion regarding the participants' efforts to teach diverse groups of students. We look at the images, share
stories of our own backgrounds and experiences, and discuss racial stereotypes
when they inevitably emerge.

The discussion of stereotypes can be a minefield in any conversation about
race. In the first year of the project a white woman made a double exposure,
portraying her "white self" at the top of a set of stairs and her "black self" at
the bottom. A black woman portrayed her "white self" as a wealthy sorority
sister. Students of color were disturbed by what the white woman's portraits
revealed about her sense of place in the world and her relationship to people
of color. White students were offended by the sorority portrait and the
assumptions of wealth it seemed to convey. So often conversations on race
lapse into divisiveness, but engaging divergent perspectives is central to struggling productively with race categories, rather than treating them as fixed or
simple identities.[3] The collaborative interaction of the portrait-making process
defuses some of the tension of race talk while encouraging participants to
challenge their assumptions. We ask participants to reflect on their first memory of race and/or racism, or their first sense of a racial "identity."[4] Often, these
memories involve incidents in school settings, which sends a strong message to
participants about how issues of race might affect their students as well.

One white woman in the early days of the project spent hours laboring
over the background details in her portraits, etching line after line to make
both images visually stunning. It was in her writing that she revealed her
anxieties about racializing her identity at all; she felt unsure of "how to approach the topic of race from my own self." Realizing her discomfort with
even being "racial," she then began to think about the "privilege" and blind-
ness to her own "race" conferred on her by being "white," which she had
never questioned before. Other participants express a keen awareness of how
race has shaped their lives, experiences, and perspectives, but the portrait
task makes them, too, wrestle with their racial identities. One African American male's self-portraits depict him as "focused" and "looking forward" to
what he needs to do to accomplish his goals, but simultaneously "on guard" for
"obstacles" that might derail his progress. A Latina refers in her portraits to
the stresses she experiences every day as a person of color in a white world
but also the "peace" she has attained through knowing and believing in her
self as Latina.

Other participants try to "put themselves in the shoes" of others when
making the portraits. A multiracial woman who self-identifies as black tells us
she is eager to make both portraits so that she can explore the dimensions of
her white self. A white woman imagines her interactions with the Hispanic
immigrants she will teach when she becomes an ESL teacher in a rural North
Carolina community. She combines her ideas into a single double-exposed
portrait portraying her self as a teacher in conversation with her self as a

Latina student, an effort to stretch her perceptions and to see through the eyes of the students she will teach.

The participants work with a group of middle school students over the course of a semester to make these same double portraits with them, guiding the students' examination of racial identity while they are wrestling with notions about race themselves. Photography is a potent tool for this work. It provides a lens on perceptions of racial identities, invites empathetic or alternative interpretations of "others" and selves, and gives participants (both teachers and students) something concrete to discuss. The picture-taking is an interactive process; students work in small groups, and rich conversations take place as they fan out around the school to search for suitable backgrounds. The middle school students are particularly adept at finding symbolic settings that express their visions: a chain-link fence framing a girl who wants to show she is "torn between two worlds" as a Hispanic American; an African American girl shimmying up a light pole who later draws in white hands reaching up to pull her down; a white girl shielding her face from view by a soccer net to represent the pressures she feels at the demands of adolescence; an African American boy barely visible down a long hallway with many doors, some of which offer opportunity, others traps, a journey he hopes to convey as full of choices.

Like the adults' images, some of the children's portraits stick closely to racial identity; others probe different, but related, aspects of identity. Some reveal skepticism or defiance about how the "outside world" perceives them and seek to shed light on their "inside selves." Some view their past selves as lacking, and imbue their future selves with hopes and dreams. An African American girl professes that her black self is "much more complicated" than her white self. A white girl explores her two selves as nonracist and racist, admitting to the world that she carries biases and prejudices that she must work to shed. A boy explores what it means to be biracial in a world that would see him as either black or white, drawing strength from his dual selves and defying viewers to limit him.

Toward the end of each session, the participants organize a forum, attended by parents, teachers, and members of the wider community, to showcase the portraits. The audience is always awed by the insights these students and teachers bring to light, by the obvious bonds and connections they develop, and by the deep reciprocal learning this documentary process and its focus on race engenders for both students and future teachers. It is striking to hear how perceptive the middle school students are, how well they are coming to know themselves, and how acutely they understand the racial dynamics of their school and community. It is powerful and inspiring to hear the educators reflect on how much they gain from this "purposeful struggle" with race and how much they learn from the children with whom they work. As they probe the contours of race in their own lives, the educators learn to see their students' racial identities, too, not as fixed or static but as complex and fluid. They are also better equipped to see beyond race to the individuality of each child.

RESOURCES

Child Development Institute. 2003. *An Unlikely Friendship: A Curriculum and Video Guide* [Motion Picture]. Chapel Hill, NC: FPG. A documentary film and free teaching guide exploring how two people from extremely different backgrounds struggle with their own racial perspectives and form a lasting and productive relationship. The teaching guide is available free online at: www.fpg.unc.edu/~walkingthewalk/pdfs/unlikely_friendship.pdf.

W. Ewald and A. Lightfoot. 2001. *I Wanna Take Me a Picture: Teaching Photography and Writing to Children*. Boston: Beacon Press. A resource on how to use photography in the classroom or community.

On the Regarding Race project: cds.aas.duke.edu/regardingrace/index.html.

DISCUSSION QUESTIONS

1. **Principle:** Why is it necessary to work to see racial identities as complex and fluid, rather than fixed or static?

2. **Strategy:** What is gained, academically, when students and teachers use school time to do such inquiry into racial identity?

3. **Try tomorrow:** How could you implement some aspect of this type of project in your own school or classroom with students and/or colleagues?

Alexandra Lightfoot received her doctorate from the Harvard Graduate School of Education. As an independent researcher/consultant, she facilitates projects that use participatory photography as a tool for research, education, and community building. She directs the Regarding Race project out of the Center for Documentary Studies in Durham, North Carolina.

27

Exploring Racial Identity Through Writing

Jennifer A. Mott-Smith

In coming to the United States, immigrant students encounter a system of racial categories that often positions them in unfamiliar or undesirable ways. A Colombian student told me this story about applying for admission to the university where I teach English as a Second Language (ESL). In filling out the application form she checked the box for "white," as she was considered white in Colombia. However, when she came face to face with the admissions officer, he took out a red pen and changed her categorization to "Latino/a." The student was confused by the fact that she was not considered white and outraged that her choice of racial category was not accepted.

Immigrant students frequently experience everyday interactions that classify them racially. While some students may embrace the new categorization and identify with a particular U.S. racial group,[1] the fact remains that the U.S. race system invidiously positions people classified as non-"white." Many immigrant students are subordinated and further marginalized through this process of racial categorization.

As students experience racial categorization in schools, they may feel angry because they recognize that they are being positioned as inferior. The Colombian student may not have known that being Latina would make her eligible for some benefits, but she did know that being white was desirable. Students may feel angry because they are miscategorized, as when Haitian students are categorized as African American. Or they may feel angry and confused because they do not see where they fit into the U.S. mosaic: for example, what race is a person from Kurdistan? Encountering the new categories may lead some students to feel confused about their identities; they may struggle between embracing the identity of their country of origin and an Americanized racial-ethnic identity.

Writing offers immigrants a way to work through racial-ethnic identity categories and to explore and challenge the classification and ranking system. Students also develop writing voice, and become more deeply invested in school, when they can discuss their lived identity struggles through their schoolwork.

A student I had in a first-year English Composition course a few years ago exemplifies the ways that writing about identity can benefit immigrant students. As a nineteen-year-old immigrant from Vietnam who had been in the United States for seventeen years, Ho (a pseudonym) was a "generation 1.5" student—that is, a student who had migrated prior to puberty. He lived in a hybrid urban culture and was torn between identifying as Vietnamese, Vietnamese American, and Asian American. He was particularly concerned with presenting himself as "cool," and he knew that he would be judged differently by peers and teachers depending on the racial-ethnic identity category with which he identified.

Unlike many students in the class who were more recent immigrants, Ho had the ability to correct his English writing by ear. However, while his classmates wrote five-page essays on an assigned topic, he wrote only paragraphs. I wrote comments with suggestions for how he might expand his ideas in the next draft, but to no avail. So I asked him to meet with our class tutor, who was also a Vietnamese immigrant. A few weeks later, Ho came to my office to explain that he was having trouble working with the tutor, and we began to talk about his writing. I wanted to help him develop his ideas; he insisted that he had nothing to say. Finally I asked him, "What if I told you that writing is about knowing who you are?" I was stunned to hear his immediate reply: "I don't know who I am."

As our discussion continued, I learned that he was proud to be "Americanized" because he felt that this made him "cool." Moreover, like the white and ethnically Vietnamese students he had associated with in high school, he did not consider being successful at school "cool." In addition, he said that he both resented and envied "FOB" (Fresh Off the Boat) Vietnamese immigrants who were not cool but who got better grades in English class than he did. He saw our class tutor as a "FOB."

This student reminds me of the second-generation Mexican American students described by immigration researchers Carola and Marcelo Suárez-Orozco.[2] Their study comparing Mexican immigrants with second-generation Mexican Americans found that second-generation Mexican American students had lower motivation to achieve in school. The authors explain that this lower motivation was likely an outcome both of the acquisition of poor school attitudes from white students and the racialization of the second generation:

A shift occurs in the psychosocial patterning of achievement motivation of Mexican-origin populations after they acquire minority status in the United States. Mexican American youths may take on the white American adolescents' ambivalence toward authority and schools. In addition, other factors such as the stresses of minority status, discrimination, alienating schools, economic hardship, and pressure to work may all contribute to the high school dropout rate in this population.[3]

My student may have been influenced by these factors, but the immediate things holding him back from writing were his concern for maintaining a "cool" identity and his confusion over how to enact his Vietnamese American identity. By listening to him, I realized that although he felt that he did not know who he was, he actually knew a lot about Vietnamese immigrant identities. I told him that he could set aside the assignments on the syllabus for now and write about his identity instead. He proceeded to write his first developed essay on the complex relationships between so-called FOBs and "Bananas"—Asian immigrants who, he explained, were "white" on the inside and "yellow" on the outside. The essay allowed him to develop a school investment by encouraging him to bring his own lived experiences into his school assignments. And by requiring him to organize his thoughts in writing, the essay helped him to work through his own identifications while improving his academic skills.

Since this experience, I have realized the importance of structuring my writing class so that immigrant students are encouraged to explore their racial-ethnic identities in their writing if they wish. To develop writing on this topic, I spend much time in class discussion with the students exploring racial and other social categories, and I respond to each individual student's writing in margin comments on papers and in one-on-one conferences. I encourage students to voice their own current understandings and press them to go beyond these understandings. I want them to consider the complexity of racial categories and to think critically about systems of subordination.

This kind of teaching also involves urging students to confront their own prejudices, or holes in their knowledge. The Colombian student who identified as "white" made clear that she wanted to dissociate herself from lower-class "drug-dealing" Colombians. In order to help her think critically about this desire, we had to discuss class as well as racial prejudices. A Japanese student claimed that there was no ethnic diversity in Japan, ignoring the indigenous Ainu and the Koreans forcibly displaced during World War II. It was important for this student to confront the ethnic diversity within her own country in order for her to understand her position as culturally Japanese within Japan, as well as her new position within the United States.

I keep two things in mind in discussions with students. First, as a white teacher, I must not forget that my race shapes the class discussion. After a semester in which I taught a number of Haitian students, I learned from another student that the Haitian students had read my casual manner in class discussions about race, particularly regarding life in Haiti and in the United States, as a manifestation of white privilege. For them, race was a difficult topic, not to be entered into lightly. These students had concluded that the class was not one that would affirm their voices, which worked directly against my desire to support them in exploring racial identities in writing. I should have spent more time establishing trust and rapport across racial lines.

Second, the teacher exploring racial identity with immigrant students—or, indeed, with all students—should respect student decisions not to reveal information about their identities. In listening to students' identity statements, in writing or in class, teachers should respect what students choose not to reveal or explore, and avoid naming an omission in front of the whole class. A teacher might approach the student and have a private discussion about the significance of the omission. In this way, teachers not only learn about the students' understandings but engage them in respectful dialogue.

Immigrant students need to be able to negotiate U.S. racial categories and to speak back to people who label them. Teachers can help immigrant students, or indeed all students, explore racial-ethnic identity categories by encouraging them to write about them if they wish to.

RESOURCES

Carl E. James and Adrienne Shadd, eds. 2001. *Talking about Identity: Encounters in Race, Ethnicity, and Language.* Toronto: Between the Lines.

DISCUSSION QUESTIONS

1. **Principle:** As a teacher, how can you invite students to explore issues of identity in their writing, without pressuring them to do so?
2. **Strategy:** How can you, as a teacher, explore your own identity in front of your students when encouraging them to explore theirs?
3. **Try tomorrow:** What would you do if, in exploring their own racial identities, students offered denigrating ideas about self or others? For example, how might you discuss with students the connotations of words like "FOB" or "Banana"?

Jennifer A. Mott-Smith is ESOL coordinator and assistant professor of English at Towson University. Her teaching and research interests include racial/ethnic identities of multilingual students, minority access to higher education, teachers' understandings of race and whiteness, and language ideologies.

28

Involving Students in Selecting Reading Materials

Christine E. Sleeter

It is the beginning of the school year. Although much of my curriculum is already planned, I want to make it relevant to the lived experiences and points of view of students in my class, which includes attending to the class's racial composition. I also want to stretch students to see viewpoints beyond their own.

Racial group membership affects many dimensions of experience, ranging from access to social institutions through interpersonal interactions to cultural practices. For that reason, race is often an important filter through which students see the world and through which authors write, whether about personal experiences, historical interpretations, or less obviously racialized topics, such as applications of science. Racial group membership does not determine how people think, but shared experiences can give rise to shared points of view. When considering reading materials for her curriculum, a teacher at any level needs to navigate a tension between assuming that racial group experience shapes the point of view of students and authors and understanding that every student and author is a unique individual with his or her own perspective. In my own university classes, I resolve this tension by assuming a "both/and" rather than "either/or" stance when selecting curricular materials.

A conceptualization of curriculum as offering students both "windows" and "mirrors," written by researcher Emily Style (see Resources), provides a helpful framework for selecting curricular materials in a way that both acknowledges what experiences students bring and stretches them beyond their own viewpoints. She writes, "If the student is understood as occupying a dwelling of self, education needs to enable the student to look through window frames in order to see the realities of others and into mirrors in order to see her/his own reality reflected." Generally speaking, textbooks reflect points of view and experiences of white Americans more than those of other racial groups; students who are Latino, Asian American, African American, or Native American may see little of their histories and everyday experiences mirrored in textbooks.[1] Not only are whites more numerous in texts than people of color, but generally speaking, the ideas chosen for inclusion are more common among whites than among communities of color. For example, California's state-adopted history curriculum treats everyone as immigrants or descendants of immigrants, trivializing and distorting histories of Native Americans and African Americans who respectively arrived on the continent millennia earlier and came involuntarily as slaves.[2] Evidence suggests that students learn more, attend more regularly, and participate more actively when they can relate to curriculum by seeing themselves and their communities mirrored in it than when they do not.[3] College students of color often tell me that they lost interest in school during adolescence because most subject matter did not relate to their experiences in the slightest, and later discovered a thirst for knowledge when ethnic studies material connected closely with their lived experiences.

At the same time, students need to learn about experiences and points of view of people from racial groups different from their own. Young people are often curious about those who differ from themselves. Citizens in a diverse society must learn to understand where others are "coming from" and why in order to fashion systems and institutions that work better for all of us. Research has shown that curricula that provide students with counter-stereotypic information about people from other racial groups—and particularly with information about those groups' experiences of racism and successful challenges to it—have a positive impact on the intergroup attitudes of both children of color and white children, providing a foundation for shared citizenship in our democracy.[4]

Adjusting curriculum to offer students both mirrors and windows is tricky because it is easy to make inaccurate and stereotypical assumptions. First, it is dangerous to assume that, by looking at students and reading their names, I can accurately identify their racial backgrounds. For example, in a college class I was teaching at the time of this writing, three students looked African American, but after talking with them I discovered that one is Black Puerto Rican and another is Black and Japanese. These students might treat literature about African Americans not as a "mirror" but as a "window." Visual cues and names provide only a rough estimate of students' racial identities, often hiding the mixed ancestry of students and indicating nothing about what individual students actually want to read.

We cannot make assumptions about how salient race is to students. Some teachers claim that their students do not see race or care what their backgrounds are. Other teachers assume that racial identity is salient to all their students, or that race is salient to students of color but not to white students. All assumptions can be wrong. I have worked with students of varied ages who are interested in learning about people who are racially like themselves, or racially different from themselves. I have also worked with students of varied ancestry who are insulted when teachers assume that their racial identity matters to them.

What, then, is a teacher to do? Recently I observed a second-grade teacher whose consideration of race I found instructive. Her classroom was very diverse. An inveterate collector of multicultural children's literature, she had amassed a rich collection of books. In her class, students read teacher-selected material in common and student-selected material that varied. I noted as I watched students during a half-hour one morning:

> One girl (from the Philippines) was reading out loud to herself the English part of a book that is written in English and Spanish. She concentrated on the book very well, tuned out everything else around her. A girl from Mexico took a book about a boy in Cameroon to her desk, and seemed pretty absorbed in it. A Black girl picked *Chato's Kitchen* by [Latino author] Gary Soto, and a kid from Mexico picked *Happy Birthday Martin Luther King.* . . . My impression was that the kids liked the books, and that reading them was a treat. There was a lot to pick from.[5]

Although everyone read the same thing (the state-adopted Houghton Mifflin language arts package) during much of the day, the teacher built choice into her curriculum. She realized that sometimes students would be drawn to materials reflecting people like themselves while at other times they would want to read about someone different from themselves.

Recently, I selected three books to put on my own college syllabus and asked each student to select one of the books to read. On the basis of past experience, I anticipated that many students would choose the first book, which focused on African American, Mexican American, and American Indian history, and others would choose the second book because of their familiarity with the author. I selected a third book focusing on indigenous peoples of the world, assuming that some immigrant and international students might find it more relevant than U.S.-based readings. For most students, these choices worked; each student felt satisfied when given a choice, although several chose differently than I had anticipated.

However, when I asked students whether they would need a fourth choice, an Arab immigrant student pointed out that none of the readings featured Arab peoples. She helped me select a fourth book examining Islam in the United States that met the requirements of the course; two additional students then chose it to read. When I asked her why she chose this book and what she was learning from it, she explained that it began with experiences she was familiar with and then moved to the diversity of Islamic people in the United States. She said she had learned a good deal that was new, particularly from the chapter on Black Muslims, and the book helped her situate herself within a racially diverse American context.

Although I design my curriculum with the expectation that about two-thirds of the material is read in common, I always offer choices. I select required materials to provide both "windows" and "mirrors." Most academic concepts can be presented from more than one point of view, or developed with reference to more than one racial group's experience. By combining teacher-selected readings that attempt to provide students both "windows" and "mirrors" with student-selected readings, teachers can offer curriculum that both relates to students and stretches them to understand the experiences of others.

Finally, I regularly invite students to voice their perspectives about relationships between what we read and their own life experiences. Doing so gives students a place to discuss the extent to which the experience or viewpoint in the text actually fits their own, and opens up class discussion to multiple perspectives and interpretations of academic ideas.

RESOURCES

Emily Style. 1996. "Curriculum as Window and Mirror." The S.E.E.D. Project on Inclusive Curriculum. Accessed November 20, 2003, at http://www.wcwonline.org/seed/curriculum.html.

DISCUSSION QUESTIONS

1. **Principle:** How do we weigh the goals of having our students learn about themselves and having them learn about others? Are both equally important? How do we balance these goals with the standard curriculum?

2. **Strategy:** How could the idea of "windows and mirrors" be misused to reinforce stereotypical assumptions about students' identities or what they might want to read?

3. **Try tomorrow:** How might you involve students in your own classroom in selecting reading materials?

Christine E. Sleeter is professor emerita in the College of Professional Studies at California State University–Monterey Bay. She writes and lectures nationally and internationally about antiracist multicultural education and teacher education.

Part XII

Create Curriculum That Analyzes Opportunity Denial

Students, like all of us, live in a world that is complicated, unfair, and overwhelming to address. Curriculum needs to help students analyze issues of opportunity denial. The essays in this part share a core principle of everyday antiracism: *individuals live lives in racially unequal opportunity structures, and they must analyze those structures in order to challenge them.*

How can educators help students analyze and challenge unequal structures of opportunity?

1. Teach critical analysis of systems of racial oppression.

   Jeff Duncan-Andrade suggests that students should never be taught about unequal opportunity structures without being encouraged to undertake "critical analysis" of those systems and how to change them.

2. Include critical popular culture in your curriculum.

   Ernest Morrell encourages teachers to include, in curriculum, popular culture texts that carry messages of social analysis and critique.

3. Engage youth in participatory inquiry across differences.

   María Torre and Michelle Fine urge that students be encouraged to investigate and explore complex social issues via "participatory action research" and artistic performance.

29

Teaching Critical Analysis
of Racial Oppression

Jeff Duncan-Andrade

What is often missing in classroom discussions of racial issues is a critical examination of how the concept of "race" has been linked to the distribution of resources. Although our schools are rhetorically committed to the principles of multiculturalism, little substantive state or national curriculum guides educators and students to confront issues of racism and racial inequality. Today, schools—especially schools that serve poor children—fail to present critical perspectives on these issues.

As a university professor and a high school teacher in Oakland, California, I recognize that working with students to confront the contemporary legacy of racism is one of my primary duties in contributing to the development of a just nation. Although I believe that all teachers in all demographic situations should critically confront racism, I focus here on a literature unit I found effective with urban students of color. This unit was part of a year-long twelfth-grade curriculum aimed at developing young people's abilities to evaluate, understand, and confront oppressive structures of racial inequality.

The literature unit, based on Richard Wright's novel *Native Son,* was titled "Social Limitations and Their Explosiveness: An Examination of the Damaging Effects of Social Inequalities" when I last taught it in an Oakland high school English class in 1998. One-third of my students were black and the other two-thirds were Southeast Asians (mostly Mien, Cambodian, and Vietnamese), Chicana/o or Mexicana/o, and El Salvadorian. I began the unit with a lecture on how suffering can affect a person's worldview and anticipated life outcomes. Crucially, this lecture did not focus on the suffering of Wright's protagonist, Bigger Thomas, but on prompting a larger analysis of the personal costs of social inequality.

In our schools, commentaries about the suffering of people of color, whether in discussions about literature or in informal comments educators make to students about their lives, are usually delivered with one of two underlying, destructive messages. The first, the Horatio Alger myth of a person pulling himself "up by his own bootstraps," argues that the suffering of individual people of color can be overcome through hard work alone. The second is a criminalizing analysis that portrays the individual sufferer as deserving his fate. Both of these representations of social suffering disregard how structural inequalities help determine personal biographies. They leave students with no analysis of social systems and no critique of injustice, providing them only with justifications for unequal social outcomes.

The lecture I gave emphasized that social inequalities produce individual and collective suffering, and that this suffering often results from unquestioned conditions providing opportunities to the privileged and denying them to the poor (e.g., access to high-quality education, housing, nutrition, and so on). I presented data on the various forms of social inequality that face urban communities like Oakland, such as homelessness, poverty, crime, joblessness, under-resourced schools, and environmental toxins. After reviewing this data, we focused on the passage from Wright's introduction ("How 'Bigger' Was Born") in which Wright explains his use of his own experiences as a black man raised in the South to guide the creation of his protagonist, Bigger. Wright reflects on how his move from the South to Chicago led him to understand the role of unequal social conditions in producing personal social suffering like Bigger's:

> I began to feel with my mind the inner tensions of the people I met. I don't mean to say that I think that environment makes consciousness (I suppose God makes that, if there is a God), but I do say that I felt and still feel that the environment supplies the instrumentalities through which the organism expresses itself, and if that environment is warped or tranquil, the mode and manner of behavior will be affected toward deadlocking tensions or orderly fulfillment and satisfaction.[1]

As we started to unpack both Wright's analysis of the importance of environment and my lecture on the contemporary inequalities producing suffering for the urban poor, we laid the groundwork for a critical analysis of Bigger's life that would examine not only how his circumstances caused his suffering, but also how Bigger might join others to challenge those circumstances.

For the remainder of the unit, the class spent twenty to twenty-five minutes a day watching A Time to Kill, a movie about a black man's legal battle after he kills members of the Klan. This film has themes similar to those in Native Son, and its trial scenes helped set the stage for a simulated trial at the end of the unit. For homework, students read from Native Son and prepared responses to guiding questions that linked the film and the book. After watching the film (with the lights on, while taking notes) for about half of the period, we discussed interpretations and reactions to the film, guided by questions that allowed students to discuss race and inequality in the context of the film, the book, and their own lives. We asked questions about how race influenced the ways that the movie protagonist, Bigger Thomas, and students themselves are treated in society. We asked how the impact of race has changed in U.S. society over time, and how it has stayed the same. We debated the decisions of the protagonists, and debated what actions and alternative actions they could have taken to achieve justice for themselves and their communities. We also debated what actions we could take in our own community to address racial inequities.

Helping students make personal connections to the characters enlivened the discussion of inequality. The unit ended with a classroom court trial to decide the fate of Bigger Thomas: how should he, as an individual living within an oppressive social structure, be judged?

Teaching literature by connecting the text to the material conditions of students' lives is a method Brazilian educator Paulo Freire referred to as "reading the word and the world." Freire argued that in order for students to make sense of what they are learning, they must learn to see the text as an extension of their lived experience and their lived experience as an extension of the text.[2] Every day in the United States, students of color experience unequal social conditions and patterned denial of access to opportunity as if they are less worthy human beings than "whites." These systemic conditions emerge from the colonialist mentality of white supremacy; they can often overwhelm. To prepare students to critique those conditions and to struggle against them collectively, educators can link discussions of texts about inequality to students' experiences of inequality. This move raises critical consciousness and can empower students to act collectively to transform these structures. Educators must also prompt discussion of how such inequalities could be collectively addressed (e.g., walkouts, petitions, research teams; see also Torre and Fine, Chapter 31). An emphasis on critical awareness and collective struggle against structures of inequality should replace the current overemphasis on individual striving as the sole way to transcend the conditions of poverty and racism.

Critical consciousness and collective action are vital as historically racially isolated communities become more ethnically diverse. In the context of my racially diverse urban classroom, to teach about black suffering as disconnected from the struggles of other groups of color would have been a missed opportunity. Bigger is black, and there is no getting around the significance of his race in the book. Within the first two pages of the first chapter, Wright makes five references to the skin color of Bigger and his family. Wright explicitly states, however, that his story was about exposing the structural conditions facing all urban people of color, a scheme of oppression "far vaster and in many respects more ruthless and impersonal" than the Southern racism he had experienced.[3]

My students in Oakland did not have identical experiences with racism, but they shared experiences with social inequality within racist structures, including their severely under-resourced urban school system. Illuminating this commonality provided an opportunity for unifying diverse students around a shared critique of injustice. This aspect of teaching about race and racial oppression is underutilized in urban schools; schools typically teach students about oppression one group at a time and thus often promote divisiveness. Teaching black, Chicano, or other youth about racial discrimination experienced specifically by their group is important. But antiracist educators should encourage students to be in solidarity with and respond to the suffering of all peoples. Wright believed that Bigger's "hopes, fears, and despairs" could establish revolutionary "alliances between the American Negro and other people possessing a kindred consciousness."[4] No group is better positioned to form these alliances than urban youth of color when they critically analyze the social forces that constrain individuals and communities within oppressive systems of racial inequality.

In the wake of Hurricane Katrina, the nation's apartheid-like social structure was once again brutally exposed. Educators must make room for students to engage in critical conversation about the social forces that create such apartheid and impose suffering on people of color. To meet this challenge, educators must be prepared and supported to implement a curriculum and pedagogy that deliberately confronts structures of racism. These educators will develop connections between students by engaging them in critical analyses of how racist structures of inequality work and by facilitating understandings of their relationship to each other as people who have endured the suffering caused by racism. Ultimately, effective educators teach the concept of race as a social paradox: a socially bankrupt concept used to divide and conquer people of color, but also an opportunity for connecting students of color to their shared experiences with racism. These discussions help students learn to identify with the suffering of other youth around the globe. It will take a national commitment to these kinds of teaching principles if urban schools aim to prepare a citizenry that will topple the racism, white supremacy, and colonialist mentality that still permeate virtually every major social structure in this nation.

RESOURCES

Teachers in all classrooms can use the following sites to seek books and curricula that can be used to address issues of oppression:
Advanced Placement Curricula: http://apcentral.collegeboard.com/apc/public/homepage/34798.html.
History is a Weapon: www.historyisaweapon.com.
Teachers for Social Justice: www.t4sj.org.
Teaching for Change: www.teachingforchange.org.

DISCUSSION QUESTIONS

1. **Principle:** What is lost if students do not take school time to analyze racially unequal social conditions?
2. **Strategy:** What types of preparation and support would you need to implement a curriculum that encourages students to critically analyze local or national structures of racial inequality? What are the main challenges in implementing curriculum that actively encourages students to analyze and confront such social conditions?
3. **Try tomorrow:** What specific questions would you like to encourage your students to ask regarding racially unequal opportunity structures? What sorts of "collective action" against unequal opportunity could you imagine encouraging your students to take?

Jeffrey Duncan-Andrade is assistant professor in Raza Studies and the College of Education, and Co-Director of the Educational Equity Initiative at San Francisco State University's Cesar Chavez Institute. He also teaches an eleventh-grade Sociology of E ducation course at East Oakland Community High School.

30

Using Critical Hip-Hop in the Curriculum

Ernest Morrell

In my work as a high school teacher and researcher, I have found that using hip-hop thoughtfully in the curriculum—getting students to analyze its lyrics, its music, and its verbal and artistic practices—allows educators to fashion an academically rigorous and culturally relevant pedagogy suitable for ethnically heterogeneous classrooms, given hip-hop's transracial appeal.[1] In particular, educators can tap the knowledge about contemporary oppression and resistance lodged in *critical* hip-hop, a subgenre of hip-hop that highlights the social, economic, and racial injustice prevalent in our society and advocates indigenous struggles for social transformation.

One of the elder spokespersons of hip-hop culture, KRS One, has defined hip-hop as "[T]he name of our collective consciousness. It is generally expressed through the unique elements of Breakin, Emceein, Graffiti Art, Deejayin, Beatboxin, Street Fashion, Street Language, Street Knowledge, and Street Entrepreneurialism (Hip-hop's nine elements). . . . Hip-hop is a state of mind." Antiracist educators should consider teaching hip-hop because it has powerful pedagogical potential, is popular with and relevant to students, and often deals with interracial relations in contemporary American society. The critical investigation of hip-hop texts can also form the core of a much-needed media education curriculum at the primary and secondary levels. This instruction will help students become more critical thinkers as well as more informed consumers, especially given the reach of hip-hop's influence. More broadly, the curriculum should explore popular art and media forms that protest against racism against all groups.

Critical hip-hop shows the limits of racial thinking even as it helps youth analyze racism. Many elements of youth popular culture, like hip-hop, are interethnic or even transethnic activities; at the same time, much of youth popular culture, undertaken largely by members of ethnically marginalized groups, is explicitly critical of the racially oppressive norms in society. Because of its genesis and ethos, critical hip-hop contains many antiracist messages that are of value to educators interested in fostering an antiracist pedagogy. Those who experience hip-hop culture claim it has dynamic and wide-ranging antiracist effects on the young people who practice it.

Although the genre and culture are much maligned in elite circles, I suggest that antiracist educators would be better served to acknowledge critical hip-hop as a critical cultural form. Critical hip-hop originated as a critique of postindustrialism; artists lamented and resisted the economic and structural conditions that have strained life and limited financial opportunities for those who hail from inner-city ghettos.[2] Hip-hop culture has stood as a voice of resistance against poverty, injustice, racism, police brutality, and an inequitable educational system.[3] Critical hip-hop texts articulate the structural and cultural causes of injustice and inequity while exhorting listeners to become free thinkers, lovers of themselves and humanity, and agents of social change.

Those who see themselves as producers of critical hip-hop view their charge as a pedagogical one. KRS One's album *Edutainment* serves as a model for critical hip-hop artists who view themselves as both public entertainers and public pedagogues. Classic artists such as X-Clan and contemporary artists such as Lauryn Hill, Dead Prez, Immortal Technique, and Mos Def send messages about forging closer ties with an African homeland or about young black girls learning to love and reeducate themselves. Much such hip-hop encourages young people of all ethnicities to become students of African American history.[4] For thirty years, critical hip-hop artists have been using lyrics to promote political messages and political action. Public Enemy's role in the late 1980s of transforming rap into a political tour de force, KRS One's explicitly political "Free Mumia," and Lauryn Hill's "Rebel" are good examples of how hip-hop artists and songs foster social activism and encourage listeners to see themselves as agents of change who can fight against injustice and oppression.

Educators can pull in hip-hop videos and articles in hip-hop-focused magazines such as *Vibe* and *Source* that deal with racial profiling, police brutality, urban poverty, and culturally irrelevant school curricula. These hip-hop pieces speak powerfully to and for students because they address the terrible effects of racism in the first person, from insiders who actually experience racism in their daily lives. Just as *The Diary of Anne Frank* exposes outsiders to the horrors of racial hatred during World War II, critical hip-hop narratives expose outsiders to the horrors of racial hatred during our own time. Teachers can use these powerful narratives to have students analyze their own daily lives.

Teachers can bring in supplementary material to have students investigate the differences in living conditions between racialized minorities and whites in our country that are mentioned in hip-hop lyrics. Reports on incarceration rates and educational attainment that are disaggregated by race are particularly relevant. For final projects, students can conduct original research on issues touched upon in hip-hop texts. Students as young as the early elementary grades have created very powerful original research that deals with issues raised in hip-hop texts. A class in Watts, California, researched the role of corporations and the government in the proliferation of guns in urban communities with large concentrations of nonwhite residents. Classes can design social action projects that confront these issues. For example, in predominantly white schools, students might consider how to develop a media education campaign to bring attention to an issue like racial profiling.

K–12 educators can draw upon hip-hop music and culture to get young hip-hop fans more excited about school, as well as engaged with antiracist themes. For example, students can create their own hip-hop and spoken word poetry, which can build sophisticated academic literacies and can spread positive, critical, and empowering messages about racial and gender equality.[5] In Southern California, educators have created curricula that use spoken word poetry to develop young people as literate citizens, artists, and advocates for racial justice. Educators can also show students vibrant examples of spoken word poetry that articulate these issues (see Resources list).

Finally, antiracist educators can utilize student interest in hip-hop music and culture to make connections to academic texts and disciplinary content. Educators I know have drawn upon hip-hop music and culture to make connections to canonical poetry, for example. In my own high school classes, students used their knowledge of hip-hop as a poetic form to examine and critique classic poets such as Shakespeare and T.S. Eliot. After discussing the merits of hip-hop as a postmodern genre, students then compared and contrasted canonical poetry texts with contemporary hip-hop texts (see Resources list). Educators have used hip-hop texts as a springboard to develop the skills of literary interpretation and expository essay writing. Students are just as able to write sophisticated analytical essays about a hip-hop text as a classic novel, poem, or play. The Algebra Project (see Resources list) shows how hip-hop can be used to increase the mathematical achievement of racially marginalized groups.

Certainly teachers face challenges when teaching hip-hop music and culture. First, negative perceptions of hip-hop prevail among educators. Many feel that hip-hop is more of a problem than a solution to racism. With popular songs that seemingly glorify violence and misogyny, the genre is written off as more pathological than pedagogical. While there are indeed many problematic hip-hop songs, critical hip-hop artists deal explicitly with complex social problems and exemplify impressive literacy and artistry. As with any other genre, educators need to be careful in their selection of texts and their use of the texts they select.

A second challenge concerns the lack of experience most educators have with hip-hop music and culture. That lack of experience can be the source of understandable fear. As with any other form of multicultural or antiracist education, it behooves educators to study the cultural practices of others. Excellent books, websites, and videos outline hip-hop's history and social foundations (see Resources list). Hip-hop organizations would be happy to point toward valuable resources or come to classes to facilitate conversations about hip-hop. Finally, in any classroom, students who are active participants in hip-hop culture can serve as valuable resources. Educators need only ask who is interested in the genre.

RESOURCES

3rd Eye Unlimited: For examples of hip-hop in youth engagement, see www .3rdeyeunlimited.com.

The Algebra Project: on hip-hop and mathematics, see the Algebra Project at www .algebra.org.

Davey D's Hip Hop Daily News: www.daveyd.com.

Hip Hop Archive: http://www.hiphoparchive.org/.

Ernest Morrell. 2002. "Toward a Critical Pedagogy of Popular Culture: Literacy Development among Urban Youth." Discusses using hip-hop to engage canonical poetry. http://www.readingonline.org/newliteracies/jaal/9-02_column/.

————. 2004. *Linking Literacy and Popular Culture: Finding Connections for Lifelong Learning.* Norwood, MA: Christopher-Gordon.

Source: a Hip Hop magazine, www.thesource.com.

Vibe: a Hip-Hop magazine, www.vibe.com.

Youth Speaks: www.youthspeaks.org offers excellent resources for educators interested in bringing spoken word poetry into their classrooms. The HBO hit Def Poetry Slam also puts out DVDs of past episodes.

DISCUSSION QUESTIONS

1. **Principle:** Morrell suggests that educators can use critical hip-hop texts as a springboard to develop students' academic skills as well as their critical thinking capacity. What do you think of the idea that pulling in critical hip-hop, or other popular culture forms, might enhance students' engagement and learning?

2. **Strategy:** What assignment or unit could you develop for your classroom that would use hip-hop, or other popular culture forms, to build academic or critical thinking skills?

3. **Try tomorrow:** How could you intertwine such efforts with your more standard curriculum?

Ernest Morrell is an associate professor in the Graduate School of Education and Information Studies at the University of California at Los Angeles. His work examines the intersections between urban adolescent literacies, youth popular culture, and academic and critical literacy development.

31

Engaging Youth in Participatory Inquiry for Social Justice

María Elena Torre and Michelle Fine

Young people carry important knowledge about the social injustices they experience in their everyday lives. Too often, this knowledge is ignored. At times it is actively silenced. With this essay, we suggest an alternative. We invite educators to consider undertaking participatory research projects with students to recognize the critical insights young people have about racial injustice and to generate cross-generational communities of inquiry around research, critique, and action. These projects can take place inside classrooms, within whole schools, or in collaboration with other schools; inquiry can proceed both through formal research and through the arts. Here we introduce *Echoes of Brown*, a performance of poetry and movement that capped a participatory research project with a diverse group of high school students in the metropolitan New York area. Student researchers investigated educational opportunity gaps and the thorny issues of integration that remain fifty years after *Brown*. The critical research, feedback sessions, writing, protests, public performance, and final book/DVD were all elements of "Participatory Action Research" (PAR), a method that involves people as researchers of the social issues they themselves experience. PAR can be replicated in classroom, school, and community settings.[1]

Engaging and investigating difference and justice together with youth, in settings that promote critical inquiry and courageous conversations, is crucial to the collective struggle against racism and all other forms of oppression. While much of our work has been with purposefully integrated groups, integrated spaces for inquiry should not always be preferred over racially specific spaces. In many instances, homogeneous groupings are important, even necessary. We have found that once youth are invited to interrogate questions of power, history, and their multiple identities, even the most seemingly homogeneous site is filled with diversity. Here, however, we draw attention to the particular transformative power of integrated inquiry groups for students and educators when they explicitly examine issues of difference and inequality, power, and participation.

When radically diverse groups of young people come together to discuss their experiences of power and injustice on the basis of their identity-group memberships (i.e., race/ethnicity, class, gender, sexuality, "disability," track level, social clique), and then *engage* and *interrogate* these differences in debating how to pursue shared social justice goals, complex social psychological identity negotiations take place. Not only does this style of participation stimulate friendships and reduce prejudice among youth, it encourages youth to investigate social problems, critically examine their ideas in larger social, historical, and political contexts, and create research-based actions and products. In this inquiry process, youth reposition themselves in relation to one another and to the hierarchical structures that govern their (and all of our) lives, schools, and communities. Witness this repositioning in the comments of one young White participant. At first, she described her involvement with *Echoes* as "working *for*" other students suffering educational injustice, but by the end, she described it as "working *with*" these students, recognizing that unequal educational practices negatively affect everyone. Although she had benefited from being in top-tier classes, when she returned to school she questioned her principal and PTA about the negative consequences of tracking.[2]

These transformations were possible because with *Echoes* we created "justice spaces"—integrated, antiracist spaces—where we openly discussed (1) how our varying relationships to power and privilege—moments when we experience more and less power because of our racial-ethnic identities, gender, sexuality, social class, age, health, history of arrest, and so on—shape our experiences, understandings, and actions; (2) how each of us brings valuable knowledge and critique of social issues that is particular to our lived experiences as individuals and members of various groups—for example, as students in special education or accelerated courses; (3) how the analytic perspectives brought by diversity within the research team would challenge participants to question that which seems "natural" or "normal." We emphasized that no individual should be reduced simply to one of their identities—i.e., "the straight A student" or the "Spanish girl."

When complex identities are acknowledged and valued and power is engaged and interrogated rather than ignored, young people are able to take risks and ask hard questions about racism, oppression, and inequality, all the while pursuing deeper understandings of complex identities. They build trust and alliances with individuals and groups across their various lines of difference. This point was underscored by Natasha, a young African American woman who shared with us her mother's protective caution to enjoy her work with *Echoes* but to be wary of the "White guilt" that may be lurking behind the facilitators' "good intentions." Natasha mentioned the open conversations that moved beyond "Black and White" and complicated participants' notions of identity, power, responsibility, and action as helping her "see where people were coming from" and trust that the project was about justice, not charity.[3] Snapshots of the *Echoes* project illustrate the rich intellectual and political potential of gathering diverse groups of youth for participatory inquiry and action.

In the summer of 2003, with the fiftieth anniversary of *Brown* approaching, we gathered a group of young people ages thirteen to twenty-one with community elders, spoken word artists, and dancers to create *Echoes*. Our goal was to reexamine "Opportunity Gap" data previous students had collected and to create a performance of the findings through poetry and dance. Together, we studied the data, including 9,000 surveys of educational attitudes and experiences from high school students, examined focus group transcripts, and studied the legal, social, and political history of segregation and integration of public schools and the continued unfulfilled promise of *Brown*.[4]

The youth in *Echoes* were an intentionally diverse group recruited from high schools and after-school programs. Two of the thirteen had been researchers in the prior Opportunity Gap project, making them experts on the data alongside adults from the Graduate Center. Collectively, they represented varied racial-ethnic backgrounds, spoke multiple languages, lived in some of the wealthiest and poorest zip codes in New York, were in AP and special education classes and, in one case, had left school, and were both experienced and brand-new writers, dancers, and performers. The only requirements for participation: a passion for inquiry, a willingness to push themselves and one another, and a desire to educate and activate audiences about the educational consequences of persistent racism. Our efforts resulted in a book and DVD of youth research, poetry, and photos of youth and elders engaged in the historic struggle for racial and class justice in public schools.[5]

The work of the *Echoes* collective took place largely over a five-day Arts and Social Justice Institute, with participants presenting a rough draft of the performance to friends and families on a warm Saturday afternoon at the Nuyorican Café, an arts organization on the Lower East Side. Pieces of the performance were workshopped and refined over a series of Saturdays. Institute mornings were dedicated to roundtable discussions about the day's agenda and relevant current events, knowledge-building sessions on the Opportunity Gap data, and presentations and discussions with lawyers, activists, historians, and writers about struggles for educational justice. Afternoons were spent on writing activities (e.g., "write a poem using a piece of the survey data that you found surprising"; "write a poem to an administrator about what you would like to see changed in your school") and with dance and movement exercises (e.g., "communicate your poem to the group without using any words"). Youth went home with reading and writing assignments that they completed after taking care of household responsibilities, while working night jobs, or on the train to and from the institute.

The combination of diverse types of activities, from writing to movement and from research to performance, provided participants with the opportunities to highlight their various identities. By placing equal value on different types of knowledge and ways of participating, the atmosphere encouraged youth to take risks, such as trying out an unpolished idea about racism, or sharing secrets about their fears and dreams. Sometimes these personal experiments were celebrated as successes, other times as works in progress. The more participants witnessed each others' layers of complexity, the more it became difficult to look across the circle at "the rich girl," or "the boy in special ed."

The poetry read-arounds, group feedback sessions, and discussions of survey findings afforded everyone, from youth participants to adults, the opportunity to debate, comment, and contribute ideas. The pedagogy fostered cross-generational inquiry through deep participation and critical research that opened up ideas about unjust educational practices such as tracking that have become normalized. Youth could develop their ideas individually and collectively and rethink their own roles in the struggle against racism without feeling pigeon-holed in a particular position.

The collaborative work of a pair of young women from the *Echoes* collective embodies the potential of participatory inquiry across difference for interrogating racism and sparking social change. The collaborative poem written by Natasha Alexander and Elinor Marboe used statistics from the youth-generated Opportunity Gap survey.

ELINOR: *42% of White American teenagers in public schools speak up when they hear racist comments.*

NATASHA: *Bold*

> *Decisive*

> > *Be fierce*

> > > *Be confident*

BOTH: <u>*Be honest*</u>.

ELINOR: *But what kind of schools do we have where 58% of White students don't speak out against hatred?*

NATASHA: *Being quiet is a strong choice*

ELINOR: *—except when it isn't.*

Elinor, who is White, attended a large, tracked, desegregated suburban high school located in a wealthy, largely White county. Natasha, who is African American, attended a small integrated school in New York City. By mid-week, after studying the history of *Brown* and participating in conversations about contemporary issues of racial and class injustice in education, both young women happened to write poems about the politics of silence. The facilitator, a poet-educator from a spoken word program, recognized similar language in their pieces and challenged them to work together, as artists, to explore the places their poems fit together and where they did not. How did each poet understand silence? Who talked about choosing silence, or about being silenced? In what ways did their poems address the broader issues of educational injustice that they had been discussing? How were the data from the Opportunity Gap survey that they selected relevant to the ideas they were trying to communicate? Natasha and Elinor's performative debate about the racialized dynamics of silence prompted new understandings about speaking out and remaining quiet in profoundly racist schools and communities.

The conversation about racial injustice in schools was new to Elinor, as her high school experience had served her well. In an early version of her original poem, Elinor reflected on times in her high school when she sat back observing her peers and surroundings, opting out of participation. Throughout the institute, she struggled to find a meaningful role and voice in the struggle for integration and against racism. The collective provided her an opportunity to engage, research, and express her own ideas through rich intergenerational conversations; others could then talk, think, write, and perform their reactions to her inquiry. Elinor used the institute to consider her position in larger social structures, the silence of privilege, the privilege of silence, and the vulnerability involved in speaking against racist attitudes and practices. She used the collaborative writing exercise with Natasha to think about her own subjective choice not to speak and the consequences of that silence when chosen by people with privilege. An excerpt from her original individual poem reads:

> *It doesn't feel good to be silent*
> *Except for when it does.*
> *Can't I be my own best friend?*
> *To keep thoughts and beliefs inside,*
> *Sometimes means more power to me.*

Natasha was all too familiar with racial injustice both inside and outside of school. Articulate and animated as a student and performer, Natasha told us about riding all-Black buses across town to the "better" middle school and about watching a mother pull a White child away from her on a playground. Her experiences fueled a very different individual poem than Elinor's. An excerpt of her original poem reads:

> *It doesn't feel good to be silent.*
> *But after a while it stops feeling bad*

Because you've had to eat it so long
You've become accustomed to the taste
The flavor becomes familiar, like an old friend's face.

The facilitator asked Elinor and Natasha to reimagine their poems together. When the two young women sat and read their pieces aloud, they noticed how their different takes on silence were directly related to their prior racialized experiences. While each poem articulated the potential power in silence, the poems spoke to very different forms of silence as power. They decided to join their pieces as a way of challenging and thinking through each other's racialized social positions. Natasha and Elinor used the knowledge embedded in their differences, as well as their own writings, conversations, and data from the Opportunity Gap study, to ask the audience: What is the difference between choosing silence and being silenced? When is silence personally powerful for one's own development, and when does it result in an avoidance of social responsibility? In the performance of the final version of their poem, Elinor, who initially took the position that being silent was a way to feel strong, spoke the last line of the poem, publicly challenging her original position.

Hundreds of young people we have worked with (almost all of whom attend desegregated high schools!), have told us how rare it is to be in integrated spaces where they can talk about the rough edges of racism and difference in safe, yet meaningful ways; where they can enter openings in identity categories that invite multiplicities within and across individuals and groups; and where they can explore the dynamics of injustice and resistance in history. Youth, like adults, seek nurturing spaces with similar others, but they also long to engage difference rather than act as if it did not exist.

Participatory action research introduces a methodology that supports democratic practice, assumes that knowledge comes from all social locations, celebrates and encourages individual capacity and contributions, necessitates collective discussion of complementary and contradictory ideas, produces action that speaks back to histories of injustice, and projects futures of possibility. The work of the *Echoes* collective reminds us that the struggle for integration and diversity matters only if this struggle sits within a larger movement, seeking to transform all conditions of oppression. With *Echoes* we practiced living, learning, working, and fighting together across our differences—using them to understand, question, and act—developing a powerful strategy to resist and dismantle racism and other oppressive hierarchies. We offer PAR as a strategic move for educators and youth wishing to spark inquiry for social change.

RESOURCES

Access to Quality Education—A Human Right? see www.amnestyusa.org/education/
pdf/summer2005.pdf.

Echoes of Brown: see web.gc.cuny.edu/che/Faultlines.pdf.
Participatory Action Research Collective website: web.gc.cuny.edu/che/start.htm.

DISCUSSION QUESTIONS

1. **Principle:** Why might the techniques of "participatory action research" and artistic inquiry be useful to get young people to investigate tough questions and social problems?
2. **Strategy:** How could time be created in the curriculum for such endeavors?
3. **Try tomorrow:** What specific social questions would you like to have your students investigate, research, and/or engage artistically? What might you need to do to start putting such a project together?

María Elena Torre is the chair of Education Studies at Eugene Lang College, the New School for Liberal Arts. She was the research director of the Educational Opportunity Gap project and Echoes of Brown: Youth Documenting and Performing the Legacy of Brown v. Board of Education.

Michelle Fine is Distinguished Professor of Psychology, Urban Education and Women's Studies at the Graduate Center, City University of New York. She works with participatory action research methods in schools, communities, and prisons.

Part XIII

Create Curriculum That Represents a Diverse Range of People Thoroughly and Complexly

We often use curriculum as an important way to learn about our diverse world. But we need to be sure to engage diversity thoroughly and well. The essays in this part share a core principle of everyday antiracism: *representations of groups must always be complex and thorough, never reductive or stereotypic.*

How can educators examine the representations of groups in their curriculum?

1. Interrogate Arab invisibility and hypervisibility.

    Thea Abu El-Haj, using Arabs as a key example, reminds us how both ignoring and misrepresenting a group in curriculum can be harmful.

2. Consider how representations of communities in texts can be harmful, and invite community members to class to represent themselves.

    Teresa McCarty urges that educators assess whether the images of groups in classroom texts are accurate and respectful. She uses representations of Native Americans as an example, and suggests that community members can be invited to class to discuss their own complex lives.

3. Teach representations of cultural difference in films without fixing the identity or reducing the complexity of "minority cultures."

    Sanjay Sharma urges that educators use films not to show quick "facts" about groups, but to get students to analyze how "minority cultures" get represented.

4. Think twice about that poster.

    Donna Deyhle suggests that educators consider, with students, whether posters and other public images in their schools and classrooms are motivating and accurate representations of group members.

5. Take up the challenge of teaching racially sensitive literature.

    Jocelyn Chadwick suggests how educators can prepare to discuss great literature that is racially "sensitive."

32

Arab Visibility and Invisibility

Thea Abu El-Haj

Arabs are rarely included in antiracist education. Anti-Arab racism in U.S. society and schools is pervasive, however, and has recently been intensified by global politics. Educators and students can learn to analyze this politicized landscape in ways that support the development of a more informed and thoughtful understanding of Arab and Arab American communities. A key strategy is to focus on how both the invisibility and the hypervisibility of Arabs in a wide variety of texts (e.g., media, films, textbooks, literature, political debates, everyday talk) can perpetuate distorted and disparaging views of Arabs. We can help students develop the tools for "reading" these texts with a critical, antiracist eye.[1]

To illustrate the harmful effects of failing to develop a critical stance on the dominant images of Arabs in the public imagination, I begin with a story about a U.S. citizen of Palestinian descent, a student in a large, urban public high school where I have been working with Arab American youth. Adam arrived home one afternoon to find Secret Service agents searching his house. His mother, confused and terrified, was unable to communicate with the agents since she does not speak English. Apparently, the school district had called the Secret Service alleging that Adam's brother, Ibrahim, had threatened to kill the president. According to the brothers and other students present at the time of the incident in an ESL class, some students, referring to newspaper articles about kidnappings and assassinations of foreigners in Iraq, accused Arabs of being prone to violence. In the midst of a heated political argument, Ibrahim asked the group how they would feel if one of their leaders were killed, pointing to the extreme level of violence that Iraqis had experienced since the war began. The teacher waited several days to report the incident to the dean's office. According to her very different account, Ibrahim was reading a newspaper when he suddenly stated that he would like to kill the president of the United States. After her report, filed several days after the alleged threat occurred, Ibrahim was summarily transferred to an alternative school and the Secret Service was called.

I tell this story to emphasize the contemporary political context that looms large for Muslim, Arab, and South Asian youth and their families, noncitizen and citizen alike. The threat of house searches, indefinite detentions without access to legal counsel, and extraordinary rendition have become part of the fabric of everyday life for these communities in the aftermath of the September 11, 2001, attacks on the World Trade Center and the Pentagon. This story also illustrates how Arab youth (as well as adults) get framed by negative, demeaning, and reductive images of their communities that saturate the media, film, and political dialogue. Whatever was said in that classroom, the response from school personnel was overdetermined by pervasive images of Arab males as terrorists. In that fearful school climate, Ibrahim was viewed not as an individual student, but as a member of a suspect class of persons. Instead of engaging in genuine educational dialogue with Ibrahim (for example, about the different perspectives on what had happened and conflicting understandings of contemporary politics), adults responded in a punitive way that had serious consequences for him and his family. In a sense, Ibrahim was both invisible—as an adolescent with a particular political perspective—and hypervisible as a supposed dangerous terrorist.

The Arab students with whom I work struggle every day with the unenviable position that Arabs occupy in the public imagination as terrorists, enemies of the state, opponents of freedom and democracy, oppressors of women, and so forth. Paradoxically, they also feel invisible, as the richly textured histories, literature, and political perspectives of their communities are largely absent from curriculum materials, media, and other public texts. Antiracist educators must dismantle the distorted and damaging frameworks that operate explicitly and implicitly in classrooms, while simultaneously working to help all students develop a rich, nuanced understanding of Arab communities. I would like to suggest some strategies to help teachers educate themselves and their students, Arab and non-Arab alike, to analyze critically the ways that visibility and invisibility work to create, maintain, and ultimately justify demeaning and dangerous attitudes, behaviors, and policies directed at Arab and Muslim communities.

Arabs and Arab Americans face several kinds of invisibility problems in the United States. First, there is general confusion and lack of understanding about who Arabs are, which arises in large part from the tendency to equate Arab and Muslim identities. What unites diverse Arab communities from North Africa and the Middle East is a shared language: Arabic. Yet prevailing misconceptions of Arabs are often erroneously expansive: for example, falsely including Iran, Afghanistan, and Pakistan in the Arab world. On the other hand, Arabs are often viewed monolithically as Muslims, when in fact Arab communities are highly varied in their religious beliefs and cultural practices. The general lack of knowledge about Arabs renders invisible the rich variability of Arab communities across the globe and in the United States.

Second, although Arabs have long experienced racist practices in the United States, they are rarely recognized as a racialized minority.[2] Violence against people perceived to be Arab, Muslim, or Middle Eastern is an ongoing problem in the United States.[3] Perhaps the most vivid illustration of the reality that Arabs and non-Arab immigrant Muslims together comprise a racialized minority is the frequency of violent attacks following September 11, 2001, on people across the country who appeared to fit the generic mold of Arab, Muslim, and Middle Easterner. In reality, the victims belonged to a wide range of ethnic and religious groups; the dead alone included people who were Christian, Muslim, and Hindu and were of Arab, Pakistani, Sikh, and Indian descent. But, because they were perceived as Arab or Muslim, or Middle Eastern, they were regarded as "enemy" aliens in the public imagination.[4] Unfortunately, despite their history as victims of group-based persecution, Arabs have often been excluded from antiracist initiatives.

Third, most people in the United States know very little about the history, literature, contemporary politics, and amazing diversity of the Arab world. Although the first wave of Arab immigration began in 1880, Arab Americans have seldom been recognized as a minority racial-ethnic group. The 2000 U.S. census recorded 1.2 million Americans of Arab descent, a figure that represents a 40 percent increase over the past two decades. Yet Arab voices and perspectives are absent from our school curricula, as well as from public discourse.

As educators, we can no longer afford to ignore Arab invisibility; Arabs are simply too important a subset of U.S. and world society today. However, we must also examine carefully how Arabs and Arab Americans are made visible in the realm of politics, popular media, and in our schools.

Today, Arabs are often made hypervisible through extremely negative images and caricatures that equate Arabs with terrorists. Terrorism is often explained as rooted in Muslim or Arab culture, as if becoming a suicide bomber were a "cultural trait" shared by Arabs and other Muslims, not an action pursued by only a small minority of individuals under particular historical and political circumstances.[5] As educators, we must investigate these hypervisible images that, in our minds, turn Arabs and other Muslims into the "enemy other."

The equation of Arab with terrorist and the assumption that Muslim or Arab culture "breeds" terrorism are clearly damaging. Less obvious are the damaging effects of some of the ways educators try to shed positive light on Arab culture. Even in well-meaning attempts to make Arabs visible in the curriculum, students are taught about Arab culture in ways that may also reinforce, rather than dislodge, demeaning and distorted views of Arab communities.[6] All too often, Arab culture is represented as a static set of traditions, values, norms, and practices to which all Arabs, particularly Muslim Arabs, adhere. For example, in *Educating for Diversity*, one of the few multicultural texts that include a chapter on Arab Americans, the authors portray Arab social life as bound by religion and "Old World traditions" that emphasize patriarchy and family honor.[7] Their analysis implies that when Arab and Arab American families experience a loosening of these traditional patriarchal bonds, it is due primarily to processes of Westernization and assimilation to U.S. society rather than due to generative processes of change within Arab communities. The Arab world is often portrayed as stranded in some bygone era, clinging to a set of outdated practices and beliefs, and even as less "civilized" than Europe and the United States.

Teaching about Arab cultural practices in this way denies the complexity and heterogeneity of Arab communities across the globe. For example, gender relations—social relationships between women and men and norms of masculinity and femininity—in Arab communities cannot be easily described. Arabs are highly diverse in terms of religion, socioeconomic class, national origin, and migration patterns. All of these factors contribute to widely variable gender patterns. Arab families represent a full range from highly patriarchal to egalitarian gender relations. However, this variability is often rendered invisible by educational programs that produce uniform, static images of Arab peoples and cultures.

Antiracist education must address the need for better information about the cultures and history of Arabs and Arab Americans. The issue, then, is not simply that practitioners should make Arabs more visible. Rather, educators need to develop in-depth, nuanced knowledge about Arab history and culture to make Arabs visible in rich, complex, and humanizing ways.

Educators can play an important role in countering anti-Arab racism by teaching themselves and their students to analyze the ways that both the invisibility and reductive portrayals of Arabs perpetuate racist notions of who Arabs are, what they want, and what they do. Asking the following kinds of questions can help students critically explore the portrayal or absence of Arabs in texts, including classroom discourse, printed and visual materials, and music.

Who is invisible in this text? Ask who is represented and who is not. Are Arabs represented at all in your curriculum? Are students exposed to any texts that address any region of the Arab world, or any portrayal of Arab American communities? Even when texts do address Arab peoples, it is important to probe further. Do real Arabs still remain essentially invisible? Whose perspectives are represented in these texts about Arabs? Are Arab voices included? Is their expertise invited? In the context of the U.S. war in Iraq (or elsewhere), whose deaths are reported? Who remains invisible? Who is the focus of reporting? These kinds of questions prompt students to examine the myriad ways in which Arabs are made invisible in texts, either by narratives that literally exclude them or through representations that do not accord them full weight as human beings whose lives and diverse perspectives matter.

Who is visible in this text and is that visibility reductive? Ask what stories are told. Do they support narratives about Arabs that emphasize a tradition-bound "culture" that is static, monolithic, and antithetical to the modern world? Do these stories focus primarily on negative portrayals of women's oppression, suicide bombers, strict religious codes, and ethnic or religious antagonisms? Alternately, are Arabs visible primarily as background figures with whom Westerners experience exciting and exotic adventures? Students need both a fuller view of Arab peoples and histories and deeper analyses that do not explain multifaceted problems such as women's oppression by blaming Arab "tradition" and "culture" instead of treating them as complex phenomena involving political, social, economic, cultural, and historical dynamics. Many social problems can be found in all communities, not just Arab communities, demonstrating that quick "cultural" explanations are misplaced.

Are diverse voices within Arab communities represented? Ask if Arabs are allowed to speak for themselves. Ask if diversity within Arab and Arab American communities is visible. Is diversity, not only of religion, region, and daily practices, but also of perspectives and opinions, reflected in the voices represented?

Visibility and invisibility can be critical ways in which the subordination of Arabs and other racially oppressed groups[8] is perpetuated in everyday life. The feminist political philosopher Iris Young offers a useful definition of this aspect of oppression, which is known as cultural imperialism: "To experience cultural imperialism means to experience how the dominant meanings of society render the particular perspectives of one's own group invisible at the same time as they stereotype one's group and mark it out as the Other."[9]

Antiracist educators must work assiduously against cultural imperialism that harms Arabs as well as other racially oppressed groups. In their everyday practice, teachers can attend to the ways that Arab and Arab American perspectives—and here I deliberately emphasize the plurality of perspectives that exist in what are widely variable Arab communities—are often absent in both curriculum and public debate. Likewise, they must examine critically the ways in which Arabs and Arab Americans are made hypervisible.

RESOURCES

Al-Bustan, Seeds of Culture: www.albustanseeds.org.
Arab American Anti-Discrimination Committee: www.adc.org.
Arab American National Museum: www.arabamericanmuseum.org.

DISCUSSION QUESTIONS

1. **Principle:** When a group is either invisible or portrayed inaccurately in curricula, how does it harm students who belong to that group? What is the impact on students from other groups?

2. **Strategy:** How could you engage students in analyzing the representation or absence of Arabs in your curriculum, and in the media?

3. **Try tomorrow:** Consider the representation or absence of Arabs in your own curriculum. Try asking the questions Abu El-Haj provides. Then consider: who else is invisible, or hypervisible, in your curriculum or the textbooks you use? How could you find more accurate information on these populations?

Thea Renda Abu El-Haj is an assistant professor in the Department of Educational Theory, Policy and Administration at Rutgers, the State University of New Jersey. Her research focuses on immigration and transnationalism; critical analyses of race, gender, class, and disability in schooling; and conceptualizations of equity in everyday educational practice.

33

Evaluating Images of Groups
in Your Curriculum

Teresa L. McCarty

How do we teach about "others" without reducing them to one-dimensional stereotypes? How can we make learning about peoples whose cultural, linguistic, and historical experiences differ significantly from those of our students more meaningful?

Based on more than twenty-five years of research, teaching, and collaborative work with Native American communities, I propose antiracist strategies that educators can employ to avoid simplistic and erroneous representations of Native Americans, while engaging students in thoughtful explorations of Indigenous peoples' cultures and experiences. I use the terms Indigenous, Native, and Native American interchangeably to refer to those whose ancestry on this continent predates colonial invasions and whose oral traditions place them as the first occupants of ancestral homelands. Many terms for Native peoples in the United States—American Indian, Alaska Native, Native Hawaiian—refer less to subjective self-identifications than to the federal government's acknowledgement of the unique status of Native Americans. More than four million Native Americans live in the United States, representing 561 federally recognized tribes and 175 languages. Despite their naming by outsiders, Native peoples have retained their own naming traditions, and "it is these names rather than any externally imposed labels that serve to reference indigenous identities."[1]

Simplified and distorted representations of Native Americans, which are still common in U.S. schools, harm both Native and non-Native students. Conversely, both Native and non-Native students gain when representations of Native Americans are realistically complex and directly informed by the perspectives and experiences of Indigenous community members themselves. I begin with examples of what not to do when representing Native Americans. When Native students are present in class, we should not assume that it is their responsibility to teach non-Native classmates about Indigenous peoples' experiences, any more than we would have parallel expectations for children of European American, African American, Latin American, or Asian American descent. At the same time, in the context of thoughtful engagements, teachers can and should validate Native students' insights on Native Americans when they are voluntarily offered.

Each semester in my university classes, at least one student reports an instance of everyday racism regarding the representation of Indigenous peoples in school curricula. Some examples my students share are gross stereotypes on worksheets: an outline intended to depict a Native American child, with words printed on a feathered headdress indicating colors to be crayoned in; the number five indicated by five Hopi kachina dancers, gourd and feathers in hand. These cartoons dehumanize Native peoples; they treat the headdress worn by respected members of some Native nations as a generic indicator of Indian identity and trivialize Hopi ceremonial regalia. Other examples include American Indian mascots depicted as animals. A greeting-card image of Wampanoag people gleefully welcoming the Pilgrims at Plymouth Rock evades the history of genocide against Native Americans, suggesting that the invasion of their lands by Europeans was—and is—cause for celebration. Some representations raise complex issues for parents as well. How should a parent talk with a child about a literature study group that uses the award-winning but racially stereotypic book by Virginia Grossman and Sylvia Long, *Ten Little Rabbits*?[2] "Counting Indians" and portraying them as "charming" look-alike animals that reproduce themselves perpetuates demeaning ethnic stereotypes.

Recently, in a university class discussion about multicultural education, a student recounted memories of a "really cool" high school social studies teacher who believed firmly in the virtues of cultural and linguistic diversity, went to great lengths to incorporate diverse perspectives in her curriculum, and strove to make lessons relevant and interesting to students. During a unit on Native Americans, the teacher, who was not Native, asked her students, none of whom was Native, to come to school dressed as American Indians. Students pieced together what they believed to be American Indian attire, as many do on Halloween. (Indeed, my files are stocked with advertisements from craft stores depicting trick-or-treaters dressed in fringed buckskin with feathered headbands, hands gesturing a war whoop. In such imitations, troubling stereotypes of Native peoples abound.) The not-so-subtle lessons in this activity that teachers should avoid were that (1) all Native people look and dress alike and are interchangeable and that (2) Native attire is a costume to be tried on playfully, rather than a real part of people's lives that should be observed and investigated respectfully.

We can begin to determine which classroom portrayals of Native Americans are harmful by unpacking the impact of representations on our students. Stuart Hall, a cultural theorist who is both Black and British, explains that to represent something is to describe or depict it, to call it up mentally by description, portrayal, or imagination.[3] These processes are powerfully activated by visual symbols as well as spoken and written language. What understandings about Native peoples does a given image convey? I suggest that teachers ask themselves and students this question about every representation of groups in their classrooms and avoid representations that seem inaccurate or inauthentic.

Inaccurate representations are at odds with lived experience, perpetuate pejorative stereotypes that falsely depict all individuals in a particular group as having the same attributes, and exaggerate differences between groups. Inauthentic representations lack credibility in their source, and make claims about Native peoples without warrant. Authenticity is a particularly slippery concept, raising questions about who can and should speak about, write about, or otherwise represent members of particular cultural or ethnic groups.[4] Some researchers and educators argue that only cultural "insiders" can accurately represent experience from that cultural standpoint: that only a Native American can accurately represent other Native Americans. Clearly those who are born and raised in a cultural system possess more intimate knowledge than can be derived from books. Most books about Indigenous peoples have been written by "outsiders" and often present distorted views. But the position that only a Native person can accurately represent other Native Americans ignores diversity among Native peoples. As Abenaki writer Joseph Bruchac emphasizes, "there is really no such thing as *The* American Indian or *The* Native American. Seeing all Indians as being alike is as foolish as not being able to see them at all."[5] Moreover, not all non-Native accounts are inaccurate and inauthentic. The key for teachers and students is striving to tell the difference— that is, inquiring into the accuracy and authenticity of representations of Native Americans.

Educators should seek complex representations of groups, moving beyond visual representations and engaging students in a complex exploration of Native American experiences. The teacher who invited her students to dress up as imaginary Indians might instead have had them read autobiographies of Native people, such as those in Patricia Riley's *Growing up Native American*,[6] or Bruchac's *Our Stories Remember*,[7] and asked them to compare these accounts with media depictions. Many Native nations and organizations maintain websites on Indigenous teaching resources (see Resource list). One of the most readily accessible and helpful organizations is Oyate, whose mission is to evaluate texts and resource materials by and about Native peoples and to provide professional in-service training on this topic. Teachers might read the growing professional literature by Indigenous researchers and educators, such as Gregory Cajete's *Look to the Mountain*[8] and Maenette Benham and Joanne Cooper's *Indigenous Educational Models for Contemporary Practice*,[9] in order to learn more about creative new approaches to teaching Indigenous subject matter. Slapin, Seale, and Gonzales's *How to Tell the Difference: A Checklist for Evaluating Native American Children's Books*[10] is an excellent guidebook available in many libraries.

Best of all, a teacher seeking to promote complex inquiry into a group's contemporary life can invite community members to discuss their own life experiences and perspectives with the class. Native American people reside in every state of the union and its territories. Many school districts maintain directories or have Native American programs and personnel. Community-based American Indian centers, institutions of higher education with American Indian or Ethnic Studies programs, and tribal museums and education offices offer accurate and authentic materials and referrals to people who are willing to speak with students. (For educators working in Native communities, these resources are readily available.)

Educators should heed Bruchac's advice that there is no single, static Native American story. This renowned Native writer acknowledges that "there are so many stories, as many as the leaves on trees."[11] Teachers can help students understand that they should not expect one person to be representative of all Native Americans, or to be the expert on everything Native American. Some preparatory reading and discussion will pave the way for a productive visit by a Native community member.

Sisika (Blackfeet) educator Vivian Ayoungman advises that community resource people—particularly elders, the most revered culture-bearers— "appreciate having specific information on what is expected of them so that they can contribute productively. . . . Arrangements should also be made to assist [with] travel and ensure their comfort."[12] Tell your guest what students have been reading and the types of questions they have raised. Explain where this visit fits within the broader curriculum and your instructional goals (see also Levinson, Chapter 23). Let your guest know that he or she should not feel pressured to focus only on historic cultural traditions, but that your students will benefit from learning about contemporary Native American issues as well. Encourage the guest to speak from her or his own personal perspective. I observed one teacher successfully negotiate this process in an ethnically mixed urban middle school language arts class that included Native and non-Native students:

> The African American teacher leads the class in a discussion of Scott O'Dell's *Island of the Blue Dolphins*. Based on historical events involving the Chumash of the central California coast, the book's plot captivates students; they easily relate to the main character, Karana, who survives against all odds after being [stranded] on a deserted island. On this particular day, the class is joined by a respected local Indian educator, who provides cultural information on the Chumash and asks students to critically consider the impact of missionization on California Indians. He shares stories about such customs as the naming rituals referenced in the book, using examples from his native Lakota Sioux oral tradition. Later, the students will work in small

groups to research questions arising from this discussion and their reading. As the bell rings, the teacher tells us that over the next few weeks, he plans to introduce other multicultural literature to encourage cross-cultural inquiry.[13]

Classroom visits by Native colleagues and elders can develop into ongoing exchanges of benefit to school districts, Indigenous nations, and local communities. At one urban high school with which I worked, visits from members of nearby Native communities prompted several teachers and their students to form a Native American Student Activity Club. Native and non-Native students worked together on school-wide projects, including an information clearinghouse on accurate and authentic teaching resources. At another school, following a series of presentations by Native resource people on "Critical Issues in Native America Today," a group of students became involved in researching diabetes prevention—a pressing issue in Native communities—and organizing health fairs in conjunction with tribal councils and the local American Indian center.

A genuinely transformative pedagogy challenges and reverses the historical relations of exclusion that have characterized schooling for Native peoples in the past. Many of these suggestions are applicable to other groups who are typically represented solely or primarily in textbooks. These initiatives require considerable time and thought, much knowledge gathering, and a commitment to learn from one another by teachers, students, and community members alike. But they have the power to teach about group experiences in more rich and authentic ways and to break down dangerous ethnic stereotypes—and those are worthy antiracist goals.

RESOURCES

American Indians in Children's Literature: Critical Discussion of American Indians in Children's Books, the School Curriculum, Popular Culture, and Society-at-Large, a website maintained by University of Illinois at Urbana-Champaign American Indian Studies professor Debbie Reese (Nambe Pueblo), americanindiansinchildrensliterature.blogspot.com.

Native American Authors—Teacher Resources: the Internet School Library Media Center's Native American author page: falcon.jmu.edu/~ramseyil/native.htm.

Oyate: www.oyate.org. See especially Oyate's *Teaching Respect for Native Peoples*, which lists "dos and don'ts."

Recommendations and Sources for Native Children's Books, a website maintained by Northern Arizona University American Indian Education professor Jon Reyhner, which includes bibliographies, recommended books, bookstores, "Questions to Ask when Selecting American Indian Books for Classrooms," and links to additional information on American Indian education: jan.ucc.nau.edu/~jar/AIE/ICB.html.

DISCUSSION QUESTIONS

1. **Principle:** How does your own curriculum represent the racial or ethnic groups that comprise your school or classroom population? How does your curriculum represent groups not present in your school or classroom? What is one consequence of those representations?

2. **Strategy:** Think of a "group" represented in some manner in your own curriculum. How might you ensure that this representation is as complex and true-to-life as the community itself?

3. **Try tomorrow:** What kinds of things could you invite a parent, community member, or other cultural resource person to talk about in your classroom? How could you invite such a representative from a given community to your class without placing him or her in the position of representing all group members, or of oversimplifying the group's current practices?

Teresa L. McCarty is the Alice Wiley Snell Professor of Education Policy Studies at Arizona State University. She has been a teacher, curriculum developer, and program administrator in American Indian education at the local, state, and national levels. Her current work focuses on Indigenous/bilingual/multicultural education, literacy studies, and language education policy.

34

Teaching Representations of Cultural Difference Through Film

Sanjay Sharma

Student: But they are Indian parents who, um . . . discriminate against their daughter, what with all that arranged marriage stuff, it's just backward.
—Class discussion of the film, *Bend It Like Beckham*

Including popular media representations of minority cultures in the classroom offers both difficulties and possibilities. *Bend It Like Beckham* (*BILB*), directed by Gurinder Chadha (2002), offers complex portrayals of a community of South Asians in Britain. (South Asians in the U.K. are primarily people with roots in Bangladesh, India, and Pakistan. In this essay, I also use the term "Asian" to describe these populations.) The plot of *BILB* revolves around Jess, a feisty seventeen-year-old British Asian living in West London, who yearns to become a professional soccer player. The premise of the film is that her parents do not share this ambition and wish her to attend university, train as a medical doctor, and marry "a good Indian boy." Much of the comedy is based on Jess deceiving her parents and continuing to play soccer in defiance of their demands. The director carefully avoids depicting a stereotypically patriarchal South Asian family. Jess's relationship with her father is handled sensitively.

But using *BILB* in the classroom at any level can still trap educators in reductively representing diasporic South Asian culture, for example by reinforcing stereotypes about arranged marriage. Alternatively, it can open up a successful discussion about what it means to represent a minority culture at all. I argue that we need to ask students to consider how any film represents any group. In *BILB*'s case, what kinds of differences are highlighted? How does the film portray "Asianness"? Does it deal with existing stereotypes of South Asians? How does it explore social issues within Asian communities?

Antiracist educators aim to support students in learning to live with differences while pursuing social justice and equality. Multicultural teaching has typically been concerned with highlighting the plurality of cultures and their ways of life in contemporary society, encouraging students to appreciate "minority cultures." Teaching about diverse cultures invariably involves representing them, whether through textbooks, narratives, images, or films.

These representations are never neutral, and students do not encounter them innocently for the first time in the classroom. Images are racially loaded, replete with meanings that the educator cannot fully know or manage. For example, when students watch an image of the Indian American convenience store owner Apu in the television series *The Simpsons*, popular ideologies about South Asians circulating in society influence how students interpret it, even if Apu is presented in a positive manner.

Critical multicultural teaching encounters the challenge of not *objectifying* groups marked as racial-ethnic minorities. (In the contemporary United States, *ethnic* identity is *racialized*: fluid ethnic characteristics such as national or regional origin, linguistic background, religious affiliation, and cultural practices are fixed and attributed to spurious "racial" origins.) Objectification reduces the diversity and complexity of a group. *Racialized* objectification typically involves depicting minority groups through stereotypes: Indian Americans are imagined as hardworking, traditional, and conniving. Students interpret even Apu's somewhat positive portrayal through these dominant stereotypes.

Multicultural educators often claim that it is possible to counter reductive stereotypes by offering positive images and more accurate knowledge about minorities. But the representation of minority cultures is more complicated than an ongoing battle between supposedly positive and negative accounts. Educators should not assume that acquiring more accurate knowledge about minority cultures directly leads students to adopt an antiracist stance.[1] Rather, we must discuss the representations of minorities circulating in the wider media and popular culture.

Even though *BILB* presents a variety of British South Asian characters and tries to portray those characters more "accurately" and positively than many previous films, these characters for most viewers remain ethnically marked by their "Asianness," irrespective of how differentiated the characters appear in terms of class, gender, and sexuality. By contrast, in the 1997 film *Titanic*, the characters are not racially marked by their whiteness; instead, differences of class and gender prevail.

An antiracist consideration of a text about a "minority culture" stimulates students to think critically about how minority groups are so often represented solely in racial-ethnic terms in texts, as all about being racial. An antiracist educator refuses to represent minority groups only in terms of their culture and ethnicity, a key risk in what we often call "multicultural" education. We must do more than recognize and celebrate cultural diversity, as if minorities are no more than their racial-ethnic identity.[2]

Looking more closely at the example of using *BILB* in the classroom enables us to tease out the challenges of racialized representation. *BILB* presents a nuanced account of family life that is sympathetic to the parents as well as celebratory of Jess's autonomy. It depicts a young British Asian woman who is alienated from neither her Asian roots nor British culture. The film contests the typical narrative of a "clash between cultures," which implies that the children of immigrants are unable to negotiate between their supposedly "traditional" home environment and "modern" British—implicitly, white—ways of life. The viewer learns that Jess's father initially refused to allow her to pursue a soccer career, not for sexist reasons, but because of his own encounters with racism in sport upon arriving in Britain, and over time he comes to accept and support Jess's aspirations. The film explores inconsistencies in the uses of "tradition," highlighting different kinds of femininities among Asian families. For example, after being banned from playing soccer, Jess protests that her sister and her friends openly flaunt their sexuality, yet are not admonished by their parents. She is upset by her parents' inability to appreciate that she acts as a dutiful daughter is expected to. "It's out of order! Anything I want is just not Indian enough for them. I mean, I never bunked-off school to go to daytimers [discos] like Pinky or Bubbly. I don't wear makeup, or tight clothes like them! They [parents] don't see all those things," she says.

While the film avoids reproducing classic stereotypes of South Asians, the student comment at the beginning of this essay demonstrates that BILB can still be interpreted stereotypically as revealing negative aspects of South Asian culture. In spite of the film's diverse representations of South Asian life in Britain, its depiction of so-called traditional cultural elements, such as arranged marriages, attracts the disapproving attention of some students.

Students may also treat the film as representing "truths" about South Asian culture in general, even if the film attempts to demonstrate a South Asian family's negotiations and debates in their full complexity. Non–South Asian students may especially frame these practices in terms of the "ethnic" difference of "others" from the white British norm. Mainstream audiences are unlikely to see BILB as just a film about a teenager seeking her independence.

Discussions of South Asians in exclusively or predominantly white classrooms are likely to dwell upon such so-called cultural characteristics as being "traditional," "religious," and "patriarchal." These characteristics are not unique to what is labeled South Asian culture. Religion plays a significant role in the lives of some white North Americans, but religiosity is not deemed an ethnic characteristic of this group. In contrast, religion is constructed as a core trait defining South Asian identity. This representation ignores the reality that many South Asians are either not religious or practice religion in other ways. Because whites are the dominant racial-ethnic group, their practices escape being ethnically and racially marked.

The fundamental pedagogical problem lies with constructing any group's culture as a static set of practices that can be enumerated: "this is how Muslims pray"; "Hindus are vegetarians"; "Tattooing is a traditional art form of the Maoris." These "facts" about other cultures end up acting as cultural "truths" rather than social issues and concerns to be debated.[3] Group practices come to seem static, rather than constantly remade.

Ultimately, the portrayal of "others" in multicultural texts delimits the real complexities of their differences.[4] The experiences and perspectives of minority groups can never be fully represented or completely grasped, whether in a film or in our teaching activities. Multicultural teaching should resist presenting "facts" about the cultures of minorities and instead spark conversation about how minorities get represented.

In a conversation regarding *BILB* about how minorities get represented reductively, students would be asked to consider, for example, whether and why they are marking Jess's father's practices of restricting her autonomy as culturally "South Asian." Students could discuss how struggles to restrict children's autonomy or over children's marriages are not specific to South Asian culture. The teacher could explore with students how parent-child relations are being contested in many communities. They could explore how Jess's British Asian identity makes it impossible for us to talk about either "British" or "Asian" culture, as if they were distinct and opposite. The contradictions within so-called Asian tradition visible in the film could be highlighted in order to explore how all cultures abound with differences and conflicts. There is always a struggle within cultures to define and represent themselves.

Finally, the question of arranged marriages in *BILB* can be used to open up not just a question about "what do South Asians do?" but a larger question of how young women negotiate the impending expectations and demands of adulthood. Such a discussion would not deny Jess's "Asianness," but it would not trap her identity in "Asianness." For example, Jess's resistance to arranged marriage illustrates the choices countless young women make against parental demands, rather than simply a rejection of "backward" South Asian culture. It demonstrates that marriage traditions in any community are resisted, ignored, and adapted.

Multicultural teaching involves taking risks with our students,[5] because representing other cultures runs the danger of fixing their differences and reducing the real complexities of minority group identity. Teaching about difference is difficult. Throughout use of any media text that represents "groups," teachers should induce students to question their assumptions about those cultures, and ask them to consider how media reinforces those assumptions. Used this way, *BILB* would provide a means for deconstructing the production of ideas about other cultures, rather than a source for learning what minority cultures are supposedly really like.

RESOURCES

Darkmatter Journal: http://www.darkmatter101.org.
Hanif Kureshi. 1990. *The Buddha of Suburbia*. London: Faber & Faber.

Sarfraz Manzoor. 2006. *Why do Asian Writers Have to be "Authentic" to Succeed?*
   observer.guardian.co.uk/review/story/0,1764420,00.html.
Meera Syal. 1999. *Anita and Me*. New York: The New Press.

DISCUSSION QUESTIONS

1. **Principle:** Sharma argues that even the most complex texts we use in class can prompt reductive conversations about cultural groups. Have you seen this occur? What happened, and how did you handle it?
2. **Strategy:** Consider a film or other text you use in class to teach about "groups." What would you now say about how that text represents the group?
3. **Try tomorrow:** What sorts of preparatory or follow-up questions could you ask the next time you use this text in class, to get students thinking about how groups get represented?

Sanjay Sharma is a senior lecturer in sociology and communications at Brunel University in the United Kingdom. His research substantively addresses issues of cultural politics, racialization, and difference, and critically considers questions of representation, globalization, radical pedagogy, identity, and subjectivity.

35

What Is on Your Classroom Wall?
Problematic Posters

Donna Deyhle

One day in Utah some years ago, I sat in a high school counselor's office listening to a career interview with Chris, an eighth-grade Navajo student. I was an ethnographer doing research on the schooling of Navajo students, so I had been invited to attend the counseling session. On the wall behind the counselor's gray metal desk hung a large "inspirational" poster of a young American Indian man with fine facial features and with long braids, adorned with a single feather, dressed in a buckskin loincloth and beaded moccasins. His physical features and clothing reflected Hollywood's "classic" image, stereotypically modeled on Plains Indians. Standing on the top of a mountain, he faced away from the viewer and stood with his arms raised to the sky, seemingly to bless the rising or setting sun; the image seemed designed to make the viewer think of tradition and honor. Seeing me stare at the poster, the white counselor smiled, "The more traditional Navajos wake up to the sunrise with prayers every morning." He sighed and leaned back in his chair. "I often wonder if we are doing them a disservice. It is so beautiful down there. They have such a simple and pure life. We should have left them alone." Chris did not return his smile. During lunch later that day we talked about the interview. Without prompting he blurted out, "That picture isn't us!"

Since then, Chris's words have echoed in my mind during my research with Navajo youth. His words expressed frustration about the racism that he and many of his peers told me—and still tell me—they felt every day in school.[1] For the most part, they reported, educators refused to believe that being Navajo in today's contemporary world was something desirable or likely to lead to much academic or career success. Students were directed to the vocational rather than college track because, educators told me, Navajos worked well with their hands and were not interested in careers. Students who left school insisted they felt unwanted and pushed out of school by uncaring teachers. Embedded involuntarily and at times unwittingly in a history of racial and cultural conflicts between American Indians and white people, including land thefts and genocide perpetrated by whites in the past,[2] even well-meaning white educators created stumbling blocks for Navajo students. They did so even through their most seemingly mundane actions, such as putting up posters of Native Americans in their offices and commenting on them.

There were many specific problems with this poster and the counselor's use of it. For one, in commenting on the poster as an image of local "Navajos," the counselor falsely portrayed the very diverse American Indian population as internally homogeneous. A picture of a Plains Indian is not the same as a picture of a Navajo, and to comment on it as a representation of Navajos was to deny the Navajo student with whom the counselor was speaking his specific language, history, religion, matrilineal familial relationships, and local sacred landscape. There are over 500 different American Indian nations, speaking hundreds of different languages. This interaction over a simple poster on the wall broadcast the counselor's assumption that all Indians are the same.

The counselor's poster, and his comments on it, also depicted Indian cultures as frozen in time. The counselor's commentary about "traditional" Navajos made clear that the poster represented to him a timeless construction of "real Indians"—living serenely, without technology and wearing leather clothing, close to animals and the land, and best "left alone." This anachronistic image obscured the diversity within contemporary Navajo experiences. The Internet, Ivy League and community colleges and universities, multicultural global communities, and advice from grandparents are all parts of young American Indian men's and women's ways of being in the world today.

The counselor also implied that the Navajo student in front of him would do best if he remained true to this imagined historic portrait. The counselor, invoking the troubled, common metaphor of "walking in two worlds,"[3] implied that Chris himself had only two life choices: to remain totally "Indian" ("traditional"), or become totally "white" (assimilate). For young Native Americans, these two choices are not real alternatives: real life is a combination. The full world of their grandparents is out of reach, even though they respect their ancestors' ways of being; the world of the larger white community is often only marginally available because of poverty, discrimination, and lower teacher expectations of their potential for success. Indian students' real lives are ignored, and the students themselves disempowered, if they are expected only to fit in either idealized world.

To Chris, this anachronistic image, even if presented somewhat sympathetically by the counselor, could never be him or his Navajo friends and family. For Chris, this sense of being not seen by his counselor— or worse, being seen through a lens of inaccuracies—was harmful. He refused to enter the counselor's office again and left school during his sophomore year.

American Indians are more likely than many groups to be misrepresented on posters as both frozen in time and internally homogeneous, but this example raises questions about how other populations are represented or misrepresented on our schools' walls. I doubt that classroom teachers or counselors would display and remark upon pictures of white Pilgrims as "pure ancestors" representing all white students, and expect white students to hold up these reflections as images of themselves in order to be "real" whites. The argument would be made that many different European nations colonized the North American continent. People remarking upon such a poster would also be likely to note it was historical.

When teachers or counselors put up posters of groups, particularly non-white groups, to counter the all-too-typical lack of images of nonwhite peoples, we must look twice at the representations we choose. Is the image frozen in time, rather than appropriately labeled as a historical image? Is it used as a generic portrait of a "group," rather than as a portrait of some members of that group? Is it a portrait that misrepresents group members' real lives in the contemporary world? Does it present students with limited choices of possible selves? Will students "see" themselves with pride or shame when they look at the poster?

We might even involve students in examining these representations before they are chosen for display, and ask students to scrutinize the images of selves and others that surround them inside and outside of schools. How accurate are these representations? How do they make students feel? If we include students in debates over images and choose carefully which images remain on the walls, students of all groups might have a chance to say, with pride and confidence, "That's part of who I am—or who I want to be."

RESOURCES

Center for Media Literacy: www.medialit.org.
One World Poster Set: A teaching guide for all grades. For a teaching guide that helps prompt analysis of images on the walls, see: http://www.tolerance.org/teach/resources/posters.jsp.

DISCUSSION QUESTIONS

1. **Principle:** How do posters, as public images, matter to how students experience learning environments?
2. **Strategy:** What sorts of general questions would you like to ask students about a poster or public image displayed somewhere at your school?
3. **Try tomorrow:** How would you actually start a conversation with students about this image? Role-play the discussion.

Donna Deyhle is a professor in the Department of Educational Studies and the Ethnic Studies Program, and Co-Director of the American Indian Resource Center at the University of Utah. Her major professional interests focus on anthropology and education, cultural conflict, racism, critical theory, the education of American Indians, and Navajos.

36

Teaching Racially Sensitive Literature
Jocelyn Chadwick

Much of the great canonical and contemporary literature we teach includes racially sensitive subjects, themes, language, and images. How can teachers create safe and trusting learning environments while exploring such literature? Literature classes expose students to ideas, periods, situations, and characters that they must consider, question, and challenge so they develop as skilled readers, critical thinkers, and astute participants in society. Many famous texts may include content considered racially *insensitive* by parents and communities; we must take special care with students when teaching those texts.

Generally, concerned parents and citizens challenge texts based on the use of racial slurs, as in Mark Twain's *Adventures of Huckleberry Finn*.[1] Others challenge works of literature based on their perceived use of racial stereotypes, or perceived lack of positive role models. I say "perceived" because, as researchers have found, many of the challengers have misconstrued the work. Few students challenge these texts on the same grounds. More often, students challenge the pedagogy of the educator teaching the work.

Almost any work can be considered racially sensitive; there is no longer any "safe" text. *A Raisin in the Sun, Othello, Beloved, The Contender, The Scarlet Letter, The Joy Luck Club, Bless Me, Ultima, Always Running, House on Mango Street, To Kill a Mockingbird*, and *Grapes of Wrath* are but a few of the texts challengers have sought to ban from schools, districts, and libraries because they argue that these texts, many of which feature people of color, are too contentious to be taught. Yet the danger seems to lie not in the text itself, but in the pedagogy of teaching it.

I suggest some steps that teachers can follow to help students gain the most from great literature with racially sensitive content.

First, establish appropriate and respectful classroom decorum. Teachers must articulate their expectations and standards clearly. From the beginning of the school year, teachers must make clear that, although some of the literature students will read throughout the year contains sensitive scenes and troubling moments in history, intolerance or inconsideration of other students in the classroom is totally unacceptable. Students have told me that in the absence of such preparation, after reading literature containing racial slurs (such as *Huckleberry Finn*), their classmates feel empowered to use these terms toward them and teachers do not intervene or use the first incident as a teachable moment to insist on racial tolerance and sensitivity. Teachers must set the tone of classroom decorum on the very first day. They must make a normal part of their daily regimen a firm and unyielding rule that everyone respects all classmates—no use of racial or ethnic slurs, and no profanity under any circumstances.

Teachers should also explain to students what type of literature they will encounter and what expectations you have for class discussions. Prepare students to read racially sensitive and controversial literature at the beginning of the course, not at the moment they begin a text. Explain why each text is the best example of the theme, period, or genre being presented. Teachers should always prepare a parallel text so that if parents of any ethnicity refuse to allow their children to read the assigned text, an alternative text will provide a learning experience as close as possible to the assigned one. For example, I often recommend that teachers use Frances E.W. Harper's *Iola Leroy, or Shadows Uplifted* as a parallel text for Twain's *Adventures of Huckleberry Finn*. Teachers can use both books in tandem, or they can assign Harper's text separately.

Before teaching a literary work, review its social and historical context yourself and then establish the context for your students. For American works, especially, bring in primary sources and secondary resources to enhance students' comprehension. In teaching Toni Morrison's *Beloved*, for example, introduce students to Margaret Garner, Frances Ellen Watkins Harper's poems on enslaved mothers, and information about plantation life. It is essential for students to understand Sethe's motivation as she attempts to kill her own children, one of the most distressing moments of the book. As Sethe states in the novel, her children are her "best things," and no one, not even the slave owner, Teacher, has a right to them.

Prepare students by covering vocabulary, characters, and controversial scenes, as well as setting the historical context. Teachers must know the etymology and historical usages of any racial slurs used in the text, such as "nigger," "kike," "spic," "guinea wop," "beaner," "poor white trash," and "wetback," and present them in context. Teachers must read controversial sections with students, using Socratic questioning to guide them in constructing their own conclusions and interpretations. Students should never be asked to navigate these kinds of scenes without guidance. Teachers must be prepared to answer both the direct questions students ask and the implied inquiries they may want to ask but are too reticent to pose out loud.

I am a proponent of mini–research projects: sending students to the library to uncover the history, terms, and events mentioned in the text. With racially sensitive texts, however, teachers must think through these activities carefully before assigning them. Asking students to do their own etymological research on the term "nigger," for example, is burdensome and inappropriate. Doing research on family life on slave plantations, on the other hand, is eye-opening for students.

Discuss problematic aspects of a text before students start reading it. Teachers should walk students through sensitive scenes that require framing and contextualizing, listening intently to their questions. Attention to and awareness of students' interpretations, ideas, and responses to these discussions and the reading itself are essential at this point.

Monitor students' responses in class and on writing and group assignments. Attend to their comprehension, anxiety, and resistance. From the first day of class, teachers must begin creating a bond of trust with students. Maintaining that bond is essential when teaching racially sensitive literature. As teachers facilitate the reading of the texts, we must read students' verbal responses, their tones of voice, and their body language. Listen carefully to their comments. Withdrawal from class participation or reticence to respond to questions are signs that a student may be in trouble and needs more care from the teacher.

As you read and discuss texts, divest yourself of preconceived ideas about the students in the room, and instead monitor students' actual reactions to the text and discussion. Students often complain that white teachers assume falsely that students of color know everything there is to know about their own history. Some teachers assume all students of color have the same experiences with poverty, single-parent families, and uneducated elders. For example, with Lorraine Hansberry's *A Raisin in the Sun*, African American students told me they felt so uncomfortable when their teacher assumed that they understood the Black family's poverty that they either refused to continue reading the play or refused to participate in class discussions. We should approach our students as people with their own opinions and ideas, without imposing racial stereotypes.

As you learn more about how students react to texts, you can start to reread texts from a racially sensitive perspective that anticipates how students of various groups might experience them and considers how best to prepare all students for fraught scenes, characters, or issues in texts. Think about the potential reactions of the entire class, both white students and students of color. Teachers must include all students in discussions, rather than spotlighting (or ignoring) students of color (see D. Carter, Chapter 43).

English teachers must ensure that their students have positive learning experiences with racially sensitive literature. Our goal is to help students think critically about universal themes. When students read texts about real life throughout history and feel comfortable enough to explore complex or even troubling themes in our classrooms, then we have created positive reading and discussion experiences.

RESOURCES

Jocelyn Chadwick. January 2006. "*Adventures of Huckleberry Finn*: A New Perspec-
     tive on an Old Classic and Teaching Racially Sensitive Literature: A Teacher's
     Guide." *Classroom Notes Plus: A Quarterly of Teaching Ideas* 23(3).
Langston Hughes. 1995. *A Pictorial History of African Americans.* New York: Crown.
Clarence Major. 1994. *From Juba to Jive: A Dictionary of African American Slang.*
     New York: Viking.

DISCUSSION QUESTIONS

1. **Principle:** Some educators simply refuse to teach racially sensitive literature or to address racially sensitive topics in other subjects. What
   learning opportunities may be lost when this occurs?
2. **Strategy:** How might teachers extend Chadwick's recommendations
   generally to discussions of racially sensitive topics in other subject areas?
3. **Try tomorrow:** Consider a specific racially fraught issue or moment in
   a text or unit you teach. How might you better prepare yourself and
   your students to approach this content?

*Jocelyn A. Chadwick is a Mark Twain scholar whose publications and work in
classrooms around the country focus on teaching racially sensitive literature.
Formerly a high school teacher and university professor, she is presently with
Discovery Education, a division of Discovery Communications, as director of
curriculum for English and social studies.*

Part XIV

Create Curriculum That Discusses History Accurately and Thoroughly

Curriculum has to present information about race and racial inequality that is accurate and thorough. Good information on our history is as important as good information about the present. The essays in this part share a core principle of everyday antiracism: *inaccurate or limited information about racial groups' histories and experiences must be replaced with accurate and thorough information.*

How can educators engage students in accurate and thorough inquiry about the past and present situation of any group?

1. Make race relevant in all-white classrooms by teaching local history.

   Mara Tieken urges that educators and students in all-white settings investigate their community's own racial past and present.

2. Teach facts, not stereotypes, about groups' experiences.

   Paul Ongtooguk and Claudia Dybdahl demonstrate how educators can teach facts, not stereotypes, about a group's experience. For example, educators can use facts to counter myths about Native Americans' constitutional status in the United States.

37

Making Race Relevant in All-White Classrooms: Using Local History

Mara Tieken

It was near Martin Luther King Day, and I was reading a biography about King to my third-graders to expose them to the history of race relations in the United States. The sea of white faces was attentive and curious; several children asked questions. But their curiosity was limited to the "tourist" variety. As I struggled to engage them in conversations about fairness and equity, they were more interested in the landscape of Montgomery and Atlanta. Rather than asking why Black Americans had to sit at the back of the bus, they wanted to know why grownups rode buses at all. But they were interested, so I tried to turn the discussion back to the history that preceded the bus boycott. Then my lone Black student, who had been silent during the lesson, offered: "My great-granny was a slave." Suddenly the room became quiet. His comment made King and the boycott less remote. I could only sit there and wonder, *What should I say?*

I was a White teacher in an overwhelmingly White school in an almost entirely White town in rural Tennessee. Virtually every resident shared this racial identity. Any explicit discussion of race—racial groups' history in the United States, cross-cultural comparisons, or even efforts to address stereotyping—was absent from school curriculum. Usually Black History Month passed by unnoticed. For the most part, these were not malicious omissions. People saw no need to discuss race, as they felt it held little relevance to their daily lives and experiences. White people may not think about themselves in racial terms; we often assume that race pertains only to people of color.[1] If race is considered irrelevant for White students, addressing it in all-white schools may seem unnecessary.

Yet all-white schools and all-white towns are racial phenomena. The demography evinces de facto segregation, whose origins lie in a complicated mix of history, economics, choice, coercion, distrust, and prejudice. This profile is not "natural," but the result of a series of historical events that actively removed or discouraged people of color from living there, including the forced removal of Native tribes, slavery, Jim Crow laws, and racist hiring, lending, or transportation practices.

But when a White teacher looks around the classroom and sees only white faces staring back, there are plenty of rationalizations to avoid "talk about race," all of which I heard as a teacher: "The achievement tests are coming up." "Race has never been a problem here." "Kids are naturally 'colorblind' anyhow, so I don't want to make them focus on difference." "It seems a little contrived to talk about race when there aren't any Black kids or Latino kids in the room." "Isn't it just better to not talk about race at all? Then it'll just never occur to students to discriminate."

Despite and perhaps because of such ideas, conversations about race are deeply necessary in such communities, both to get students thinking more critically about social issues and to prepare them to interact more successfully with peers of color when they leave. One of the best ways I found to get my students talking critically and concretely about issues of race was to address the very "whiteness" of the town, to examine, with students, how this demographic profile was created. It took me two years of uncomfortable silences and missed opportunities to stumble upon the realization that this town's history was just as racial as the history of a multicultural urban center.

Antiracist teachers in all-white towns can begin to expose the reasons behind their current demographic composition through a curriculum in local history. As a class traces the migrations of different groups in and out of their area, students learn about the relationships among these groups and talk about the rules and practices that shaped these interactions. Through such exploration, they begin to see the actions that led to their town's homogeneity. The racial exclusiveness or segregation of a town can be understood as a result of choices made by figures in history rather than an accident.

The town in which I was teaching lacked a complete historical account, so I began by researching local history myself. I used sources from the county library, enlisting the help of the librarian and seeking out materials that were more inclusive than the standard biographies of White men. I researched the Native Americans indigenous to the area and learned as much as possible about their cultures and histories. I traced their forced emigration following the influx of White "settlers." I sought to identify the regional practices of slavery, as well as what happened to freed African Americans after the Civil War. I wanted to create a balanced, accurate, and complete local history. How, I kept asking, did this nearly all-white little town arrive at its present situation?

This story became our history curriculum. I shared the outlines of the story at the beginning of the year, and we added to it through interviews with family and community members. We created time lines, and we traced the history of the school itself. During Thanksgiving, we discussed real interactions between White newcomers and the people native to the area. We examined the rationales of the White families moving into the area; we examined the customs of local tribes. We discovered that the nearby iron furnace supplied the Confederates with arms and that a mansion in a neighboring town was appropriated as a Union hospital near the end of the Civil War. When we read about Booker T. Washington, we studied what happened to freemen and women during and after Reconstruction. We put every historical event we studied in our local context. Students realized that the current demographics were the result of a history just as racialized as the history of Montgomery, Alabama. Because this history was situated in the familiar, students were able to understand it, discuss it, and give it life.

To present this history was risky, especially for a teacher new to the profession who was also new to the area. Teaching a more inclusive local history can anger those who stand to gain from keeping this history quiet, as well as those who are uncomfortable with and feel threatened by conversations that involve questions of racial injustice. An antiracist teacher must be careful to ensure that this local historical account is balanced. Just as people of color deserve fair and accurate depictions of their lives, the lives of local White citizens cannot become caricatures either. One-sided depictions of locals as uniformly racist or simple-minded will only close minds and fuel angry responses from parents, teachers, and administrators. Bringing in examples of citizens—especially White citizens—who resisted racial injustice is important.[2] Just as discussing "race" in and of itself is productive only if this discussion is thoughtful and thorough,[3] a local history curriculum usefully prompts discussion only if its content is respectful and accurate.

When my students learned that many different peoples had once lived in the area, they began to think differently about stereotypical comments, racist slurs, and other forms of racial discrimination. Personal revelations about family experiences now incited more conversation rather than uncomfortable silence. Our discussion about Martin Luther King no longer seemed remote, for the students saw themselves and their town reflected in the larger history of race relations in America.

RESOURCES

Civil Rights Museum: variety of topics and civil rights issues:
    http://www.civilrightsmuseum.org.
Louise Derman-Sparks and Patricia G. Ramsey. 2006. *What if All the Kids Are White? Anti-bias Multicultural Education with Young Children and Families.* New York: Teachers College Press.
James Loewen. 1995. *Lies My Teacher Told Me.* New York: The New Press.
———. Personal Website: www.uvm.edu/~jloewen/.
National Center for History in the Schools: http://nchs.ucla.edu.
Howard Zinn. 2003. *People's History of America: Abridged Teaching Edition.* New York: The New Press.

DISCUSSION QUESTIONS

1. **Principle:** How are all-white schools and towns racial phenomena?
2. **Strategy:** What might be gained in your classroom or school if you undertook a study of local history? What challenges specific to your school and district might you encounter during this investigation?
3. **Try tomorrow:** Where or how would you start an investigation into your school community's past?

Mara Tieken is a doctoral student at the Harvard Graduate School of Education. She is studying the relationship between rural schools and communities, focusing on the role of school reform and community organizing in this context. Before entering graduate school, she taught third grade and adult education in rural Tennessee.

38

Teaching Facts, Not Myths, about Native Americans

Paul Ongtooguk and Claudia S. Dybdahl

Racial stereotypes about Native Americans, like many other groups, are prevalent and enduring in our society and are too rarely countered with factual information. We have seen K–12 students and adults, when asked to talk about understandings of Native Americans, generate stereotypical words and phrases like "alcoholics," "shiftless," "unemployed," "living off the government," "dependent," "enjoying special hunting privileges," "getting free health care," and "running casinos." More positive stereotypes include "close to the wilderness" and "brave."[1]

Even those students who learn to avoid blatant stereotyping may be left with nagging questions about the facts of Native Americans' actual lives and actual status—in the case of Native Americans, their "free health care," "casinos," and "special hunting rights." Without any grounding in factual information, Non-Native Americans are often confused and resentful of what they perceive as the unwarranted "privileging" of Native Americans.

The key to unseating these misunderstandings is factual information, and in Native Americans' case, the Constitution of the United States.[2] Legally, Native Americans have a unique status conveyed in the Commerce Clause, Article 1, Section 8. A number of American laws applicable only to tribes and persons are related to this constitutional status. Federal recognition of Indian tribes continues today, and thousands of Native Americans are considered citizens of both their tribe and the United States. Federally recognized tribes have distinct rights and responsibilities that other groups do not have. For example, federal Indian law allows for "Indian gaming," even when gaming may be prohibited on surrounding state land.

Unlike most popular notions about racialized groups, which are historically uninformed or totally wrong, Native Americans do have a special status within this country. Many of our students simply do not understand the full facts about that status. Students' questions about Native Americans' "privileges" need to be addressed directly by referring to history and law. For example, students rarely know that in the terms of treaties in which tribes ceded their land, the U.S. government promised, as partial payment, to provide medical care and education.

Since these treaties are still in effect, the tribes do not reclaim the land and the U.S. government continues to provide for health and education.

Students often ask significant questions about Native Americans and their status within the modern United States. Rather than providing factual answers, schools often perpetuate paternalistic attitudes by entreating students, as good citizens in a multicultural society, to just "accept" Native Americans. The problem is that students are asked to accept what they may perceive as special treatment or unfair advantage, which may generate resentment and exacerbate conflicts and stereotypes. Teachers are not well prepared to respond to factual questions about Native Americans (for information, see Resource list; also see McCarty, Chapter 33, for more resources).

Teachers might start by learning three pieces of relevant contemporary information:

- There are 562 Indian tribes that are recognized by the U.S. Congress (Federal Register 2002). Many thousands of Native Americans are dual citizens.
- U.S. laws and precedents, referred to as federal Indian law, deal only with Native people. This field is the subject of many books, and people who are studying to become lawyers may specialize in federal Indian law.
- Indian gaming generates billions of dollars each year and employs thousands of people. Casinos are owned by specific Indian tribes, and the tribes keep the profits. States try to negotiate with the tribes to receive a percentage of the profits. Millions of Americans, both Native and non-Native, visit these casinos each year.

These pieces of information suggest some real differences between Native Americans and non-Natives that seem to violate our view of American society as a place where all are treated the same. How did we get to this point? Answering this question requires learning some basic historical facts.

The Constitution's framers—all white male property owners—created this framework in 1787 at the Constitutional Convention. Native American people were not invited to this convention, and they were not granted U.S. citizenship under the Constitution. The founding fathers recognized, however, that Native Americans and newly arrived Americans would have to coexist within the boundaries that they had established for this new country. They reasoned that there should be some consistent way for the two groups to conduct relations. They decided to give the Congress of the United States, rather than each state, the constitutional power to deal with Indian tribes. Indian tribes were recognized as sovereign entities by the framers of the Constitution.

Contemporary issues related to Native American societies must be understood within this Constitutional framework. Federally recognized tribes continue to exist and have the authority to sponsor tribal governments. Native Americans, under certain conditions, are eligible to enroll in these tribes. Tribal governments and their members may be exempt from some state legal codes, and tribes may have the authority, under certain conditions, to establish their own laws and their own court systems. Some treaties that indigenous nations made with the federal government are still in effect. These treaties often explain why tribes continue to deal directly with the federal government in certain matters, including health care and child welfare.

Some state laws apply to some Indian tribes, but others do not. The result is a complex and dynamic network of relations between the federal government, state governments, and particular tribes. Changing circumstances raise new questions. For example, New York State levies a sales tax on all cigarettes. However, the state recognizes the right of the Seneca Indian tribe to sell cigarettes without the sales tax on Seneca Indian land. Since these cigarettes are significantly cheaper, non-Native people travel to Seneca Indian land to buy them. But New York State asserts that the Senecas can sell tax-exempt cigarettes only to tribal members. Disputes of this type are negotiated between the tribe and the state, resolved in federal court, or settled by Acts of Congress.

Two hundred years after the establishment of this country, the degree of tribal autonomy is still disputed. Federal policies have been inconsistent. Current policy, which was set by the Indian Self-Determination Act of 1973, recognizes the rights of Indian tribes to make key decisions about their future. Within this context of self-determination, it seems logical that tribes would retain the right to decide who lives on tribal land. And yet decisions on this issue from tribal courts often involve prolonged court battles in the state and federal court systems. Native Americans must still fight to defend and define their constitutional status and their sovereign rights as tribes.

Utilizing the full corpus of American history and law (see Resources) offers a framework for discussion that does not rest on assumptions and unwarranted claims, but generates informed dialogue.

As you negotiate this new terrain, be prepared for roadblocks. Roadblock issues should not be avoided, but they should be managed so that learning is not impeded or discussion derailed. In a study of Native American sovereignty, many students will come face to face with unexamined assumptions that they hold regarding American history and society. For example, the doctrine of "Manifest Destiny" and its philosophy that the European settlement of America was a "natural" event will be challenged through an examination of Native American experiences of colonization. Students need to be coached to suspend assumptions in order to learn new information and to consider different perspectives, not just about Native Americans but about American society in general.

As teachers and students work together to combat racial stereotyping in our society, they must learn correct information in order to unlearn a multitude of myths that surround Indian peoples—like many other groups—in the media. Schools can begin this process with students by replacing ignorance with a few basic facts.

RESOURCES

Alaskool: Materials about Native Alaska History, Education, Languages, and
    Cultures: www.alaskool.org.
Dee Brown. 2001. *Bury My Heart at Wounded Knee: An Indian History of the*
    American West. New York: Henry Holt.
Edward S. Curtis. 1907–1930. *The North American Indian.* 20 vols. Washington, DC:
    Library of Congress. Text and digitized images available online at
    curtis.library/northwestern.edu.
A.J. McClanahan. *Growing up Native in Alaska.* Anchorage, AK: The CIRI Foundation.
The Native American Rights Fund: www.narf.org.
Newberry Library D'Arcy McNickle Center: www.newberry.org/mcnickle/darcyhome
    .html.
Francis Paul Prucha. 1995. *The Great Father: The United States Government and the*
    American Indians. Lincoln: University of Nebraska Press. His multivolume
    history, which has been abridged.
————., ed. 2000. *Documents of United States Indian Policy.* In David Damas, ed.,
    Handbook of North American Indians. 3rd ed. Lincoln: University of Nebraska
    Press. This is the standard account of federal Indian policy. It is an invaluable
    resource for information on Arctic Indian and Eskimo peoples. The "Handbook"
    set consists of twenty volumes and is published by the Smithsonian Institution
    (William Sturtevant, General Editor).
Other resources for "insider" views of American Indian cultures are well-known
    authors Sherman Alexie, Vine Deloria Jr., Louise Erdrich, and Velma Wallace.

DISCUSSION QUESTIONS

1. **Principle:** Why is it so necessary for an educator to counter stereotypes or myths with facts?
2. **Strategy:** Consider an instance in which you may have taught a stereotype because you had insufficient information about a particular group. What do you wish you had done differently?
3. **Try tomorrow:** What specific issues about Native Americans, or some other group, might you like to investigate with your students to counter some common misperceptions with facts?

Paul C. Ongtooguk is an assistant professor of education at the University of Alaska–Anchorage, where he teaches courses and conducts research on Alaska

Native education. Ongtooguk is the son of Tommy Ongtooguk of Teller, Alaska.

Dr. Claudia S. Dybdahl is a professor in the College of Education at the University of Alaska–Anchorage, where she teaches classes and conducts research in literacy education. Dr. Dybdahl began her teaching career in a K–12 school in rural Alaska and is a long-time resident of the state.

SECTION D

Race and the School Experience:
The Need for Inquiry

Part XV

Investigate Learning Experiences
in Your Classroom

To ensure that students receive necessary learning opportunities and that students experience classrooms as empowering rather than denigrating, educators need to inquire into students' school experiences. You can start by asking questions about how students experience classroom interactions with you. The essays in this part share a core principle of everyday antiracism: *no classroom interaction is necessarily racially harmful or unequal, but some classroom interactions might be. The educator must investigate, without forcing a racial lens on the interactions.*

How can educators investigate how students are experiencing their classrooms?

1. Use student inquiry to investigate the learning experience.

   Makeba Jones and Susan Yonezawa suggest that educators organize student inquiry groups to assess students' learning experiences particularly in racially mixed classrooms.

2. Interrogate the meanings of students' silences.

   Kathy Schultz proposes that educators investigate student silences without forcing analysis of that silence as being or not being "racially" based.

3. Question sweeping generalizations about cultural groups; instead, ask group members how they are personally experiencing your classroom.

   Doug Foley suggests that educators ask students about their classroom experiences, rather than assuming that members of "cultures" will behave in particular ways in the classroom.

4. Keep trying to make predominantly white classrooms safe spaces for students of color.

   Pamela Perry urges educators to stay open to feedback on whether predominantly white classrooms feel like "safe" spaces for students of color.

5. Consider when racially spotlighting and racially ignoring students in classrooms may harm them.

   Dorinda Carter reminds us that educators must navigate between two potential harms: "spotlighting" students of color as racial group members, and ignoring students of color because of their race.

Inviting Students to Analyze Their Learning Experience

Makeba Jones and Susan Yonezawa

We work at the Center for Research on Educational Equity, Assessment, and Teaching Excellence (CREATE) at the University of California–San Diego (UCSD). In 1998, in a state-funded effort to increase college eligibility rates in under-performing schools, CREATE-UCSD formed partnerships with eighteen elementary and secondary schools in San Diego County whose students came predominantly from low-income families and where racial-ethnic minority students comprised the majority.[1] When the work started, approximately 40 percent of the partner high schools' students were scoring below grade level. These schools served students from a range of ethnic and linguistic backgrounds, including Filipino, Pacific Islander, Vietnamese, Mexican, African, African American, and white. We at CREATE sought to collaborate with teachers and administrators to improve students' learning experiences and achievement. We began by listening to students discuss their learning experiences.

We had heard so much pessimism from teachers about the prospects of raising the test scores of their students of color that we wanted to hear those students' own analyses of the problem. Student inquiry groups—small discussion forums facilitated by students, and designed to solicit student perspectives on the learning experience—provide a space for students' voices to be heard on core issues of teaching and learning. These voices are often otherwise silent to teachers, particularly in racially mixed classrooms.[2] We found that high school students could analyze their school and classroom experiences and provide insights that educators found extremely useful.[3]

Inquiry groups can assist the learning process generally and also serve other antiracist goals. Often, educators listening to diverse students discuss teaching and learning reconsider their own assumptions and beliefs about students' capability and motivation, which are often grounded in unintentionally negative preconceptions about students' race, ethnicity, and/or culture.[4] In an inquiry group, every student is an expert on his or her learning; the insights of a Latino student failing in school are as important as those of a white student with straight As. Student inquiry groups offer teachers diverse opinions about how various students experience specific academic practices, as well as about the meaning to various students of teachers' social behaviors, such as disproportionately referring certain students for disciplinary consequences or, more positively, standing at the door to greet every student as she enters the classroom. Students' perspectives provide useful suggestions for improving their motivation, learning, and engagement. For all of these reasons, we suggest that teachers set up inquiry groups in all classrooms, but particularly in racially mixed classrooms, as an antiracist practice.

We started with student inquiry groups because we saw students' voices as a neutral way for us to prompt reflection among adults on whether the school served students across racial and language groups equally well. In the end, we presented the results to school faculties, sharing both quotations and summary statements from the student inquiry groups. Students' and teachers' names and other identifying markers were removed; the goal was to prompt reflection about teaching and learning, not to condemn teachers. Educators themselves can convene and conduct student inquiry groups along the same lines.

First, teachers must decide what issue or topic they would like to learn about from their students' perspectives. For example, do you wonder whether your homework assignments help students learn concepts and skills taught during class? Do you want to know why students generally do better on assignments than on quizzes? Are you interested in hearing suggestions for motivating students to work harder? Do you want to know if students perceive your discipline as racially fair? If a teacher is interested in students' perspectives on her curriculum, she could have inquiry groups discuss questions such as "Do you feel like you are learning in this class? Why or why not?" or "Have there been assignments that you have enjoyed doing? If yes, provide one example. If no, can you think of an example of an assignment or activity you would like to do?" Start by listing questions yourself and then cluster the questions into topics, e.g., relationships with students, curriculum, instructional strategies, motivation. Sorting questions into categories assists your decision making about which questions to select.

Teachers have to decide if students will be allowed to select topics for discussion. How you communicate the purpose of the inquiry to your students is important to the effectiveness of the groups. Students are more likely to take the discussion seriously when they believe their teachers are open to improving their teaching by listening to students' perspectives. Whether or not you choose the topics and questions, and regardless of students' grades, attendance, or behavior, students will want to hear that you believe that every student is an expert about her learning.

We met with approximately eight to fifteen students for regular, open-ended, forty-five-to-eighty-minute conversations about their views on a range of topics, including their relationships with teachers, administrators, and counselors, their perceptions of curriculum and instructional strategies that motivated them to learn, and their opinions about relationships among students in the school. We told students we were interested in learning about these topics from their perspectives, and that we wanted them to feel comfortable introducing additional education-related topics. In contrast to the more rigid question-and-answer discussion formats used in focus groups, we wanted students to shape the conversation.

As facilitators, we were prepared to take risks and follow where students wanted to take the conversation. But we also sought to ensure that no one felt embarrassed or hurt by anything someone else said during the discussion. Creating a safe environment that was comfortable for every student, with an atmosphere of openness to disagreement and acceptance of differences of opinion, was crucial to our success. We decided that we should not impose a dialogue about race on the inquiry because doing so would assume that all students perceived racial identities and interracial interactions as influencing their experience in the classroom. We anticipated that students who wanted to introduce a race-related topic into the discussion would do so.

There were tense moments during some inquiry groups as students challenged one another's opinions about whether or not the school was racially segregated. During these moments, we had to decide whether the safety of the group environment would be compromised if we did not intervene. We admit, in retrospect, that we should have intervened sooner than we did in some sessions.[5] With faith that our pedagogical principles would steer us in the right direction, we learned by trial and error.

While our work has been with high school students, elementary and middle school teachers can set up student inquiry groups as well.[6] Questions and topics for inquiry should be appropriate to grade level, age, and content area. As a general rule, we advise teachers to stay in the classroom but not to sit with students during the discussion. Students facilitate the inquiry discussion themselves.

To prepare facilitators to model openness to others' perspectives, we used explicit ground rules in the inquiry groups to set the tone for the inquiry space as safe and open to every participant's perspective. Rules should be discussed with students in advance. These might include: there are no right or wrong perspectives, agree to disagree, do not interrupt one another, everyone has the opportunity to speak, always give your full attention to the speaker, and speak from personal experience only without criticizing what others say about their experiences. Practicing with these ground rules in classroom discussion can familiarize students with talking in open and respectful ways and allow teachers and students to engage honestly with one another.

We recommend groups of three to five students, which helps students feel at ease. The small number also reduces the likelihood that someone will dominate the discussion and alienate others. Use your best judgment to group students; depending on students' personalities and relationships, some classes may do well with student-formed groups, while others need teacher-formed groups. Try arranging groups with a mix of outgoing and introverted students, students of different ethnicities and achievement levels, and relatively equal numbers of boys and girls. The groups could spend fifteen minutes discussing two or three questions or forty-five minutes discussing five or six.

Have students generate a written record of their dialogue. One method is to ask every student to take the last five to ten minutes of the discussion time to write down one final answer for each question. Alternatively, you could ask each group to create a list of ideas and suggestions. A second method is to ask one or two students in each group to take notes during the discussion. Students paraphrase what was said and do not identify who made specific comments. Asking two students creates a shared responsibility for capturing the group's discussion and increases the likelihood of getting good notes. Each group could then take the last ten minutes to hear the note-taker's notes, decide if anything is missing or inaccurate, and offer additional comments and suggestions.

Teachers should respond to students' suggestions. What action will you take? Some suggestions are easier to try than others. What should a teacher do if students perceive that the teacher grades according to racially uneven expectations? After reflecting on her grading system, she could change her grading practices. If she feels worried that the students are perceiving bias (see Cohen, Chapter 16), she could talk with the whole class about the grading system or talk to individual students as she hands back their work, demonstrating that she has considered their suggestions and is trying to communicate better about her expectations. Communicate with your students about what you are considering changing and why these changes may take time. If you are unsure about some of the suggestions, ask students to write an anonymous letter or approach you in private to clarify them.

Asking for expertise requires listening to students' opinions. If teachers are not ready to hear what students have to say, the groups could backfire. Teachers might feel upset by students' opinions and dismiss them, and students might react angrily. We wanted students to share what troubled them about their classroom experiences, even if they had become disengaged and hostile toward school. Teachers sometimes dismiss student opinions because what troubles students about the learning experience may not trouble teachers. We caution teachers before embarking on student inquiry groups to think about how much honesty you can take about your classroom. Know your limits. Start with topics that are comfortable. We hope that over time you will venture outside your comfort zone.

We end with two brief examples of positive changes that occurred after we conducted faculty presentations on students' perspectives about their classroom experiences. A science teacher was so moved by students' descriptions of positive relationships in which teachers knew pupils as individuals rather than as nameless, faceless students that he started taking digital photos of students at the beginning of the year. Learning their names and faces quickly helped him develop positive relationships with them. At another school, inexperienced teachers were surprisingly affirmed by students' comments in the inquiry groups that the teachers' "small" gestures, such as saying "good morning" or showing an interest in students' families, made a real difference in relationships with students and students' motivation to learn and to succeed. When organized in a spirit of openness to learning, self-reflection, and communication, student inquiry groups can promote countless positive changes in classrooms of any demographic.

RESOURCES

Jeffrey Shultz and Alison Cook-Sather. 2001. *In Our Own Words: Students' Perspectives on School.* Lanham, MD: Rowan & Littlefield.

DISCUSSION QUESTIONS

1. **Principle:** Why, if at all, might racially mixed classrooms particularly benefit from using student inquiry groups to reveal students' perspectives on the learning experience?
2. **Strategy:** What would you like to learn generally about your classroom from a student inquiry group?
3. **Try tomorrow:** What specific questions would you like students to engage in inquiry groups? Generate a list.

Dr. Makeba Jones is an assistant project scientist at the Center for Research on Educational Equity, Assessment, and Teaching Excellence (CREATE) at the University of California–San Diego, and one of the directors of the San Diego Area Writing Project, an affiliate of the National Writing Project.

Dr. Susan Yonezawa is an associate project scientist at the University of California–San Diego, Center for Research on Educational Equity, Assessment and Teaching Excellence (CREATE). Her research interests include school reform and educator and student inquiry.

40

Interrogating Students' Silences

Katherine Schultz

For a teacher, students' silences can have a range of meanings. Silence might signal that students are engaged in their individual work; alternatively, it might indicate disinterest, boredom, and even hostility. Although teachers often focus on students' talk, silences can provide as much information about students' learning and understanding. When we fail to investigate the meanings of silences, we may limit students' learning and even dissuade them from participation in our classrooms.

Teachers must navigate two dilemmas in relation to silence. First, teachers must determine when silence is a productive marker of learning and when a student's silence reflects disengagement or a lack of understanding. Second, teachers must determine when a student's silence is an indication of individual style and when silence is a marker of racialized classroom dynamics. Moreover, a teacher should ask herself whether she herself interprets silence accurately through a racial lens, or too quickly. For instance, teachers and the public in general tend to assume that quiet Asian American girls are engaged in learning and quiet Black students are disaffected from school, rather than wondering whether a student's silence is simply an individual's response to the particular moment or a group member's response to racialized classroom dynamics.

A vignette illustrates the complexity of crafting an antiracist response to a student's silence, particularly when the teacher is teaching across racial boundaries.

A Mexican American boy sits in the back of the high school government class. Students are speaking rapidly about J. Edgar Hoover and the FBI. Vying for the floor, his peers' voices spill over each other. His notebook open, the student remains nearly mute for weeks on end. It is not until close to the end of the first semester that he utters his first statement to the whole group. He delivers a powerful indictment of the growing consensus in the class, reminding everyone, including the teacher, of the film they recently viewed which revealed Hoover's anti-gay stance. In a rare moment of quiet, his classmates listen carefully to his words. His statement changes the course of the conversation, which picks up quickly when he finishes speaking.[1]

As a researcher in this classroom who had spent ten years as an elementary school teacher and several more as a teacher educator, I joined the teacher, who is also White, in interpreting the student's silence in several different ways over the course of the semester. Initially, I interpreted his stance—slumped deep into his seat in the back of the room, wearing clothing generally labeled by teachers as "gang-related," and looking bored—to mean that he was disengaged from school. Occasionally I wondered if he lacked the cultural knowledge required to participate in the rapid-fire discussions that characterized this multiracial, yet predominantly African American classroom. I speculated that his lack of facility with English contributed to his infrequent participation in classroom talk. At first, neither his teacher nor I asked him to explain his own silence.

Until he spoke up at the conclusion of this conversation, I failed to see the power that resided in his choice to remain silent. I saw his initial silence as indicative of a failure to participate, rather than as indicating his reflective thinking about the topic and a decision to time his response to have a deeper impact on the conversation. Later I understood that as an individual and potentially at times as a group member, this student was both disengaged and engaged in discussions. His silence might have registered his personal style of reflection and his desire to choose his words carefully. Alternatively, his response might register his position as a Mexican American student in a school where there was ongoing tension between and among groups of Latino and African American students, or stand as a rejection of his White teacher and the White curriculum. His response may have been a self-protective refusal to engage in the complicated racial and cultural dynamics of the classroom, rather than a refusal to participate in its academic activities. His silence could have been explained by any or all of the above.

Both his teacher and I unconsciously defaulted to making assumptions about his silence, rather than asking him whether his participation and silence reflected his individual style or his response to the racial dynamics of the classroom—or better yet, asking him what his silence did reflect about his classroom experience. Having since talked to many students about the meanings of their silences, I can now see the importance of understanding that silence might indicate both a personal style and a result of racialized dynamics that are likely to include the teacher herself. I understand the ways in which his silence might be interpreted positively as well as negatively, as a strength rather than simply as a weakness.

Silence holds multiple meanings for individuals within and across racial, ethnic, and cultural groups and at any given moment in a classroom interaction. In schools, however, silence is often assigned a limited number of meanings. Silence is most often thought of only as the absence of talk, and almost always as problematic rather than potentially powerful. Student silence is typically interpreted either as a result of his or her group membership, or as a result of individual characteristics, rather than a combination of stances toward participation. Teachers either tend to read classroom silences through individual lenses, assuming that a student is shy or reticent to speak, or understand student silences through group lenses, assuming that the student's group membership (i.e., as Asian American) translates into a particular style of participation or silence in class. Too often, it seems, the silence of White students is read through an individual lens ("that girl is naturally quiet") while the silence of students of color gets read through a racialized lens ("those kinds of girls never participate"). To avoid these pitfalls, educators should explore the multiple meanings silence holds for students. As antiracist teachers seeking to understand and shape our teaching in response to our students, we should allow both group membership and individual characteristics to enter the analysis when we are interpreting students' silences. The assumption that we understand a student's silence keeps us from asking difficult questions about students both as individuals and as group members and, especially, about classroom dynamics.

Beginning in the late 1960s, anthropological and linguistic research offered primarily group-based explanations for students' silence in school.[2] This research problematized the silence of marginalized groups of students in classrooms and highlighted teachers' roles in this silencing. The result was a focus on creating inclusive participation structures, providing opportunities for talk and interaction.[3] Often these participation structures were designed with certain groups in mind so that classrooms could become more culturally responsive. The intent was to set up classrooms that were respectful, building on students' strengths rather than remediating perceived deficits that students brought from their home communities. Most often the goal was simply to increase talk. The implication was that the talk is a proxy for learning and that different groups talk or remain silent in different ways.

Rather than privileging talk, I suggest that we include an analysis of silence in our investigation of classroom interaction. Understanding different forms of participation practiced by individuals and, occasionally, by group members allows us to recognize a wider range of student engagement. For instance, knowledge of the conventions of participation among Navajos may help a teacher to understand a Navajo student's silences as respectful and as a decision not to put oneself in front of others. Yet, the assumption that all Navajos participate through silence keeps us from recognizing the particular modes of participation enacted by individual Navajo students (see also Foley, Chapter 41). If we read silence only through a racialized lens—assuming, for instance, that American Indians are silent[4] and Black girls are loud[5]—we are likely to misread the choices made by individuals within those groups, and we miss the opportunity to analyze how silence and participation are produced in our classrooms. Conversely, students can be harmed if we understand silence or

loudness only through an individual lens, because then we might avoid considering the group norms from which the child sometimes operates or the
context of racialized interactions in our own classrooms. As teachers beginning to learn to interrogate student silence, we must attend to our limiting
readings of silence and participation.

When should we interpret silence as a reflection of racial dynamics in the
classroom, and when should we understand silence as an individual choice?
When do we accept silence and wait for talk, and when do we push students to
speak so that their voices are heard? To answer both questions, I suggest we initiate conversations with our students about how, when, and why students
choose to participate through both talk and silence. Rather than simply wondering about the meanings of silence, we should ask students directly about it.

I conclude with a few suggestions for interrogating silence. First, teachers
can begin by looking for silences that occur between and among students and
teachers. When are there silences in conversations? Who is silent? Ask the
student privately about the meanings and intentions of his silences. Alternatively, have students lead a group conversation about the meanings of silence
in the classroom (for tips on student inquiry groups, see Jones and Yonezawa,
Chapter 39). They might ask, "when are we silent as a class, and what does
that reflect? What might it mean when (unnamed) individuals or groups of individuals are silent at certain times and in certain conversations?" Teachers
and students can interrogate, together, what has been made "sayable" in their
classroom and when and how students choose silence. A discussion of the differences between choosing silence and being silenced can lead to an examination of classroom dynamics and participation norms.

Second, I suggest that teachers redefine participation in classrooms to include silence, that they consider how and when silence might constitute a valid
and even useful form of participation and when it should be interrupted.[6] Re-
turning to the opening vignette of the silent boy, we can ask whether and when
the teacher might have interrupted his silence and invited him to speak; what
participation structures his teacher might have introduced to the classroom in
order to allow his voice to be heard earlier in the year; and how she might have
patiently listened to and counted his silence as a form of participation, while
attending to his writing and informal conversations with peers outside of class.
As teachers, navigating this complex terrain requires ongoing inquiry. We
should ask ourselves: do we only validate the students who respond quickly to
our questions, filling in the silences with ready answers? How can we set up
classrooms to invite a wider range of participation styles? How do we respond
to the quiet students who listen first, pausing for reflection before speaking?
Can we imagine how a silent student might be contributing in a useful way?
Are there indicators in a student's silence that can help us understand the
interpersonal dynamics of our classrooms? How can we invite students to interrogate the racial aspects of such interpersonal dynamics?

As we include silence as a valid form of participation in our classrooms, we should be careful not to let students purposefully get away with silence as a way to opt out of learning. Leaving room for silence is a potentially dangerous path to follow; it might even be interpreted as a way to limit participation by individuals or groups of students. For instance, a teacher might find it easier to allow a particularly contentious student or group of students to remain silent instead of engaging with their critical contributions. Rather than advocating silence, I suggest that teachers inquire about the meanings of silence and attempt to understand what it indicates about students' responses to ongoing classroom interactions. I urge teachers to listen deeply to both talk and silence. Above all, inquiring into silence might lead to classrooms where engaged and equitable participation is defined as broadly as possible.

RESOURCES

P.F. Carini. 2001. *Starting Strong: A Different Look at Children, Schools and Standards*. New York: Teachers College Press.

M. Himley, ed. 2002. *Prospect's Descriptive Processes: The Child, the Art of Teaching, and the Classroom and School*. North Bennington, VT: The Prospect Center.

M. Himley, with P.F. Carini, eds. 2000. *From Another Angle: Children's Strengths and School Standards*. New York: Teachers College Press.

K. Schultz. 2003. *Listening: A Framework for Teaching across Differences*. New York: Teachers College Press.

DISCUSSION QUESTIONS

1. **Principle:** How might a silent student be participating in a useful way? How might a student's silence indicate a problem with classroom dynamics, for individuals or for racial group members? When should students or teachers be pushed to practice new participation styles?
2. **Strategy:** How have you typically responded to student silence?
3. **Try tomorrow:** How might you investigate the origins of your students' silences? What questions would gently open up conversation about what a student is experiencing and what you are doing? How might an investigation into students' silence backfire?

Katherine Schultz is an associate professor and director of the Center for Collaborative Research and Practice at the University of Pennsylvania's Graduate School of Education. Her research interests include the preparation of teachers for urban public schools; the discourses of "race" among students and preservice and experienced teachers; and adolescent literacies.

41

Questioning "Cultural" Explanations of Classroom Behaviors

Doug Foley

As an educational anthropologist, I have spent thirty years researching and teaching about working with culturally diverse students. Making generalizations about cultural groups is no simple matter. This story focuses on what one in-service workshop on Native Americans taught white teachers and how they applied this cultural knowledge in their classrooms.

Historically, in-service teacher education in America has taught a deficit view of the cultures and languages of low-income students of color. This perspective views middle-class whites' child-rearing, language, family, and community practices as superior to those of working-class families and communities of color. Many multicultural educators consider the cultural deficit perspective pernicious, pseudo-scientific, and racist. Social scientists have been attacking it for years, but it is still prevalent in American society.[1] During my research on the Mesquaki in Tama, Iowa, the teacher in-service workshop that I observed was trying to move away from a deficit view of cultural difference.[2] The workshop offered teachers what the organizers considered a more culturally neutral, positive portrait of the cultural and linguistic differences between Native Americans and "mainstream" whites. Pleased at first to see my hometown address the needs of the Mesquakis, I studied how the white teachers in the workshop understood and implemented what they learned about Native American culture and language.

One instructional problem that most workshop participants acknowledged was the difficulty of getting Mesquaki students to participate in classroom discussions. The instructors responded by presenting a powerful, sweeping image of the silent, taciturn "Indian speech style" to explain the students' reticence. They referred to claims by anthropologists and sociolinguists that Indians rarely speak in white-dominated classrooms because of their respect for elders, stoicism, preference for indirection, and avoidance of conflict. The leaders taught that Indians have a distinct "learning style" that shies away from individual assertiveness and achievement. In short, the workshop suggested that it was normal cultural behavior for Native Americans to be reserved, unassertive, and silent. The teachers were encouraged to draw these students out in a careful, respectful manner.

To find out how teachers absorbed these ideas, I interviewed ten of the twenty workshop participants, all of whom were white K–12 teachers. Several of the teachers interviewed retained their cultural deficit view of the Mesquaki students' silence and lack of participation. They continued to blame the Mesquaki students and saw them as lacking English language skills, motivation to succeed, self-esteem, parental guidance, and community support for education. Other white teachers embraced the message of the workshop: that Mesquaki youth were silent because this was the "Indian" way of communicating and learning. These teachers both admired the Mesquakis' more respectful, restrained speech style and pitied them for being less assertive, competitive, and academically engaged than white students.

As these teachers talked with new confidence about their silent, passive Indian students, they slipped into a white discourse about Indians that has been circulating in American popular culture for 150 years.[3] After whites conquered Indian lands, liberal whites began writing novels, newspaper articles, and stage plays that romanticized Indians as stoic "noble savages" forced to live among whites. Anthropologist Renato Rosaldo has aptly labeled this liberal white discourse "imperialist nostalgia."[4] According to Rosaldo, when whites think their superior culture has destroyed a more backward culture, they nostalgically seek to preserve what is left of their notion of the cultural tradition. Several teachers spoke about Indians and Indian culture in precisely this way. They incorporated what the cultural sensitivity workshop taught them about a noble, traditional Indian speech style into their romantic ideas about vanishing Indian culture. The experts who ran the workshop and drew on sociolinguists' notion of a distinct Indian speech style had no intention of feeding the imperialist nostalgia of white teachers, but that seems to be what happened.

The workshop had given these liberal white teachers a sweeping way of thinking about a vexing problem in their classrooms. When asked how these ideas had affected their relations to Mesquaki students, they said they became "less pushy" and "less demanding" as teachers. They saw this approach as respecting the Mesquaki way of communicating and learning, and they prided themselves in being more sensitive than their deficit-oriented peers. Their cultural sensitivity training apparently gave them a respectable cultural theory that lowered their expectations for Mesquaki student participation and achievement. The workshop presented little information about racial barriers and discrimination against Mesquaki students. Above all, teachers armed with their "cultural" theory now felt no need to find out how each student was personally experiencing the school and their classroom. It did nothing to challenge these white teachers' tendencies to be "race blind" and "colormute" about these factors.[5] These teachers continued to avoid seeing and talking about exclusionary racial practices in their classroom and school.

After hearing how white teachers explained the silence and low classroom participation of Indian students, I asked individual Mesquaki students why they were silent in predominantly white classrooms. They responded to my questions with their own: "Wouldn't you be silent if you were a student in our tribal school and surrounded by non-Indians?" "Wouldn't you be silent if you were treated like dumb, dirty Indians every day?" After many interviews and observations of classrooms, it became clear that various Mesquaki students were not silent simply because of an Indian speech and learning style. Many were responding to the long and continuing history of racist practices in my hometown, which are documented extensively in my book *The Heartland Chronicles*.[6] I initially concluded that racism, not some cultural speech style, was producing "the silent Indian." But, as I learned more about the lives and feelings of individual Mesquaki students, I began to lose faith in my own sweeping theory that racial prejudice alone explained the silence. I came to see students' nonparticipation as produced by a complex mix of cultural, linguistic, gender, and personality factors, as well as racist treatment (see also Schultz, Chapter 40). Some were silent for very personal reasons: some lacked confidence; some were shy; some were strung out on drugs; some were indifferent to success.[7] In the end, although the issues of racist treatment seemed the most important to students, I concluded that no single theory by itself explained the silence of Indians in white classrooms.

Sweeping characterizations of cultural groups invariably oversimplify why particular members of that group act the way they do. Theories about cultural difference and cultural sensitivity training are useful to some extent: some aggregate differences in the ways people who belong to different cultural groups behave are important for educators to consider. There is a kernel of truth in the sociolinguistic model of an Indian speech style that is respectful and taciturn; Mesquakis in the aggregate have a shared style of communicating and interacting. Teachers must be careful, however, not to take such theories literally and apply them uncritically. Sweeping cultural theories are not good prescriptions for how to behave with individual students. In relying upon cultural explanations, well-intentioned liberal white teachers saw less need to get to know how each student was responding to their classroom and the school.

Rather than giving a list of standard prescriptions for becoming a more culturally aware teacher, I offer some advice about what to do with cultural generalizations. When you go to your next multicultural in-service workshop, be open to what is being taught, but be critical as well. Do not take what is being said literally as a description of how all group members behave, or as a formula for how to behave with your students. Sweeping theories about cultures oversimplify human behavior. Theories are ideas to think with, and always partial explanations. Discuss the ideas presented in workshops and courses with peers and with members of the cultural group being portrayed. Engaging in a dialogue about the ideas people are advocating is critical.

The next step is to apply all those grand theories to the everyday reality of your classroom with healthy skepticism. The students in your classrooms are individuals living in complicated historical and contemporary situations. Students sometimes respond to school and classroom environments as members of groups; at other times they respond as individuals. Get to know every student in your classroom and ask how he is responding to your school setting. Sink your teeth into the perplexing riddles in your classroom, such as the "silent Indian." Listen to the students' explanations for them. Always keep looking for complex and multiple reasons why students act the way they do in a particular classroom and school.

RESOURCES

Louise Derman-Sparks and the A.B.C. Taskforce. 1989. *Anti-Bias Curriculum: Tools for Empowering Young Children.* Washington DC: NAEYC.

T. Richard Milner. 2003. "Reflection, Racial Competence, and Critical Pedagogy: How Do We Prepare Pre-service Teachers to Pose Tough Questions?" *Race, Ethnicity and Education* 6(2): 193–208.

Margo Okazawa-Rey. 1998. "Personal Cultural History Exercise." In E. Lee, D. Menkart, and M. Okazawa-Rey, eds., *Beyond Heroes and Holidays: A Practical Guide to K–12 Anti-racist, Multicultural Education and Staff Development,* pp. 66–67. Washington DC: Network of Educators on the Americas.

DISCUSSION QUESTIONS

1. **Principle:** When and how do theories about culturally specific ways of acting and interacting help us serve children? When are cultural explanations for behavior incomplete, oversimplified, or even harmful?

2. **Strategy:** Foley argues that in anticipating culturally specific behaviors from students, educators may fail to investigate what underlies individual students' behaviors. Describe such a case.

3. **Try tomorrow:** Think of a student exhibiting a particular behavior in your classroom. How might you start a discussion with him or her to investigate the multiple, complex causes of this behavior?

Douglas Foley is a professor of anthropology and of education at the University of Texas–Austin, with research interests in class theory, class cultures, social movements, ethnic groups, and inequality in American public schools.

42

Creating Safe Spaces in Predominantly White Classrooms

Pamela Perry

The students in my university classroom were talking excitedly among themselves when I announced that it was time to start the class. Everyone quieted down to listen except for two young women sitting kitty-corner to me. One, whose back was to me, was engaging the other, whose face I could clearly see. I loudly repeated that I would like everyone to stop talking, but the two women did not notice. In a split second, I decided to call out their names to get their attention and, in that moment, blanked on the name of the woman whose back was to me. All that came out of my mouth was "Carolyn," the name of the woman facing me. Both instantly stopped talking and whipped their heads my way. I said, "So what are you doing?" They haltingly replied that they were discussing the presentation they were supposed to give that day in class. I asked them to please hold it for now so I could get class underway.

Much to my surprise, Carolyn approached me after class a few days later in the hall and indirectly but clearly accused me of racism. What I left out of my account of the incident is that Carolyn is African American, that she was the only African American in the class, and that I am white. I told the story as I experienced it—that is, without any conscious consideration of the racial identities of the two women involved. Although, from my perspective, Carolyn's racial identity had no bearing upon my calling her name out— except for the fact that because she was the only black person in a class of twenty-five students it was easy for me to remember her name—Carolyn interpreted my behavior very differently. She asked me why I had singled her out and yelled at her when Sara, the white woman with her back to me, had initiated the conversation and was speaking at the time.

I apologized profusely and explained that, in the moment, I had drawn a blank on Sara's name. Carolyn responded by saying that it had been her experience, especially in classes in which she was one of the only black students, that teachers "singled [her] out" as I had done and "ostracized" her because she was black. Her voice trembled and cracked, and her eyes began to fill with tears. She noted that I had called her name out in a disciplinary tone when a white student, whose name I did not call out, was equally deserving of disciplinary attention.

This story illustrates the importance of white teachers being open to considering how classroom interactions that feel ordinary and harmless to them can be experienced by students of color as exclusionary and ostracizing. Even the most committed antiracist educators can unwittingly provoke such responses. I do research on racism and identify myself as a social justice educator, yet my behavior evoked fear and pain in one of my students of color. All teachers can learn a great deal from being open to student feedback on negative classroom experiences. Such feedback might be direct, such as what Carolyn gave me, or indirect, such as silence or nonverbal signs of anger or alienation. Student feedback is particularly valuable for white teachers, who particularly can unintentionally and unknowingly harm students of color by acting in ways that make them feel racially marked, isolated, or victimized. Especially in predominantly white spaces, even momentary actions by a teacher—particularly a white teacher—can quickly mark racial minorities as "other."

As scholars of color, such as W.E.B. Du Bois, Franz Fanon, James Baldwin, and most recently bell hooks, have long argued, a fear of being dominated and harmed by whites is pervasive for many people of color experiencing white-controlled spaces. Spaces with predominantly white demographics increase this threat, as such spaces exclude people of color by definition if not by design.[1] Granted, a white student too might feel fear upon hearing his or her name called out by a white teacher in a disciplinary tone. For black and other children of color in classes run by white teachers and dominated by white students, however, that fear is often compounded by the possibility of being what bell hooks calls "terrorized by whiteness."[2] Carolyn was outspoken in class and had demonstrated a strong drive to fight societal racism, yet I had aggravated a longstanding and painful racial wound.

White teachers and white students are often oblivious to the painful and alienating effects that white-dominated classrooms can have on students of color. Classes can be white-dominated numerically, culturally, and/or socially; yet to white people in those spaces, the norms that regulate the space can feel normal and neutral rather than race-specific.[3] White teachers in predominantly white classrooms must thus stay open to the feedback of students of color in order to learn when our behaviors unintentionally make them feel afraid.

To avoid inflicting harm, teachers must first recognize that students of color may be particularly vulnerable in white-dominated spaces to experiencing student and teacher behaviors as exclusionary or stigmatizing. To mitigate this, teachers can help proactively create an atmosphere in the classroom in which minority students feel equally heard and respected by the teacher and the other students. They must do so, paradoxically, without highlighting students' position as the "only" people of color in the room (see Dorinda Carter, Chapter 43).

I offer two examples from my own practice with college-age students that can be adapted to younger students. Clearly, these strategies will not prevent students of color from feeling vulnerable or threatened, as my experience with Carolyn demonstrated. But they at least help create a climate where students of color may feel more comfortable approaching a white teacher to discuss their experience of the classroom environment.

An important everyday act for teachers is to use multiple strategies to welcome all voices in the classroom. One effective activity I have used is called the "quiet conversation." To start, the teacher or class chooses a controversial topic that will excite a wide range of opinions. Each student writes a statement on a piece of paper that expresses his or her knowledge or thoughts about the topic. Students can choose to write their name(s) on the paper or not. When each person finishes writing his or her statement, he or she looks up to meet someone else's eyes, and the two swap papers. The students now respond to the statement on the paper they just received, and when they are done, they look up to meet someone's eyes and swap again. After five or six swaps, the teacher can stop the activity and read some of the written conversations to the class. This exercise enables all students, including those who are shy or fearful of speaking up in class, the opportunity to express their views and engage in a conversation in a way that feels nonthreatening.

To create a safe space in a predominantly white classroom where issues of race are being discussed, it is also important to lead class discussions that explicitly address racism as a nationwide, shared problem. Teaching students about racism in society not only helps racial minority students feel seen and respected for their experiences, but also helps white students become more cognizant of the facts and causes of racial inequalities. When discussing racism and inequality, teachers should give equal time to the positive and negative effects of racism on white people. I have found that too much emphasis on the negative effects of racism on people of color can add to racial minority students' sensation of dangerously being "singled out" as a "problem." In these discussions, white teachers should also correct stereotypical assumptions students express in class about race, people of color, and even white people. We are not formally trained to facilitate our classes in this way, but gaining these skills is imperative for making classrooms safe spaces for students of color as well as white students.

These practices can also open up minefields. Once white teachers are aware of the potential for evoking fear in students of color in white-dominated classrooms, they can become overly self-conscious about their behavior, especially when a situation requires teachers to call on or discipline a student of color. In the quest to create safe spaces, different situations call for different actions. In matters of discipline, I now try to take the matter up privately with the student or draw attention to group dynamics rather than to individuals. For example, I would now proactively talk privately to Carolyn after class about our exchange; I would also now call out both Carolyn's and Sara's names to distribute responsibility for their talking out of turn. But I have found no fail-safe method. The important thing to remember is to stay open to feedback from students of color regarding the safety of spaces, whether that feedback is direct or indirect, positive or negative.

Another potential minefield for a white teacher and/or white students is actually listening to this feedback—to hear that they have said or done things students of color experience as racist or at least insensitive. Still, creating safer spaces for students of color in predominantly white classrooms means, above all, being open to learning from moments when students of color feel that they are not safe.

RESOURCES

Marshall Rosenberg and Arun Gandhi. 2003. *Nonviolent Communication: A Language of Life*. Encinitas, CA: PuddleDancer Press.

DISCUSSION QUESTIONS

1. **Principle:** If a student of color indicated to a teacher that she experienced her classroom environment as unsafe or experienced the teacher's actions as racially harmful, how could the teacher best respond?
2. **Strategy:** What are some nonverbal ways students indicate that they may be feeling hurt, left out, or unfairly treated in a class? If you see such cues, how could you respectfully start to inquire about the student's experiences?
3. **Try tomorrow:** Whether you teach in a predominantly white classroom or not, how could you help make students of color, or any students, feel welcome to inform you about moments when they have felt unsafe or unfairly treated? Role-play such an interaction.

Pamela Perry is a sociologist whose research and teaching interests include whiteness, racism, and antiracism, particularly the social processes by which whites develop "antiracist" political consciousness and behaviors; the long-term effects of school desegregation; and youth activism.

43

On Spotlighting and Ignoring Racial Group Members in the Classroom

Dorinda J. Carter

The experience of being Black in a majority-White environment affects Black students in both harmful and helpful ways. Often, these students are simultaneously affirmed and devalued as Black students and both included and isolated in classrooms. A Black student constantly wonders if and how race is operating in her daily treatment, which can have negative psychological and academic effects.

I attended predominantly White schools from grades eight through twelve in Stone Mountain, Georgia. In the late 1980s, my parents enrolled me in the Minority-to-Majority busing program, believing that my sister and I would receive a better education in a racially integrated environment. Attending predominantly White schools had many benefits: access to highly qualified teachers, current textbooks and technology, field trips that introduced me to the social and cultural capital of mainstream America, extracurricular activities, advanced placement and honors courses. But the experience entailed emotional challenges. I was acutely aware of my minority status. As a high-achieving Black student, I was often referred to by teachers as "the only one" or "one of few" in this category, which characterized me as succeeding despite their expectations. In the classroom, I was not always allowed to be an individual, but was often defined by my racial group membership. More often than not, I felt compelled to speak and behave in ways that would situate me as the representative of my racial group.

This racial framing of me as a Black student who was more likely to fail than to achieve forced me to worry about many things. I often wondered if my White peers thought my work was comparable to their own. I wondered if a teacher marked an A on my paper because the work met his standards for the assignment or if he thought this was the best a Black student could do. I sometimes hesitated to answer questions posed by the teacher, wondering if anyone would deem my response inadequate coming from my Black body. Yet, when I was not asked to share my ideas with the class, I wondered if it was because the teacher felt that a Black person had little to add to the discussion. I wondered if I was invisible in the classroom. I sometimes wondered if the teacher called on me to answer a question so that I would not feel marginalized or silenced as a Black student.

The questions that plagued me at school represent the kind of "race wrestling"[1] that Black students often engage in while navigating predominantly White schools. Although race is not necessarily always on the mind of any individual student of color, my experiences resemble those documented by educational researchers who study the experiences of Black students in predominantly White public, private, and elite school settings.[2] Teachers in any demographic situation must consciously consider how treating students as racial group members in classrooms may be helpful and/or harmful to the learning process.

Figuring out when it is helpful or harmful to spotlight Black students *as Black* or to ignore Black students' racial identities is a true dilemma facing classroom teachers today. Often, teachers are unaware of classroom moments when Black students perceive that they are being treated as racial beings when they do not want to be, or when Black students perceive that they are being *ignored* because they are Black or treated as "just a student" when they want their experience to be acknowledged in racial terms. How does a teacher know when to racialize and when not to racialize Black students so as not to cause them harm and to value their presence equally? These are essential questions with no prescriptive answers.

Here I address the dilemma of spotlighting and ignoring as it relates to the experiences of Black students in predominantly white high schools. Although my research focuses on high-achieving students, students at all achievement levels report wrestling with race-related worries in the classroom. Teachers who work in other demographic settings and with students at other achievement levels can also benefit from understanding the ramifications of racially spotlighting and racially ignoring students of color in an educational environment.

When a Black student perceives that he is being positioned as racially hypervisible, particularly by a White teacher or White students, this is racial spotlighting. When a Black student perceives that she is being positioned as racially invisible in the classroom, particularly by a White teacher or White students, when she desires to be visible *as* a racial group member or to be visible, period, this is racial ignoring. My use of these terms is informed by Mica Pollock's research in a California high school in which adults in the school both focused negatively on Black students and actively ignored them.[3] I expand these ideas to focus on Black students' perceptions of their racialization in the classroom and their desires to be perceived in racial or nonracial terms in different situations. In my research, I found that students perceived that their White teachers and White peers racially spotlighted and racially ignored them in classroom situations, making them feel alternately hypervisible and invisible.[4] These feelings impeded academic engagement and led some Black students to remain silent in class discussion or resist homework assignments.

One way in which students describe experiencing racial spotlighting is by being positioned by White teachers and White peers as native informants. The Black feminist cultural critic bell hooks describes spotlighting in which the person of color is objectified and cast in the role of racial spokesperson.[5] When class discussion centers on her racial group, the student's perception is that White peers and the teacher expect her to share the experience that is being discussed and explain whatever they do not understand. For example, during a classroom discussion of a racial profiling incident that occurred in another high school, a Black male student was asked by his teacher to relate the incident to his own life; he felt that "her question was kinda weird."[6] Many Black students report being positioned as native informants during class discussions of racially sensitive topics. When slavery was discussed in history or English class, one student said, "It always makes me feel uncomfortable being the only African American student in the classroom. . . . like, it feels weird because people ask me questions about it, and like, how do you figure that I would know more about it? I'm learning the same thing you are, and it just makes me feel funny."[7] Another student reported that, during discussions about Africans and European colonialism, "I'm expected to know everything . . . I guess they [Whites] assume just cuz we're Black that we know everything about Africa, what went on in Africa."[8] In these instances, students perceive that their White peers and teachers focus uninvited attention on them to provide an expert opinion on topics that involve African Americans simply because they identify or are identified as members of that racial group.

These students experience physical and psychological discomfort in the classroom as a result of this spotlighting. Hypervisibility can have serious academic consequences: one student silenced herself in the classroom for fear that if she spoke out she would have the "wrong answer" as a Black person. When White peers or the teacher assume that having a Black identity makes anyone an expert on "Blackness," Black students are burdened by being asked to explain a history that may have little to do with their own experiences. The native informant form of racial spotlighting disregards Black students' complex identities.

Racial spotlighting also arose during English class discussions of racially sensitive literature (see also Chadwick, Chapter 36). Black students reported being the target of stares from their White peers when Jim, the African American character in *Huckleberry Finn*, was discussed. One boy reported, "it felt kinda awkward as they were discussing it, cuz, um . . . you know . . . it took place back in the 1800s, so he was treated kind of like a slave or a lesser human being . . . and it just felt kinda like their eyes were on me when there was a discussion around the Jim character. I saw them looking at me."[9] As this student pondered whether or not his peers equated Jim's life experiences with his own, his peers' stares made him feel hypervisible in the classroom, which caused great anxiety. "I just didn't feel like saying much of anything. The teachers, like, brush it off quickly and move to another topic."[10] This student noticed that his teacher was aware of other students staring at him, but she did nothing.

Racial spotlighting that is negative, reductive, or simply unwanted creates physical and psychological discomfort that limits students' engagement in the learning process. Teachers can reduce the negative effects of racial spotlighting by consistently monitoring this dimension of their instructional behaviors. Teachers should also be conscious of the verbal and visual interactions occurring between students during classroom discussions of racially sensitive material. Rather than live in fear that all treatment of Black students as Black is harmful or racist, teachers should remember that when racial spotlighting affirms individuals as members of racial groups in ways they desire, and when questions about racial group experiences allow people to voice a position they want to express, it can be helpful to the teaching and learning process. In these instances, students feel valued.

The teacher who seeks anxiously to ignore Black students' identities or experiences as Black students runs the risk of ignoring Black students themselves. That is, she risks creating an atmosphere where she nervously avoids interactions with Black students, and where Black students feel invisible or feel that their contributions are dismissed because they are Black. A young man in my study reported that the White teacher did not recognize him when he raised his hand during class discussion. He spoke to the teacher to change the situation. "It does make a difference, you know? Even that little thing proves something to me, you know?"[11] Another young woman described a classroom experience in which her peers exacerbated her feeling of invisibility. She and a White student made the same comment, but the White student received affirmation from her peers after speaking:

> I don't know what their problem is. I don't know if it's because I don't talk as much . . . they might think I'm wrong or something. It's annoying after a while—that I would say it, and they would all pretend that they're thinking about it or whatever. Then somebody else [a White student] would say it, and it's like, "oh yeah, write it down." And it's like I just said that five minutes ago! It's upsetting, aggravating, because it doesn't happen just one time. It happens more than once. And I feel like my answer is not good enough coming from me or something like that.[12]

This incident resulted in the student being less vocal in the class. A Black student whose voice is invalidated during a class discussion or who is never called upon when his or her hand is raised feels invisible; he or she wants to be acknowledged just like other students as having valuable thoughts about the topic at hand and is likely to interpret the ignoring as occurring because he or she is Black. Remedying this problem sometimes requires making certain to call equally on a student so that she or he can voice an individual position that she chooses to express.

Teachers and students may perceive how race is operating in their interactions differently. A teacher cannot always predict when a Black student will perceive actions as racially motivated. Neither can a teacher assume that race will be salient for all students of color in the same way or at the same moments. Nonetheless, a teacher can ensure that she is attempting to be antiracist by being more conscious about the dynamics of racial spotlighting and racial ignoring. After monitoring classroom interactions, the educator might attend to students of color to counteract ignoring, and ignore students' racial group membership to counteract spotlighting. Flexibility is central to antiracist instruction; as long as the educator consciously considers whether her moves are harmful or helpful to the student in the learning process, she will do better by her students. This minefield must be navigated constantly, so keep asking yourself and others about it.

RESOURCES

Derek Bok Center for Teaching and Learning, Harvard University. 1992. *Race in the Classroom: The Multiplicity of Experience* [Motion Picture]. Cambridge, MA: Harvard University. bokcenter.harvard.edu/icb/icb.do.

DISCUSSION QUESTIONS

1. **Principle:** Since both spotlighting and ignoring students as racial group members can be harmful, Carter suggests that educators primarily must remain conscious of the potential of both types of harm. What do you make of her conclusion that "flexibility" is the answer?

2. **Strategy:** Can you think of a time when you or someone you know felt racially spotlighted or racially ignored in a classroom? What could the teacher have done differently in this situation?

3. **Try tomorrow:** How could you start an open inquiry with a student, to examine his or her experience of your classroom interactions? How could you avoid further "spotlighting" the student in this inquiry? Role-play the interaction.

Dr. Dorinda J. Carter is an assistant professor of teacher education at Michigan State University. She explores the interrelatedness of racial and achievement self-conceptions, achievement ideology, and school behaviors for Black students in suburban and urban schools. She also examines the coursework and field experiences needed to prepare students to be effective urban educators.

Part XVI

Spearhead Conversations with Students about Racism in Their Lives and Yours

Even people close to one another often have very different views of which actions or situations are "racist" and "antiracist." In order to work together to counteract racial inequality and racism via schools, people need to share these views. The essays in this part share a core principle of everyday antiracism: *competing definitions of racism and antiracism should be discussed.*

What tactics can educators employ when trying to discuss racism and antiracism with others in their school?

1. Brainstorm and discuss racial incidents as a way to push toward deeper understandings of racism and antiracism.

   Larry Blum suggests that educators and students brainstorm and discuss everyday experiences with racism in their own lives and competing ideas about what to do in such situations.

2. Debate racially charged topics directly and carefully in a structured format.

   Ian Haney López suggests that students can learn to analyze and discuss conflicting positions on fraught racial issues.

3. Let students help define and debate the antiracist policies necessary for improving your school.

   David Gillborn urges that students and educators, together, write school-wide policies regarding racism, antiracism, and equal treatment.

44

Racial Incidents as Teachable Moments

Lawrence Blum

In a class on "race" and racism I teach for high school seniors at a racially diverse school, I ask students to brainstorm together, as a class, "racial incidents" that individuals among them have experienced or witnessed. The exercise prompts deeper analysis of what racism is, what it looks like in students' daily lives, and what students experiencing or witnessing such incidents might do about them. It encourages students to move toward taking some responsibility for addressing race-related wrongs. This exercise is part of antiracist practice, broadly construed. Students confront such incidents all the time but seldom have an opportunity to think them through in an academic setting. Like adults, they often have oversimplified views of what racism is; they seldom have the opportunity to unpack and examine this question in a facilitated group discussion.

I first ask my students individually to write about a single "racial incident" to which they were either a party or a bystander. I ask them to focus on an incident within their peer group or involving adults and peers, in order to make the discussion about intervening in the incident more compelling. I purposefully leave open what is to count as a "racial incident" because I want to let the students define it. However, I specify that it has to be a situation in which "race" was involved in someone feeling harm. I mention that the incident can be "minor," such as someone saying something racial that someone else objects to, or "heavier," such as a fight or excluding someone from something important. The question of what is minor or heavy is debated in our discussion. This take-home assignment asks students to describe the "racial incident" in detail and consider how a particular party or bystander to the incident "might have reacted in a constructive way" to the situation.

I pick four or five incidents that raise a range of distinct and interesting issues for discussion. If the teacher has sufficient time, it is probably best to analyze all of the students' incidents. I rewrite these incidents so as to mask the identity of the student providing the incident. Sometimes, when anonymity seems impossible, I ask the student privately if she minds my using her incident even though other students may be able to identify her. I rewrite the incident in the second person, both to encourage the student reader to identify with the subject of the incident and to enable us to discuss the incidents more freely.

Here are some examples of incidents that my students have offered.

1. You are a Black teenager vacationing in a beach town with very few Blacks. Drinking a Fresca, you and a friend, who is also Black, enter a convenience store looking for something to eat, but you do not find anything to your liking there. As you and your friend look around the store, you feel people looking at you in a hostile manner. The clerk asks if you have paid for the Fresca; you say you brought it from another store. You add that you have not taken anything from the store, but the clerk will not let you leave until he has ascertained that the store does not carry the item that you have on you.

2. You are a White teenager working in a store. You consider your White manager racist. One day you make an "attitudey" remark to the manager, and she snaps back at you to "leave the n°gg°r attitude with the n°gg°rs."

3. At a Latino-centered school dance, with mostly Latino students participating, you are among a group of White students who are dancing. Some Latino students tease you and the other White students for the way you dance, saying you have "stiff White people hips." You and your friends are hurt and offended.

4. You are an Asian student. In an English class, the teacher has students read and discuss an article about Bill Cosby criticizing lower-class Blacks. In the discussion, you say that you agree with Cosby. You agree that many Black students are more concerned about their looks than their education, and that it is partly their parents' fault for buying their kids $50 shoes and then saying they are poor. Your Black friend tells you that you have no right to have any opinion on this subject because you are not Black. You get mad and say, "Just because I am not Black, I cannot have an opinion on that subject? Now who is discriminating?"

In the discussion about racial incidents, I have some general goals. One is to make the students pinpoint what exactly has gone wrong in the incident described. Often they initially offer a reductive and simplistic analysis: for example, they simply say that someone has been "racist." I prod them to push that analysis further. What exactly do they mean when they say that something or someone is racist? Just saying an act or a person is racist does not tell us much. For example, sometimes students mean that the perpetrator is a racially prejudiced individual; sometimes they mean that the perpetrator hurts someone else even if he is not prejudiced. Some of the students have been introduced to a power analysis of racism; they say that since White people have power and Blacks and Latinos do not, hurtful remarks made to

White students, as in example 3, are not racist and not a serious matter that merits attention.

I criticize overuse and misuse of the word "racist" in my book, *"I'm Not a Racist, but . . .": The Moral Quandary of Race*.[1] I argue that racism should be understood either as race-based hostility or as treating racial others as inferior. However, in the class, I do not force this view on the conversation. My goal is for the students to articulate at a deeper level what exactly is going wrong in the incidents, rather than to arrive at an assessment of whether the behavior in question is appropriately called racist.

Some students argue that it is enough to say that someone is offended by a remark to call that remark "racist." I push them to consider two things that are often difficult to discuss: first, whether the person was justified in taking offense, and second, whether there was something inherently wrong with saying the thing that caused the offense. For example, even if the Black student in example 4 had a good reason to be offended by her Asian friend's agreeing with Bill Cosby, it may nevertheless not have been wrong for the Asian student to say what she believed.

As students grapple with these issues, I press them to get beyond simple and imprecise terms like "racist" and "offended." Students then typically offer more nuanced words, including "ignorant," "insensitive," "thoughtless," "hurtful," "not being recognized" for your specific racial identity and what it means to you, and other ways to express racial wrongfulness. I encourage them to consider whether and in what ways some incidents involve greater hurt or greater insensitivity than others. For example, while it is generally wrong to think in broadly generalized ways about racial and ethnic groups (and thus to stereotype White people as having stiff hips while dancing, as in example 3), the White manager's use of the much more vicious and damaging "n°gg°r°" (in example 2) is to most a more troubling moral infraction, both because Blacks are more socially vulnerable than Whites and also because the n-word has much more cultural power to insult.

As they are pushed to think and speak in more complex ways about these racial incidents, students come up with increasingly insightful analyses. For example, in discussing example 1, in one class most students agreed quickly that the store owner was making unjustified assumptions based on stereotypes of young Black males. Pushed further, students then debated whether this was due to ignorance on the owner's part, overgeneralization from a few Black males he had encountered, or racial hostility. According to one Black student, the youth should not have come into the store with an open drink, given his knowledge that store owners are often suspicious of Black youth. Others strongly disputed this cautiousness.

After analyzing the incident, I ask students to reflect on whether and how the wrong involved in the incident relates to the racial identities of the perpetrator, the target, and the bystander. For example, I ask whether it is more wrong for a White person to call someone a "n°gg°r" than for a Latino or Asian to do so. When a Black person uses the n-word, does its meaning differ? If a Black manager views Black youth who enter his store with suspicion, is this worse than a White manager's doing so? How about a situation, often brought up spontaneously by students in these discussions, in which the youth eyed with suspicion is dressed in baggy pants and possibly a hooded sweatshirt but is not Black?

These questions have no simple answers. I am asking my students to appreciate the real-life complexity embedded within an overall commitment to racial equality. In my own classroom, I try to make students question two conflicting popular views about racism. One is the view that "only those with power can be racist" and that racism is only enacted by White people. The other is the "colorblind" notion that the racial identity of the perpetrator and target of the act is not relevant to how wrong or bad it is. In my view as a scholar, which I do not push on the students but throw into the debate, different racial groups have differential power to hurt others and are differentially vulnerable to hurt. However, vulnerability is also affected by local power relations as well as White dominance in the overall society. In a school in which Whites are a minority, whites are more vulnerable to exclusion. Assessments of vulnerability have to take into account all relevant contexts, from local to societal.

After analyzing the incidents, I try to move the students toward the idea that they should consider intervening. I ask what they think they would do, and then what they should do or would do if they thought about it more. In discussing possible interventions, we all realize that we have come to naturalize some racially problematic behaviors. Once, in discussing a manager following Black youth around stores (example 1), many of the Black and Hispanic students noted that they found this behavior so ubiquitous that they had learned to think that they were not bothered by it. They regarded it as just part of the way the world operated. Others argued that this behavior is wrong and not inevitable, and that there are things one can do to try to interrupt racial profiling and make the perpetrator recognize a potential cost to themselves in continuing to engage in it, such as saying "Are you following me?" "Why are you following me?" or "So, do you follow every Black kid who comes into your store?"

In these discussions, I ask students to think about whether the racial identities of the participants in the incident do, or should, affect what the antiracist person should do. Once, we discussed whether bystanders of various racial groups should intervene if a Black student racially insulted a Latino student. Both Black and non-Black students said that only Black students should intervene to stop or criticize the Black student. Other students argued that someone of any group should act to stop the action, or protect the target of the action, but that they would not in fact do so if they were not Black.

Personally, I argue in these debates against the view that racism is an appropriate concern only of the members of the targeted group in the incident. That point of view is, unfortunately, not common, and leads many White students to think that racial issues concern groups other than themselves. But it also leads some non-White students to think that if a member of another group is victimized, that is no concern of theirs. However, we also discuss how sometimes a member of a group is able to resolve a situation constructively in a way that a nonmember could not easily do. For example, in the discussion of the "stiff White people hips" incident, it would have been far easier for a Latino student to convey a message of inclusion rather than exclusion. One Latina in the class said she would just go over to the White kids and start dancing with them, which struck me as a particularly effective solution.

Some teachers might be wary of this exercise. Nevertheless, some guidelines make the exercise accessible to teachers who would like to try it. First, we should not dismiss any student-generated incident as "not really significant." The student may see something in the incident that we teachers do not initially see; exploring the incident and articulating what students see as significant in it is the goal of the exercise. Second, the exercise does not require the teacher to be an expert on how to understand or judge racial incidents and interactions. It requires her only to guide students in exploring them, to keep asking whether other students see things differently or whether they agree with what has been said. Of course, the more we know about the world in which these incidents take place the better, and a teacher planning the exercise might benefit from discussing some of the students' incidents with colleagues of different racial groups. In the discussions, I find myself often saying, "I'm not sure what to do in that situation, but what do you think of this (a proposed intervention)?" Giving some thought beforehand to the situations we plan to discuss with students might be helpful.

Given an opportunity to generate and discuss "racial incidents" as well as constructive responses to those incidents, most students will benefit from in-depth discussion of both racism and antiracism.

RESOURCES

Mark Lukasiewicz and Eugenia Harvey. 1991. *True Colors* [Television Documentary]. Libertyville, IL: CorVision Media. TV documentary in which two young men, one black and one white but with the same level of education, job qualifications, and class standing shop and seek jobs and apartments, and are treated very differently.

Francis Ried. 1996. *Skin Deep* [Motion Picture]. Berkeley, CA: Iris Films. College students of different races and from different campuses around the country are taken to a retreat for a weekend, where they work through racial issues with one another.

DISCUSSION QUESTIONS

1. **Principle:** Why might debating real-world incidents of racism and antiracism be beneficial to students?
2. **Strategy:** What general issues would you need to consider in starting such a conversation and managing it successfully in your own classroom? How would you personally start to prepare?
3. **Try tomorrow:** How would you respond if some of the incidents students raised occurred in your own classroom or involved interactions with you? How could a critical discussion of "racial incidents" between school adults and students be useful to get you and your colleagues talking about how best to assist students?

Lawrence Blum is Distinguished Professor of Liberal Arts and Education (and professor of philosophy) at the University of Massachusetts–Boston. He works in race theory, multiculturalism, moral philosophy, and moral education. He has taught a course on Race and Racism at Cambridge Rindge and Latin High School several times.

45

Debating Racially Charged Topics

Ian F. Haney López

At one point or another, you may have to teach directly about race. Perhaps charged questions or comments about people, texts, or situations have interrupted the class and need to be addressed at greater length. Perhaps, like me as a law school professor who teaches U.S. race law, you cover material so deeply enmeshed in issues of race that there is no way to avoid the subject.[1] You might teach history that involves contentious racial events, such as the Civil Rights Movement; you might teach literature that involves characters intertwined in conflicts over racial inequality; you might teach social science, with a section that focuses on the immigrant experience in the United States. How do you do it? How, for instance, might you teach a case like *State v. John Mann* (1830)? In this case, John Mann leased an enslaved black woman for a year and put her to work. Later, believing it necessary to "chastise" her, he shot and wounded her gravely. Had Mann committed a crime? The North Carolina court said no, stating that while the woman's owner could sue Mann for damage to her "property," the state could not undercut slavery by imposing criminal penalties for violence against the enslaved. "Perfect submission requires perfect control," the court reasoned. On that basis, the court refused to entertain criminal charges against Mann.

For years, I taught *Mann* in a straightforward manner. I lectured about the facts of the case, gave some background on the judge, and analyzed the legal rhetoric for lessons about the nature of slavery as a system. This approach worked well enough, but I constantly confronted a major problem: my students would not ask any questions or venture any opinions that trod even remotely near dangerous territory. No one ever dared ask, for instance, whether the court was in some sense correct that slavery required that criminal law not protect slaves. This sort of argument circulates in the background, but is rarely voiced and examined thoughtfully.

In considering this general reticence, it seemed to me that there were two conflicting dynamics at work. On the one hand, most students seemed deeply reluctant to share their views. Seemingly unsure of themselves, they hesitated as if worried that they might misspeak. On the other hand, many students also seemed to come to class convinced that they already knew everything there was to know about race simply by having grown up in a society in which racial inequality was prevalent.

After many frustrating semesters, I abandoned lectures in favor of a course that organizes the readings around formal debates on contentious racial issues, followed by more informal, but equally critical, discussions about the opinions addressed and emotions raised by the debate. Now I have student teams argue for or against the proposition that the U.S. Constitution, including the Bill of Rights, was originally written in such a way as to facilitate slavery. Other debates involve the propositions that affirmative action is reverse discrimination and that Congress should be free to prevent the immigration of certain racial groups into the United States. Substantively, this approach forces the students to do research on various arguments for or against positions and requires them to wrestle analytically with contemporary racial problems. It pushes them to read the same materials I had assigned in the lecture course, but with an engagement engendered by the need to frame and respond to particular arguments centered on the debate resolutions.

I organize the students into debate teams at the beginning of the semester, putting two to four students on each team. During the fourteen-week semester, I hold debates during twelve of the weeks, using the first week to introduce the course and a week near the middle to provide a break from the debate format. Each team debates twice during the semester. To ensure that the rest of the class stays involved, I assign them the responsibility of asking the debaters questions. I announce at the course's outset that the final exam will consist of two of the assigned debate topics, with the requirement to write on one topic they did not argue. This requirement forces the students to do the reading and to pay close attention to the arguments even when they are not behind the podium.

I structure the debates formally. Students are responsible for developing an original six-minute argument, which they deliver from the podium. When they are done, they remain at the podium and respond to the cross-examination questions posed by the class as a whole. This lasts for four minutes. Members from each team alternate in making constructive arguments and responding to cross-examination questions until each debater has stood before the class. After the constructive arguments and cross-examinations, each team is allowed to offer a single two-minute rebuttal and summation. Each team is given four minutes total during the debates for preparation time, which they may use at any time to confer with one another. I encourage the debaters to do outside research on the arguments that are actually being made in the larger society. I also request that they provide the class with an annotated bibliography of the five most helpful resources they found in preparing for the debate.

The greatest benefit of this format lies in the cover that formal role-playing affords the students. It frees them to articulate and advocate for, or challenge and critique, positions on race that they may or may not accept but would otherwise be reluctant even to voice. I assign the students sides and encourage them to make whatever sort of arguments they have encountered in their research, irrespective of whether they agree with those arguments. The goal is to give the students a space to talk through the ideas, beliefs, and assumptions that exist, even on the fringes, which they otherwise would not have an opportunity to engage in a structured, thoughtful way. I caution them against spewing abusive language, reminding them that the point of the exercise is to debate ideas and that inherent in debating is the goal of convincing others, not offending them. But I also explain to the students that some of the arguments will be offensive and that a goal of the class is to understand how best to respond to these arguments.

Be warned, though, that debates will be a pedagogical disaster if you are not ready to facilitate a follow-up discussion in which the students can shed their roles and come back together as a group to discuss the debate dynamics. The debates serve best as ice-breakers, as short precursors to deeper conversations in which students can state their real opinions. Formal debating is too constricting a format to allow a full exploration of the ideas and, equally importantly, the emotions raised when teaching about race. Usually I follow a debate with a short break to give the students time to stretch and to mark the end of the debate and the transition to a different sort of conversational mode. Upon reconvening the class, I ask the debaters if they wish to remark, not on the substance of their arguments, but on how they felt about making them and about responding to the other side. I then ask the class if they found any of the arguments particularly upsetting and what in particular they object to. This initial effort is important in exposing and acknowledging the emotionally laden aspects of race, even as asking students to examine their reactions moves the conversation back in the direction of analysis and the exchange of ideas.

I feel real trepidation in offering this advice for teachers in K–12 settings in which racial minorities may be especially vulnerable, whether because of classroom demographics or because the teacher, as the authority figure, is white. Law students are highly skilled in analytic reasoning; they are adults on the verge of professional careers. Moreover, in the classes I teach, racial minorities often outnumber whites. As a minority scholar whose main research interests center on race, I not only am familiar with most of the arguments likely to be raised but also represent a reassuring presence for minority students. My intuition, though, is that high school students, under the guidance of a thoughtful teacher, white or not, would benefit from engaging emotionally charged yet thought-provoking conversations about race. Ultimately, you as the teacher will have to decide whether the promise of this approach significantly outweighs its perils.

RESOURCES

The Alberta Speech Association. August 2006. *A Step By Step Guide to Debate:* www
.compusmart.ab.ca/adebate/resources/debate/step_by_step_guide_to_debate.pdf.
Good for tips on organizing student debates and discussions on contentious issues.
Education World: www.educationworld.com/a_lesson/03/lp304-01.shtml. Helpful
teaching guides on setting up a debate.
We Can Work it Out: www.streetlaw.org/content.asp?contentId=162.

DISCUSSION QUESTIONS

1. **Principle:** Why might it be important for students to discuss pervasive
   perspectives on fraught race issues, even if they do not agree with those
   perspectives?
2. **Strategy:** What general adjustments would you have to make when
   tailoring this activity for high school students? Middle schoolers? What
   topics could you see debating? Could the debate activity be turned into
   a research and writing assignment with similar benefits?
3. **Try tomorrow:** In your own classroom, what specific norms would
   have to be set to make such a debate and follow-up conversation analytically enriching, yet not personally damaging? Should all topics or comments be allowed in these debates, or should some be off-limits? Which
   ones and why?

*Ian Haney López is a professor of law at the University of California–Berke-
ley, where he teaches in the areas of race and constitutional law. He has published ground-breaking books on the legal construction of race. He is
researching colorblindness as a new racial paradigm that justifies continued
white dominance.*

46

Developing Antiracist School Policy

David Gillborn

In approaching antiracist change, I work from a perspective that understands racism to include a much broader set of actions and assumptions than the narrowly based definition of racially biased hatred used by most mainstream commentators. Crude, obvious, and deliberate acts by individuals are only the tip of a much larger iceberg. While there are no biologically meaningful subdivisions to the human race (see Goodman, Chapter 1), social beliefs and daily practices construct inequities around the notion of racial difference. Racism is a complex, multifaceted, and constantly changing set of practices and beliefs that have the effect of disadvantaging, disempowering, marginalizing, and stigmatizing entire groups.[1] Racism cannot be understood in isolation from wider economic, social, and political inequalities. At the same time, one of the central messages of this collection is that racism operates in part through countless ordinary assumptions made and actions taken by people in educational settings, as well as outside them.

Dealing with racism in school is not merely a question of adopting a simple set of strategies for all situations, since what works in one setting at one time might not work elsewhere or even in the same place at another time. Antiracism entails a constant struggle to move toward greater equality. Antiracist educators must even guard against the possibility that our own actions might inadvertently support the injustices we are working against. As the African American legal scholar Derrick Bell has argued, "genuine service requires humility. We must first recognize and acknowledge (at least to ourselves) that our actions are not likely to lead to transcendent change and may, indeed, despite our best efforts, be of more help to the system we despise. . . . Then, and only then, can that realization and the dedication based on it lead to policy positions and campaigns that are less likely to worsen conditions for those we are trying to help."[2] Recognizing the scale of the problems we face as antiracist educators is not defeatist, but realistic. We know that racial inequities in education and in society at large may well outlive us, but we commit ourselves to opposing these injustices and mitigating their reach.

In this spirit, I offer one technique that educators in an English school used to work toward greater racial equity, which they defined as equalizing achievement and opposing all forms of social discrimination based on notions of "race" and racial differences. Mary Seacole Girls' School (pseudonym), located in a large English city, serves around 550 students, aged eleven to sixteen. The school is extremely diverse: just under half the students have family origins in South Asia, principally Pakistan and India; one in three students is White; and around one in five is Black, with family origins in the Caribbean and Africa. As the principal of Mary Seacole School put it, "That word can be an emotive word, 'racism.' But I think to back off it doesn't say what we are about; that is being dishonest. And at the end of the day that is what you have got to stand by. We are *anti*-racist. . . . 'Anti' sounds a rather cold word in some ways [but this] is a positive 'anti'—it is *pro* antiracism." I first visited Seacole in the 1990s when it was recommended to me as an example of a successful antiracist school. I conducted research there at a time when antiracism was being vehemently attacked in the press as a symbol of politically motivated educators who were allegedly lowering "standards." My aim was to identify and learn from schools that had made progress in raising the achievement of students who belong to racial-ethnic minority groups and in challenging racism. Seacole was such a school.

I interviewed staff and students in order to get a picture of what the school had done to change the previous inequalities of outcome and alter the perception, previously common among students and local communities, that the school did not deal equitably with its constituent groups.[3] One of the key turning points for the Seacole School was the creation of a written antiracist policy. The school had already been moving toward a greater awareness of cultural diversity, changing the curriculum in some subjects to challenge exclusively Eurocentric perspectives. However, the school was still plagued by accusations of staff racism and race-based name-calling among students. These incidents heightened teachers' awareness that the school would benefit from a clear statement of antiracist principles and practices.

With the principal's backing, a core group of staff members took responsibility for drafting a policy. Specific writing tasks were delegated to small groups, ensuring that teachers representing each subject area were asked to contribute. From the very start, no subject area or school function was assumed to be beyond improvement as far as racial equality was concerned. (See also Hawley, Chapter 50.)

A first draft of the policy was presented to the whole staff and new members were recruited to the team. Departments were kept informed of progress and asked to provide feedback. All staff members were able to participate in the development of the policy. The teachers working on the draft policy used some classroom time to solicit feedback from students regarding key issues, such as name-calling and the kinds of staff behavior that students saw as problematic. These discussions confirmed that students were interested in the issues and had valuable perspectives to contribute.

From then on, students were actively involved in shaping the antiracist policy. The student council encouraged wider distribution of the draft among students and invited student feedback. Discussions were held with each grade level and responses were relayed to those who were redrafting the policy. Any student, individually or as part of a group, could send written comments on the draft policy to a friendly and well-liked member of the staff who coordinated the effort. These comments were overwhelmingly constructive, indicated strong support for antiracism among students, and frequently highlighted the complexity of defining racism in school contexts.

Students' written responses to the policy suggested that, while strongly supporting antiracist policy and calling for harsher penalties for racist acts, many wanted to modify parts that they felt applied blanket condemnation to issues that were more complex. Students were particularly concerned by the draft's suggestion that name mispronunciation was always "racist" and that "exclusive," or mono-ethnic, friendship groups were examples of "racism":

We were a little concerned about the procedure on "exclusive groupings." We do not feel that friendship groups should be manipulated to produce an ethnic "balance"; friends should be left to sort things out for themselves. However, in a work situation, we are happy to mix freely and work with students from all backgrounds. Basically we didn't like the idea of someone telling us who our friends should be.

Just because we sit in groups does not mean we do not mix. . . .

If a group does not wish another to join them they should be told in front of everyone that they are being racist. The group should be split up and the "unwanted" girl allowed to choose where she wishes to go.

The mispronunciation of names still occurs but it shouldn't be taken that seriously as it is a matter of learning how to say the names correctly.

Serious racist attacks should be dealt with a lot more severely by the teachers.

In the library there are loads of books written in English—well I think there should be more written in Urdu or Punjabi. . . .

Catalogue every racist incident. If perpetrator is same three times, automatic suspension.

Student involvement brought unanticipated benefits. The process offered students the opportunity to discuss issues of racial injustice in the school, often made taboo for fear of negative or defensive reactions by staff. The students' energetic engagement with the issues created a widespread expectation that the situation would change. Teachers were impressed by the enthusiasm and seriousness with which students approached the draft policy. Their responses raised the profile of antiracism within the school and helped to convince all teachers that the document was needed, making it difficult for teachers to argue that the policy might simply "stir up trouble" or "rock the boat," a common argument when antiracist change is proposed. After the students became involved, it was virtually impossible for the school to pull back from antiracist work; indeed, they pushed the whole school to ask new questions about racism and antiracism.

Just as the policy brought unexpected benefits, so too it brought a series of possible dangers. The most obvious is that the creation of a written policy could become the end point, an empty gesture gathering dust on shelves while racial inequity continued unchallenged. A good way of countering the overreliance on a written document is to build in regular milestones for action and review. Educators and students can identify what progress would look like—a closing of the achievement gap, higher graduation rates, fewer expulsions—and appoint a committee to evaluate it.

A second, more fundamental threat lies in the response of white teachers and white students who may feel threatened by the creation of a public antiracist policy. Antiracism, by definition, challenges racism and the power of whites to gain, even unwittingly, from the exclusion and oppression of other people. Policy makers commonly discuss multiculturalism as if everyone always gains from a greater awareness of diversity. I call this "vanilla" multiculturalism, a soft-focus notion of universally acceptable change. Any serious assault on racial privilege will necessarily challenge the status quo. This does not mean that whites will be forced into poverty or lose their citizenship rights, as some commentators would have us believe. But it does mean that white people will have to change the way they think and act. Indeed, white children and white adults may begin thinking about themselves as "raced" for the very first time in their lives. White people commonly react by fearing that they are losing power or have been cast in the role of villains. To respond to these reactions from students, some of the most successful schools that I have worked with have listened to the white students' concerns—denying them voice merely confirms the "anti-white" stereotype—and then talked them through the antiracist procedures: What kinds of activities or statements are no longer acceptable? How will the school change as a result? At every step, the teachers point out that white students are free to use the antiracist policy as protection whenever they feel themselves unfairly excluded on the basis of race. This work not only reduces some of the initial white opposition but can become part of antiracist pedagogy by revealing just how rare it is for white people to consider themselves as raced persons in a world where "race" still exerts such a powerful negative force for millions of their peers.

Students' views and experiences are an integral part of antiracist change. Students of color understand things about racism and inequality that cannot be learned from books, no matter how conscientious the antiracist educator. Students are a vital resource and essential allies in our struggle to create more equitable schools.

Constructing and enacting a school-wide policy on countering racism requires teachers, students, and parents to begin a discussion about what racism is and how it manifests in everyday interactions and distributions of opportunity. Creating an antiracist policy is always a process. At any time, and without warning, the current understandings of what counts as racism or antiracism can be thrown into turmoil by an event in the schoolyard, the local community, or the world that raises the profile of a particular group or generates new racist stereotypes that have to be identified and countered.

The question as to whether, or, more precisely, when to treat people as members of a racial group is a complex matter. At times we must acknowledge that racial-ethnic minority students experience the world differently and consequently may have important perspectives that will not occur to teachers; it is wise to pay particular attention to the views of particular groups. On other occasions, however, framing students solely as members of racial groups, requesting their feedback from their group's perspective, or applying an antiracist policy to them as group members risks inadvertently worsening the situation by imagining that students always experience the world primarily as racial group members—rather than, say, as gendered or classed, or as people with disabilities—which is exactly the kind of assumption that antiracism often tries to deconstruct. For example, a school in England tried to heal the scar of a racist murder in which an Asian child was killed by a white child by banning all white students from the funeral. This attempt at antiracism backfired by seeming to cast all whites as guilty by association.[4]

Seacole School recognized that decisions about how to pursue antiracism are difficult and, most importantly, that youth, especially those belonging to racial-ethnic minorities, often have a more sophisticated understanding of the specific issues than do their teachers. Student participation was not originally part of the planning, but as the students' enthusiasm became visible, the teachers had the wisdom and courage to work with the situation and take it further.

RESOURCES

Stella Dadzie. 2005. *Toolkit for Tackling Racism in Schools*. Stoke-on-Trent, UK: Trentham: www.trentham-books.co.uk. A practical guide to antiracism in schools, including exercises, hints and tips, and suggestions for further resources and contacts.

Brian Richardson, ed. 2005. *Tell It Like It Is: How Our Schools Fail Black Children*. London: Bookmarks. An accessible collection of writing on the education of Black children in Britain, including contributions by activists, poets, academics, and parents. Many teachers have used the collection to spark debate in their schools.

Runnymede Trust. 2003. *Complementing Teachers: A Practical Guide to Promoting Race Equality in Schools*. London: Letts Educational. A well researched and highly accessible guide to educational inclusion and social justice issues. Includes specific guidance for every major curriculum area.

DISCUSSION QUESTIONS

1. **Principle:** What benefits can you see, for students and educators, of writing a school-wide antiracist policy? What minefields come to mind?
2. **Strategy:** How can school communities keep antiracist policies from becoming "an empty gesture gathering dust on shelves"?
3. **Try tomorrow:** If you were helping to write an antiracist policy for your school, what specific things would you want it to include? What sorts of things do you think your students might want in the policy?

David Gillborn is professor of education at the Institute of Education, University of London. He is active in antiracist politics, works with community-based groups, and has contributed to several policy-making initiatives nationally.

Part XVII

Talk Thoroughly with Colleagues about Race and Achievement

Increasingly, educators are expected to talk about racial achievement patterns. But talking more about racial achievement patterns is not helpful if the conversations fail to analyze such patterns thoroughly. The essays in this part share a core principle of everyday antiracism: *since talking reductively about racial achievement patterns makes it impossible to solve those patterns, educators must talk thoroughly about causes and solutions instead.*

How can educators pursue thorough talk about race and achievement?

1. Cultivate a school-based discourse that emphasizes educators' responsibility for students' learning.

   John Diamond proposes that educators ask always what they can do to serve students and enhance their learning, rather than focus solely on what other people should do.

2. Add structural analyses to cultural explanations of variations in student achievement.

   Vivian Louie urges that educators break the habit of quickly imagining families' "cultural" educational "values," and learn instead how real families are trying to navigate actual opportunity structures.

3. Talk about racial hierarchies when you assess school reforms.

   Rosemary Henze suggests that educators keep asking whether school reforms are actually equalizing students' opportunities inside schools.

4. Discuss regularly with colleagues the many ideas and actions it will take to enrich the education of all students in diverse schools.

   Bill Hawley suggests how educators can start to reform an entire school for equity amidst diversity.

47

Focusing on Student Learning

John B. Diamond

When students and their families are believed to be the principal cause for school success or failure, teachers feel less responsible for ensuring that students achieve at high levels. They are less likely to adjust their instructional practices to meet students' educational needs because they doubt that their efforts will pay off. To best assist students, educators should cultivate a school-based discourse that (1) emphasizes teachers' responsibility for students' learning and (2) challenges arguments that blame students' struggles primarily on students' and their parents' supposed lack of educational investment.

The explanations for racial differences in academic achievement that come up in educators' conversations about student achievement are often linked to taken-for-granted assumptions about racial groups' families and their cultures. For instance, the model minority myth[1] suggests that Asian American students are disproportionately high achievers because they and their families are more heavily invested in education than members of other groups (see also Louie, Chapter 48). When Blacks and Latino/as struggle academically, members of their communities are often thought to be less invested in educational achievement. Unfortunately, incomplete explanations about families and communities sometimes overwhelm educators' sense that their own practices make a difference. My colleagues and I have found that this presumption makes teachers less likely to consider whether their own instructional practices meet students' educational needs.[2]

When teachers in a school feel collective responsibility for their students' academic success or failure, student achievement is enhanced. When most teachers do not feel responsible, student achievement suffers. On one end of the continuum are schools where the majority of "teachers take personal responsibility for the success or failure of their own teaching"; on the other end are schools where "most teachers see . . . students' ability (or lack of it), students' family background, or their motivation" as limiting the impact of their teaching.[3] "When teachers work to make sure all of their students are learning, when they change how they teach in order to make this happen, when they believe all students deserve whatever efforts are needed to learn, students respond by learning more."[4]

Research on expectations typically focuses on teachers' beliefs as if individuals come up with these notions by themselves, but we know from experience and research that they are influenced by others. In a recent study of leadership in urban schools, my colleagues and I found that among the eighty-four teachers we interviewed in the first phase of our study, 83 percent reported that their classroom practices were influenced by principals and 80 percent reported that other teachers influenced their thinking.[5] The same study shows that when the majority of a school's students come from groups that have traditionally struggled academically (e.g., low-income African Americans and/or Latino/as), teachers tend to feel less responsible for students' outcomes.[6] Teachers report that they are influenced by others' discourse in both formal settings such as faculty meetings and informal school settings such as school parking lots.

In the schools I have studied that have experienced the most academic improvement, teachers and administrators discussing students' academic struggles focus on what schools can do. In one successful school, the principal asks teachers to reframe conversations in which their colleagues blame children and their families for students' academic struggles without discussing the implications of school practices. In conversations about student achievement, teachers and administrators at this school often interrupt an ongoing conversation to ask what they themselves could do differently. Teachers and administrators use a document they developed that links teachers' lesson plans to individual students' skill mastery as a basis for discussing areas in which students are struggling and teachers might consider changing their approaches.[7] This practice reinforces teachers' sense of responsibility for student learning. This school's assistant principal argued, "I believe . . . if [a student] didn't learn it, you have not found a way to teach it." Formal and informal conversations among teachers and between teachers and administrators emphasize how school personnel can respond in different ways to the challenges they face in the classroom.

There are some potential pitfalls to emphasizing teachers' responsibility for students' outcomes. First, it is crucial to avoid the language of blame. Taking responsibility for improving achievement should not mean blaming teachers when students struggle. It simply means that teachers must be vigilant in exploring every avenue to facilitate students' success.

Second, it is important to recognize students' challenges without letting them overwhelm the sense that school practices make a difference. In the successful urban schools I have studied, challenges that students had outside school that could affect school performance were acknowledged and addressed but not used as excuses. Acknowledging students' challenges means recognizing that some students do not have computers, hundreds of books, and fully engaged parents at home. An instructional program characterized by rigorous academic standards can take account of these realities.

Third, focusing on teachers' responsibility for student learning does not mean that parents and students have no role to play. Students' efforts and parents' engagement are vital to achievement. Teachers and administrators must seek to make meaningful connections with parents even though parental involvement may come in different forms. But rather than just ask what parents should be doing differently, they should ask, "what could we do differently to enhance parents' support of students' outcomes?"

RESOURCES

Minority Student Achievement Network: msan.wceruw.org.

DISCUSSION QUESTIONS

1. **Principle:** To what extent do you agree that it is important for educators to accept more responsibility for student learning and achievement? How can educators do this without feeling "blamed"?
2. **Strategy:** Diamond suggests that educators should acknowledge and address challenges that students have outside school that could affect school performance, but not use those challenges as excuses. Consider a type of challenge some of your students face. How might you and your colleagues better start to address that challenge?
3. **Try tomorrow:** How might you reframe a conversation about low test scores, after a colleague made a statement blaming students and their families for those scores? Role-play the interaction.

John B. Diamond is an assistant professor at the Harvard Graduate School of Education. He studies the relationship between social inequality and educational opportunity in elementary and secondary schools. In particular, his work examines how teachers' expectations, school leadership, educational policy, and parent engagement affect students' educational opportunities and outcomes.

48

Moving Beyond Quick "Cultural" Explanations

Vivian Louie

I begin with a story of a fundamental misunderstanding. When speaking for the first time to a large audience of K–12 educators serving substantial numbers of immigrant children about my book, *Compelled to Excel: Immigration, Opportunity, and Education among Chinese Americans*,[1] I offered a critique of prevailing explanations of the racial-ethnic achievement gap that center on cultural deficits and assets within families, particularly the "model minority" stereotype of Chinese immigrants. According to this popular notion, Asian American children of immigrants are disproportionately high achievers in school because of their parents' belief in the importance of education. This discourse frames Chinese immigrants as culturally programmed to succeed, especially in comparison to native-born minority groups, such as African Americans, and to other immigrant groups, such as Latinos, that are not doing as well in the aggregate.

Model minority discourse was an effective way for mainstream power brokers to deflect the claims of injustice voiced by African Americans and Latinos during the Civil Rights Movement; if members of these racial-ethnic groups just worked harder, the argument went, they too would achieve as Asian Americans did. But this cultural explanation renders variations among Asian Americans invisible. More important, it fails to explain the structural context that produces Asian American students' outcomes (whether successful or not) and shapes whatever beliefs and practices Chinese parents share. Attitudes and actions do not originate in family culture alone, and family cultures themselves are shaped within structural contexts of constraints and opportunities.

In my research, I show that social-structural analysis must be added to cultural explanations of academic achievement. In order to understand why members of any group parent as they do (typically a key aspect of "cultural" explanations), we should consider such factors as the social class background of parents, extended family members, and friends; the wealth of the community in which they live; and parents' understandings of the racial-ethnic hierarchy in the United States as privileging some and penalizing others. In the case of immigrants, we should consider the kinds of education parents carry with them from their homelands; their experiences of the symbolic and literal losses that accompany migration, such as the loss of language and the impossibility of transferring occupational skills; and what both mean for their status and attempts to become socially mobile in the United States.

When such structural issues are considered, immigrants' experiences prove to be infinitely more complex than the "programmed to achieve" story told by the model minority discourse. The Chinese immigrant parents in my study indeed all emphasized the importance of a college degree to their children, and they came from nations with a strong tradition of privileging formal education and a conception of learning as a result of hard work rather than natural ability. However, powerful social contexts in the United States lent new meanings to this cultural heritage and made it worth keeping, especially the greater accessibility of higher education (in China, access is typically limited on the basis of examinations) and the financial payoff it yields. Equally important was parents' perception of racial-ethnic inequality in the United States. Most were convinced that their children would not be given a fair chance because they were of Chinese descent, so they needed educational credentials to get around discrimination.

Further, despite sharing some ideas about the importance of pursuing college degrees in the U.S. context, working class, urban Chinese families had far less information on the actual pathway to higher education than did middle-class, suburban Chinese families. Accordingly, their children often struggled in school.

I tried to tell this more complex story in my talk. Afterward, during the buffet lunch, I continued the conversation with members of the audience. A friendly white woman approached me. At the end of our conversation, she remarked: "And now I know why my Asian immigrant students do so much better than my Latino students do—it's their family culture valuing education so much. I had always thought that, but it is good to know I was right. Thank you for allowing me to understand that." I was taken aback. This woman had articulated the notion that I had tried to contradict, or at least complicate, in my talk. Before I could respond, the woman melted away into the crowd.

In retrospect, I suspect she was not alone in holding firmly to her previous impression. Facile, reductive explanations that resort to family "culture" as the primary cause of differentials in achievement among groups circulate constantly in schools. The Chinese American students I interviewed talked about peers who could not believe anyone Asian could fail a test and about teachers who never registered their academic struggles because Asian children are supposed to be the brainy, quiet ones who never need help.

Americans have made similar arguments about various immigrant and racial-ethnic groups for decades. The logic underlying the Elementary and Secondary Education Act of 1965 was the "culture of poverty" explanation, which held that low-income and poor African American children came from homes with a "cultural deficit."[2] Low-achieving black students were misunderstood as the children of parents who, for racial and class-related reasons, did not value schooling. The dramatic increase in the number of immigrant children in the aftermath of the Immigration Act of 1965 gave rise to more cultural explanations, as the children of new immigrant groups were compared with one another and with those of native-born racial-ethnic minority groups. Depending on demographic trends, the groups being compared in cultural terms shifted, but the language and explanation remained remarkably consistent.

If we are serious about addressing and eliminating the achievement gap, then we need to take on structural issues. Not only are "group" differences in parenting habits often overstated, but student achievement results from far more than differences in parenting. Focusing entirely on the family excuses the school as an institution, where teachers, counselors, and administrators make decisions about children every day that affect whether a child does well or not. It is all too easy to make those assessments based on the prevailing cultural shorthand: she is Asian so she belongs in the AP class; he is Latino so he belongs in ESL. Second, families live in particular communities, often not by choice but because these are the only places they can afford or are allowed into, given housing costs and de facto segregation. The fact that some children are growing up in communities where public services are few and far between, without police protection, parks, and libraries, affects their development and academic achievement.

For most of us, culture is a concept that we can easily wrap our minds around; we often reduce it to food and holiday celebrations. Structure is a more difficult concept. Thinking about how the lives of students and their parents are defined by structural factors requires us to consider social class, as measured by income, occupational prestige, and educational attainment, and wealth, as measured by assets, property, and income, both inherited and earned. Doing the structural analysis of how different groups end up slotted into occupations that have greater or lesser prestige and rewards seems far more difficult than imagining how people from different "cultures" parent.

To explain differences in student achievement, K–12 educators need to add structural analyses to their cultural explanations. We can still compare different groups, or different parenting practices (if we actually investigate them), but we should always fully investigate the circumstances underlying any differences in parents' actions. For example, the model of education in which parents actively sponsor their children's schooling does not apply to all working-class immigrant parents. Working-class Asian parents are seldom involved with their children's schools; the schedules these immigrant parents work, their limited formal schooling, their unfamiliarity with American schools, and the language barrier all limit their participation. Schools should develop new strategies to promote the level and form of parental involvement that helps the child. Collaborations between schools and community-based organizations serving immigrants facilitate greater understanding of both the parents and their children.

I had these thoughts in mind when I gave a second book talk to K–12 educators. I decided to spend the last twenty minutes of my talk discussing my recent work comparing the schooling choices of working-class Chinese and working-class Dominican immigrant parents. I found that working-class Chinese parents often know Chinese adults from middle-class backgrounds who alert them to the better-performing public schools to aim for and the poorer-performing schools to avoid. Working-class Dominican parents are more likely to favor Catholic schools, a shared pattern of belief grounded in the superior quality of Catholic and private schools to poorly resourced public schools in the Dominican Republic and the poor quality of the local public schools where they now live in the United States. When immigrant Dominican parents could not afford Catholic school, they turned to the local zoned schools, often without realizing that there were other good public school options outside their neighborhood. I tried to explain group differences in school preference by including these structural factors that shape the experience of each group.

I thought I had done so successfully until a man in the back raised his hand. Identifying himself as a Dominican, he challenged me: "Are you saying that Dominican parents don't value school as much as Chinese parents do? Because that's how I am understanding you. And I don't think that's true." I was taken aback by his question. "No," I responded, "that is definitely not what I want to say. And I am sorry if that was not clear enough in my talk because your question is important, and my answer needs to be more clearly laid out. So let me give some more examples of what I mean." I described the specific structural factors influencing how each group of parents chose schools. I ended by calling upon educators to be mindful that the constant comparison pitting immigrant groups that ostensibly strive against immigrant groups that ostensibly do not is incomplete and can have negative results. Some groups lack information about how the public educational system works, but they still care about their children's schooling.

I hope that by supplementing cultural explanations of differences in academic achievement with analyses of groups' experiences navigating unequal structures, researchers, educators, and policy makers can find more effective ways of understanding achievement gaps between groups and, eventually, eliminating them.

RESOURCES

Here are some organizations in my region that can help educators learn more about immigrant families' structural circumstances. Similar organizations exist in communities nationwide.

Coalition for Asian American Children and Families, New York, NY, www.cacf.org.
Chinese Progressive Association of New York City, New York, NY 10002, Phone: (212) 274-1891.
Chinese Progressive Association of Boston, Boston, MA, www.cpaboston.org.
The Coalition for Asian Pacific American Youth (CAPAY), c/o Asian American Studies Program, UMass Boston, Phone: (617) 287-5658, E-mail: CAPAY@umb.edu.
El Centro Presente, Cambridge MA, Phone: 617-497-9080, E-mail: centro@cpresente.org.
Higher Education Resource Center, Congregacion Leon de Juda, Boston, MA, Phone: 617-442-5608.

FILMS

Jon Alpert, Yoko Maruyama, and Keiko Tsuno. 1976. *Chinatown: Immigrants in America.* New York: Produced in association with WNET/Thirteen.
Laura Simon. 1997. *Fear and Learning at Hoover Elementary.* New York, Boston: American Documentary Inc.

DISCUSSION QUESTIONS

1. **Principle:** What explanations about "cultural" ways of parenting have you heard in your school? How do these explanations affect how you or your colleagues view your students and their parents?

2. **Strategy:** What information about "structural contexts of constraints and opportunities" might you seek in order to complicate those "cultural" explanations? Consider seeking information about where your students' families live, their wealth, their circumstances of immigration (if applicable), their knowledge about the educational system, and their reception and experiences in local schools and communities.

3. **Try tomorrow:** How might you respond the next time a colleague offers a quick "cultural" explanation about how family practices or "values" cause achievement? Role-play the interaction.

Vivian Louie is an associate professor at the Harvard Graduate School of Education. A sociologist, Louie focuses on how the children of immigrants and adult migrants (1) acquire the educational credentials and skills needed for upward mobility in a globalized world, and (2) experience cultural shifts through the process of migration.

49

Naming the Racial Hierarchies That Arise During School Reforms

Rosemary Henze

Even when school reform aims to improve opportunities for all students across racial lines, educators can fail to discuss the racial hierarchies that get produced or reproduced as they proceed with their reforms. As an illustration of this problem, this essay analyzes actions taken by two middle school principals who led an urban school in Alaska in the late 1990s. The first tried to desegregate the school by organizing students according to learning style rather than race, but failed to address the racial hierarchies that then resulted. The second more explicitly considered race in order to then desegregate the school once it had resegregated. While this story does not suggest that either principal's school reform was better than the other, it does suggest that educators reforming schools must recognize and address with staff the racial hierarchies that reappear during and even despite reforms.

Allaneq Middle School is located in Vista Valley, the only part of the city where whites are a minority (all names are pseudonyms). The nonwhite population consists of Native Alaskans, African Americans, Asians and Pacific Islanders, and Latinos. Vista Valley is also the poorest part of the city. Problems with violence, drugs and alcohol, and abuse appear in the media almost daily, creating a negative impression of this neighborhood. Allaneq had the highest suspension rate and the lowest standardized test scores in the district. The student population was diverse: 34 percent of the students were classified as White, 25 percent as Native Alaskan, 18 percent as African American, 17 percent as Asian and Pacific Islander, and 5 percent as Hispanic. Sixty percent of the students were enrolled in the free and reduced lunch program, used as a proxy for poverty. Student turnover was high: almost half of the student body was new each fall, due to fluctuations in the job market and a large number of Native Alaskan families who moved back and forth between their native villages and the urban area. Students spoke forty-four different languages at home, and 20 percent of the student body was classified as limited English speaking. Among the certificated faculty, only 11 percent were considered "nonwhite."

Molly Cartwright, who served as principal of Allaneq from 1993 to 1998, had a powerful vision. She sought to change the negative image of the school as a violent and culturally bereft ghetto. She reached out and formed partnerships with local industry and cultural organizations to support the school and provide extracurricular opportunities for students. At the beginning of her tenure, she subdivided the school into learning communities. Cartwright believed that smaller teams would help teachers get to know the students and their families and that students would benefit from instruction tailored to their individual needs and interests.

Noticing that students tended to group themselves informally by race, she quietly hoped the new learning communities would encourage more crossing of racial boundaries among students. Cartwright constructed her plan for school reorganization based on her understanding of learning style theory. Adopting Howard Gardner's theory of multiple intelligences,[1] she argued that schools should value different kinds of intelligence equally.

On the basis of these ideas, Cartwright developed a new structure of teams and schools within a school that she believed would allow students to group themselves along lines of intellectual interest and pedagogical preference rather than racial-ethnic identity. Each student and family would ideally get to choose the team that best represented their preferred teaching and learning style. If a child was "right-brained" and intuitive, his family might choose the Red School, which used project-based, hands-on, thematic, and student-centered approaches to instruction. For a student who preferred a setting in which the teacher is the primary authority and the focus is on learning academics through drill and practice, the family might choose the Blue School. The Green School served students who were bilingual or who had an interest in learning another language, and the Fireweed School was designed for students who preferred a Native Alaskan style of teaching and learning. A student would usually stay with his or her cohort for two grades, maintaining consistency in teaching styles. The teachers, counselors, aides, and reading specialists on each team would all share the same students, and meet daily for an hour and a half for planning across subject areas. Faculty members would choose the school in which they taught by their preferred style of instruction and their friendships with colleagues.

In defining learning styles, the principal explicitly identified only one racialized group, Native Alaskans, with a particular learning style meriting its own school. This school became overtly racialized as many Native Alaskan parents chose this option for their children. The Native Alaskans at the school were from diverse origins: Yup'ik Eskimos, Aleuts, Inuit, Athabaskans, Tlingit, Klinkit, and many students who identified as "mixed" Native Alaskan and some other racial group. Cartwright openly rationalized the racialized grouping of the Fireweed School based on the history of Native Alaskans' poor school performance. She said she had previously taught in and served as principal of a village school, so she understood the culture shock of the transition from rural to urban and wanted to make Fireweed a safe space where Native Alaskan students could feel comfortable and not get swallowed up by the large urban school. In theory, any student and family could choose any team based on his or her learning style preference, but in practice, three-quarters of Fireweed participants were Native Alaskan.

According to teachers I interviewed, the creation of a safe space for Native Alaskan students indeed seemed to give extra attention to students who otherwise tended to get lost in the shuffle. However, another issue arose that was less often discussed among staff: the Fireweed School also ghettoized Native Alaskans, providing them with no structured opportunities to interact with non-Native peers. Further, some non-Native teachers who were repeat-edly praised in public by the principal for their "Native Alaskan teaching style" felt the Fireweed School trivialized the depth of knowledge and experience a teacher would need to have to truly integrate Native Alaskan values in a class-room situation.

As the school-within-a-school concept became institutionalized, other seri-ous problems with a sharp racial edge arose, but were rarely discussed openly among faculty. By 1998, racial segregation had reasserted itself in other schools as well. In the private words of one teacher: "Alaskan Native kids . . . are sectioned off in one part of the building. The bilinguals are in the middle of the building, with specifically the bilingual teachers. . . . There's not just a general mix on a daily basis; only for assemblies or some special activities . . . we need to work on a plan to be more inclusive." By 1999, racial-ethnic segre-gation of the school had become entrenched. The Blue School, which was supposed to focus on "traditional" teaching and learning styles, was composed almost exclusively of African American and Latino students. Recent immi-grant and bilingual students from Mexico, Asia, and Africa clustered in the Green School because of its language theme and ESL services. The Red School, focused on alternative learning styles, had more white and "mixed race" students than any of the other schools.

The most damaging aspect of this resegregation was that staff and students began to privately stereotype whole schools and the students within them. The Blue School's hallway was disparagingly dubbed "Ghetto Hall." Assump-tions quietly circulated that low-income black and Latino students needed a skills-based curriculum and that white students benefited most from progres-sive approaches employing higher-order thinking skills. Native American students were assumed to do better when sheltered from the mainstream, and immigrant students to need a bilingual approach. Learning styles and the racial-ethnic groups associated with them became quietly ranked, especially between the Red and Blue Teams. But as these racial hierarchies became entrenched, neither the principal nor the faculty discussed them directly.

When Terri Turner conducted an informal needs assessment with Allaneq teachers and students prior to taking on the principalship in the fall of 1999, one of the first problems that privately came to her attention was the "ghet-toization" of the Blue Team. The Team's students received only basic instruc-tion, and had become seen as "behavior problems." She decided to reshuffle the teams, abandoning learning styles as an organizational scheme and making each team internally diverse. This move was a deliberate and newly explicit at-tempt to de-racialize the school's organization. Turner described her rationale openly to her faculty, and argued that the new structure would pursue the main benefit of the team approach: the increased personal attention. She did not reshuffle the faculty teams, who by that time had worked out their inter-nal problems and were functioning well. She preserved the identity of the Fireweed team but increased the percentage of non-Native students to around 50 percent. Both faculty and students were enthusiastic about the changes she instituted. They especially appreciated the fact that she had listened to and reacted publicly to their quietly circulating complaints about the resegregated teams.

In the first school reform, racial segregation and reductive assumptions about students' learning or behavioral tendencies had been reproduced, with-out any public discussion to redirect the reform. Faculty had started to natu-ralize a direct connection between learning styles and racial-ethnic groups, and even to rank the schools and their students as more or less desirable. They never discussed in public this core problem of the school. Educators must call attention to the racial hierarchies that surface during school reforms; other-wise, they are likely to continue despite educators' good intentions.

RESOURCES

Hunter Cutting and Makani Themba-Nixon. 2006. *Talking the Walk: A Communica-tions Guide for Racial Justice.* Oakland, CA: AK Press.

R. Henze, A. Katz, E. Norte, S. Sather, and E. Walker. 2002. *Leading for Diversity: How School Leaders Promote Positive Interethnic Relations.* Thousand Oaks, CA: Corwin Press.

DISCUSSION QUESTIONS

1. **Principle:** If racial hierarchies in status or learning opportunity exist at your school, to what extent do you discuss or not discuss them as a faculty?

2. **Strategy:** What might be gained if you discussed existing racial hierar-chies with colleagues, students, or parents? What might be difficult about such a discussion?

3. **Try tomorrow:** How might you start a productive conversation with a colleague about how to understand and address any such racial hierarchy within your school? Role-play the interaction.

Rosemary Henze is a professor in the Linguistics and Language Development Department, San José State University, California. Her current areas of interest include school leadership; education for social justice; language and power relations; and the development of accessible forms of anthropological scholarship for the public.

50

Spearheading School-wide Reform

Willis D. Hawley

How can you and your colleagues start creating a school devoted to equal opportunity and outcomes, where students' racial and ethnic diversity enhances the learning opportunities of all? This essay compiles research on successful leaders of diverse schools to suggest how a whole faculty might get started on such school-wide reform.[1] (See also Resource list.)

Research suggests that successful principals of diverse schools engage all members of the school community in an overarching conversation about the benefits of diversity-enriched learning. That is, they clarify that a diverse school can actually provide students with learning opportunities and life advantages that students in more homogeneous schools do not have. Rather than setting up a special diversity team, they mainstream the responsibility of designing and implementing diversity-related school reforms. Together, the entire faculty has to create a comprehensive plan to help ensure that reforms will not be disconnected and episodic.

Research shows that your entire faculty and staff must be readied to take on new responsibilities, and to see their potential benefits for the entire school. Some colleagues will likely resist such change out of a belief that "race is not an issue here." A confidential student survey and discussion series on life at the school, alongside faculty discussions of data on racial and ethnic differences in student performance, retention, and discipline, can start to convince the more resistant faculty that differences in the school experiences of students of various racial and ethnic groups warrant attention.

Research shows that as a faculty and staff, you will need to initiate four types of ongoing conversation. You will need to start to (1) develop shared understandings about the benefits and challenges of improving the school experiences of your diverse student body; (2) identify, through collaborative problem solving, effective practices for enhancing interpersonal relationships and academic achievement in your diverse setting; (3) pinpoint the resources you need to implement these promising practices; and (4) create processes for continuous school improvement. So:

1. **Develop Shared Understandings.** All faculty and staff should participate in study groups to identify your school's current needs. Ideally, local experts on student learning in diverse settings can assist your study groups. The librarian can create a space in the school library for resources on teaching and learning in diverse settings. The groups should talk with students, examine research on enhancing student achievement, and look at what other successful schools are doing. You should report back to one another and, after considerable discussion, prepare a school community statement listing the general propositions you agree on. Here are some examples written by teachers:

- Improving relationships among people of different races and ethnicities in our school (both students and adults) requires the reduction of prejudice, but also the development of knowledge, understandings, and skills—i.e., "intercultural competencies"—that facilitate communication and collaboration.
- Creating a school climate that aggressively undermines racial and ethnic stereotypes and addresses the sources of intergroup tensions among teachers and students, and among students, will reduce discipline problems and, more importantly, motivate all students to achieve at high levels.
- Developing opportunities to learn with and from people of different races and ethnicities enhances everyone's capacities for complex problem solving.

As you identify shared understandings about teaching and learning in diverse settings, you and your colleagues should also add research-based statements to your school community statement, for example

- Biological differences among people of different racial and ethnic groups are virtually nonexistent.
- Even people of good will may harbor subtle and unrecognized prejudices.
- Efforts to sensitize students to the strengths and unique characteristics of different cultures are not sufficient to equalize opportunity.
- It is important to avoid over-generalizing (i.e., stereotyping) the dispositions and needs of people with similar skin color or ethnic background.

In order to promote common understanding of the implications of these propositions, the principal should post them in her office and in a public place in the school, such as the teachers' meeting room, and support continued discussion on the principles by hosting regular "community forums."

2. **Identify Effective Practices.** Research shows that a successful faculty creates new opportunities to analyze student performance and to share knowledge about how best to meet students' needs. It will be difficult initially to compare and propose ways to improve the performance and behavior of students of diverse racial groups and ethnicities, because some teachers will be uncertain about being perceived as confrontational, insensitive, naive, or racist. You and school leaders should encourage openness about uncertainty and norms of trust and mutual respect (for more guidelines, see Singleton and Hays, Chapter 4).

   A faculty engaged in collaborative efforts to identify effective practices for their diverse environment should recognize, discuss, and continue to elaborate on research-based propositions like the following:

- Teachers, administrators, and staff must share responsibility for student learning throughout the school.
- Instruction and curricula should ensure that all students have rigorous opportunities to learn.
- Understanding students' predispositions, ways of knowing, and personal histories enhances students' motivation to achieve and teachers' effectiveness. This requires that teachers know their students well.
- Instructional strategies should maximize the opportunities students of all racial groups and ethnicities have to learn with and from one another. These strategies include, among others, cooperative learning, differentiated instruction (tailoring instructional approaches to individual students' needs), peer tutoring, reciprocal teaching (where teacher and students share the role of instructor), and complex instruction (see Cohen and Lotan, in Resources).
- Efforts to improve racial and ethnic relations among teachers and students, and among students, should be integral to the overall school mission to enhance student learning, rather than compartmentalized in parts of the curriculum or in particular student groups or activities.

3. **Develop Necessary Resources.** Research shows that successful reformers work to strengthen professional development, form partnerships with families and community organizations, and secure district support for the school's reform efforts. Most professional development can occur through collaborative faculty problem solving about meeting specific instructional, developmental, and interpersonal challenges identified by the continuous analysis of student performance. You can

restructure the school schedule to provide for common planning times and weekly professional development, so that the school community has time to engage in this collaborative learning and action.

Research shows that administrators should also work to identify ways that families and community organizations could inform and support the reform. For example, reform will require efforts to improve communication with families with limited English proficiency, to design student assignments that help all families help their children to learn, and to help community organizations engage in activities that support students' in-school learning experiences.

The principal will have to remember that district support will also determine the reform's eventual success or failure. She should work closely with senior district staff to help them understand how the reform contributes to the development of skills that are essential to success in life and to higher academic performance.

4. **Make School Improvement Continuous.** Since many good ideas lose momentum over time, your faculty, in collaboration with your principal, will have to pursue several strategies to sustain the reform effort. You should initiate regular faculty, staff, and student discussions of potentially controversial issues. You should also develop processes for mediating interpersonal conflict and dealing with perceived internal inequity and discrimination. Above all, you should continuously, and collaboratively, analyze information about racial patterns in student achievement, student discipline, and the demographic composition of extracurricular activities. You must remain committed to discussing, on a regular basis, all the ideas and actions that will be necessary to improve student learning and performance.

RESOURCES

James A. Banks, Peter Cookson, Geneva Gay, Willis D. Hawley, Jacqueline Jordan Irvine, Sonia Nieto, Janet Ward Schofield, and Walter G. Stephan. 2001. *Diversity Within Unity: Essential Principles for Teaching and Learning in a Multicultural Society.* Seattle: University of Washington, Center for Multicultural Education. Accessed November 24, 2006, at http://www.educ.washington.edu/coetestwebsite/pdf/DiversityUnity.pdf.

Elizabeth Cohen and Rachel Lotan, eds. 1997. *Waiting for Equity in Heterogeneous Classrooms: Sociological Theory in Action.* New York: Teachers College Press.

Rosemary Henze, Anne Katz, Edmundo Norte, Susan E. Sather, and Ernest Walker. 2002. *Leading for Diversity: How School Leaders Promote Positive Interethnic Relations.* Thousand Oaks, CA: Corwin Press.

Randall B. Lindsey, Kikanza N. Robins, and Raymond D. Terrell. 2003. *Cultural Proficiency: A Manual for School Leaders.* 2nd ed. Thousand Oaks, CA: Corwin Press.

Teaching Tolerance: www.tolerance.org/. Teaching Tolerance has free resources for classroom teachers—a website, videos, and a quarterly magazine.

DISCUSSION QUESTIONS

1. **Principle:** Why is it necessary to integrate diversity-related school reforms with general school reform efforts, rather than separate the two agendas?
2. **Strategy:** How can educators best convince colleagues to join together in school-wide efforts related to diversity and equity?
3. **Try tomorrow:** If you were to spearhead a school-wide effort to capitalize on the diversity of your school's population, how would you start that discussion with your colleagues and administrators? What goals or school-wide needs would you examine first?

Willis D. Hawley is Emeritus Professor of Education and Public Policy at the University of Maryland. His research deals with the design and implementation of policies and practices that affect school improvement, race relations, school integration, and the professional development of teachers and school administrators.

Part XVIII

Analyze, with Colleagues and Students, How Your Race Affects Your Teaching

Educators often spend far more time discussing their students' racial identities and experiences than discussing their own. The essays in this part share a core principle of everyday antiracism: *educators need to discuss how their own teaching orientations might be linked to their experiences in the world as a racial group member.*

How can educators start discussing, with colleagues or students, the role their own "race" might play in their teaching?

1. Discuss students' use of the "n-word."
   Wendy Luttrell proposes that teachers can spark needed conversations about how their "race" affects their authority by discussing what they do when students say the "n-word."

2. Engage in cross-racial dialogue with your colleagues.
   Alice McIntyre suggests that teachers regularly convene interracial discussion groups to share ideas about teaching.

3. Identify who you are in relation to the curriculum.
   Priya Parmar and Shirley Steinberg propose that educators discuss, with students, how their own backgrounds position them in relation to the material they are teaching.

4. Notice how racial lenses shape ideas about "good" teaching.
   Lee Bell suggests that educators discuss, with colleagues, varying definitions of "good teaching."

51

Responding to the "N-Word"

Wendy Luttrell

On the first day back at school, students greet one another after the long summer break. A common racial epithet spoken without apparent malice punctuates black students' dialogue as they hail each other and renew their friendships. A white, female teacher walking down the hall bristles when she hears the "n-word" but remains silent. An African American female teacher calls out, "Hey, watch your mouth." "Sorry, Miss," a student replies. The two teachers exchange glances, and the white teacher says to the African American teacher, "they'll listen to you, but if I say anything, they say, 'c'mon, that's just how we talk.'"

What do you do when you hear students use the "n-word"? (I use this form throughout the chapter; I prefer not to use the word itself because I find it hurtful and because the term "n-word" was commonly used by the teachers who are represented in this essay.) Does it matter what racial group the speaker belongs to? Does it matter what racial group you belong to? Does it matter whether you hear the word in the hallway or your classroom? What determines your response as an educator?

Some teachers argue that there are more pressing concerns than responding to their students' use of the n-word. Perhaps. But discussing how to respond to students' use of the n-word is a valuable entry point for dialogue among teachers about the relevance of race to their teaching practice, especially their exercise of authority and efforts to establish trust with students.

Teachers can engage in conversations with students about the n-word by discussing the complex distinctions between the violence-stained use of the term "nigger" throughout history and the contemporary, sometimes empowering appropriation of the term "niggah" in youth culture (see Resource list for suggestions). But that is not the task of this essay. Here I consider why it is important for teachers to talk among themselves about racially loaded incidents such as students' use of the n-word. These discussions bring to the surface a whole range of perspectives and emotions raised by teaching across racial lines. As teachers enter these conversations, it is important to acknowledge that there is no one "right" way for a teacher to respond to a student's use of the n-word, and that responses depend on the context of the usage; teachers should consider a wide range of strategies and anticipate that the intervention may raise a lot of anxieties. Discussing the issue as a staff has great potential for building a community in which teachers can talk openly across racial lines about the role of race in their work.

Between 2000 and 2003, Janie Ward and I convened monthly meetings with teachers in Boston-area public schools to discuss their experiences as urban educators. The research project, "Accessing Strengths and Supporting Resistance in Teaching," aimed to develop professional materials grounded in teacher knowledge and inquiry. The gender and racial composition of the groups differed in different schools, but participants reflected the city's teaching force, which is 75 percent female, 70.5 percent white, 15.1 percent black, non-Hispanic, 10.4 percent Hispanic, and 2.2 percent Asian.[1] We wanted to know, from their perspective, what the "hot-button" issues were in their schools and what role, if any, they believed they should have in addressing them. Teachers expressed a wide range of concerns about the influence of youth culture on school climate and, some argued, on student achievement: issues of language use, do-rags, hoods, or "x-rated" mannerisms were prominent in our discussions.[2] The n-word issue particularly opened discussion about white teachers' racial self-awareness. The participating white teachers had had little opportunity to discuss this topic, which is likely to be avoided by white Americans in interracial settings.[3]

The predominantly female teachers in our study, regardless of race, agreed that the n-word holds different meanings for their students than it does for them. But the white teachers expressed more hesitation than their African American or Latina peers about reprimanding students, particularly black students, when they used this term. The conversations were framed as if it were assumed that students of color were the ones using the n-word, as evidenced by such statements as "of course if I heard a *white* student use it, like hate speech, I would intervene." Some white teachers admitted haltingly that they refrained from reprimanding students precisely because they were white and female and believed they stood no chance of being listened to. In response, the participating teachers of color, especially the African American teachers, said they were quick to chastise students who used it, not only because they felt at ease as a consequence of sharing racial group membership but also because they found the word wrong and hurtful.

Some of the white teachers had explicit rules forbidding the use of the n-word in their classrooms but actively ignored its use in hallways and the cafeteria. One white teacher said that she used to explain her reasons to students, including the need for students to develop vocabulary that was more suited for "professional" settings like schools and workplaces, but she no longer felt she had time to "waste" on the topic. Another white teacher explained why she had stopped trying to respond at all: "I used to intervene, and then I got so many

threats and I got called so many names and I got no backup and I said, 'OK.' . . .
And now it is hand[s] off. But if it happens in my classroom, it is different."

As these discussions unfolded and more strategies were exchanged, we
found that one recurring theme galvanized debate: white women's position
and authority vis-à-vis their students of color. One white teacher wondered
aloud about how "hard a line" she should take with her black students generally and wrestled with her place as a white woman to "judge" "respectful" behavior: "The classroom is like my home and I spend a lot of time here. I just
don't want to hear these words. Actually I don't want to hear them at home either. But maybe what I'm trying to say is, yes, I would like them to have a
more respectful way of dealing with each other. But then, I'm not quite sure.
Am I passing . . . (long pause)—maybe the judgment I pass is not entirely useful." Another white female teacher said haltingly, "I don't feel like I'm in a position to tell them whether or not they can use that word." Another white
female teacher summed up her colleagues' basic concerns more explicitly:
"How much do I really know about this thing? Am I equipped to be someone
who can give a [black] child wisdom about this?"

These explanations raised a crucial issue for these colleagues to discuss:
how and whether white teachers are warranted, or warranted differently from
teachers of color, to guide or discipline students of color. The white female
teachers agreed that it took time to establish the trust that was required for
them to feel comfortable asserting their authority. As one white teacher explained, "my gender, race, and class are against me." She described how, over
time, she had to work to get students to trust her "despite my race and class":
"I feel that I have to show them that I respect them for who they are as people for a long time . . . before they and I can get through the race and class
thing. . . . It gets much easier as we've made that leap into trusting . . . and to
them trusting in my care for them, despite my race and class."

White teachers felt unease and even pain associated with the need to prove
to students of color that they have their best interests at heart. They had had
few opportunities to discuss their doubts with their colleagues. Some white
teachers acknowledged that they were plagued by feelings of vulnerability, insecurity, and fear of being exposed as an unwitting racist. Many cited cultural
axioms stressing the difficulty of understanding others across race lines, such
as "it's a black thing" and "white people don't understand," as suggesting that
they were unwarranted in advising black students to act differently or even in
teaching them at all. Not all the participating white teachers explicitly con-
fessed this vulnerability; some embraced colorblindness, insisting they did not
"see color" at all. In this anxious conversation, space was opened for these
difficult emotions to be considered rather than avoided.

As the teachers discussed one another's efforts to establish trust and safety
in the classroom so that black students would view white teachers' power as
legitimate rather than simply coercive, some teachers of color expressed a

concern that white teachers might be avoiding their role as authorities and advisors. Ella, an African American teacher, posed a question to her white colleagues: "I was thinking when I was listening to the pieces about trust . . . that has never come up for me in working with students of color or for white students. I don't know if it's racial . . . these issues of trust and concerns about safe spaces that I hear a lot from white teachers."

Ella suggested that students trusted her and, more importantly, that she trusted her own judgment, exercise of authority, and connection with both students of color and white students. She then reflected on her own strategy for exercising authority, invoking a "mamma attitude" that she believes makes her an effective teacher of racially diverse children: "It's my stern voice . . . and I can imagine their mother figure using it during times of trouble. I know that they know I mean business when this momma attitude comes from me towards them." While the strategy Ella offered was an individual one, it draws upon her affiliation with other African American "mother figures." Her comfort with this strategy was in some part racially based. She suggested that she and her African American students shared ideas about power and authority, such as what it means to "mean business." Yet her suggestion for matter-of-factly exercising power and authority resonates with research on the specific behaviors that successful black and white teachers employ to foster black students' schooling success, including seeing oneself as a surrogate parent, which some call "othermothering."[4] At the heart of Ella's strategy is her confidence in her authority, and that was the main message she wanted to pass on to her white colleagues. Stirred by her comments, other teachers of color began asking why white teachers tolerated disruptive or self-defeating behaviors from students of color, which opened up important issues.

The scholarly literature suggests three possible explanations for white teachers' reluctance to exercise authority: "racial fear, moral distance, and the presumption that black children are by nature 'bad.'"[5] To this I would add another reason raised in our conversations about the n-word: having no chance to discuss feelings of disconnection and vulnerability as white teachers. Sekani Moyenda has argued that because there is typically no vehicle in white people's lives for actively discussing and interpreting racism with people of color, white teachers are unpracticed and at times fearful of what they will learn about their own racism.[6]

Both white teachers and teachers of color need practice holding discussions outside of their "comfort zones" about the relevance of race to their teaching. These conversations should be ongoing and undertaken with commitment to gaining the wisdom that it takes to educate children both within and across racial lines for the obstacles they face and opportunities they seek. These conversations carry risks of falling into familiar, destructive patterns of cross-racial dialogue; white guilt and paralysis and black anger can highjack the effort if people back away. White colleagues may resist by initially embracing colorblindness, and colleagues of color involuntarily positioned as authorities on the subject may express resentment and withdraw. To promote and help guide these conversations, we have designed an online teacher professional development course, *Understanding Self, Race, Gender, and Class to Leverage Student Achievement*, which was successfully piloted in the Milwaukee Public Schools in 2005–2006. (See Resource list.) Online communication allows for a continuous cycle of reflection and response that deepens dialogue and supports new action. It can help many teachers to discuss racism with people outside their comfort zones, increasing their confidence and willingness to talk with their own colleagues in person.

As the participants in our conversations agreed, responding to students with caring authority can take various forms. Some teachers simply tell students not to use the n-word in school spaces; others engage students in critical inquiry about the n-word, its history, and its usage in contemporary youth culture; still other teachers might better ignore its usage at certain moments. As you figure out your own strategy, what is most important is that you and your colleagues start discussing, with one another, all the complex feelings about race and authority that these interactions raise for teachers.

RESOURCES

Randall Kennedy. 2002. *Nigger: The Strange Career of a Troublesome Word*. New York: Pantheon Books.
Understanding Self, Race, Gender, and Class to Leverage Student Achievement. For access contact Wendy Luttrell at wendy.luttrell@gmail.com.

DISCUSSION QUESTIONS

1. **Principle:** When does your own racial group membership seem to matter as you guide student behavior? When does it not seem to matter?
2. **Strategy:** In general, what do you think a teacher should do when she hears the n-word?
3. **Try tomorrow:** What other specific issues of race and authority would you most like to discuss with your colleagues? What question would you ask to start this conversation once you were assembled? Role-play the situation.

Wendy Luttrell is Aronson Associate Professor of Human Development and Education at the Harvard Graduate School of Education, and studies the relationship between culture, identity, and schooling. Her books and publications explore how schools shape students' beliefs about worth, value, knowledge, and power, especially regarding gender, race, ethnicity, class, and sexuality.

52

Engaging Diverse Groups of Colleagues in Conversation

Alice McIntyre

For many years, I taught a multicultural education course in a graduate school of education that was populated predominantly by white middle-class students. During a discussion about racism and urban education, one of the white students stated that it was not racism that kept some students from learning: "Inner-city kids, and most of them are kids of color, and this is not racism, this is a fact, most inner-city kids don't want to learn. They just don't care."

I heard variations on this comment, which matter-of-factly dismissed the intellectual aspirations of youth of color, many times, in my classroom and in my research with prospective teachers.[1] In my classroom, often, students would continue as if their peer's comment were a realistic assessment of the issue under discussion. In this case, when no one challenged or questioned the student's remark, I invited her and the rest of the class to discuss how they knew that inner-city students of color did not want to learn. This invitation led to a difficult but informative discussion that is ongoing and takes place in many of the courses I teach today.

I credit my ability to prompt inquiry on fraught racial remarks to my being an active member of a cross-racial dialogue group.[2] The group I belonged to emerged out of conflict. At the time of its inception, the women of color with whom I attended graduate school were frustrated with the ways in which some of the white students, including me, were failing to address racial issues. Out of their frustration, the women of color asked a faculty member to organize a meeting with white students aimed at exploring strategies for addressing the racism they were experiencing in the school environment.

The four women of color and the four European American women who ultimately became the ongoing participants in the group came to the dialogue with varied agendas, shifting levels of trust and mistrust, and a desire to address racial injustices in our personal and professional lives. Over the course of four years, we explored a host of issues related to racism and whiteness. One issue that we struggled with was how to intervene when students or colleagues make comments denigrating, stereotyping, or inaccurately representing people of color in class, faculty meetings, or informal discussions.

The women of color felt that most white students and white faculty members are too afraid to speak up when a colleague or student makes a racist remark. They consistently challenged the white women in the group to "do something" rather than remain silent. Silence, they argued, was a form of complicity. The white women in the group agreed that we had a responsibility to speak up when we heard racist comments. Yet we disagreed about how and when to do so. We agreed that white faculty members, more than their peers of color, need to take a visible stand against racism in the settings in which we find ourselves. Yet we found it difficult to find a fixed response that would fit every situation. All of us realized that each woman in the group had a distinct personality and a particular way of engaging the world, and that those individual factors shape our responses to racist comments.

We did not always resolve the dilemmas that we presented to one another in our meetings. When I discussed the incident with which this essay begins, some of the women in the group thought it would have been better for me to stop the class immediately and address the student's comment. Others thought that I should have waited until the end of the class, hoping that one of the other students would question the statement.

At times we became frustrated with one another, with a specific issue, and with our lack of clarity about how to address various forms of racism. During those moments, we withdrew into silence, changed the subject, cracked a joke, or simply agreed to disagree. At times, those responses were distancing. Yet we forged relationships as women committed to accompanying one another in the process of unlearning and undoing racism. We learned to tolerate moments of disconnection and to integrate them into an ongoing process of dialogue and collaboration.

As a white educator, I find that dialogues with other white teachers are important but not sufficient for me to become more effective as an antiracist educator. Homogeneity within the teaching profession can too easily mute self-evaluation and collective critique.[3] Many antiracist white people want to be perceived as different from "those other whites," the racist ones (see Thompson, Chapter 61). White people are often unable to notice, name, and challenge our racist assumptions and beliefs when we talk only to one another.

It is essential for me and, I believe, for other white people to talk with people of color as we work for individual, institutional, and social change. People of color bring to the table profoundly different life experiences and perspectives that whites need to hear. Just as importantly, mutual dialogue with white people who are committed to challenging racial injustice can free educators of color from a role as racial group representatives and native informants that they are often forced into in their interactions with white educators who are less interested in this challenge.

We should take responsibility for initiating dialogues about race and teaching with both white and nonwhite colleagues. Although our environments may be racially unbalanced, we must always attempt to expand intra-group discussions into interracial dialogues.

The questions that guided many discussions in our cross-racial group include: how does our racial group membership influence our teaching? How does being a white teacher or a teacher of color affect our relationships with other teachers? With students who belong to the same and different racial-ethnic groups? How do we, as teachers, address racism in our school, and how can we do so more successfully? What racial incidents have taken place recently in our school, and how well were they handled?

Some schools have no faculty of color, a situation whose roots we should examine. In such situations, white teachers can together tackle racism in the institutions where we work. We can examine our own racial histories and explore what it means for us to be white. We can read first-person accounts of white people who have reflected on their own racial histories and have committed themselves to engaging in antiracist activities. (See Resource list for two recent examples.)[4] We can engage in professional development activities that provide us with opportunities to explore and undo racist attitudes and actions.[5] But engaging in ongoing cross-racial dialogue with committed friends and colleagues will particularly encourage us to challenge racism in our classrooms and professional communities.

RESOURCES

Ruth Frankenberg. 1996. "When We are Capable of Stopping, We Begin to See: Being White, Seeing Whiteness." In Becky W. Thompson and Sangeeta Tyagi, eds., *Names We Call Home: Autobiography on Racial Identity*, 3–17. New York: Routledge.

Mab Segrest. 1994. *Memoir of a Race Traitor.* Boston: South End Press.

DISCUSSION QUESTIONS

1. **Principle:** How can we pursue dialogue in a multiracial group without implying that group members are responsible for speaking for the racial group to which they belong?

2. **Strategy:** What particular learning experiences do you think a cross-racial dialogue group of colleagues at your school might offer? In which circumstances, if any, might dialogues within a racial-ethnic group be a useful starting point?

3. **Try tomorrow:** If you were to form a cross-racial dialogue group at your school, how would you solicit participants? What might be the first thing you would say at the first meeting? Role-play the interaction.

Alice McIntyre is professor and chairperson of the Elementary Education Program at Hellenic College in Brookline, MA. She has written extensively about whiteness, education, and the use of participatory action research (PAR) to address issues salient to inner-city youth in the United States and women in the north of Ireland.

53

Locating Yourself for Your Students

Priya Parmar and Shirley Steinberg

As teachers, we have found that identifying ourselves to students in terms of our own positionality—that is, naming exactly who we are in terms of the racial, ethnic, and religious group memberships that affect our social position—has been a way to carve a safe space for students in which to discuss sensitive racial and ethnic matters. We have also found that as educators, we cannot possibly begin to teach with frankness unless we name who we are in relation to our curriculum and admit what we do and do not know.

We are both professors of education; Steinberg identifies herself as Jewish and White, Parmar as Asian Indian. We have been working in the public high schools of Brooklyn and the Bronx using hip-hop as a way to interest students in literacy. In four schools, we have been collaborating with a spoken word collective and high school teachers to write, perform, and publish poetry via poetry slams. When we start working with the students in these classes, we meet them, explain our program, and explain our vision of using hip-hop to create art. This essay focuses not on our curriculum but on how we introduce ourselves. What we thought was just part of being authentic educators has become one of the most essential parts of our pedagogy.

Shirley: When I began to work with adolescents in an all-Black and Latino/a high school in the poorest part of the Bronx, I knew I was not only old—a product of the sixties—but also White and Jewish. My goal was to utilize students' knowledge of hip-hop as a vehicle for literacy. The first time I worked with a class, I waited for the teacher to introduce me. He mentioned I was a professor, and the students were understandably bored. I have never felt so White, so over-thirty, or so not hip-hop. After he called me to the front, a few students clapped, but most did not even look up.

I stood in front of about thirty students, looked around, and began: "I'll bet you're wondering what a frizzy-haired Jewish woman is doing up here talking to you about hip-hop." There was not a sound in the room, and then a girl turned to the class: "No, she didn't." The students hooted, clapped, and laughed. She added she had never heard a white person say they were White, and the other students agreed. Interestingly, I had not said I was White;

I said I was Jewish. But I was obviously White, and that is what she saw and heard. We began to discuss race. They said they knew at every moment of their lives that they were not White, but they felt White people did not know that they were White. Months later they would still recall the time I said I was Jewish, laugh, and shake their heads that no other White person had ever told them that. They said they appreciated that in our classroom, they did not have to act as if it were a secret that I was White, while they were expected to talk about being Black, Latino, or Asian—topics that the hip-hop curriculum naturally raised.

Priya: As I began work with adolescents in three Brooklyn high schools predominantly composed of Black and/or Latino/a students, I introduced myself to the classes in a way that I felt would link me to the students. Before coming up to the front, I saw that I was the only Indian or South Asian in the room. I wondered to myself if the school had any Indian students. Raised in a rural town in central Pennsylvania, I was always aware that I was different. Feeling very alone as a youth, I turned to hip-hop and found music and words that fit how I related to the world. After finishing my dissertation on KRS-One and hip-hop culture, I felt my experiences, expertise, and scholarship would work well in our school collaborations.

Like Shirley, I was introduced to the class by the teacher. The students were equally unexcited. I faced them and, feeling like I could read their minds, I knew I had to name who I was. I began to speak about my feelings of alienation as a woman of color in a White school. The students were visibly shocked. As Latino/as and African Americans, they had never thought of South Asians as persons of color. My comment about my own color was surprising to them, as was my knowledge of hip-hop and familiarity with their musical tastes and idols. Unlike Shirley, I discussed my positionality as one of shared oppression and alienation. My candor, like Shirley's, reached the students, and they were immediately more comfortable with my efforts to engage them in these conversations as an educator.

Both of us realized that our willingness to discuss our race and ethnicity with our students allowed them to feel more comfortable as we worked together. Race was not always discussed, but in this hip-hop curriculum, much of the writing the students chose to do centered on racial identity and, at times, gender and class, and critiques of racism. Their poetry and writing naturally went to their own identity issues, self-identification, and positionality. As adolescents they were acutely conscious of how they appeared to peers. But this was the first time for many that they were able to self-identify to adult educators and be confident that we would listen. Our students began to write and perform passionately about the recovery of their own ethnic identities, and their struggles as young women and men of color living in a male-dominated and white-dominated society.

As we engage students with hip-hop and literacy, we now always name our positionality; when introducing our curriculum, we say who we are in relation to it. We say what we know and what we do not know. This self-identification has helped us bridge the gaps that we feared would be too broad as we undertook a curriculum that was seemingly the students' own. These experiences have kept us thinking about how educators are often afraid of racial differences and fearful of naming them. Because whiteness is so often treated as invisible, as if only non-Whites are racially and ethnically positioned, White teachers often are particularly afraid to name their own positionality. Identity, including whiteness, is not absolute or fixed; rather, identity is always changing and evolving. Yet we contend that the denial of the existence of the educator's own positionality creates more barriers and a lack of trust, especially when students are asked so often to name theirs. When an educator's whiteness is unnamed, it remains in a dominant position, reinforcing that it is the noncolor color by which all other colors are measured. We have seen that when White teachers in racially mixed classrooms are unable or unwilling to name their own position in relation to the curriculum, they fail to engage their students in important inquiry that challenges the boundaries of all categories, including whiteness, frames all identity as changing and evolving, and critically examines the often unnamed dominance of whiteness in popular ideology.[1] Alternatively, to spark such inquiry, it is often equally important for non-White educators to name their positionality.

The desire of many adolescents of color to choose race and ethnicity as a theme in their writing is strong. After educators position themselves regarding these issues, students are freer to discuss issues of race beyond their own identities. Particularly when White educators name their identities in conversations with students and disclose how they view their knowledge in relation to the curriculum they teach, students feel freer to discuss how they view not only the educator, but also themselves and the world.

RESOURCES

Gary Howard. 2006. *We Can't Teach What We Don't Know: White Teachers in Multicultural Classrooms*. 2nd ed. New York: Teachers College Press.

R. Jensen. 2005. *The Heart of Whiteness: Confronting Race, Racism and White Privilege*. San Francisco: City Lights Books.

T. Wise. 2004. *White Like Me: Reflections on Race from a Privileged Son*. New York: Soft Skull Books.

DISCUSSION QUESTIONS

1. **Principle:** How can you imagine it being useful to position yourself in terms of your racial-ethnic group membership, prior knowledge, or life experience in relation to your curriculum? Under what circumstances do you think it might *not* be useful to do so?

2. **Strategy:** What types of "positioning" statements made by a teacher might make your school's students feel more comfortable and ready to inquire? What types of positioning statements might reduce that comfort and spirit of inquiry?

3. **Try tomorrow:** What might you say to students in your own classroom to start to position yourself in relation to some unit or topic you teach? Try role-playing this introduction.

Priya Parmar earned her doctorate from the Pennsylvania State University in 2002 in curriculum and instruction with an emphasis in language and literacy education. Her scholarly interests include critical, multiple literacies, multicultural education, youth culture, and other contemporary issues in the field of cultural studies in which economic, political, and social justice issues are addressed.

Shirley R. Steinberg teaches at McGill University. Her areas of research encompass youth culture, social justice, and education (race, class, gender, sexuality issues), critical pedagogy, and cultural and media studies. She is the founding editor of Taboo: The Journal of Culture and Education.

54

Expanding Definitions of "Good Teaching"

Lee Anne Bell

Several years ago, I spent a school year with a multiracial group of third-through sixth-grade girls in an urban elementary school examining issues of gender, race, and achievement.[1] Over nine months of weekly meetings and multiple classroom observations, I got to know these girls and their teachers quite well. One day I asked the girls to tell me about the qualities of their favorite teacher. Before I could add, "Don't tell me a name, just the qualities," came a unanimous chorus, "Ms. Johnson! Ms. Johnson!" When I probed to find out why she was their favorite teacher, one white fourth-grader said, "Because we know she loves us!" The eager nods of other girls in the group affirmed that the speaker had gotten it right.

This conversation challenged my own assumptions about good teaching, because I had not seen Ms. Johnson as a notably good teacher. After observing Ms. Johnson's classroom two or three times, I considered her loud and over-bearing. I had a specific model of good teaching that regards warmth and positive feedback as an essential way of engaging student voices and encouraging democratic participation in the learning community. Until then, I had not considered that there might be other ways of reaching these goals, or even that warmth could be expressed in various voice tones and at other volumes. Clearly the students saw warmth and encouragement in Ms. Johnson's style that I had failed to see.

Curious to know more, I asked Ms. Johnson to sit down with me to talk about teaching, and she graciously agreed. In the course of our conversation, I asked her how she had decided to become a teacher and what her goals were for her classroom. She told me she had grown up in a cohesive, conservative, all-black working-class community in the segregated South. During her middle and high school years, she had excelled as a learner but felt that, as a black girl, she had been discouraged from developing her full potential based on gender stereotypes held by her black teachers, both male and female. She stated that she pushed her female students in ways she wished she herself had been pushed. She was convinced that this would help her students overcome barriers of sexism, racism, and poverty. Her intentions were clear to the girls—both white and of color—in her classes, who recognized the ways she challenged them as a sign of love. Ms. Johnson consciously created a classroom community in which issues of challenging societal discrimination were raised and deliberated, and the girls recognized this, too, as a "loving" pedagogy.

I have often reflected on the lessons this experience offered me as a teacher educator. I now realize that as a white educator and researcher observing the classes of Ms. Johnson, a black teacher, I had silently judged her teaching through an unconscious racialized lens that did not encompass a black educator's alternative vision of progressive pedagogy. The experience led me to see how easy it is for those from dominant groups to judge others according to unexamined notions of what constitutes good teaching.[2] In this case, I unconsciously applied assumptions about good teaching based on an unacknowledged white and middle-class norm that could see only "warm fuzzy" teaching demeanors as good. I implicitly embraced a color-blind view of progressive pedagogy that did not take into account how educators who did not grow up white or middle-class might differently approach a pedagogy grounded in shared progressive goals but different prior schooling experiences.

As a white, middle-class person, I could take for granted that my definitions of good teaching would be supported by research, journals, and books created largely by people like me and, though grounded in our particular experiences, presented as universal truths. My encounter with Ms. Johnson and her students encouraged me to examine the ways in which quick assumptions about what constitutes "good teaching" so often prevent white middle-class people like myself from listening carefully across racial and class lines to find expertise in colleagues' teaching, stunting a fuller development of our own pedagogy. I also learned the importance of gaining expertise from educators who share membership in students' racial and class communities, and have honed their abilities to connect with students on that basis.

I learned that Ms. Johnson wanted her students to become strong, independent, and able to think critically about their lives, and she wanted them to have the tools to confront injustice. Her pedagogy of challenge was backed up by a purposefully constructed classroom community in which students could raise and consider issues of prejudice, bias, and discrimination and be supported by their teacher. She had a bold presence in the classroom, spoke loudly, and demanded a lot. She knew all of her students and their families well, saw them frequently in the grocery store or at church, and felt personally responsible for their behavior and achievement. Her students of all racial groups knew that she cared about them and trusted her challenges as important to their learning.

I am embarrassed to admit how easily I jumped to conclusions about Ms. Johnson that were based on superficial knowledge and unconscious assumptions about her practice. After my encounter with Ms. Johnson, I started researching how racial location can shape perspective. My interviews with teachers from diverse racial groups revealed some of the assumptions about good teaching we bring to our classrooms. They illustrated the tendency of white teachers to invoke "colorblindness" when describing their own and other educators' practices, while showing that teachers of color more often insist that race and culture matter to teaching and must be acknowledged so as to be addressed.[3] Ms. Johnson was attuned to issues of race in the lives of her diverse students and shaped her pedagogy accordingly. She was preparing them to navigate an unequal and racist world successfully. Her pedagogical approach worked.

As educators, we should start a dialogue across racial boundaries to help us recognize ideas about good teaching that might otherwise be stifled or overlooked. We can also read about the alternative perspectives and practices of successful teachers, particularly teachers of color (see Resource list). Further, dialogue about pedagogy with colleagues of color does not have to start with queries about race per se. Ms. Johnson was far more than a "black teacher"; she was a successful teacher, with a unique set of pedagogies. To elicit Ms. Johnson's perspectives about good teaching, I simply needed to ask her what she was seeking to accomplish. Listening to individual colleagues' ideas about good teaching requires a long-term commitment to developing authentic personal relationships through dialogue.

Through our conversations, I learned that Ms. Johnson and I both believed in learning as a process of active engagement and were committed to creating classrooms that challenge and support students in developing their critical capacities. Listening to her views and the experiences that shaped them has broadened and enriched my own pedagogy in ways that I doubt I would have found on my own. I now pay much more attention to racial dynamics in my own classroom, and I think more consciously about how I as a white educator can help prepare my students from all racial groups to navigate a racist society.

RESOURCES

Lisa Delpit. 1988. *Other People's Children: Cultural Conflict in the Classroom.* New York: The New Press.

Lisa Delpit and Joanne Kilgore Dowdy, eds. 2002. *The Skin That We Speak: Thoughts on Language and Culture in the Classroom.* New York: The New Press.

Jacqueline Jordan Irvine. 2003. *Seeing with a Cultural Eye: Educating Teachers for Diversity.* New York: Teachers College Press.

Gloria Ladson-Billings. 1994. *The Dreamkeepers: Successful Teachers of African-American Children.* San Francisco: Jossey-Bass.

DISCUSSION QUESTIONS

1. **Principle:** What assumptions do you carry about what good teaching is? Where might those assumptions have come from?
2. **Strategy:** Thinking back, how might you have overlooked the "good teaching" in another teacher's practices? Why?
3. **Try tomorrow:** Think of one of your colleagues from another racial group whose pedagogy you admire. How could you start a conversation with him or her about it? Role-play the situation.

Lee Anne Bell is professor and director of education at Barnard College, Columbia University. Her research and teaching focus on issues of race, racism, and social justice in teacher education. She supervises student teachers in New York City public schools and mentors new teachers through the Barnard New Teacher Network.

SECTION E

Engaging Communities for Real

Part XIX

Inquire Fully about Home Communities

We know families are crucial, but as educators, we often make insufficient efforts to actually connect to families and communities. Often, we neglect to get to know students' communities in any real detail, or even imply unwittingly that communities are not worth getting to know. The essays in this part share a core principle of everyday antiracism: *reductive or denigrating ideas about home communities must be replaced by thorough inquiry into home communities.*

How can educators get started in thorough inquiry about students' home communities?

1. Respect and seek to learn about students' home worlds.

   Eugene García suggests that educators remember that single actions can convey to students the teacher's sense of the worthiness or unworthiness of their families.

2. Start getting to know your students' communities.

   Leisy Wyman and Grant Kashatok lay out a full set of issues and minefields educators must consider in trying to get to know their students' communities.

3. Help students to investigate and document their complex communities.

   Kathleen Cushman proposes methods for getting students to research and analyze their own communities.

55

Valuing Students' Home Worlds

Eugene E. García

My sister looked forward to her first day at school. Her older brothers and sisters reminded her that school was important, even though they went to their farm work as usual. My mother accompanied her to the one-room schoolhouse. The teacher was held in high esteem by both the farm and ranch owners and the laborers of this rural Colorado community. While her siblings had picked up some English in school, my sister, like the rest of the family, spoke primarily Spanish. Our European and indigenous ancestors had decided to stay in the territory Mexico ceded to the United States by the Treaty of Guadalupe Hidalgo in 1848, at the end of the war. Spanish had been the language of this part of the country for centuries; English was the language of the new immigrants from other parts of the United States.

As always, the question "What is your name?" greeted my sister on her first day of school. "Ciprianita," she answered happily. The teacher tried to pronounce the name and then politely requested, "Can I call you Elsie? It is my favorite name." In that instant, my sister's linguistic and cultural heritage was challenged and, in my mother's presence, her child's *raíces*, roots, were metaphorically severed. Ciprianita had developed her social roots in her Spanish-speaking family. The teacher meant no harm. She wanted to replace Ciprianita's unfamiliar name with a more familiar one. It probably did not seem significant to the teacher. But my sister can never forget that first day of school: to her, it represented the moment when she was told to leave her full self at home. A teacher's response to a student's home background can make a critical difference. To this day, my sister still goes by the name "Elsie," and retelling this story always brings tears to her eyes. She and other Latino children learned that they had to leave their Spanish-speaking selves at the schoolhouse door.

In the most positive interpretation, changing a student's name when she enters school could signify the educational philosophy that who you are—rich or poor, Anglo or Latino—does not matter in school. Despite the group-based differences embodied in names, everyone will be treated as equals, so names are not really important. In the most negative interpretation, changing a student's name could signal an unwillingness to respect the student's cultural and linguistic background and set the stage for other instructional and institutional practices that do the same thing, such as ignoring the child's family history of immigration, or exclusively using literature that students cannot identify with. It might suggest to the student and her family that they do not belong in the school because the deepest marker of the home self, a child's given name, does not belong. Our family was left with a sense of loss as we struggled to interpret how to react to a new name thrust into our family.

Ciprianita's experience highlights why it is so important to broadcast in everyday ways that we respect the home practices and linguistic roots of our students and seek to understand them. Names signify the personal and cultural identities students carry from home. Teachers must respect and seek to understand many other roots that students bring into the classroom. After this first moment that Ciprianita was disrespected, "Elsie" never did well in school, and she did not graduate from high school. My mother often refused to visit the school with any of us from then on, feeling disrespected by the teachers' offhanded erasures of her children's home lives. Still, our mother always asked us if we had behaved ourselves at school; she never asked what we were learning, assuming this was the teacher's role, just as her role at home was to teach us what we needed to be successful in the home environment. Neither my mother nor my siblings and I lost the conviction that education was important, though our relationships with educators were strained. My mother continued to send all her younger children to school. Elsie left school when she felt that work was more important.

As I share this story with Latinos and others with immigrant family backgrounds, heads begin to nod, suggesting similar things happened to them and to their family members. While we are in many ways the same as non-Latinos or standard English speakers, we also live different lives that demand educators' attention and respect. Many of us speak a home language different from most teachers. We regard teachers as elders to be respected, too; but when non-Latino teachers want us to be like them, and even when we want to do exactly that, something gets in the way. Not difference itself, but the respect that we desire for who we are, not just who we want to become. Unfortunately, we often pay a heavy academic price. Any overt signal of disrespect for one's home life from an individual in authority indicates to those receiving the message that they are not wanted and even do not belong in school. It need not be that way.

A teacher can take care to show equal respect. One basic place to begin is to consider "what's in a name": to ask students about the origins of their names, their parents' names, and their grandparents' names and to honor the diversity of those origins. Research shows that students begin to develop self-concepts, positive and negative, based on how others perceive them, and that the names and treatment we receive from others lead us even to perform or underperform on specific academic tasks.[1] Packed into something like an involuntary name change is a deeply negative perception that students quickly internalize: my name and all it stands for must not be worthy of serious consideration.

Students are always making determinations regarding the worthiness of who they are individually and of the racial-ethnic group to which they are considered to belong. They get many signals of worthiness or unworthiness from their teachers. Families do what they can to protect their children's sense of worth; in our case, the family *raíces* was very strong and helped all of us to survive and even prosper. As an extended family, we held together through work: we negotiated with large-scale farms to thin sugar beets and pick peaches, apples, and pears together. We worked hard, without serious dissent and with clear accountability. Unfortunately, this family protective advantage was not available when it came to helping us navigate our lives in schools, particularly when it came to our interactions with teachers. Our family valued education and regarded it as the gateway out of farm labor. A high school diploma was a prized possession. None of the adult members of the extended family had the opportunity to attend school on a continuous basis. But they clearly understood the value of formal education. My father would say to all of us, "Núnca te pueden quitar la educación"—"They can never take away your education, what you have learned." My father and the extended family taught us respect for family, elders, and others, hard work, patience, and persistence. But they could not teach us literacy, mathematics, science, and the entire culture of schooling. Teachers had to do that. Since many teachers did not respect the home worlds from which we emerged, we were put at a distinct disadvantage in comparison to those students whose lives mirrored teachers' out-of-school lives and linguistic roots.

Interactions over language were key to this disrespect. My home language was never spoken at school, or even acknowledged. One of my *tios* (uncles) told us how he was punished for speaking Spanish on the school grounds. We were careful never to do that. The *raíces*, cultural and linguistic roots, of my entire existence outside of school was specifically discounted, even held in contempt. The fact that I worked in the fields with my father, mother, and brothers was seen as a failure to achieve economic security, not as a positive effort to utilize family resources to meet economic insecurity. Since I did not speak English, this absence was emphasized at the cost of understanding that I spoke fluent Spanish. Too often my needs were overemphasized and perceived as deficits, rather than searching for the assets I brought, and utilizing them in the classroom. Through disparaging interactions with teachers, I realized that I did not do things at home that had value in the school culture. I had no summer vacations; we worked the hardest and longest in the summer.

I did not go visit Grandma; she lived with us. I never visited the library; we lived ten miles from the nearest library, and the only vehicle we had was shared for purposes of making a living.

Significantly, I was always respected by my teachers as an individual; in that sense, I was treated equally. But the linguistic and cultural milieu in which I lived was not given equal respect. Typically it was dismissed, or considered irrelevant, but sometimes it was explicitly negatively regarded. I recall the high school football coach responding to a group of us "Mexicans"—that was his term for us—after we informed him that we could not come to the required football practices because we were all picking peaches with our families: "You are either football players or peach pickers, you decide." That stopped our participation in the football team. There was no choice for us. As a young student, I was quiet and complacent, accommodating to the classroom and school but never feeling a part of it, never thriving there.

Investigating and utilizing the knowledge that children bring from the language and family milieu from which they come makes for better learning and achievement because it builds on the student's existing "funds of knowledge."[2] One successful school had teachers writing weekly journals to their children's parents, opening a window of communication between teacher and parent. (See García, on Resource list.) Even parents who were illiterate found a relative or a neighbor to respond to the teacher. The journals shared personal happenings and served as a way to get to know each other on a continuous basis. This knowledge allowed teacher and parent to make more informed assessments of one another. Parents and teachers both reported that they enjoyed and valued the exercise. In another case, teachers visited students' homes on a regular basis. (See Moll, on Resource list; for further suggestions on doing this, see Wyman and Kashatok, Chapter 56.) The cumulative knowledge teachers amassed in these visits assisted them in constructing instruction that built on the students' family backgrounds. Knowing your students and the families, communities, and circumstances in which they live demonstrates that educators value students' home practices. Learning students' language or key elements of it facilitates communication with them and their parents. The very act of attempting to learn their language will enhance your interactions. Never make assumptions about their culture; always ask in a respectful way about what you do not understand.

I suggest that educators work to get to know Latino students'—and all students'—home worlds, both as individuals and as group members. Educators should not assume that all Latinos have the same relationship to Spanish and similar cultural repertoires. Latinos have very diverse roots. The process of respectfully seeking to know may start with a name, but it requires much, much more.

RESOURCES

Center for Applied Linguistics: www.cal.org.

Eugene García. 2001. *Hispanic Education in the United States: Raíces y Alas.*
Boulder, CO: Rowman & Littlefield.

Shirley Brice Heath. 1996. *Ways with Words: Language, Life, and Work in
Communities and Classrooms.* New York: Cambridge University Press.

Luis Moll. 1992. "Funds of Knowledge for Teaching: Using a Qualitative Approach to
Connect Homes and Classrooms." *Theory into Practice* 31(2): 132–41.

DISCUSSION QUESTIONS

1. **Principle:** Besides changing students' names, what everyday acts by
   educators can signal disrespect for students' "home worlds"?
2. **Strategy:** How can educators start to learn more about the home
   worlds of their actual students rather than learning generic information
   about the "groups" from which students come?
3. **Try tomorrow:** What is one specific way you might "broadcast" that
   you respect the home practices and linguistic roots of your students and
   seek to understand them?

*Dr. Eugene García is vice president for education partnerships at Arizona
State University. His research and scholarship centers on issues related to the
education of linguistically and culturally diverse children.*

56

Getting to Know Students' Communities

Leisy Wyman and Grant Kashatok

Teachers who do not share their students' backgrounds can get to know their students' communities and draw on those developing relationships to redirect and improve their own teaching.[1] Since venturing outside the school demands courage and perseverance, we suggest some conceptual and concrete approaches, outline some common pitfalls, and name some indicators that educators can use to mark their progress along the way.

The co-authors of this essay have worked together and apart as educators and researchers in various Native Alaskan communities over the past fifteen years. Wyman, a white woman, first came to the Yup'ik region as a teacher in 1992. She has researched Yup'ik youth, bilingualism, and education and collaborated with Yup'ik community members to document the knowledge of local elders.[2] Kashatok, a Yup'ik man, has conducted research on cross-cultural communication at the University of Alaska–Fairbanks and worked in the Yup'ik region as a teacher and administrator. Currently, as part of his job as principal of a K–12 school in a Yup'ik village, he helps incoming groups of non-Native teachers get to know the new community. This essay draws on our combined experiences to discuss non-Native teachers working in relatively small and remote Native Alaskan communities. We encourage teachers to adapt the methods we describe to their local communities.

In many Native Alaskan villages and some Native American communities, non-Native teachers live in the communities they serve, far from any place where they might enjoy majority status. Unfortunately, some teachers respond to the multilayered tensions between schools and communities by becoming what our colleague Paul Ongtooguk describes as "triangle teachers," rarely venturing beyond the triangular path between their homes, the school, and the local store. They underscore their positions as outsiders by remaining insulated during the year, never getting to know the communities of their students, and leaving the communities they serve at every opportunity. Triangle teachers are often beleaguered by discipline problems and motivational challenges in their classrooms. Some are eventually pressured to leave Native communities by students, parents, and school board members and flee from Native Alaskan communities, hurling accusations of reverse racism over their shoulders as they go.

Non-Native teachers who get to know Native Alaskan communities connect classroom activities to their students' lives, which decreases discipline challenges and increases student motivation. Many develop continuing collaborative relationships with community members; some are eventually accepted as community members and allies.

These teachers adopt what we call a "triangulating" stance. In qualitative research, triangulation refers to gathering information from a multiplicity of perspectives. Triangulating teachers seek constantly to learn about communities, always resisting quick blanket explanations for local practices. By triangulating, teachers can learn to see students and members of their communities as individuals as well as racial group members.

Begin by establishing relationships with community members who work in the school. Teachers, school board members, aides, and staff members who share students' backgrounds often have valuable insights about the community and considerable information concerning the individual, family, and school histories of particular students. Even communities that seem homogeneous from the outside, however, may contain internal lines of division along lines of class, gender, generation, education, place of origin, linguistic background, familial background, and religious orientation. By depending on one or two community members for inside information, teachers risk taking on the biases and blind spots of individuals. In one interview with Wyman, a retired Yup'ik teacher reported realizing that unemployed young men played an active role in the informal economy of her village by helping their extended families with childcare and eldercare needs and participating in subsistence activities. As a teacher busy in the school all day, she had assumed that these young men were "doing nothing."

Insiders may also feel insulted when they are asked to provide quick, oversimplified portrayals of their own communities. As a Yup'ik educator, Kashatok has often been approached by non-Native teachers as an authority on "how Yup'ik people think/see/do/feel about x." While Kashatok helps newcomers adjust to life in Yup'ik communities, he is wary of teachers who expect to acquire knowledge from "locals" with little effort of their own. Like many village residents, he waits to see if people are committed to learning through many channels and staying in the community before spending the considerable time required to teach non-Native teachers how to recognize, understand, and work with community patterns of communication and socialization.

Triangulating teachers physically venture out of the school and into the everyday life of the communities they serve. During her early years as a teacher, Wyman was often asked by a Yup'ik administrator in her district, "Are you getting invited over to families' houses?" In interacting with families, teachers should explain that they want to learn more about their students' backgrounds in order to become better teachers. Importantly, teachers should present themselves as learners ready to appreciate the strengths found in everyday practices, rather than as authority figures seeking to intervene in presumed deficiencies[3] or tourists fascinated with "exotic" customs. During visits in Yup'ik villages, household members often watch for subtle signs that teachers regard their everyday practices as "strange." Through joking comments such as "So you want to learn how Eskimos live? Did you think we lived in igloos?" they may test teachers' assumptions and critique prevalent stereotypes of Yupiit and Inuit.

Given the pressing demands on dedicated teachers' schedules, it is not easy to find the time to get to know students' families. Teachers must negotiate the evolving expectations of these new relationships while getting to know a broad range of community members. These challenges require time management skills and diplomacy, but they are signs of progress. The knowledge that grows through these relationships not only makes teachers more effective but deepens their connections with students and increases the personal rewards of teaching.

Attending community events that are open to outsiders offers another possible starting point. While it is normal to feel obtrusive at first, over time, you may be welcomed by community members who understand your presence as a sign of your ongoing interest in their children and respect for them. As one non-Native principal with a particularly strong relationship to a Yup'ik village stated about attending feasts, "At first, they weren't quite used to me showing up and they kind of wondered why I was there. Now I'd better go or people will wonder why I didn't participate!"

Unfamiliar communication patterns can make it difficult for teachers to know which events are open to their participation. In Yup'ik communities, teachers are often welcome to attend feasts, weddings, and funerals, but people may issue social invitations indirectly by stating when an activity will happen and assuming that teachers will know they can participate. Some events may be off-limits to outsiders, and showing up unexpectedly could be interpreted as disrespectful or invasive. Teachers should ask students, parents, and other adults for recommendations of events at which they would be welcome and then take the initiative to attend on their own.

Joining a routine activity that involves community members can serve as an important, sustained entry into local life. In Native Alaskan villages, teachers have joined sports teams, church choirs, and Native dance groups. Many teachers have been invited to join students' families in subsistence hunting. One teacher told Kashatok that going out hunting made him appreciate what his students know about survival and navigation in the subarctic environment. By participating in activities that lie at the heart of communities, teachers demonstrate a deep willingness to get to know individuals and local ways of doing things. Teachers can also encourage community members to bring their knowledge and experience into the school and classroom.

Some teachers may feel intense anxiety about their physical safety when considering venturing into local communities. Teachers in this situation can start by going to public places with colleagues or students' parents.[4] These fears can also provide an important starting point for teachers to reflect on their own racialized privilege.

For teachers who work in bilingual communities, learning a language that students hear at home can be one of the most powerful avenues available for developing relationships with community members. In Yup'ik-speaking communities, even teachers' modest continuing efforts to speak Yup'ik are generally interpreted as a welcome sign of respect. Still, there are many reasons why, in any given instance, a community member may not speak, or speak at length, in a heritage language with a teacher. First attempts to speak any language are likely to sound comical or unusual. At other times, teachers' attempts to use a heritage language may bring out feelings of insecurity, confusion, loss, or anger. If the language of instruction of the school is English, this may be contributing to heritage language loss within families and local communities. Matter-of-factly trying out a heritage language on a community member might also be interpreted as racial "othering": "Why is this teacher assuming I speak or want to speak Yup'ik/Chinese/Spanish based on my appearance?" Being mindful of these and other contextual factors can help teachers stay attuned to when their well-meaning efforts are opening channels of communication, and when they might be going awry.

As teachers work to get to know communities of color, it helps to understand ongoing dynamics of distrust. In Native communities, distrust toward incoming teachers stems from local histories of schooling as well as contemporary inequalities. Historically, Native Alaskans experienced formal educational systems that were deliberately designed to erase their languages and ways of being. In one village where the authors worked together, even seemingly innocuous debates about such details as whether students should need a hall pass to go to the bathroom could call up adults' memories of abuse by school personnel. These memories led to emotionally charged discussions in which non-Native teachers struggled to understand how they had unknowingly trod onto what one administrator referred to as the "hot spots of history."

Complicated dynamics of unequal power within schools as state institutions persist in spite of efforts to improve the relationships between village schools and the communities. One school district in Alaska that serves an almost entirely Yup'ik population has been recognized state and nationwide for supporting Indigenous language programs, training and hiring Native Alaskan teachers, and creating curriculum reflecting Yuuyaraq (*the way to be a good human*), a system of beliefs and practices specific to the Yup'ik way of life. Still, three-fourths of the teachers and all but two administrators are non-Native. Salaries range far above the local average, and some teachers are provided housing with running water in villages where other residents must cut ice and collect rain for water and haul their own waste. As community members observe these dramatic discrepancies, they are acutely aware of the unequal relationships of power and privilege between them and incoming non-Native educators.

Teachers are often unaware of how they, as de facto representatives of state institutions, are stepping into long-standing struggles over the purposes and control of Native education. For many Native communities, schools are potential sites of linguistic and cultural maintenance where Indigenous rights to self-determination must be negotiated with changing federal, state, and district mandates and funding policies.[5] Racial tensions are part of this broader picture, and can complicate teachers' attempts to get to know their students' communities. In one Yup'ik village where Wyman and Kashatok worked together, over the course of a few years, a series of non-Native teachers and administrators were pressured to leave the community. Teacher-student relations remained racially charged. After many negative previous experiences with white teachers, some students expressed longing for a day when there would be "no more *kass'aq* (white/outsider) teachers" and spoke of visions of a future with "all *kass'aqs* out" of the village. Some non-Native teachers who felt rejected by the community suppressed analysis of this dynamic by banning the word *kass'aq* from the classroom. To move beyond such defensive postures, teachers should learn enough about community experiences, struggles, and hopes to talk about these tensions with students and community members.

Developing trust is a two-way street. Community members may have their own varying assumptions about the motivations of the outsiders who teach students of color. In remote Native Alaskan and Native American communities, community members sometimes assume, based on bitter experience, that non-Native teachers are there for the money, to experience romanticized "Native" lives, or because they were not hired anywhere else. Many are suspicious of those who claim that they have come primarily to "help" Native villages, rather than to learn from and work with community members. Getting to know people provides teachers with natural opportunities to share and reflect upon their personal motivations for teaching.

White teachers are often unprepared for the emotional hurdles they encounter in trying to get to know communities of color. It takes courage to enter spaces where a welcome is not assured, and participating in any new community puts us in the vulnerable position of learner. Teachers should expect to make mistakes, to be laughed at for their fumbling efforts, to encounter rejection, and to wrestle with ongoing questions about the racial positions of themselves and their students. The process takes time, and we strongly encourage teachers not to retreat back into their comfortable triangle paths too soon.

Since getting to know your students' communities is a never-ending process, it is helpful to be able to recognize markers of progress. You will know your strategy is succeeding when people who initially dismissed you start to see you as an individual and potential colleague and ally. Another sign of progress is when you start seeing your students both as community members and as individuals with particular experiences, backgrounds, and strengths. Even in isolated communities, culture is dynamic, and people respond to change in varying ways.

Youth in Yup'ik communities may respect elders as a group, and also recognize individual elders for their special skills in storytelling, legal strategizing, counseling, translating, teaching, sermonizing, skin-sewing, hunting, running a business, and fixing machinery. Teachers who learn to recognize both the patterns and the immense diversity that exists within communities that initially appear homogeneous gain confidence navigating this complex landscape.

Ultimately, you will know you are succeeding when your growing and deepening relationship with the community helps you with your work in the classroom. The most important question to ask yourself along the way is, "How can I use my new knowledge to positively affect the everyday learning experiences of my students?" Getting to know your students' communities opens doors to a whole host of answers.

RESOURCES

Alaska Native Knowledge Network: http://ankn.uaf.edu/.
Alaskool Website: www.alaskool.org.
E. McIntyre, A. Rosebery, and N. González, eds. 2001. *Classroom Diversity: Connecting Curriculum to Students' Lives.* Portsmouth, NH: Heinemann.

DISCUSSION QUESTIONS

1. **Principle:** What classroom benefits might result if you get to know community members in real depth?
2. **Strategy:** Which of the tactics suggested here for "getting to know" your students' communities strike you as most promising? Which, if any, of the suggestions make you anxious, or skeptical, and why?
3. **Try tomorrow:** What is one way you could start getting to know people in your students' communities?

Leisy Wyman is an assistant professor in the department of Language, Reading and Culture at the University of Arizona. She received her PhD from Stanford University in 2004. Her academic interests include linguistic anthropology of education, bilingualism, youth culture, and indigenous education.

Grant Kashatok taught for ten years in village schools in southwestern Alaska before receiving his master's degree in education leadership from the University of Alaska–Anchorage in 2005. Currently he is site administrator for Newtok Ayaprun School in Newtok, Alaska, where he works on issues of teacher and community engagement.

57

Helping Students Research
Their Communities

Kathleen Cushman

"Where do I come from, and where am I going?" In their passage to adulthood, teenagers ask these two questions all the time. For some years I have been listening to teenagers around the country—primarily students of color from families without economic privilege—and gathering their voices into books about their lives and learning. Our conversations take various forms, but two central themes—the desire to collect and share knowledge about themselves and their communities, and the desire to get respect when sharing it—consistently emerge when kids say what they need from the adults who teach them.

In our book *Fires in the Bathroom* (see Resource list), my high school co-authors suggest that teachers find out more about where students are coming from: not just their interests and activities, but also their cultures and neighborhoods. If teachers come from backgrounds and places different from those of their students, they have even more responsibility to listen and learn. The students cautioned teachers to be thorough when investigating students' origins.

Vance, who grew up in Harlem and is black, noted two problems: educators never talking about students' communities, and educators too quickly and reductively remarking on them. "When you talk about your neighborhood, it's a more open way to approach learning personal things," Vance said. "But it's easy to assume things about a student based on their neighborhood or their race and class. . . . They say, 'You don't talk like someone from Harlem.' We don't have to be reminded by you of what the stereotypes are."

Students realize that the reality of their communities is more complicated than the stereotypes, and they long for opportunities to show both their teachers and their peers the "inside" of their communities rather than just the "outside." "People don't want to come to my neighborhood because they're afraid of it," said Lauraliz, who lives in the Bronx. "Our apartment is beautiful and spotless, there are mirrors all around, and it's kind of like a house. But the outside of it is just horrible, so my mother doesn't like to invite people."

Teachers can offer students the opportunity to research, analyze, and portray their own communities in all their complexity, to their teachers and one another. In the process, students also discover crucial information about their communities that they do not know. A good example came my way from Meghan Caven, a student teacher at Brown University, who assigned her high school students to do research and create a poster about some aspect of housing in Providence, R.I.

> [One student] looked at ownership vs. resident populations in different Providence neighborhoods, broken down by race. He was surprised to discover that though only 12 percent of the population of the West End/Southside is white, 35 percent of the houses there are white-owned. We discussed what this meant and how it applied to segregation. He was impressively astute in his interpretation of the "Providence Plan," questioning why "Hispanic" was not represented on its graphs. He directed his poster toward Latino residents of these communities, his own neighborhood, encouraging them to purchase houses. Another student made a poster that highlighted the uncertain future of public housing in Providence.

As they gathered more facts, students and teacher learned to make explicit, and then to dismantle, their own and others' uninformed or inaccurate assumptions about their communities. Through research, this class challenged prevailing beliefs and demonstrated that neighborhoods are not spaces in which people of a particular racial-ethnic group lead their lives in easily summarized ways. Mounting their findings on posters in the community provided an authentic audience that gave their learning a public as well as private purpose.

Investigations of communities can go much deeper. Students and teachers can turn to historical sources—museums, archives, books, local residents—to complicate the story of how their community evolved (see also Tieken, Chapter 37). In Edcouch and Elsa, Texas, high school students research and self-publish the bilingual *Llano Grande Journal* (see Resource list), which presents local history largely missing from their textbooks. Using archives and oral histories, they have documented how the local economy grew on the backs of migrant laborers who had to fight for basic rights. These students build their academic knowledge and skills through this investigation, and at the same time they fuel themselves to push back against continuing discrimination against laborers in their community. Younger children read their *Journal* in literature classes; older residents gain a deeper understanding of one another and the social structures and cultural patterns that unite and divide them.

Students can investigate complex social questions in their communities in person (see also Torre and Fine, Chapter 31). In 2005, three classrooms of immigrant students in New York City took cameras and tape recorders into their neighborhoods to document the lives and labor of their parents, relatives, and neighbors. They recorded, transcribed, and translated conversations in which, often for the first time, these immigrants shared with the next generation their motivations and struggles in leaving their countries and coming to New York. As I helped shape and publish the resulting essays in *Forty-Cent Tip: Stories of New York City Immigrant Workers* (2006), I saw profound effects on my own attitudes and those of other readers, which is often an important outcome of student research. Workers in our neighborhoods who were previously invisible or disdained—street hawkers, office cleaners, laundry workers—revealed their courage, dignity, and sacrifices. Young people's pride in their own communities grew as they contributed new knowledge to counter the ignorance of others. One student and his father stopped in at Barnes and Noble, found five copies of the book on the shelves, and spent half an hour in conversation with buyers who were fascinated to meet an author. Making the work public had broad and deep effects. Even without our book, the project could easily have taken shape as a modest photo exhibit with text alongside.

In working with students to investigate and portray their own communities, I see them become more outspoken about those communities' complexity. Our work is serious: in my case, students earn an hourly wage for their work. They check our manuscripts for accuracy; their names and pictures appear in the books. Through the publication process, they take their authorial roles ever more seriously, refining what we publish and deepening our collective understanding as they ask questions and make suggestions.

The young people with whom I create these books come from situations much different from my own, and hearing what they say about their communities is not always comfortable. Often, students challenge me to push my own thinking on how communities are defined. One contributor, who had immigrated to this country four years earlier, objected to her identification as an English language learner in the biographical notes at the end of our book. I had thought to honor her rapid mastery of her new language; she saw the note as diminishing and disrespecting her voice, as narrowing her own presentation of her "community." We took it out.

My core recommendation for K–12 educators is to find tools and time to help students of all ages delve into the complexity of their own communities and then make public their expressions of those investigations. A class might opt for web publishing, local exhibits, or community newspapers as alternative public forums. When teachers afford students the opportunity to inquire thoroughly into communities and to answer the question, "Where do I come from?" they also begin to guide students toward answering the freeing, open-ended question that is central to education: "Where am I going?"

RESOURCES

Kathleen Cushman. 2005. *First in the Family: Advice about College from First-generation Students*. 2 vols. Providence, RI: Next Generation Press.

Kathleen Cushman, the students of "What Kids Can Do," and Lisa Delpit. 2003. *Fires in the Bathroom: Advice for Teachers of High School Students*. New York: The New Press.

Llano Grande Center for Research and Development. *Llano Grande Journal. Hard Work and Dignity: Perspectives from the Fields of South Texas*. Edcouch-Elsa High School, Edcouch, Texas. Accessed on What Kids Can Do website: http://www/whatkidscando.org/studentwork/Llano.html.

What Kids Can Do, ed. 2006. *Forty-Cent Tip: Stories of New York City Immigrant Workers*. Providence, RI: Next Generation Press. A book by the students of three New York public international high schools.

DISCUSSION QUESTIONS

1. **Principle:** Why might it be important for students to research their communities in the classroom context?
2. **Strategy:** How could you design a community inquiry and public presentation to simultaneously satisfy academic requirements?
3. **Try tomorrow:** What specific community questions might you work with your own students to investigate? How might you involve students in selecting local issues to examine?

Kathleen Cushman writes for a national audience about the lives and learning of adolescents. After fourteen years documenting educational change efforts around the country, in 2001 she helped start What Kids Can Do, Inc. (www.whatkidscando.org), a nonprofit organization that aims to make public the work and voices of youth.

Part XX

Discuss Parents' Experiences of Racially Unequal Opportunity

Part of getting to know parents, and collaborating with them in assisting children, is listening to their analyses of the school experience. Those analyses may be positive or negative; the negative kind are far harder for educators to hear. The essays in this part share a core principle of everyday antiracism: *parents, too, may experience educational systems as racially unequal; educators must engage parents in discussions about those experiences.*

How can educators start to engage parents in discussions about how they experience their child's classroom or school?

1. Actively cultivate the trust of parents of color.

   Beverly Tatum urges, for example, that educators listen to black parents when they express distrust of the school system and of educators' decisions about their children.

2. Help parents who struggle against damaging stereotypes of their children.

   Janie Ward, using parents of black boys as a key example, proposes that many parents must be supported as they struggle to deal with negative popular views of their children and families.

3. Undermine racially stratified tracking through minority parent involvement.

   Roz Mickelson and Linwood Cousins suggest that educators should help offer parents of color equal knowledge about how to access opportunities inside schools and districts.

58

Cultivating the Trust of Black Parents

Beverly Daniel Tatum

I received a phone call from an African American parent seeking my professional services as a psychologist. "My son's teacher called me today, and she says she wants to have my son tested at school for special needs. There's nothing wrong with my son, and I am not going to let that teacher label him that way! I need some help. What should I do?" I understood her distress. As an African American mother of sons, I know that black boys are more likely to be referred for special education than any other group of students, and among the least likely to be identified as "gifted." Our conversation followed that pattern. This mother saw her son's strengths, but felt the school and specifically his white teacher focused on his weaknesses, whether real or imagined. This mother was puzzled and suspicious. What was this conversation really about, she wondered? Was this white teacher unable to see her child because of her preconceived notions about black boys? Was the school going to label her child in ways that would limit his future? Could that teacher be trusted?

The caller was seeking a second opinion from someone she thought she could trust: a black female psychologist. Since the case was outside my expertise, I referred her to another psychologist I knew, affirming the wisdom of her plan to get an independent assessment in addition to whatever testing the school might do. Not long after this conversation, when I mentioned this incident to a group of white teachers in a workshop on effective antiracist classroom practice, one of the participants responded with agitation, "Why would you tell her to get a second opinion? You are encouraging her not to trust the school!" The idea that a well-intentioned white teacher might be viewed with suspicion by an African American parent offended her. She thought that the teacher had the child's best interest at heart and could not understand why any parent would question a teacher's professional judgment. The idea that the teacher's racial group membership might make a black parent suspicious troubled her. From this teacher's point of view, I had validated the mother's worst fears of racial bias, rather than encouraging her to place her faith in her son's teacher and his school.

This mother's lack of trust is based on the long and troubled history of

African Americans' relationships with white-run schools. There is substantial contemporary evidence to support her suspicions about her son's treatment. According to civil rights research, African Americans and Latinos identified as special education students are twice as likely as white students to be removed from the general education program and be taught in a restrictive, substantially separate, and lower-quality setting.[1] Black parents are justifiably wary of white educators' treatment of black children, especially when they make a referral for special education, or a teacher appears to have underestimated a black child's ability. Similar suspicions might arise when a black child is tracked away from a "high-ability" group into a lower one. Black parents' distrust of white-run schools is rooted in generations of institutionalized policies and practices that have denied equal access to quality education, and resulted in the over-referral of black children for special education and the under-identification of black children as gifted and talented. The distrust must be acknowledged and then countered with explicit efforts to build trust.

Before a teacher can help a child, she must gain the parents' trust. Parents must be partners with teachers in developing and implementing an appropriate educational plan. Otherwise, an overt or covert battle between parents and teachers is likely to ensue. Parental distrust can easily degenerate into disrespect, which inevitably contaminates the relationship between teacher and student. A trusting relationship between the teacher and the parents will certainly strengthen her effectiveness with the child and increase the possibility of a successful educational intervention.

What can an antiracist educator do to work effectively with black parents when questions arise about a child's capabilities in the classroom? Working proactively to cultivate a trusting relationship before such a situation arises is essential.

Put your values on the walls. Black parents and their children have often experienced classrooms where most, if not all, of the images in the books and on the walls are of white people. Too often, the invisibility of blacks and other people of color has been the norm. The teacher who includes positive representations of children and adults of color (non-stereotypical representations; see Deyhle, Chapter 35) signals his understanding of the importance of affirming the identities of all the children in the school. This small gesture conveys an encouraging message to a wary parent who is looking for evidence that a teacher about children of color. The presence of multicultural books on the shelves, photos of multiracial children on the walls, and social justice literature on your desk sends positive signals to parents of color even before the conversation begins.

Name the problem of distrust. Some white teachers are nervous about sharing critical feedback about a black student's performance with the student's parents for fear that they may be accused of racial bias. But honest feedback is

necessary for improvement, and to deny the child and the parents the opportunity to learn from it is unfair. What if the child does need special assistance?
Tension could be defused if the teacher began by acknowledging the problem
that improper and unnecessary special education referrals are all too common
for black children and it would not surprise her if the parents were wary of her
recommendation. After acknowledging the validity of their concerns about labeling and the low expectations too often projected onto black children, the
teacher could present concrete evidence and examples of the student's difficulties to his parents. Wary parents may feel that the teacher who has acknowledged the possibility of parental distrust will listen respectfully to their
perspective.

If you are accused of racial bias, do not take it personally. Rather than
reacting in a defensive manner, acknowledge the possibility that your judgment may be biased and ask for more information from the parent's perspective. It is hard to grow up in a race-conscious society without being
influenced by stereotypes. "There's not a prejudiced bone in my body!" is a
familiar refrain; such categorical denials only reinforce suspicion on the part
of black parents who view them as naive at best. How much more effective
it would be to ask sincerely, "Help me understand what I did that made you
think so." An invitation to enter into dialogue rather than a rush to defend
oneself goes a long way in cultivating trust even in the midst of a difficult
interaction.

Though we may not always recognize it, each of us carries the weight
of the history of interracial relations with us into our cross-racial interactions.
The burden of cultivating the trust of black parents in an educational system
that has too often failed their children falls particularly on the shoulders of
white teachers, who represent the vast majority of today's teaching force and
who, as members of the racially dominant group, carry the particular weight
of history. The white antiracist educator can lighten that load by being clear
and consistent in the expression of her own values. By listening carefully to
the concerns of the families she serves, even when her professional judgment
is challenged, the antiracist educator opens the door to productive dialogue,
which will help ensure that the best interest of the child—as defined by the
parents as well as by the teacher—is served.

RESOURCES

Anne Henderson, Vivian Johnson, Karen L. Mapp, and Don Davies. 2007. *Beyond
    the Bake Sale: The Essential Guide to Family/School Partnerships.* New York:
    The New Press.
Beverly Daniel Tatum. 2007. *Can We Talk About Race? And Other Conversations in
    an Era of School Resegregation.* Boston: Beacon.

DISCUSSION QUESTIONS

1. **Principle:** What proactive steps can an educator take to cultivate trust in her relationships with black parents or other parents of color?
2. **Strategy:** How could you fight the urge to react defensively against a parent's accusation of bias or racism?
3. **Try tomorrow:** Think of a parent-teacher interaction that did not go well. What could you have said to start off this conversation on the best possible footing, and to prepare to collaborate with the parents to meet the needs of their child?

Beverly Daniel Tatum is president of Spelman College in Atlanta, Georgia. A clinical psychologist with a research focus on race relations and racial identity, she has worked extensively with K–12 educators on developing antiracist classroom practices in predominantly white classroom settings.

59

Helping Parents Fight Stereotypes about Their Children

Janie Victoria Ward

Across the nation, when I visit schools, churches, community meetings, and other venues where black parents convene and talk about schools, I hear expressions of anxiety and distress. We leave these gatherings angry, fearful, and depressed; we cannot seem to escape negative perceptions of our children and our families. Black parents cringe when we receive the dreaded call from the school's discipline dean complaining about the "bad behavior" of our son, or the group of boys he rolls with. We swell with frustration when we hear from our son's principal the all-too-familiar refrain, "He's just not living up to his potential." We seethe in anger as we sit in PTA meetings and parent-teacher conferences listening to teachers complain about the behavior of "some" boys—and we know damn well which boys they are alluding to. Even black parents whose sons are bringing home report cards filled with As and Bs feel the sting of the negative perception educators try so hard not to say aloud: that black "bad boys" are lazy, disruptive, and apathetic about their education.

Toxic, pejorative pronouncements about our children and families are everywhere, for everyone to see and hear. When we turn on the television, pick up the newspaper, or read magazines, we are bombarded with reports about the failure of black boys. In schools, we are constantly reminded, they are disproportionately placed in special education, more likely than any other group to be suspended and expelled, and often completely missing from advanced placement and honors courses. Held personally responsible for most of the social problems they face, black boys are scapegoated, blamed, and punished at every turn. They are framed as thugs and criminals, sexually irresponsible, intellectually inferior, unemployed and unemployable. The discourse of black male underachievement and its pathologizing narrative of crisis plays over and over in our heads.

We worry about how white educators in particular will respond to the distorted messages they hear. We panic, thinking they will never see our boys as children, seeing them instead as willfully bad mini-adults in desperate need of social control.

Lately, I have been reflecting on the wide range of ways in which black parents and caregivers respond to the negative messages we hear. Some of us ignore these messages outright. Others become overwhelmed by a belief that the messages we face are too great to overcome. Most of us are somewhere in the middle, acutely aware of the racist misperceptions that surround us, certain that they paint an incomplete picture of the lives we lead, and filled with fury that such misrepresentations are allowed to stand.

Yet we find ourselves still caught in the stranglehold of these negative representations. The work of confronting damaging ideas about our children—particularly our sons—continues to be a major stressor for black parents, on top of the normal stresses encountered by all parents raising adolescents. Whether we like it or not, black parents are engaged in a never-ending battle to overcome the demons of damaging stereotypes. This battle can play out in relations among ourselves, educators, and our children, as many of us adopt survival-oriented resistance strategies to protect our children in schools.

I have seen black parents, fearful, frustrated, and determined not to see their children fail, levy fierce, sometimes humiliating, and sometimes unintentionally debilitating criticism of their children's behavior and schoolwork, hoping that these tough words will turn their children around. I have seen other black parents resist internalizing negative messages of black males by dismissing altogether any negative comments teachers make about their children's school behavior. Others of us work with our children to debate and discern what incidents should be addressed, rather than discounted and ignored, and how, as young black men, they can best respond in racially charged situations while maintaining their sense of pride, integrity, and identity.

Educators need to know that our work as black parents is to prevent racist ideology from negatively shaping our children's schooling experiences. Educators also need to know that for parents of black boys, resisting the relentless rumors of inferiority about our children and about ourselves as parents is exhausting.

In my book, *The Skin We're In*,[1] I suggest a four-step model to help black children and parents resist racist notions about ourselves. Educators must know that many black parents are already doing these things so that their children can survive and thrive. By understanding this ongoing resistance work, educators can understand tensions that arise with parents over the treatment of their children in school. They can also support black parents' ongoing resistance to the negative images of their children in schools and society. Black parents are struggling to:

See it. Black parents need to look carefully and honestly at what is going on with our boys. In school, we must (and often do) observe closely, looking for patterns or recurring events. What do our school's disciplinary statistics say about who gets punished and what they get punished for? Are our boys being treated fairly? Are they well represented in upper-level courses, or concentrated in special education? How do teachers and administrators feel about our children? What do they actually say? What do they actually do? Then, we struggle to:

Name it. When we have done this analysis and think we see racism, we must call it out. Different parents have different definitions of "racism." Naming racism is painful, but naming it frees us from the psychological morass of confusion and distress. So, to protect our children, we often do name racism when we see it in schools. We also struggle to:

Oppose it. As a way of opposing any potentially negative treatment of our sons, we can try to work with teachers to assure our sons' educational success. We can raise educators' expectations for our sons and help them discipline our boys more effectively. As we try to undertake these efforts, we must do extra work that other parents do not have to do: we have to fight the omnipresent racist notion that there is something inherently wrong with us just because of who we are. So, finally, we struggle to:

Replace it. Black parents best replace the falsehoods of racial ideology by holding fast to the belief that we and our children are so much more than the relentless stereotypes would lead us to believe. Like educators, we must remind ourselves daily that our boys are not bad; they are capable of maturity, focused intellectual acuity, deep caring, and great love. We, too, must never forget that black folks have a proud history of boys and men who have persevered against odds far worse than those they face today; that we have overcome before and we will again. Our relations with teachers are often characterized by our shows of strength.

Educators have an important role to play in supporting, and actively participating in, the ongoing resistance work of black parents. Educators can begin by becoming aware of our constant struggle against negative stereotypes of our children. That way, they can join that struggle rather than become its target.

RESOURCES

Janie Victoria Ward. 2000. *The Skin We're In: Teaching Our Children to be Emotionally Strong, Socially Smart, Spiritually Connected.* New York: Free Press.

DISCUSSION QUESTIONS

1. **Principle:** Ward says that for black parents, "resisting the relentless rumors of inferiority—about our children, and about ourselves as parents—is exhausting." How might this exhausting effort affect parents' relationships with educators?

2. **Strategy:** What stereotypes about black boys are circulating in your school? How do you think they affect these boys, their educational experiences, and their parents' relationships with teachers?

3. **Try tomorrow:** In your next conversation with a parent, how might you communicate to her that you are her ally in the "struggle against negative stereotypes" of her children?

Janie Victoria Ward teaches in the Africana Studies Department at Simmons College in Boston, Massachusetts. In addition, she teaches courses in social justice. Adolescent development, particularly the racial identity and moral development of black adolescents and young adults, is her primary research interest.

60

Informing Parents about Available Opportunities

Roslyn Arlin Mickelson and Linwood H. Cousins

Tracking and ability groups are almost universal features of public education. School tracking refers to the differentiation of the core curricula into courses that offer a given subject at various levels of rigor. Typically, higher tracks cover the curriculum in a broader and deeper fashion than lower-track classes in the same subject. Lower tracks generally prepare students for nontechnical careers and not for college. Whether by design or unintended consequence, academic tracking (and "ability" grouping, which starts the process in the early grades) typically result in children of color and lower-income students being placed in lower tracks compared to their white and middle-class peers.[1] Racially stratified grouping and tracking are highly consequential because lower groups and tracks offer far fewer opportunities for rigorous learning. These racial disparities in access to learning opportunities represent structural aspects of everyday racism in education.

The Charlotte-Mecklenburg schools of North Carolina form an urban-suburban district with roughly equal proportions of black and white students and a smaller number of Hispanic students (43 percent, 39 percent, and 10 percent respectively in 2004–2005). The district has a long history of segregation but a deep commitment to integration and academic excellence; still, whites have proportionately higher enrollments in advanced math and science courses than blacks. This pattern is even more pronounced at the Advanced Placement level.[2] From 2002 through 2005, along with Anne Velasco and Brian Williams, we developed and implemented the Math/Science Equity Project (MSEP). MSEP's goal was to close the racial disparities in higher-level math and science course enrollments through increasing the involvement of African American parents in the course selection process. We expected that parents who participated in MSEP would be more likely to convince their children to enroll in higher-track math and science courses and more effective in communicating their wishes to educators.

Disturbingly, children of color are disproportionately found in lower groups and tracks even when their ability, interests, and prior achievement suggest they should be in higher ones.[3] While parents, students, and educators work to end tracking, eliminating the racism associated with assignment may ameliorate racial stratification (see also Tyson, Chapter 24). There is ample evidence that detracked classes and heterogeneous groupings offer more effective and equitable approaches to teaching and learning[4] (see also Rubin, Chapter 18).

Tracking is rarely done in an overtly racist manner. Adolescents, their parents, and educators often jointly select courses and tracks for high school students. School personnel take students' prior performance, test scores, and interests into account. Students base their decisions on parents' and educators' advice, their own interests, and peer influences. In theory, parents are key participants in the process. But in practice, parents' awareness of what to do regarding course placement and how to manage and support their children's educational careers varies widely and is strongly related to parents' racial group membership and social class backgrounds. In coffee shop gatherings, soccer games, and impromptu discussions at school events, some parents exchange information with knowledgeable friends, neighbors, and relatives about the quality and characteristics of teachers, courses, administrators, and schools. Research in Charlotte confirms that middle-class, white parents typically have the experience, education, and network connections that help them get their children into top groups and tracks,[5] while racial-ethnic minority and working-class parents are less likely to have access to the official information, social networks, and experiences that are increasingly necessary for them to guide their children's educational choices.[6] To counter this racialized discrepancy in Charlotte-Mecklenberg, MSEP offered valuable information about secondary course tracking practices to African American parents.

Why did we offer parent information workshops only to black parents? Previous research indicates that racial-ethnic minority parents are far more likely than middle-class white parents to defer to educators' decisions about their children's course placement.[7] Minority parents often assume that because educators' professional expertise trumps their own knowledge and experiences, they should not, or cannot effectively, advocate for a higher track placement for their child. Working-class parents of color (including those with limited English language proficiency, who were not a large population in Charlotte-Mecklenburg) are the least likely of all parents to have the sense of school-based empowerment necessary to become involved in course placement decisions or to question school personnel about them.

Targeting our workshops to minority parents attempts to level a very uneven playing field. Workshops provide minority parents with the information, networks, and negotiation skills many white, middle-class parents already use to their children's advantage. Whether or not ability grouping and tracking were designed to protect and advance white educational privilege is not the point; they operate in ways that do just that. School system personnel who treat all parents as equally knowledgeable about curricular choices and tracking are in effect advantaging those who are middle-class and white.

MSEP fought such unintended racism in two ways. First, we modeled how a diverse group of adults could work together collaboratively to get students of color into more advanced courses. The MSEP leadership team included the two lead researchers (a white woman and an African American man); one postdoctoral fellow (an African American man), and one project manager (a white woman); the twelve student research assistants included seven African Americans, four whites, and one Asian Indian. We collaborated with community organizations including the public libraries, parks and recreation department, churches, and nonprofit organizations, all of which had ethnically diverse personnel.

The second, more important way that MSEP fought racism was through conducting a series of two- and six-week community-based parent enrichment workshops designed to enhance minority parents' involvement in the secondary course placement process. MSEP workshops were offered to African American parents with children in three high schools and their feeder middle schools. Participating adults were guardians of black students capable of academic success in top-level math and science courses, but not enrolled in them. Parents were recruited through community organizations, local media, and the target schools' guidance departments.

MSEP workshops offered parents information on their educational rights under the North Carolina constitution; North Carolina's high school courses of study (Career Tech Prep, College Tech Prep, College/University Prep); the systems of elementary, middle school, and high school tracking; key decision points requiring parental involvement; and the math and science secondary course sequences. Parents engaged in hands-on math and science activities and participated in role-playing designed to help them manage the course selection and placement process. Workshops included sessions on supporting children educationally during early and middle adolescence. Childcare and educational enrichment activities offered to participants' children during these workshops eventually blossomed into parallel hands-on math and science activities in response to children's requests to do the same "fun" math and science that their parents were doing.

Workshop sites varied to maximize convenience for parents. They included the UNC Charlotte campus, community recreation centers, public schools, public libraries, and local churches. All parent participants and their children shared a meal with the MSEP team during breaks. We provided transportation if needed. We established a website at www.msep.uncc.edu and developed a project newsletter, *Letters From HOME*, which we mailed out every two months. Several parent graduates of the workshops worked in collaboration with MSEP staff to develop a new parent organization to later replace the workshops as a source of information, leadership training, and networking.

One of the most difficult hurdles we faced arose from the workshops' focus on African American parents. Because we recruited parents in public forums, parents from all ethnic backgrounds learned about MSEP. During these sessions, some white parents expressed feelings of frustration and exclusion when informed that the workshops were not available to them. We explained that our ultimate goal was to offer parent workshops to all families in Charlotte through a partnership with the Charlotte-Mecklenburg Schools after we had demonstrated that MSEP was effective. At the same time, we explained our initial focus on African American families as an attempt to address the racial gaps in AP course enrollment. Despite these explanations, the rationale underlying current minority parent focus, and our promises to include them in future workshops, some white parents accused MSEP of reverse racism.

We also faced negative reactions from some African American adults who expressed cynicism about yet another group of "experts" coming into the black community to "treat" them for their "shortcomings." Although these skeptics acknowledged the racial disparity in top-track enrollments and achievement, they questioned the intentions of MSEP leaders and staff. They assumed that the MSEP team would carry out its program, collect data, enrich their careers, and then leave the community and its people no better than before. Skeptics said this pattern had occurred with many "experts" who had worked in their community previously.

Others questioned the authenticity of our multiracial leadership team, suggesting that the black members of the MSEP were a public relations gimmick camouflaging the real power held by white team leaders. When parent and neighborhood activists voiced their fear of tokenism at community forums, luncheons, and other recruitment events, we responded by candidly engaging their concerns about the project's leadership and their expectations that MSEP, like other organizations, would abandon the community after the culmination of the project.

Eventually, persistence helped to generate more community support. During MSEP's second annual luncheon, several of the original cynics praised the workshop team for its dedication and endurance. When, after three years, MSEP ceased offering workshops and the leadership team partnered with parent-graduates to form a community-based, parent-led organization and network that continues to disseminate the skills, knowledge, and enrichment materials related to higher-track enrollment, the continued presence of the MSEP team reinforced the positive perception of the project among former critics.

The old chestnut—be careful what you ask for, because you may get it—aptly describes the final racial minefield MSEP sought to avoid. The program's goal of equipping minority parents to enroll their children in top tracks, especially Advanced Placement classes, held both constructive and destructive potentials. If more minority students took the most rigorous academic courses and thrived in them, racial gaps in enrollment, test scores, and college attainment would narrow. However, if racial-ethnic minority students who took these classes were underprepared for them and did not perform well, they risked undermining their own self-confidence and reinforcing racial stereotypes about cognitive ability. MSEP addressed this dilemma by repeatedly emphasizing that parents knew best whether their children were prepared for a given course and track.

We are still assessing whether the MSEP program caused more African American students to enroll and thrive in higher-level math and science courses in Charlotte-Mecklenburg; but we know that more African American students did enroll. Parents' responses to assessments we conducted indicated that our workshops were an important part of this process: they left the workshops better informed and empowered. Some parents were angry that the school system had failed to inform them about tracking and course selection. Workshop graduates expressed their intent to encourage their children to enroll in higher-level math and science courses. Follow-up interviews suggest that many parents persuaded their children to enroll in more challenging courses.

Educators can join with parents in efforts to challenge the exclusions inherent in ability grouping and tracking. From MSEP's inception, school administrators, teachers, and staff were involved in recruiting parents to the workshops and, in a few instances, developing and delivering the workshop curricula, but educators can do far more. Teachers and counselors can join parents as allies rather than adversaries in the struggle for equal access to high tracks and, beyond that, for well-run heterogeneous classrooms (see Rubin, Chapter 18). We envision educators and parents working collaboratively to eliminate tracking practices entirely, but also making the flawed system more inclusive.

RESOURCES

Joyce L. Epstein. 2001. *School, Family, and Community Partnerships.* Boulder, CO: Westview.
Robert L. Moses and Charles E. Cobb. 2001. *Radical Equations: Civil Rights from Mississippi to the Algebra Project.* Boston: Beacon Press.

DISCUSSION QUESTIONS

1. **Principle:** If your school practices ability grouping or tracking, do you think such practices fairly treat the students in "lower" groups and tracks?
2. **Strategy:** When such tracking systems exist, who should decide what qualifies students for higher tracks or ability groups? What conflicts

might arise if your school eliminated tracking or ability grouping practices? In general, what could be done about such conflicts?

3. **Try tomorrow:** What specific information might your students' parents need in order to support their children's educational placement? How might you get involved in providing them with this information?

Roslyn Arlin Mickelson is a professor of sociology and an adjunct professor of public policy, information technology, and women's studies at the University of North Carolina–Charlotte. Her interests include minority educational issues, school and classroom compositional effects on achievement, gender, education policy, and school reform.

Linwood H. Cousins, currently associate professor at Longwood University, is a social worker and anthropologist whose teaching and research focus on the interaction of race, ethnicity, class, and culture with American life and schooling.

SECTION F

Keeping It Going

Part XXI

Struggle to Change a System That Is Unequal, While Working Within It

Working within a racially unequal system can be overwhelming. Still, it is important to remember that you, in collaboration with others, can make a difference. The essays in this part share a core principle of everyday antiracism: *everyday action inside schools is not the only way to counteract racism and racial inequality in society, but it is one crucial way.*

How can educators keep inquiring about everyday antiracist action?

1. Create a context for collective, collegial responses to racism.

   Audrey Thompson argues that antiracist educators, particularly white educators, must cooperate with colleagues rather than strike out as lone "heroes."

2. Remember that even antiracist educators reproduce a racialized social system.

   Eduardo Bonilla-Silva and David Embrick suggest that antiracist educators must remain aware of their participation in unequal systems.

3. Stay hopeful.

   Ron Glass urges educators to remain hopeful that everyday action matters.

61

Resisting the "Lone Hero" Stance

Audrey Thompson

After studying white privilege in a graduate multicultural education class, Patrick, a white third-grade teacher, was determined to shake things up at Fillmore Elementary School (all names are pseudonyms). At the next faculty meeting, he came out blazing. The new policy they were discussing was racist, he announced; it catered to white privilege and dominance. At subsequent meetings, he distributed articles on whiteness and identified examples of racism in the school. The other white teachers responded with muted hostility. They were not racist, they protested. Believing that they already knew what he was going to say, his colleagues stopped listening to him. Because he worked on an all-white faculty, Patrick was perhaps more likely to encounter overt hostility and resistance than he would in a more diverse setting. In polite mixed-race settings, skeptical whites may refrain from overtly dismissing antiracist claims or statements so as to not be thought racist. At the end of the semester, Patrick abandoned his attempts to discuss racism with the faculty, deciding to concentrate on what he could accomplish alone in his classroom.

Initially Penny, too, was excited at the prospect of challenging racism. A white student teacher impatient to make a difference, she quickly grew disenchanted with her university classes. "All we're doing is *talking* about racism," she complained. "I want to go out there and really connect with students of color. We can sit around and theorize all we want, but it doesn't help the kids." Her impatient idealism alarmed several of her classmates. "You're not *ready* to teach our kids," one of the students of color told her. "The only one of us you listen to is Regina. How are we going to trust you with our kids when you won't let go of any of your white privilege?" When addressed as if she were no different from countless other white teachers—well intentioned but ignorant—Penny disengaged. She attended the remaining class meetings in silence, her arms wrapped tightly around her body.

Like Patrick's colleagues, Penny was offended at being addressed as white. But, rather than seeing herself as racially innocent, Penny was overwhelmed with guilt about her white privilege. She felt helpless before the realization that many of the privileges she enjoyed—her family's wealth, her access to higher education, and her fluency in the language of power—could be explained by structural racism rather than solely by personal merit. As she became aware of her own investments in whiteness, Penny lost the privilege of thinking of herself as a distinctive individual whose race was irrelevant. Anxious both to restore her sense of specialness and to distance herself from her whiteness, Penny had found refuge in the role of "exceptional white person." In this common stance, antiracist whites project any negative qualities associated with whiteness onto others, while they stand out as the rare white person who "gets" it. By acknowledging her whiteness but highlighting her difference from less enlightened or untrustworthy whites, Penny sought to evade the question of her complicity in racism.

Turning to Regina, a student of color, for acceptance and approval, Penny came to rely on her as the voice of racial authority. Although Penny longed for the support of the other students of color, she ignored their views if they conflicted with what she thought Regina thought. The more people talked about racial issues, the more complex they became. Frustrated by talk that made her feel less and less like she "got" it and fearing that her specialness might go unrecognized, she poured her energy into highlighting the contrast between herself and her white classmates, whom she saw as talking the talk but not walking the walk. In emphasizing that she alone was willing to do more than "just talk," Penny adopted the pose of lone white hero.

Although at times abject in her need for the approval of the students of color in the class, Penny did not assume a genuinely humble learning stance. Whites who position themselves as exceptions to whiteness often believe that after two or three classes about white dominance and privilege—or even one or two conversations—they are well positioned to make pronouncements about race and racism. Some of us are quick to practice surveillance over others; others want to take charge and lead the way. Many of us demand that our antiracist activism be acknowledged and celebrated. Above all, we expect our own anxieties, feelings, opinions, and questions about race to organize discussions around race and racism.

The danger in priding ourselves on our exceptionalism—a standing temptation for antiracist whites—is that we focus on the workings of dominance and privilege in other white people. Privately, perhaps unconsciously, we assume, like Penny and Patrick, that we are fine and that it is only other white people who need to change. Advanced forms of white exceptionalism dramatize this difference between ourselves and others. Posturing as lone white heroes, we underscore our willingness to take the initiative in antiracist work and to make sacrifices in doing so, even facing disapproval or punishment. Our focus, however, is less on the work to be done than on our own pivotal status in the business of change. To borrow a phrase from my friend Georgia Johnson, "The emPHAsis is on the wrong sylLAble." When white antiracist activists are seduced by the image of ourselves as heroes, we fail to interrogate the efficacy of our grand gestures. As whiteness theorist Alison Bailey asked at a gathering of white antiracist activists: "Who is this really helping? It seems like the main point of the gesture is to be able to tell your buddies, 'Wait till you hear what I did today!'"

Although would-be heroes may engage in important work, our desire for personal attention threatens to undermine other antiracist processes that depend on collective work and a degree of anonymity. What disturbed Penny's classmates was that she seemed intolerant of the long, sometimes slow, often undramatic, behind-the-scene process of social and institutional change. In her impatience to do something recognizably antiracist, Penny was unwilling to take the time to develop the complex understandings she needed to do antiracist work well. Invested in an image of herself as an informed, reliable, courageous, and committed antiracist, Penny expected people of color as a group to immediately recognize her as one of "us." When most of her black and brown classmates refused to offer her the approval she sought, Penny's heroic persona collapsed.

When we posture, we do so for an audience. While Penny looked to Regina in particular and to students of color more generally as her audience, for Patrick there were two audiences, both predominantly white. The audience to whom he reported his antiracist work consisted of other antiracist educators, but the more immediate audience for his interventions was his white, race-evasive colleagues at Fillmore. Because Patrick expected his colleagues to condemn his antiracist initiatives, he was more successful than Penny at maintaining his new antiracist identity. He remained committed to antiracist pedagogy, but his interventions failed to change school discourses about race, serving only to alienate his white peers. Despite the "we" statements that Patrick conscientiously employed, it was clear to the other teachers and administrators that he saw himself as not-that-kind-of-white. Patrick genuinely wanted his colleagues to address racism and was frustrated by their refusal to do so, yet their resistance helped him display his own courage and commitment. Faced with the hostility of his white colleagues, Patrick could embrace an image of himself as a white hero battling incredible odds and maintaining his moral and political integrity.

Both Patrick and Penny were excited by the idea of becoming antiracist crusaders. Unfortunately, their impatience to make their mark undermined their efficacy. Eager to distance themselves from their former white obliviousness, they also distanced themselves from their white colleagues. This exceptionalist impulse has been encouraged by some researchers, who believe that antiracist whites must develop a positive self-image in place of an abject one. Yet celebrating heroism as the antidote to guilt often serves to recenter white privilege, as the struggle against racism becomes an occasion for exceptional whites to get extra credit as good, hardworking people qualified beyond doubt to lead.

Dramatic heroism is not the best or the only alternative to despair. Important as it is for white antiracists to respond to racism decisively and courageously, much of antiracist work is not dramatic. It is slow, patient, and systematic. An emphasis on white heroism suppresses the everyday labor necessary to create the conditions for change. The preoccupation with white agency also highlights white righteousness and downplays the vital role of people of color. Whites who perform the role of lone antiracist hero in classroom and school settings risk treating racism as an occasion for the display of their own virtue, much in the way that movies like *Ghosts of Mississippi* and *Amistad* foreground white saviors and ignore the agency of people of color. The long-standing and continuing antiracist activism of numerous people of color becomes a mere backdrop for the courageous moral stand taken by a white person.

Because dominant racial narratives encourage whites to approach antiracism in heroic rather than everyday terms, white antiracist teachers need to work at not thinking of ourselves as heroes and not wanting others to view us as exceptional. We must create a context for collective, collegial responses to racism, rather than setting ourselves up as judges who stand apart from other whites. The systematic work of inviting guest speakers, setting up workshops or study groups, attending conferences, arranging to collaborate on racial issues with a sister institution, hiring new faculty, working with parents and leaders in communities of color, and enlisting the support of administrators all helps create such a context. So does talking with colleagues outside of faculty meetings, learning about one another's teaching, and engaging in the extended conversations that are not possible in faculty meetings.

Because antiracist work requires that whites relinquish many of our claims to innocence and unquestioned competence, white teachers who humbly address their racial privilege and ignorance are likely to feel extraordinarily vulnerable. As Karen Teel, a white middle school teacher, said of her three-year collaboration with Jennifer Obidah, an African American educator: "The biggest risk by far for me was the possibility of disillusionment with myself as a teacher, as a researcher, as a human being."[1]

By contrast, white exceptionalist stances emphasize competence and a form of innocence on the part of the lone enlightened white person. In adopting such a stance, we take ourselves out of relationships, most obviously but not only relationships with other whites. We frame our white colleagues "as 'people who don't get race the way *we* get race,'" positioning them in terms of their lack of enlightenment.[2] Although other white teachers' care and concern for students may be similar to ours only a few months earlier, our posturing as heroes leaves them with few ways to move.

Teachers of color are also burdened by white heroism. When teachers of color are expected to serve as unpaid consultants to white antiracist teachers and to praise our antiracist efforts, their energies are drained and they are relegated to a supporting role. While white teachers are celebrated for their courage and commitment in confronting their own and others' racism, the skill and effort that teachers of color invest in coaching whites is largely taken for granted. Even white antiracists who forego a heroic posture may end up burdening people of color with their demands for enlightenment and affirmation; it is possible to take a humble position about racial understanding as a way of insisting that people of color teach us everything we need to know. As Obidah says of her commitment to teach Teel how to work with African American students, people assume "that I wasn't affected by having to do that over and over again."[3] Because the white teacher is volunteering her labor, her courage and commitment are made visible, while the antiracist labor of the African American teacher is taken for granted.

Changing the racial order in schools calls for patience, tenacity, and a humble recognition of how much there is to learn. Longing to do something dramatic assumes that no significant work is yet under way but that, now that an enlightened white person is on board, things can really start happening. Chip Berlet, a long-time white activist, explains:

> There's always gonna be oppression. There will be oppressions we haven't even imagined. It's a process that never ends. The metaphor I use is canoeing upstream. If you stop paddling, you go backward. But if you build into a day-to-day kind of reality that you are paddling upstream, after a while you don't notice it. It's what you have to do.[4]

"We tend to think that the highly charged moments are the most significant," one white antiracist teacher observes, "but it's sometimes just the opposite."[5] The most important changes to the racial order may be the ones we never notice: changes that occur behind the scenes, become second nature, or involve silence rather than speaking. To insist on seeing change that we find personally gratifying and to assume that we are at the forefront of change is to privilege our own need for control over the process. Bringing about lasting change takes time. As Jesse Wimberley, a long-time activist, observes: "We don't try to get as many large showcase victories as we do people saying, 'I get it. We need to work together.'"[6]

RESOURCES

Julie Landsman. 2001. *A White Teacher Talks about Race*. Lanham, MD: Scarecrow Press.

Jennifer E. Obidah and Karen Manheim Teel. 2001. *Because of the Kids: Facing Racial and Cultural Differences in Schools*. New York: Teachers College Press.

Cooper Thompson, Emmett Schaefer, and Harry Brod. 2003. *White Men Challenging Racism: 35 Personal Stories*. Durham, NC: Duke University Press.

DISCUSSION QUESTIONS

1. **Principle:** If you are a white teacher struggling to pursue antiracism, how do you feel after reading this piece? What is at stake for you in this work, and what ideas about yourself and your efforts do you find it hard to call into question? If you are a teacher of color, do you see any related issues in your own antiracist work?

2. **Strategy:** How can white teachers become energized to fight racism, or stay energized, without falling into the traps that Thompson describes as "lone white heroism"?

3. **Try tomorrow:** How could you invite colleagues to join you in ongoing "systematic work" against racial inequality in your school? What specifically would you invite them to do? Try role-playing the invitation.

Audrey Thompson is a professor of philosophy of education and gender studies at the University of Utah, where she teaches courses on African American and feminist epistemologies, whiteness theory, and the history of women in education. Her research interests include progressive pedagogy, children's literature, race narratives, and cross-race listening.

62

Recognizing the Likelihood of Reproducing Racism

Eduardo Bonilla-Silva and David G. Embrick

This book is filled with suggestions for the everyday ways in which teachers might change the racial status quo; it is also full of indications that teachers' everyday actions and ideas help maintain the racial status quo. Contrary to the popular belief that educators across the world have typically been agents for progressive racial change, the weight of the evidence suggests that most educational systems and most educators operate to maintain racial hierarchy rather than to challenge it.

Since schools typically reproduce a society's racial structure, antiracist educators should not envision schools as places where that structure will be easily challenged. Rather, in order to "fight the power" of racial inequality through schools, educators must always consider how they unwittingly assist in the reproduction of the racial order through their everyday interactions with students. Indeed, educators should realize that schools are typically central in the reproduction of racism rather than places where racism is challenged.

Educators at all levels, despite our protestations to the contrary, do not represent a special category of people who remain magically uninfluenced by broader social norms. While most Americans falsely view racism as isolated acts of individual prejudice, racism actually entails constant relations of domination and subordination between members of social groups defined as superior and inferior.[1] Educators are part of this set of relations. White educators in particular, as members of the dominant group, can never fully escape their dominant position nor fully abandon practices that keep the racial order in place. Moreover, when white educators go home after school, it is usually to segregated communities where they will replenish negative views and perceptions about racial minorities, even when they wish not to.[2] Teachers of color working within a racially unequal system can also unwittingly reproduce the racial status quo through their everyday acts.

"The educators must be educated" is a famous line from Marx that Paulo Freire incorporated in his book, *The Pedagogy of the Oppressed*.[3] Rather than simply setting forth to transform the world by educating others, antiracist teachers must always attend to the roles they play in reproducing the current racial order. Antiracist educators must remember that they work inside a racialized social structure that they are likely to reproduce. At the same time, if teachers question the social order, some of the material they teach and the critical spirit they bring to the fore will rub off on their students.[4] But self-criticism about our own roles in reproducing the racial status quo is central to the process of developing new educational practices that can change it.

We offer a few specific suggestions for white antiracist educators joining the struggle against the racially unequal status quo, since they comprise the majority of the teaching force; several of these suggestions can be extended to teachers of color as well.

First, while the classroom is important, be ready to play an active role in broad social movements outside of the formal school environment, too. Second, be patient. Do not expect students or parents of color to accept you in social solidarity until you prove yourself under fire as someone committed both to change and to critical self-analysis. Do not try leading the oppressed rather than learning from them. However, know that after you have proven yourself as a self-critical participant in the fight for justice and equality, you will be accepted as a "brother" or "sister." Third, remember that since every educator is part of the racial order, whether you like it or not, you benefit from the way things are set up. White teachers must accept the fact that you too accrue some of the material and psychological "wages of Whiteness"[5] each day and should not believe for a second that you are "beyond race."

Finally, and most important, to be an antiracist educator you must be antiracist in your everyday experiences outside of schools as well as inside them. A white teacher in particular must ask himself: do I live in a desegregated neighborhood? Do I take an active stance against racial stereotypes and racist jokes by friends, family, and co-workers? Do I support programs designed to give minorities an equal opportunity? Do I support interracial friendships, dating, and marriage?

Becoming an antiracist educator is not simply a matter of becoming enlightened about one's own prejudice, or about teaching students not to be racist. Rather, it is about always attending to the hardest thing of all to stomach: how and when one's own everyday lived experiences as an educator help reproduce the racial status quo.

RESOURCES

Teaching for Change is a nonprofit that provides ideas and information on practicing anti-racism in the classroom: www.teachingforchange.org.

DISCUSSION QUESTIONS

1. **Principle:** The authors imply, in the end, that schools may not be the best places for meaningful social change. Do you agree? Why or why not? How does the suggestion make you feel?

2. **Strategy:** The authors suggest that antiracist educators must be antiracist outside as well as inside schools. If professed antiracist educators do not work against racial inequality throughout their everyday lives, have they somehow failed? Why or why not?

3. **Try tomorrow:** Can you think of anything you did recently that may have contributed to an unequal racial order, rather than challenge it? What could you have done differently?

Eduardo Bonilla-Silva is professor of sociology at Duke University. He is best known for his book Racism Without Racists: Color-blind Racism and the Persistence of Racial Inequality in the United States.

David G. Embrick is an assistant professor in the sociology department at Loyola University–Chicago. He is currently examining discrepancies between corporations' public views and statements on diversity and their implementation of diversity as a policy, and participating in a multi-university project examining student racial attitudes in different academic environments.

63

Staying Hopeful

Ronald David Glass

As Paulo Freire put it, "Hope is an ontological need."[1] The path forward in antiracist work is always a bit unclear. Freire and Myles Horton remind us that the road to racial equality can only be made "by walking."[2] Antiracist work must take place without the benefit of any absolute certainties about the routes. Thompson (Chapter 61) suggests that antiracist work is particularly complex for white educators, who cannot fully absolve themselves of complicity in the very structures they are opposing (see also Bonilla-Silva and Embrick, Chapter 62). For all educators, constructing an antiracist road requires humility about the inescapable limits and constraints that bind our work. It also requires battling inevitable despair.

Despair often overtakes educators who realize the enormity of the task of overcoming racism, which is embedded throughout the fabric of the culture and reaches into the most intimate domains of everyday life. Despair overtakes all educators who feel that they can never make a difference that will make fundamental changes, that they cannot bear the weight of a racist history in each moment of the day and in every interaction. Despair leads us to wonder if perhaps we should devote ourselves to some more obtainable goal in striving to make the world a better place.

Antiracist work is not something you do for part of the day and then go home; it is a way of life and has to permeate every aspect of what you do. There is no beginning and no end in the struggle for justice. Yes, this is hard and difficult work, morally challenging and emotionally draining.

But we cannot employ the privilege of giving in to this despair. This issue calls to my mind the stock greeting, "Down but not out!" between my friend Marc and me during the two years we battled cancer. Marc's ferocious malignancy overcame him; my less virulent disease was vanquished. When death pounds your defenses, the life remaining offers hope enough for taking the fight forward another day, or simply another moment. This is the nature of revolutionary hope, and it is the most reliable antidote to despair in the struggle for justice. As long as we are alive, we have the opportunity to continue to challenge the "isms" that shape the contours of injustice and are the terrain of our journey without maps. What makes hope an ontological need is that it helps us to reach beyond the limits of the moment; it reaffirms that the evils and injustice of the day have not yet extinguished us.

Decades of antiracist resistance have exacted a heavy toll from me. I anticipate the pain ahead for Ben, my "mixed-race" son. He will wrestle with his identity in the face of a dominant ideology trying to coerce him into categories given by an unjust racial order. That force is formidable and inflicts deep harms. Yet racist ideology has also suffered major defeats that have opened up social, economic, and political possibilities that were barely imaginable only a generation earlier. Revolutionary hope cannot take away the suffering along the journey toward justice, but it recognizes that despair only undermines the efficacy of the struggle and comforts the enemies of change.

Human beings build the history, culture, and situations that they live. Critical consciousness emerges from the effort to grasp that the given limits are not fated realities but obstacles and boundaries created in the course of human events. The struggle for justice is realized "by way of a breach with the real, concrete economic, political, social, [and] ideological . . . order"[3] and embodied in specific actions that aim at remaking the world. Justice is not achieved once and for all in some cataclysmic upheaval, but rather step by step, situation by situation, particular context by particular context. Sometimes, in unpredictable moments of history, localized changes expand rapidly into transformative leaps that reshape an era. But even these leaps rely entirely on the innumerable small steps that precede and sustain them. Revolutionary hope identifies possible actions despite situational limits; it recognizes that justice requires ongoing work and struggle. It is precisely the embodiment of this work and struggle in a way of life that avoids the trap of despair.

The small steps I took in my own youth carried minimal weight, yet still packed sufficient force to transform my immediate situations. As a white person, I discovered the power of my voice to disrupt conspiracies of silence in the face of racism when I challenged the tellers of racist jokes and questioned stereotypes passed off as truth. My courage grew with each experience, and as my fears became less fearsome, my power increased and I engaged a broader and riskier range of situations. By my senior year of high school, I interrupted my basketball coach's halftime rant about "losing to a bunch of niggers" in a championship game, which he regarded as an affront to our racial superiority as well as to our undefeated season. Speaking truth to power not only preserved my own sense of integrity but also showed my white teammates that racism need not be tolerated from anyone at any time. This action demonstrated my willingness to take risks as an ally, since I had used my relative privilege to provide some minimal protection for my one black teammate. I was the only player to give him lifts to his house, which sat at the end of a dirt road at the edge of the community, keeping him from a long bus trip and walk home after practices. I befriended the handful of other black students in the school and intervened physically when white toughs assaulted them, even though on one occasion knives were being wielded. These steps were part of a family pattern: my parents took me to a small local civil rights march associated with the Selma demonstration and quietly hired a big-city lawyer to defend innocent black residents being victimized by an unscrupulous landlord. My father took me with him to the black shantytown as he made an emergency house call for an injured child, far beyond the normal limits of his neurosurgical practice. It was impressed upon me that these were not acts of charity but of self-interested solidarity; they were not demonstrations of exceptionalism, but acts of moral and political obligation. As Jews, I was told, we were only safe to the degree that the society was just for all. We were responsible for using every means at our disposal to affect whatever immediate situation we faced.

As I entered the workforce, the scope of my challenges to racism expanded. I became a counselor in a large family services agency, where I faced battles over hiring the agency's first black professional and providing focused programming on racism as a type of community mental-social health problem. As a leader in the anti–nuclear weapons movement, I struggled to link racism and militarism in our research, programs, and civil disobedience actions. I served on the board of trustees of a synagogue, where I convened a committee of Jews and Blacks that collaborated on programs to address poverty and homelessness and created an interracial, interfaith Passover seder that for two years drew more than 250 participants. My university research, writing, and teaching explicitly attempted to contribute to antiracist struggle. I led faculty retreats and seminars on racial issues, chaired college and university diversity committees, monitored compliance with affirmative action principles, and mentored faculty and students of color. With local schools, I facilitated projects to address diversity issues related to professional development, student achievement, and parental involvement. I provided background information and research to reporters for local and statewide media outlets to help shape coverage of race-related issues.

Does any of this work make me exceptional or even exemplary? No! I am only one among countless unnamed people who have fought against racial inequality across the generations. The struggle for justice is not some particular action; it is a way of life that finds room for transformative action in every domain. Does racism still exist? Yes! Am I personally still infected by racist ideology? Yes! Have my efforts or these projects achieved all their aims? No! There is more that could and should be done in each context and situation. But I now have a deeper grasp of the realities of racism and the difficulties of antiracist struggle, which enables me to be more powerful and effective in future efforts. So I continue to leverage the opening within each situation to push beyond the limits of racism and expand the space for justice. Should I despair over what remains unachieved? No! I only hope to fight another day. If each of us were dedicated daily to the tasks immediately within our reach, the wheel of history would turn more quickly; the dream of justice would be pursued, despite its obscurities and the obstacles to its realization. Neither alone nor together can people accomplish all that must be done, but this limit relieves no one from the obligation to do whatever she or he can.

RESOURCES

Lucy Phenix, Cumberland Mountain Educational Cooperative. 1985. *You Got to Move!* [Motion Picture]. New York: Icarus Films.

DISCUSSION QUESTIONS

1. **Principle:** How can an educator fight despair in the face of the enormity of this country's racial inequality?
2. **Strategy:** As an educator, what experiences have fostered "revolutionary hope" in you?
3. **Try tomorrow:** What is one thing you could do to inspire "revolutionary hope" in your colleagues, your students, or yourself?

Ron Glass is an associate professor of philosophy of education at the University of California–Santa Cruz, and chair of the Social Context and Policy Studies Ph.D. program. His work focuses on ideological formation, and the role of education in developing a just, pluralistic democracy.

64

What Is Next?

Mica Pollock

Now that you are done reading this book, you may be both inspired and over-whelmed. I have felt that way as I put this book together over the past three years. I asked authors to "get real" about dealing with race in school. As I worked through the complexities of their proposed solutions, I was struck again by how complicated and ongoing this work has to be.

I hope that this book has helped you hone your *everyday race consciousness*—your awareness of how on a daily basis, complex individuals live lives as racial group members, treat one another in racial terms, and experience racially unequal systems. I also hope that you keep asking yourself: *in such a world, which actions inside schools and classrooms counteract racism and racial inequality?*

Educators have an exciting role to play in today's struggle for a more equitable society, for we can help equalize opportunity on a moment-to-moment basis. We can treat all students as equally complex and worthy. We can teach them to treat other people that same way. We can team with outside opportunity providers to secure opportunities schools cannot provide; but above all we can ensure that our schools and classrooms are sites for counteracting inequalities on a daily basis.

Your daily job is a perfect springboard to do this work. I hope that along with your colleagues and your students and their communities, you keep inquiring about the opportunity consequences of everyday actions inside schools, as I will.

Complete List of Everyday Antiracist Strategies*

Remember That Racial Categories Are Not Biological Realities

Race categories are not biological or genetic realities. They are categories that humans made up.

- Teach students why race is an obsolete biological concept.
- Resist the programmed assumption that different racial groups have different intellectual abilities.
- Try not using the word "Caucasian."

Get Ready to Talk about a Racialized Society

Teachers need to discuss the relevance of race in school with students, parents, and each other.

- Start developing the will, skill, and capacity to engage in courageous conversations about race.
- Start talking precisely about moving students to opportunity.
- Start thinking critically about what it means to "care" for students.

Remember That People Do Not Fit Neatly and Easily into Racial Groups

People do not fit easily and neatly into racial groups, even though they also often experience the world as racial group members.

- Try to follow children's leads in conversations about race.
- Observe the complex ways that students interact informally.

Remember That People Are Treated as Racial Group Members and Need to Examine That Experience

Students (and teachers) need to process their experiences in the world as racial group members.

*This list compiles strategies and principles proposed in this book. Please extend it over time with your colleagues, your students, and their communities.

- Create cocoons for strengthening identities.
- Be aware that students of color may need to heal from internalized oppression.
- Urge students to see and treat one another as equally worthy.

Emphasize Individuality

We must get to know one another as individuals, not just as "racial group" members.

- Refuse to see individuals as automatic representatives of "achievement gaps."
- Cultivate a mindset of curiosity about your students as individuals.
- Cultivate individualized points of personal connection with your students.

Remember That Students Experience Racially Unequal Expectations about Their Brainpower

Educators must remember that students may have experienced unequal expectations based on their race. Educators need to counter student anxiety about unequal intelligence or potential.

- To promote persistent achievement among students of color, be a perfectionist, but help students meet high standards.
- When giving feedback to students of color, emphasize high standards and assert your belief in their ability to reach them.

Counter Racially Patterned Skill Gaps

Educators must give students skills they have previously been denied or failed to acquire.

- Never confuse teaching academic skills with holding low expectations for student achievement.
- Think carefully about how you use groups in detracked classrooms.

Help Students Gain Fluency in "Standard" Behaviors While Honoring the "Nonstandard" Behaviors They Already Have

Educators must help students to be successful on "standard measures"—even as we remember that often, students have and need far more skills than we may be assessing.

- Teach to standards, but also honor nonstandard knowledge.
- Do not disparage the nonstandard varieties of English students speak.
- Do not disparage students' own cultural codes; help them become fluent in multiple cultural codes.

Defy Racially Based Notions of Potential Careers and Contributions

Students may sense that their future careers and contributions are limited to certain "races," and teachers must open up that sense of limited possibility.

- Challenge cultural messages of who can and cannot do science.
- Introduce students to "ordinary" role models; then have them practice what they learn.

Analyze Racial Disparities in Opportunities to Learn

If certain school practices are denying opportunity to students along racial lines, those practices must be shifted so that children are provided opportunity instead.

- Push for optimal learning opportunities for all children as if they were your own.
- Avoid disproportionately disciplining students of color, and always use discipline to reconnect students to the benefits of learning.

Create Curriculum That Invites Students to Explore Complex Identities *and* Consider Racial Group Experiences

Racial identities are always in flux and complex, never fixed or simple, and they should be discussed that way in the classroom.

- Use photography to wrestle with questions of racial identity.
- Encourage students to explore racial identities in their writing.
- Involve students in selecting reading materials.

Create Curriculum That Analyzes Opportunity Denial

Individuals live lives in racially unequal opportunity structures, and they must analyze those structures in order to challenge them.

- Teach critical analysis of systems of racial oppression.
- Include critical popular culture in your curriculum.
- Engage youth in participatory inquiry across differences.

Create Curriculum That Represents a Diverse Range of People Thoroughly and Complexly

Representations of groups must always be complex and thorough, never reductive or stereotypic.

- Interrogate Arab invisibility and hypervisibility.
- Consider how representations of communities in texts can be harmful, and invite community members to class to represent themselves.
- Teach representations of cultural difference in films without fixing the identity or reducing the complexity of "minority cultures."
- Think twice about that poster.
- Take up the challenge of teaching racially sensitive literature.

Create Curriculum That Discusses History Accurately and Thoroughly

Inaccurate or limited information about racial groups' histories and experiences must be replaced with accurate and thorough information.

- Make race relevant in all-white classrooms by teaching local history.
- Teach facts, not stereotypes, about groups' experiences.

Investigate Learning Experiences in Your Classroom

No classroom interaction is necessarily racially harmful or unequal, but some classroom interactions might be. The educator must investigate, without forcing a racial lens on the interactions.

- Use student inquiry to investigate the learning experience.
- Interrogate the meanings of students' silences.
- Question sweeping generalizations about cultural groups; instead, ask group members how they are personally experiencing your classroom.
- Keep trying to make predominantly white classrooms safe spaces for students of color.
- Consider when racially spotlighting and racially ignoring students in classrooms may harm them.

Spearhead Conversations with Students about Racism in Their Lives and Yours

Competing definitions of racism and antiracism should be discussed.

- Brainstorm and discuss racial incidents as a way to push toward deeper understandings of racism and antiracism.

- Debate racially charged topics directly and carefully in a structured format.
- Let students help define and debate the antiracist policies necessary for improving your school.

Talk Thoroughly with Colleagues about Race and Achievement

Since talking reductively about racial achievement patterns makes it impossible to solve those patterns, educators must talk thoroughly about causes and solutions instead.

- Cultivate a school-based discourse that emphasizes educators' responsibility for students' learning.
- Add structural analyses to cultural explanations of variations in student achievement.
- Talk about racial hierarchies when you assess school reforms.
- Discuss regularly with colleagues the many ideas and actions it will take to enrich the education of all students in diverse schools.

Analyze, with Colleagues and Students, How Your Race Affects Your Teaching

Educators need to discuss how their own teaching orientations might be linked to their experiences in the world as a racial group member.

- Discuss students' use of the "n-word."
- Engage in cross-racial dialogue with your colleagues.
- Identify who you are in relation to the curriculum.
- Notice how racial lenses shape ideas about "good" teaching.

Inquire Fully about Home Communities

Reductive or denigrating ideas about home communities must be replaced by thorough inquiry into home communities.

- Respect and seek to learn about students' home worlds.
- Start getting to know your students' communities.
- Help students to investigate and document their complex communities.

Discuss Parents' Experiences of Racially Unequal Opportunity

Parents, too, may experience educational systems as racially unequal; educators must engage parents in discussions about those experiences.

- Actively cultivate the trust of parents of color.
- Help parents who struggle against damaging stereotypes of their children.
- Undermine racially stratified tracking through minority parent involvement.

Struggle to Change a System That Is Unequal, While Working Within It

Everyday action inside schools is not the only way to equalize opportunity racially, but it is one crucial way.

- Create a context for collective, collegial responses to racism.
- Remember that even antiracist educators reproduce a racialized social system.
- Stay hopeful.

Notes

Introduction

1. West 1992.

SECTION A: RACE CATEGORIES: WE ARE ALL THE SAME, BUT OUR LIVES ARE DIFFERENT

PART I

2. Mica Pollock

1. Banaji 2001.
2. Gould 1996.
3. Lemann 1999.
4. Donato 1997.
5. Tyack 1993.
6. Steele and Aronson 1995.
7. Lee 1996.
8. Smedley 1999.

3. Carol C. Mukhopadhyay

1. Mukhopadhyay, Henze, and Moses 2007.
2. Ibid. See also Gould 1996.

PART II

4. Glenn E. Singleton and Cyndie Hays

1. West 1993, 155–56.
2. West 1993, 3.
3. Pollock 2004a.

5. Mica Pollock

1. Pollock 2004a; Olsen 1995.
2. Kirp 2007.
3. Braga and Pineda 2006.
4. Pollock 2004a.

6. Sonia Nieto

1. Ginley 1999, 85–86.
2. For a review of the research, see Nieto 2004.
3. Weinberg 1982.
4. Noddings 1992; Valenzuela 1999.
5. Rolón-Dow 2005.

PART III

7. Kimberly Chang and Rachel Conrad

1. Rizvi 1993; Van Ausdale and Feagin 2002.
2. Reddy 1994, 46.
3. Ayers 1999, 139.
4. Mura 1999, 91.
5. Ayers 1999, 141.
6. Ayers 1999, 142.

8. Ben Rampton

1. Gilroy 1987.
2. Hewitt 1986, 178; Sutton-Smith 1982.
3. Cutler 2003.
4. Hill 2003.
5. Hall 1988, 2.

PART IV

9. Patricia Gándara

1. Gándara 2004.
2. Gándara and Moreno 2002.
3. Gándara and Bial 2001.
4. Gándara 1995; Phelan, Davidson, and Yu 1997.
5. Erikson 1968.

10. Angela Valenzuela

1. Córdova 2005; Fanon 1991; Memmi 1965; Torres 2003.
2. Macedo 1994; Olsen 1998; Valenzuela 1999.
3. Macedo 1994; Torres 2003.
4. Valenzuela 1999.
5. Anzaldúa 1999; Anzaldúa and Moraga 1983.

11. L. Janelle Dance

1. Tatum 2003.

PART V

12. Samuel R. Lucas

1. Walters, McCammon, and James 1990.
2. Moses 1941.
3. Lucas and Paret 2005.
4. Jencks and Phillips 1998.
5. Daniels, Devlin, and Roeder 1997; Nisbett 1998.
6. McFadden et al. 1992 versus Ferguson 1998.
7. Fordham and Ogbu 1986 versus Cook and Ludwig 1998.
8. Fischer et al. 1996 versus Phillips et al. 1998.
9. Lucas 2000.
10. Schiele 1991.
11. McFadden et al. 1992.
12. Lacy and Middleton 1981.
13. Pollock 2001.
14. Arrow 1973; Blank, Dabady, and Citro 2004, 61–63.
15. Useem 1992; Lucas 1999, 2001.

13. Joshua Aronson

1. Aronson 2002; Steele and Aronson 1995.
2. Cohen, Steele, and Ross 1999.
3. Dee 2004.

14. Heather M. Pleasants

1. Ladson-Billings 1994.

SECTION B: HOW OPPORTUNITIES ARE PROVIDED AND DENIED INSIDE SCHOOLS

PART VI

15. Ronald F. Ferguson

1. Ferguson and Wimer 2006.

16. Geoffrey L. Cohen

1. Cohen, Steele, and Ross 1999; Cohen and Steele 2002; see also Crocker et al. 1991.
2. Ferguson 1998.
3. Cohen, Steele, and Ross 1999.
4. Cohen and Steele 2002.
5. Cohen and Garcia 2005.
6. Harber 1998; Massey, Scott, and Dornbusch 1975; Cohen and Steele 2002.
7. See also Crocker et al. 1991.
8. Cohen, Steele, and Ross 1999.
9. Walton and Cohen 2007.

10. Walton and Cohen 2007.
11. Aronson and Inzlicht 2004.
12. Cohen et al. 2006.

PART VII

17. Amanda Taylor

1. Ferguson 2003; Jussim, Eccles, and Madon 1996.
2. Ladson-Billings 1994.
3. Good 1987, 3.
4. Ferguson 2003.
5. Delpit 1988.

18. Beth C. Rubin

1. Wheelock 1992; Cohen and Lotan 1995.
2. Mickelson 2005.
3. Rubin 2003.
4. Oakes 1985; Mehan 1992; Slavin 1993; Tate 1994; Welner and Oakes 1996.

PART VIII

19. Edmund T. Hamann

1. See Valdés 2001.
2. Valdés 2001.
3. Valdés 2003.
4. Sarroub 2005.
5. TESOL Board 1997.

20. John Baugh

1. Labov et al. 1968.
2. Williams 1975.
3. Baugh 2000, Smitherman 2000.
4. African American Educational Task Force 1996, 40.
5. *New York Times*, 24 Dec. 1996, A22.
6. Smitherman 1977.
7. Stockman 1996; Wyatt 1995.
8. Ball et al. 2003.
9. Baugh 2000.
10. Alim 2004.

21. Prudence Carter

1. P. Carter 2005.
2. Alexander, Entwisle, and Thompson 1987; Farkas et al. 1990; Roscigno and Ainsworth-Darnell 1999.

3. Warikoo 2005.
4. Delpit 1997.

PART IX

22. Maria Ong

1. Fausto-Sterling and English 1986.
2. Fullilove 1987; Jackson 2004.
3. LaFollette 1988; Margolis and Fisher 2002; Seymour and Hewitt 1997.
4. Ong 2005.
5. Ivie and Ray 2005.
6. Gordon 2005.
7. Childstats.gov 2005; National Science Foundation 2004.
8. Lee 1996.
9. Nakanishi and Nishido 1995; and Takaki 1990.
10. Nelson 2006.
11. Oakes 1985.
12. Lucas 1999.
13. Ong 2005.
14. Krajcik, Czerniak, and Berger 1998; Roth et al. 1991.
15. Stack 1996.
16. Leggon 2001; Ong 2005.
17. Holbrook 2005.
18. Smith 1958, 69.
19. Nelson 2006.
20. Gould 1996.

23. Meira Levinson

1. Verba, Schlozman, and Brady 1995.
2. Levinson 2004.

PART X

24. Karolyn Tyson

1. Irvine 1990.
2. Donovan and Cross 2002.
3. Darity et al. 2001.
4. Hallinan and Kubitschek 1999; Resnick 1995.
5. Tyson, Darity, and Castellino 2005.
6. Lareau 2003, 1987.

25. Pedro A. Noguera

1. Johnson, Boyden, and Pittz 2001.
2. Meier, Stewart, and England 1989.

3. Hirschi 1969.
4. Singer 1996.
5. Ferguson 2000.
6. Metropolitan Life 2001.
7. Rawls 1971.
8. Pollack 1999.
9. Ferguson 2000.
10. McLaughlin and Heath 1999.
11. Kohlberg 1973.
12. Applied Research Council 1999.
13. Shores 2003.

SECTION C: CURRICULUM THAT ASKS CRUCIAL QUESTIONS ABOUT RACE

PART XI

26. Alexandra Lightfoot

1. Pollock 2004b.
2. Fraser 2002.
3. Pollock 2004b.
4. Derman-Sparks, Phillips, and Hilliard 1997.

27. Jennifer A. Mott-Smith

1. See Ibrahim 1999, on African students in Canada identifying as "Black."
2. Suárez-Orozco and Suárez-Orozco 1995.
3. Suárez-Orozco and Suárez-Orozco 1995, 183.

28. Christine E. Sleeter

1. Sleeter 2005; Zimmerman 2002.
2. Sleeter 2002.
3. Gay 2000.
4. Milligan and Bigler 2007.
5. Sleeter 2005, 155–56.

PART XII

29. Jeff Duncan-Andrade

1. Wright 1940, xvi.
2. Freire and Macedo 1987.
3. Wright 1940, xv.
4. Wright 1940, xv.

30. Ernest Morrell

1. Morrell 2004.
2. Rose 1994.

3. George 1998.
4. Dagbovie 2005.
5. Jocson 2005; Fisher 2005.

31. María Elena Torre and Michelle Fine

1. Anand et al. 2002; Fine et al. 2005; Fine et al. 2004; Torre 2005; Torre et al. 2007; Guishard et al. 2005.
2. Torre 2005.
3. Torre et al. 2007.
4. Fine et al. 2005.
5. Fine et al. 2004.

PART XIII

32. Thea Abu El-Haj

1. Some of the ideas in this chapter and several paragraphs appeared in Abu El-Haj 2006.
2. Naber 2000; Samhan 1999.
3. Ahmad 2002; Naber 2000.
4. Ahmad 2002; Ibish 2003; Volpp 2002.
5. Mamdani 2004.
6. Abu El-Haj 2005.
7. Adeeb and Smith 1995.
8. Brayboy 2003.
9. Young 1990, 58–59.

33. Teresa L. McCarty

1. McCarty and Zepeda 1999, 200.
2. McCarty 1995.
3. Hall 1997.
4. For a helpful examination of these issues, see Fox and Short 2003.
5. Bruchac 2003, 8.
6. Riley 1993.
7. Bruchac 2003.
8. Cajete 1994.
9. Benham and Cooper 2000.
10. Slapin, Seale, and Gonzales 1992.
11. Bruchac 2003, 8–9.
12. Ayoungman 1995, 84.
13. McCarty and Watahomigie 2004, 98–99.

34. Sanjay Sharma

1. Cohen 1992.
2. Rey Chow 1998.
3. Sharma 2004, 2006.
4. Bhabha 1994.
5. Grossberg 1994.

35. Donna Deyhle

1. Deyhle 1995.
2. Nichols 2003.
3. Henze and Vanett 1993.

36. Jocelyn Chadwick

1. See Chadwick-Joshua 1998.

PART XIV

37. Mara Tieken

1. Frankenberg 1993.
2. Derman-Sparks and Ramsey 2006.
3. Pollock 2004a.

38. Paul Ongtooguk and Claudia S. Dybdahl

1. Ongtooguk 1994.
2. Cohen 1941.

SECTION D: RACE AND THE SCHOOL EXPERIENCE: THE NEED FOR INQUIRY

PART XV

39. Makeba Jones and Susan Yonezawa

1. Jones et al. 2002.
2. Jones and Yonezawa 2002.
3. Yonezawa and Jones 2007.
4. Nieto 1994; Jones and Yonezawa 2002.
5. Jones and Yonezawa 2002.
6. Douillard 2002.

40. Katherine Schultz

1. Schultz 2003.
2. Gilmore 1985; Philips 1983; Tannen and Saville-Troike 1985.
3. Au and Mason 1981; Erickson and Mohatt 1982; Philips 1983.
4. Philips 1983.
5. Fordham 1993.
6. Schultz 2003.

41. Doug Foley

1. Foley 1997.
2. Foley 1995.

3. Berkhoffer 1978.
4. Rosaldo 1989.
5. Pollock 2004a.
6. Foley 1995.
7. Foley 1996.

42. Pamela Perry

1. powell 2005.
2. hooks 1992, 175.
3. Frankenberg 1993; Perry 2002.

43. Dorinda J. Carter

1. Pollock 2004b.
2. Cookson and Persell 1991; Horvat and Antonio 1999; Zweigenhaft and Domhoff 1991.
3. Pollock 2004a.
4. D. Carter 2005.
5. hooks 1994.
6. D. Carter 2005, 174.
7. D. Carter 2005, 164–65.
8. D. Carter 2005, 163.
9. D. Carter 2005, 173.
10. D. Carter 2005, 174.
11. D. Carter 2005, 184.
12. D. Carter 2005, 182.

PART XVI

44. Lawrence Blum

1. Blum 2002.

45. Ian F. Haney López

1. see Haney López 2003, 1997.

46. David Gillborn

1. For more on this conceptualization of racism, see Gillborn 2008, 2006; Delgado and Stefancic 2001.
2. Bell 1992, 198–99.
3. Gillborn 1995.
4. Macdonald et al. 1989.

PART XVII

47. John B. Diamond

1. Lee 1996.
2. Diamond, Randolph, and Spillane 2004.

3. Lee and Loeb 2000, 8.
4. Lee and Smith 2001, 153.
5. Spillane, Hallett, and Diamond 2003.
6. Diamond, Randolph, and Spillane 2004.
7. Diamond 2007.

48. Vivian Louie

1. Louie 2004.
2. Louie 2005.

49. Rosemary Henze

1. Gardner 1985.

50. Willis D. Hawley

1. Hawley 2007; Schofield 2004; Stephan, Renfro, and Stephan 2004; Dovidio et al. 2004; Weissglass 2003; Lindsey, Robins, and Terrell 2003; Henze 2002; McKenzie and Schuerich 2003; Banks et al. 2001; Hawley et al. 1995.

PART XVIII

51. Wendy Luttrell

1. NCES 2006.
2. Luttrell, Holland, and Ward 2006.
3. Henze et al. 2002; Pollock 2004a; Eliasoph 1999.
4. Beauboeuf-Lafontant 2002; Foster 1997; Irvine 2002; Ladson-Billings 1994; Villegas and Lucas 2002.
5. Ward 2005.
6. Berlak and Moyenda 2001, 64.

52. Alice McIntyre

1. McIntyre 2002.
2. McIntyre et al. 1998.
3. Hurd and McIntyre 1996.
4. Dees 1991; Frankenberg 1996; King 1972; Segrest 1994; Stalvey 1970.
5. McIntyre 1997.

53. Priya Parmar and Shirley Steinberg

1. Kincheloe and Steinberg 1998.

54. Lee Anne Bell

1. Bell 1991.
2. Bell 2002.
3. Bell 2003.

SECTION E: ENGAGING COMMUNITIES FOR REAL

PART XIX

55. Eugene E. García

1. Steele 1997; see also McKown and Weinstein 2003.
2. Moll 2001.

56. Leisy Wyman and Grant Kashatok

1. Cleary and Peacock 1998; Gonzalez, Moll, and Amanti 2005.
2. Fredson et al. 1996.
3. Gonzalez 2005.
4. Buck and Sylvester 2005.
5. McCarty 2004; Lipka et al. 1998.

PART XX

58. Beverly Daniel Tatum

1. Losen and Orfield 2002.

59. Janie Victoria Ward

1. Ward 2000.

60. Roslyn Arlin Mickelson and Linwood H. Cousins

1. Berends et al. 2005; Jencks and Phillips 1998; Lucas 1999; Oakes 2005.
2. Mickelson 2001.
3. Mickelson 2001, Oakes 2005.
4. Boaler and Staples 2005; Burris and Welner 2005; Cohen and Lotan 1999; Hanushek and Woessmann 2005.
5. Kornhaber 1997; Mickelson 2001; Mickelson and Velasco 2006.
6. Epstein 1995; Gordon 2001; Lareau 2000.
7. Epstein 1995; Epstein and Dauber 1991; Lareau 2000.

SECTION F: KEEPING IT GOING

PART XXI

61. Audrey Thompson

1. Obidah and Teel 2001, 69.
2. Thompson 2004, 388.
3. Obidah and Teel 2001, 89.
4. Thompson, Schaefer, and Brod 2003, 92–93.
5. Fox 2001, 65.
6. Thompson, Schaefer, and Brod 2003, 75.

62. Eduardo Bonilla-Silva and David G. Embrick

1. Bonilla-Silva 1997, 2001, 2003; Goldberg 1993; Omi and Winant 1994.
2. Massey and Denton 1993, Bonilla-Silva, Goar, and Embrick 2006.
3. Freire 1993.
4. Giroux 2001.
5. Roediger 1991.

63. Ronald David Glass

1. Freire 1994, 9.
2. Horton and Freire 1990.
3. Freire 1994, 99.

Reference List

Abu El-Haj, Thea Renda. 2005. "Global Politics, Dissent, and Palestinian-American Identities: Engaging Conflict to Re-invigorate Democratic Education." In *Beyond Silenced Voices*, ed. Weis and Fine, 119–215. Rev. ed. Albany: State University of New York Press.

———. 2006. "Race, Politics, and Arab American Youth: Shifting Frameworks for Conceptualizing Educational Equity." *Educational Policy* 20(1): 13–34.

Acosta, Nikaury, Jasmine Castillo, Candace DeJesus, Emily Geneo, Monica Jones, Seequemarie Kellman, Amanda Osorio, Norman Rahman, Lisa Sheard, and Jeremy Taylor, with Janice Bloom and Lori Chajet. 2003. "Urban Students Tackle Research on Inequality: What You Thought We Didn't Know." *Rethinking Schools* 18(1): 31–32.

Adams, Maurianne, Lee Anne Bell, and Pat Griffin, eds. 1997. *Teaching for Diversity and Social Justice: A Sourcebook*. London: Routledge.

Adams, Maurianne, Warren J. Blumenfeld, Rosie Castaneda, and Heather W. Hackman, eds. 2000. *Readings for Diversity and Social Justice: An Anthology on Racism, Sexism, Anti-Semitism, Heterosexism, Classism, and Ableism*. London: Routledge.

Adeeb, Patty, and G. Pritchey Smith. 1995. "The Arab Americans." In *Educating for Diversity: An Anthology of Multicultural Voices*, ed. Carl A. Grant, 191–207. Boston: Allyn & Bacon.

African American Educational Task Force, Oakland, California. 1996. "Amended Resolution of the Board of Education Adopting the Report and Recommendations of the African American Task Force, a Policy Statement and Directing the Superintendent of Schools to Devise a Program to Improve the English Language Acquisition and Application Skills of African-American Students." No. 9697–0063. Available at http:/www/linguist.emich.edu/topics/ebonics-res2.html and http://www.edu–cyberpg.com/Linguistics/ebresolution.html, accessed November 23, 2006.

Ahmad, Muneer. 2002. "Homeland Insecurities: Racial Violence the Day after September 11." *Social Text* 72(3): 101–15.

Alexander, Karl L., Doris R. Entwisle, and Maxine S. Thompson. 1987. "School Performance, Status Relations, and the Structure of Sentiment: Bringing the Teacher Back In." *American Sociological Review* 52: 665–82.

Alim, H. Samy. 2004. *You Know My Steez: An Ethnographic and Sociolinguistic Study of Styleshifting in a Black American Speech Community*. (Publications of the American Dialect Society No. 89.) Durham, NC: Duke University Press.

Anand, Bernadette, Michelle Fine, David S. Surrey, and Tiffany Perkins. 2002. *Keeping the Struggle Alive: Studying Desegregation in Our Town. A Guide to Doing Oral History*. New York: Teachers College Press.

Anzaldúa, Gloria. 1999. *Borderlands/La Frontera*. San Francisco: Aunt Lute Books.

Anzaldúa, Gloria, and Cherie Moraga, eds. 1983. *This Bridge Called My Back: Writings by Radical Women of Color*. 2nd ed. New York: Kitchen Table, Women of Color Press.

Applied Research Council. 1999. *Turning Toward Each Other, Not On Each Other*. Oakland, CA.

Aronson, Joshua. 2002. "Stereotype Threat: Contending and Coping with Unnerving Expectations." In Aronson, *Improving Academic Achievement: Impact of Psychological Factors on Education*. San Diego: Academic Press.

Aronson, Joshua, Carrie Fried, and Catherine Good. 2002. "Reducing the Effects of Stereotype Threat on African American College Students by Shaping Theories of Intelligence." *Journal of Experimental Social Psychology* 38: 113–25.

Aronson, Joshua, and Michael Inzlicht. 2004. "The Ups and Downs of Attributional Ambiguity: Stereotype Vulnerability and the Academic Self-knowledge of African American College Students." *Psychological Science* 15: 829–36.

Aronson, Joshua, Michael J. Lustina, Catherine Good, Kelli Keough, Claude M. Steele, and Joseph L. Brown. 1999. "When White Men Can't Do Math: Necessary and Sufficient Factors in Stereotype Threat." *Journal of Experimental Social Psychology* 35: 29–46.

Arrow, Kenneth. 1973. "The Theory of Discrimination." In *Discrimination in Labor Markets*, ed. Orley Ashenfelter and Albert Rees, 3–33. Princeton, NJ: Princeton University Press.

Au, Kathryn H., and Jana M. Mason. 1981. "Social Organizational Factors in Learning to Read: The Balance of Rights Hypothesis." *Reading Research Quarterly*, 17: 115–52.

Ayers, William. 1999. "To the Bone: Reflections in Black and White." In *Racism Explained to My Daughter*, ed. T. Ben Jelloun (translated from the French by Carol Volk), 139–73. New York: The New Press.

Ayoungman, Vivian. 1995. "Native Language Renewal: Dispelling the Myths, Planning for the Future." *Bilingual Research Journal* 19: 183–87.

Ball, Arnetha F., Sinfree Makoni, Geneva Smitherman, and Arthur K. Spears. 2003. *Black Linguistics: Language, Society and Politics in Africa and the Americas*. New York: Routledge.

Banaji, Mahzarin. 2001. " 'Ordinary Prejudice': Science Briefs." *Psychological Science Agenda* (January–February): 9–11.

Banks, James A. 2001. "Diversity Within Unity: Essential Principles for Teaching and Learning in a Multicultural Society." Seattle: University of Washington, Center for Multicultural Education. Accessed November 24, 2006, at http://www.newhorizons.org/strategies/multicultural/banks.htm.

Banks, James A., Peter Cookson, Geneva Gay, Willis D. Hawley, Jacqueline Jordon Irvine, Sonia Nieto, Janet Ward Schofield, and Walter G. Stephan. 2001. *Diversity Within Unity: Essential Principles for Teaching and Learning in a Multicultural Society*. Seattle: University of Washington, Center for Multicultural Education. Accessed November 24, 2006, at http://www.educ.washington.edu/coetestwebsite/pdf/DiversityUnity.pdf.

Baugh, John. 1999. *Out of the Mouths of Slaves: African American Language and Educational Malpractice*. Austin: University of Texas Press.

———. 2000. *Beyond Ebonics: Linguistic Pride and Racial Prejudice*. New York: Oxford University Press.

Beauboeuf-Lafontant, Tamara. 2002. "A Womanist Experience of Caring: Understanding the Pedagogy of Exemplary Black Women Teachers." *Urban Review* 34(1): 71–86.

Begley, Sharon. 1995. "Three Is Not Enough." *Newsweek*, February 13, 67–69.

Bell, Derrick. 1992. *Faces at the Bottom of the Well*. New York: HarperCollins.

Bell, Lee Anne. 1991. "Changing Our Ideas About Ourselves: Group Consciousness Raising with Elementary School Girls as a Means to Empowerment." In *Empowerment Through Multicultural Education*, ed. Christine E. Sleeter, 229–50. Albany: State University of New York Press.

———. 2002. "Sincere Fictions: The Pedagogical Challenges of Preparing White Teachers for Multicultural Classrooms." *Equity and Excellence in Education* 35(3): 236–44.

———. 2003. "Telling Tales: What Stories Can Teach Us About Racism." *Race, Ethnicity and Education* 6(1): 4–25.

Benham, Maenette K.P., with Joanne E. Cooper. 2000. *Indigenous Educational Models for Contemporary Practice*. Mahwah, NJ: Lawrence Erlbaum.

Berends, Mark, Samuel R. Lucas, Thomas Sullivan, and R.J. Briggs. 2005. *Examining Gaps in Mathematics Achievement Among Racial-Ethnic Groups, 1972–1992*. Santa Monica, CA: RAND.

Berkhoffer, Robert, Jr. 1978. *The Whiteman's Indian: Images of the American Indian from Columbus to the Present*. New York: Vintage.

Berlak, Ann, and Sekani Moyenda. 2001. *Taking It Personally: Racism in the Classroom from Kindergarten to College*. Philadelphia: Temple University Press.

Bhabha, Homi. 1994. *The Location of Culture*. London: Routledge.

Blank, Rebecca M., Marilyn Dabady, and Constance F. Citro. 2004. *Measuring Racial Discrimination*. Washington, DC: National Academies Press.

Blau, Judith R., Vicki L. Lamb, Elizabeth Stearns, and Lisa Pellerin. 2001. "Cosmopolitan Environments and Adolescents' Gains in Social Studies." *Sociology of Education* 74(2): 121–38.

Blum, Lawrence. 2002. *"I'm not a racist, but . . .": The Moral Quandary of Race*. Ithaca, NY: Cornell University Press.

Boaler, Jo, and Megan Staples. 2005. "Transforming Students' Lives Through an Equitable Mathematics Approach: The Case of Railside School." Paper presented at the American Educational Research Association. Montreal, Quebec, Canada. April.

Boger, John Charles. 2002. "The New Legal Attack on Educational Diversity in America's Elementary and Secondary Schools." In *Rights at Risk: Equality in an Age of Terrorism*, ed. Diane M. Piché, William I. Taylor, and Robin A. Reed, 43–70. Washington, DC: Citizens' Commission on Civil Rights.

Bonilla-Silva, Eduardo. 1997. "Rethinking Racism: Toward a Structural Interpretation." *American Sociological Review* 62(3): 465–80.

———. 2001. *White Supremacy and Racism in the Post-Civil Rights Era*. Boulder, CO: Lynne Rienner.

———. 2003. *Racism Without Racists: Color-blind Racism and the Persistence of Racial Inequality in the USA*. Lanham, MD: Rowman & Littlefield.

Bonilla-Silva, Eduardo, Carla Goar, and David G. Embrick. 2006. "When Whites Flock Together: White Habitus and the Social Psychology of Whites' Social and Residential Segregation from Blacks." *Critical Sociology* 32(2–3): 229–54.

Braga, Leticia J., and Claudia G. Pineda. 2006. "Seek to Understand the Circumstances that Affect Children from Immigrant Households." Unpublished paper, Everyday Antiracism Working Group, Harvard Graduate School of Education.

Brayboy, B. McKinley Jones. 2003. "Visibility as a Trap: American Indian Representation in Schools." In *Invisible Children in the Society and Its Schools*, ed. Sue Books, 35–52. 2nd ed. Mahwah, NJ: Lawrence Erlbaum.

Bruchac, Joseph. 2003. *Our Stories Remember: American Indian History, Culture, and Values Through Storytelling*. Golden, CO: Fulcrum.

Buck, Patricia, and Paul Sylvester. 2005. "Pre-service Teachers Enter Urban Communities: Coupling Funds of Knowledge Research and Critical Pedagogy in Teacher Education." In *Funds of Knowledge*, ed. Gonzalez, Moll, and Amanti, 213–32. Mahwah, NJ: Lawrence Erlbaum.

Burris, Carol Corbett, and Kevin G. Welner. 2005. "Closing the Achievement Gap by De-tracking." *Phi Delta Kappan*, April 1. http://www.pdkintl.org/Kappan/k0504bur.htm.

Cajete, Gregory. 1994. *Look to the Mountain: An Ecology of Indigenous Education*. Durango, CO: Kavakí.

Carter, Dorinda J. 2005. "'In a Sea of White People': An Analysis of the Experiences and Behaviors of High-achieving Black Students in a Predominantly White High School." Ed.D. dissertation, Harvard University, Cambridge, MA.

Carter, Prudence. 2005. *Keepin' It Real: School Success Beyond Black and White*. New York: Oxford University Press.

Chadwick-Joshua, Jocelyn. 1998. *The Jim Dilemma: Reading Race in Huckleberry Finn*. Jackson: University Press of Mississippi.

Childstats.gov. 2005. *America's Children: Key National Indicators of Well-being 2005*. Federal Interagency Forum on Child and Family Statistics. http://childstats.ed.gov/ americaschildren/pop3.asp, accessed January 11, 2006.

Chow, Rey. 1998. *Ethics after Idealism*. Bloomington: Indiana University Press.

Cicourel, Aaron V. 1981. Notes on the integration of micro and macro levels of analy-sis. In *Advances in Social Theory and Methodology: Toward an Integration of Micro- and Macro-Sociologies*, ed. Karin Knorr-Cetina and Aaron V. Cicourel, 51–80. Boston: Routledge and Kegan Paul.

Cleary, Linda M., and Thomas D. Peacock. 1998. *Collected Wisdom: American In-dian Education*. Needham Heights, MA: Allyn and Bacon.

Cohen, Elizabeth G., and Rachel A. Lotan. 1995. "Producing Equal-Status Interac-tion in the Heterogeneous Classroom." *American Educational Research Journal* 32: 99–120.

———. 1999. *Designing Group Work: Strategies for the Heterogeneous Classroom*. New York: Teachers College Press.

Cohen, Felix S. 1941. *Handbook of Federal Indian Law*. Washington, DC: Govern-ment Printing Office.

Cohen, Geoffrey L., and Julio Garcia. 2005. "I Am Us: Negative Stereotypes as Collective Threats." *Journal of Personality and Social Psychology* 89: 566–82.

Cohen, Geoffrey L., Julio Garcia, Nancy Apfel, Patti Brzustoski, and Allison Master. Forthcoming. "Wise Feedback: A Field Experiment."

Cohen, Geoffrey L., Julio Garcia, Nancy Apfel, and Allison Master. 2006. "Reducing the Racial Achievement Gap: A Social-Psychological Intervention." *Science* 313: 1307–10.

Cohen, Geoffrey L., and Claude M. Steele. 2002. "A Barrier of Mistrust: How Nega-tive Stereotypes Affect Cross-Race Mentoring." In *Improving Academic Achieve-ment: Impact of Psychological Factors on Education*, ed. Joshua Aronson, 303–28. San Diego: Academic Press.

Cohen, Geoffrey L., Claude M. Steele, and Lee D. Ross. 1999. "The Mentor's Dilemma: Providing Critical Feedback Across the Racial Divide." *Personality and Social Psychology Bulletin* 25: 1302–18.

Cohen, Philip. 1992. "'It's Racism What Dunnit': Hidden Narratives in Theories of Racism." In *"Race," Culture and Difference*, ed. James Donald and Ali Rattansi, 62–103. London: Open University/Sage Publications.

Cook, Philip J., and Jens Ludwig. 1998. "The Burden of 'Acting White': Do Black Adolescents Disparage Academic Achievement?" In *The Black-White Test Score Gap*, ed. Jencks and Phillips, 375–93. Washington, D.C.: Brookings Institution Press.

Cookson, Peter W., and Caroline H. Persell. 1991. "Race and Class in America's Elite Preparatory Boarding Schools: African Americans as the 'Outsiders Within.'" *Journal of Negro Education* 60(2): 219–28.

Córdova, Teresa. 2005. "Agency, Commitment and Connection: Embracing the Roots of Chicano and Chicana Studies." Special Issue: Presence, Voice, and Politics in Chicana/o Studies, *International Journal of Qualitative Studies in Education* 18(2), March–April, 221–33.

Crocker, Jennifer, Kristin Voelkl, Maria Testa, and Brenda Major. 1991. "Social Stigma: The Affective Consequences of Attributional Ambiguity." *Journal of Personality and Social Psychology* 60: 218–28.

Curtis, Edward S. 1907–1930. *The North American Indian*. 20 vols. Washington, DC: Library of Congress. Text and digitized images available online at http://curtis .library/northwestern.edu.

Cutler, Cecelia A. 2003. "Yorkville Crossing: White Youth, Hip-Hop and African American English." In *The Language, Ethnicity and Race Reader*, ed. Harris and Rampton, 314–27. London: Routledge.

———. 2004. *Crossing Over: White Teens, Hip-Hop and African American English*. New York: New York University Press.

Dagbovie, Pero Gaglo. 2005. "'Of All Our Studies, History Is Best Qualified to Reward Our Research': Black History's Relevance to the Hip Hop Generation." *Journal of African American History* 90(3): 299–323.

Daniels, Michael, Bernie Devlin, and Kathryn Roeder. 1997. "Of Genes and IQ." In *Intelligence, Genes, and Success: Scientists respond to* The Bell Curve, ed. Bernie Devlin, Stephen E. Fienberg, Daniel P. Resnick, and Kathryn Roeder, 45–70. New York: Springer-Verlag.

Darity, William, Domini Castellino, Karolyn Tyson, Carolyn Cobb, and Brad McMillen. 2001. "Increasing Opportunity to Learn via Access to Rigorous Courses and Programs: One Strategy for Closing the Achievement Gap for At-Risk and Minority Students." Report prepared for the North Carolina Department of Public Instruction, Evaluation Section, Raleigh, NC http://www .ncpublicschools.org/Accountability/evaluation/minority/index.htm.

Dee, Thomas S. 2004. "Teacher's Race and Student Achievement in a Randomized Experiment." *Review of Economics and Statistics* 86(1): 195–210.

Dees, Morris, with Steve Fiffer. 1991. *A Season of Justice: The Life and Times of Civil Rights Lawyer Morris Dees*. New York: Charles Scribner's Sons.

de Jong, Ester J. 2004. "After Exit: Academic Achievement Patterns of Former English Language Learners." *Educational Policy Analysis Archives* 12(50). Accessed September 22, 2005, at http://epaa.asu.edu/epaa/v12n50/v12n50.pdf.

Delgado, Richard, and Jean Stefancic. 2001. *Critical Race Theory*. New York: New York University Press.

Deloria, Vine. 1988. *Custer Died for Your Sins: An Indian Manifesto*. New York: Macmillan.

Delpit, Lisa. 1988. *Other People's Children: Cultural Conflict in the Classroom*. New York: The New Press.

———. 1997. "The Silenced Dialogue: Power and Pedagogy in Educating Other People's Children." In *Education: Culture, Economy and Society*, ed. Albert Henry Halsey, Hugh Lauder, Philip Brown, and Amy Stuart Wells, 582–94. New York: Oxford University Press.

Delpit, Lisa, and Joanne Kilgore Dowdy, eds. 2002. *The Skin That We Speak: Thoughts on Language and Culture in the Classroom*. New York: The New Press.

Derman-Sparks, Louise, Carol Brunson Phillips, and Asa G. Hilliard III. 1997. *Teaching/Learning Anti-Racism: A Developmental Approach*. New York: Teachers College Press.

Derman-Sparks, Louise, and Patricia G. Ramsey. 2006. *What If All the Kids Are White? Anti-Bias Multicultural Education with Young Children and Families.* New York: Teachers College Press.

Deyhle, Donna. 1995. "Navajo Youth and Anglo Racism: Cultural Integrity and Resistance." *Harvard Educational Review* 65(3): 403–44.

Diamond, John B. 2007. "Cultivating High Expectations in an Urban Elementary School: The Case of Kelly School." In *Distributed Leadership in Practice*, ed. James P. Spillane and John B. Diamond. New York: Teachers College Press.

Diamond, John B., Antonia Randolph, and James P. Spillane. 2004. "Teachers' Expectations and Sense of Responsibility for Student Learning: The Implications of School Race, Class, and Organizational Habitus." Special Issue: Race, Power, and the Ethnography of Urban Schools. *Anthropology and Education Quarterly* 35(1): 75–98.

Donato, Ruben. 1997. *The Other Struggle for Equal Schools: Mexican Americans During the Civil Rights Era.* Albany: State University of New York Press.

Donovan, M. Suzanne, and Christopher T. Cross, eds. 2002. *Report of the National Research Council Panel on Minority Students in Special and Gifted Education.* Washington, DC: National Academy Press. http://www.nap.edu/catalog/10128.html.

Douillard, Kimberly Ann. 2002. "Going Past Done: Creating Time for Reflection in the Classroom." *Language Arts* 80: 92–98.

Dovidio, John F., Samuel L. Gaertner, Tracie L. Stewart, Vicki M. Esses, Marleen ten Vergert, and Gordon Hodson. 2004. "From Intervention to Outcome: Processes in the Reduction of Bias." In *Education Programs for Improving Intergroup Relations: Theory, Research and Practice*, ed. Walter G. Stephan and W. Paul Vogt, 243–65. New York: Teachers College Press.

Eliason, Patricia. 1995. "Difficulties with Cross-Cultural Learning Styles Assessments." In *Learning Styles in the ESL/EFL Classroom*, ed. J. Reid, 19–33. New York: Heinle and Heinle.

Eliasoph, Nina. 1999. "'Everyday Racism' in a Culture of Political Avoidance: Civil Society, Speech and Taboo." *Social Problems* 46(4): 479–502.

Epstein, Joyce L. 1986. "Parents' Reactions to Teacher Practices of Parent Involvement." *Elementary School Journal* 86: 277–94.

———. 1995. "School/Family/Community Partnerships. Caring for the Children We Share." *Phi Delta Kappan*, May, 701–12.

Epstein, Joyce L., and Susan L. Dauber. 1991. "School Programs and Teacher Practices of Parent Involvement in Inner-City Elementary and Middle Schools." *Elementary School Journal* 91: 289–305.

Erickson, Frederick, and Gerald Mohatt. 1982. "Cultural Organization of Participation Structures in Two Classrooms of Indian Students." In *Doing the Ethnography of Schooling*, ed. George Spindler, 132–74. New York: Holt, Rinehart and Winston.

Erikson, Erik. 1968. *Identity, Youth and Crisis.* New York: Norton.

Essed, Philomena. 2002. "Everyday Racism: A New Approach to the Study of Racism." In *Race Critical Theories: Text and Context*, ed. Philomena Essed and David Theo Goldberg, 176–94. Malden, MA: Blackwell Publishers.

Fanon, Franz. 1991. *Black Skin, White Masks.* New York: Grove.

Farkas, George, Robert P. Grobe, Daniel Sheehan, and Yuan Shuan. 1990. "Cultural Resources and School Success: Gender, Ethnicity, and Poverty Groups Within an Urban School District." *American Sociological Review* 55: 127–42.

Fausto-Sterling, Anne, and Lydia L. English. 1986. "Women and Minorities in Science: An Interdisciplinary Course." *Radical Teacher* 30: 16–20.

Ferguson, Ann Arnett. 2000. *Bad Boys: Public Schools in the Making of Black Masculinity*. Ann Arbor: University of Michigan Press.

Ferguson, Ronald F. 1998. "Teachers' Perceptions and Expectations and the Black-White Test Score Gap." In *The Black-White Test Score Gap*, ed. Jencks and Phillips, 273–317.

———. 2003. "Teacher Expectations and the Black-White Achievement Gap." *Urban Education* 38(4): 460–507.

Ferguson, Ronald F., and Christopher Wimer. 2006. "Peer Relations, Classroom Goal Structures, and Academic Persistence: Preliminary Findings from a Large Sample of Elementary Classrooms." Working paper, September. The Achievement Gap Initiative at Harvard University.

Fine, Michelle. 1989. "Silencing and Nurturing Voice in an Improbable Context: Urban Adolescents in Pubic School." In *Critical Pedagogy, the State, and Cultural Struggle*, ed. Giroux and McLaren, 13–37. Albany: State University of New York Press.

Fine, Michelle, Janice Bloom, April Burns, Lori Chajet, Monique Guishard, Yasser Payne, Tiffany Perkins-Munn, and María Elena Torre. 2005. "Dear Zora: A Letter to Zora Neale Hurston Fifty Years after *Brown*." *Teachers College Record* 107(3): 496–528.

Fine, Michelle, Rosemarie A. Roberts, and María Elena Torre, with Janice Bloom, April Burns, Lori Chajet, Monique Guishard, and Yasser Payne. 2004. *Echoes of Brown: Youth Documenting and Performing the Legacy of Brown v. Board of Education*. New York: Teachers College Press.

Fischer, Claude, Michael Hout, Martín Sánchez Jankowski, Samuel R. Lucas, Ann Swidler, and Kim Voss. 1996. *Inequality by Design: Cracking the Bell Curve Myth*. Princeton, NJ: Princeton University Press.

Fisher, Maisha. 2005. "From the Coffee House to the Schoolhouse: The Promise and Potential of Spoken Word Poetry in School Contexts." *English Education* 37(2): 115–31.

Foley, Douglas. 1995. *The Heartland Chronicles*. Philadelphia: University of Pennsylvania Press.

———. 1996. "The Cultural Production of the Silent Indian." In *The Cultural Production of the Educated Person: Critical Ethnographies of Schooling and Local Practice*, ed. Bradley Levinson, Douglas Foley, and Dorothy Holland. Buffalo: State University of New York Press.

———. 1997. "The Evolution of Deficit Thinking: Educational Thought and Practice." In *A Critical Appraisal of Deficit Theory in Education*, ed. Richard R. Valencia, Chapter 4. London: Falmer Press.

Fordham, Signithia. 1993. "Those Loud Black Girls: (Black) Women, Silence, and Gender 'Passing' in the Academy." *Anthropology and Education Quarterly* 24(1): 3–32.

Fordham, Signithia, and John U. Ogbu. 1986. "Black Students' School Success: Coping with the Burden of 'Acting White.'" *Urban Review* 18: 176–206.

Foster, Michele. 1997. *Black Teachers on Teaching*. New York: The New Press.

Fox, Dana L., and Kathy G. Short. 2003. *Stories Matter: The Complexity of Cultural Authenticity in Children's Literature*. Urbana, IL: National Council of Teachers of English.

Fox, Helen. 2001. *"When Race Breaks Out": Conversations about Race and Racism in College Classrooms*. New York: Peter Lang.

Frankenberg, Ruth. 1993. *White Women, Race Matters: The Social Construction of Whiteness*. Minneapolis: University of Minnesota Press.

———. 1996. "When We Are Capable of Stopping, We Begin to See: Being White, Seeing Whiteness." In *Names We Call Home: Autobiography on Racial Identity*, ed. Becky W. Thompson and Sangeeta Tyagi, 3–17. New York: Routledge.

Fraser, James W. 2002. Foreword. In *In Search of Wholeness: African American Teachers and Their Culturally Specific Classroom Practices*, ed. Jacqueline Jordan Irvine. New York: Palgrave.

Fredson, Alice, Mary J. Mann, Elena Dock, and Leisy T. Wyman. 1998. *Kipnermiut Tiganrita Igmirtitlrit: Qipnermiut Tegganrita Egmirtellrit: The Legacy of the Kipnuk Elders*. Fairbanks, AK: Alaska Native Language Center.

Freire, Paulo. 1993. *The Pedagogy of the Oppressed*. New York: Continuum.

———. 1994. *Pedagogy of Hope*. New York: Continuum.

Freire, Paulo, and Donald Macedo. 1987. *Literacy: Reading the Word and the World*. South Hadley, MA: Bergin and Garvey.

Fullilove, Robert E. 1987. "Images of Science: Factors Affecting the Choice of Science as a Career." Office of Technology Assessment Contractor Report.

Gándara, Patricia. 1995. *Over the Ivy Walls: The Educational Mobility of Low-Income Chicanos*. Albany: State University of New York Press.

———. 2004. "Building Bridges to College: The Puente Program." *Educational Leadership* 62: 56–60.

Gándara, Patricia, and José F. Moreno. 2002. "The Puente Project: Issues and Perspectives on Preparing Latino Youth for Higher Education." *Educational Policy* 16, September.

Gándara, Patricia, with Deborah Bial. 2001. *Paving the Way to Postsecondary Education: K–12 Intervention Programs for Underrepresented Youth*. Washington, DC: National Center for Education Statistics.

García, Eugene. 2001. *Hispanic Education in the United States: Raíces y Alas*. Boulder, CO: Rowman & Littlefield.

———. 2005. *Teaching and Learning in Two Languages: Bilingualism and Schooling in the United States*. New York: Teachers College Press.

Gardner, Howard. 1985. *Frames of Mind: The Theory of Multiple Intelligences*. New York: Basic Books.

Gay, Geneva. 2000. *Culturally Responsive Teaching: Theory, Research, and Practice*. New York: Teachers College Press.

George, Nelson. 1998. *Hiphopamerica*. New York: Penguin.

Gillborn, David. 1995. *Racism and Antiracism in Real Schools*. Philadelphia: Open University Press.

———. 2006. "Critical Race Theory and Education: Racism and Anti-Racism in Educational Theory and Praxis." *Discourse* 27(1): 11–32.

———. 2008. *Conspiracy? Racism and Education*. New York: Routledge.

Gilmore, Perry. 1985. "Gimme Room: School Resistance, Attitude and Access to Literacy." *Journal of Education* 167: 111–28.

Gilroy, Paul. 1987. *There Ain't No Black in the Union Jack*. London: Hutchinson.

Ginley, Mary. 1999. "Being Nice Is Not Enough." In *The Light in Their Eyes*, ed. Nieto, 85–86. New York: Teachers College Press.

Giroux, Henry. 2001. "Pedagogy of the Depressed: Beyond the New Politics of Cynicism." *College Literature* 28: 1–32.

Goldberg, David T. 1993. *Racist Culture: Philosophy and the Politics of Meaning*. Cambridge, MA: Blackwell.

Gonzales, Alberto, Marsha Houston, and Victoria Chen. 1994. *Our Voices: Essays in Culture, Ethnicity and Communication*. Los Angeles, CA: Roxbury Publishing Company.

Gonzalez, Norma. 2005. "Beyond Culture: The Hybridity of Funds of Knowledge." In *Funds of Knowledge*, ed. Gonzalez, Moll, and Amanti, 29–46.

Gonzalez, Norma, Luis C. Moll, and Cathy Amanti, eds. 2005. *Funds of Knowledge: Theorizing Practices in Households, Communities, and Classrooms*. Mahwah, NJ: Lawrence Erlbaum.

Good, Thomas L. 1987. "Two Decades of Research on Teacher Expectations: Findings and Future Directions." *Journal of Teacher Education* 38(4): 32–47.

Goodman, Alan H. 1997. "Bred in the Bone?" *The Sciences*, March/April, 20–25.

Gordon, Edmund W. 2001. "Affirmative Development of Academic Abilities." *Pedagogical Inquiry and Praxis. Informing the Development of High Academic Ability in Minority Students*. 2 (September): 1–4.

Gordon, Edward E. 2005. *The 2010 Meltdown: Solving the Impending Jobs Crisis*. Westport, CT: Praeger.

Gould, Stephen Jay. 1996. *The Mismeasure of Man*. New York: W.W. Norton.

Grossberg, Lawrence. 1994. "Introduction: Bringin' It All Back Home—Pedagogy and Cultural Studies." In *Between Borders: Pedagogy and the Politics of Cultural Studies*, ed. Giroux and McLaren, 1–25. London: Routledge.

Guishard, Monique, Michelle Fine, Christine Doyle, Jeunesse Jackson, Travis Staten, and Ashley Webb. 2005. "The Bronx on the Move: Activist Research By Youth as Organizing." *Journal of Educational and Psychological Consultation* 16(1–2): 35–54.

Hall, Stuart. 1988. "New Ethnicities." In *Black Film, British Cinema*, ed. Kobena Mercer. London: BFI/ICA Documents 7: 27–31.

———, ed. 1997. *Representation: Cultural Representations and Signifying Practices*. London: Open University/Sage.

Hallinan, Maureen, and Warren N. Kubitschek. 1999. "Curriculum Differentiation and High School Achievement." *Social Psychology of Education* 3(1–2): 41–62.

Halstead, Mark. 1988. *Education, Justice and Cultural Diversity: An Examination of the Honeyford Affair 1984–85*. Lewes: Falmer.

Haney López, Ian F. 1997. *White By Law: The Legal Construction of Race*. New York: New York University Press.

———. 2003. *Racism on Trial: The Chicano Fight for Justice*. Cambridge, MA: Harvard University Press.

Hanushek, Eric A., and Ludger Woessmann. 2005. "Does Educational Tracking Affect Performance and Inequality? Differences-in-Differences Evidence Across Countries." National Bureau of Economic Research Working Paper No. 11124.

Harber, Kent. 1998. "Feedback to Minorities: Evidence of a Positive Bias." *Journal of Personality and Social Psychology* 74: 622–28.

Harris, Roxy, and Ben Rampton, eds. 2003. *The Language, Ethnicity and Race Reader*. London: Routledge.

Hawley, W.D. 2007. Designing Schools That Use Student Diversity to Enhance the Learning of All Students. In *Lessons in Integration: Realizing the Promise of Racial Diversity in American Schools*, ed. Erica Frankenberg and Gary Orfield, 31–56. Charlottesville: University of Virginia Press.

Hawley, Willis D., James Banks, P. Padillo, D. Pope-Davis, and J. Schofield. 1995. "Strategies for Reducing Racial Prejudice: Essential Principles for Program Design." In *Toward a Common Destiny: Improving Race and Ethnic Relations in America*, ed. Willis D. Hawley and A. W. Jackson, 423–30. San Francisco: Jossey-Bass.

Henze, Rosemary C. 2000. "Leading for Diversity: How School Leaders Achieve Racial and Ethnic Harmony." *Research Brief* 6, January. Santa Cruz, CA: Center for Research on Education, Diversity, and Excellence.

Henze, Rosemary, Anne Katz, Edmundo Norte, Susan E. Sather, and Ernest Walker. 2002. Understanding Racial and Ethnic Conflict. In *Leading for Diversity: How School Leaders Promote Positive Interethnic Relations*, ed. Henze et al. Thousand Oaks, CA: Corwin Press.

Henze, Rosemary C., and Lauren Vanett. 1993. "To Walk in Two Worlds—Or More? Challenging a Common Metaphor of Native Education." *Anthropology & Education Quarterly* 24: 116–34.

Hewitt, Roger. 1986. *White Talk, Black Talk: Interracial Friendship and Communication Amongst Adolescents.* Cambridge, UK: Cambridge University Press.

Hill, Jane. 2003. "Mock Spanish, Covert Racism, and the (Leaky) Boundary Between Public and Private Spheres." In *Language, Ethnicity and Race Reader*, ed. Harris and Rampton, 199–210.

Hirschi, Travis. 1969. *Causes of Delinquency.* Berkeley: University of California Press.

Hochschild, Jennifer, and Nathan Scovronick. 2003. *The American Dream and the Public Schools.* New York: Oxford University Press.

Holbrook, Jarita. C. 2005. "Astronomy, Africa: Modern, Traditional, and Cultural." In *Africana: The Encyclopedia of the African and African American Experience*, ed. Anthony Appiah and Henry Louis Gates. Oxford: Oxford University Press.

hooks, bell. 1992. "Representation of Whiteness in the Black Imagination." In bell hooks, *Black Looks: Race and Representation.* Boston, MA: South End.

———. 1994. *Teaching to Transgress: Education as the Practice of Freedom.* New York: Routledge.

Horton, Myles, and Paulo Freire. 1990. *We Make the Road by Walking: Conversations on Education and Social Change*, ed. Brenda Bell, John Gaventa, and John Peters. Philadelphia: Temple University Press.

Horvat, Erin McNamara, and Anthony L. Antonio. 1999. "'Hey, Those Shoes Are Out of Uniform': African American Girls in an Elite High School and the Importance of Habitus." *Anthropology & Education Quarterly* 30(2): 317–42.

Hurd, Tracey L., and Alice McIntyre. 1996. "The Seduction of Sameness: Similarity and Representing the Other." *Feminism & Psychology* 6(1): 86–92.

Ibish, H. 2003. *Report on Hate Crimes and Discrimination Against Arab-Americans: The Post-September 11 Backlash.* Washington DC: Arab American Anti-Discrimination Committee.

Ibrahim, Awad El Karim. 1999. "Becoming Black: Rap and Hip-Hop, Race, Gender, Identity, and the Politics of ESL Learning." *TESOL Quarterly* 33(3): 349–69.

Irvine, Jacqueline Jordan. 1990. *Black Students and School Failure: Policies, Practices, and Prescriptions.* New York: Greenwood.

———. 2002. *In Search of Wholeness: African American Teachers and Their Culturally Specific Classroom Practices.* New York: Palgrave.

———. 2003. *Seeing with a Cultural Eye: Educating Teachers for Diversity.* New York: Teachers College Press.

Ivie, Rachel, and Kim Nies Ray. 2005. *Women in Physics and Astronomy, 2005.* College Park, MD: American Institute of Physics. AIP Publication Number R-430.02.

Jackson, Shirley Ann. 2004. "Sustaining Our National Capacity for Innovation." Paper presented at Harvard University Kennedy School of Government, Cambridge, MA, May 3.

Jencks, Christopher, and Meredith Phillips, eds. 1998. *The Black-White Test Score Gap.* Washington, DC: Brookings Institution Press.

Jocson, Korina M. 2005. "'Taking it to the Mic': Pedagogy of June Jordan's Poetry for the People and Partnership with an Urban High School." *English Education* 37(2): 132–48.

Johnson, Tammy, Jennifer Emiko Boyden, and William J. Pittz, eds. 2001. *Racial Profiling and Punishment in U.S. Public Schools: How Zero Tolerance Policies and High Stakes Testing Subvert Academic Excellence and Racial Equity*. Oakland, CA: Applied Research Center.

Jones, Makeba, and Susan Yonezawa. 2002. "Student Voice, Cultural Change: Using Inquiry in School Reform." *Equity and Excellence in Education* 35(3): 245–54.

Jones, Makeba, Susan Yonezawa, Elizabeth Ballesteros, and Hugh Mehan. 2002. "Shaping Pathways to Higher Education." *Educational Researcher* 31(2): 3–11.

Jussim, Lee, Jacquelynne Eccles, and Stephanie Madon. 1996. "Social Perception, Social Stereotypes, and Teacher Expectations: Accuracy and the Quest for the Powerful Self-Fulfilling Prophecy Effect." *Advances in Experimental Social Psychology* 28: 281–388.

Kendall, Frances E. 2006. *Understanding White Privilege: Building Authentic Relationships Across Race*. New York: Routledge.

Kincheloe, Joe L., and Shirley Steinberg. 1998. "Addressing the Crisis of Whiteness: Reconfiguring White Identity in a Pedagogy of Whiteness." In *White Reign: Deploying Whiteness in America*, ed. Joe L. Kincheloe, Shirley Steinberg, Nelson M. Rodriguez, and Ronald E. Chennault, 3–30. New York: St. Martin's Griffin.

King, Larry L. 1972. *Confessions of a White Racist*. New York: Viking.

Kirp, David L. 2007. *The Sandbox Investment: The Preschool Movement and Kids-First Politics*. Cambridge: Harvard University Press.

Kivel, Paul. 2002. *Uprooting Racism: How White People Can Work for Racial Justice*. Rev. ed. Gabriola Island, British Columbia, Canada: New Society Publishers.

Kohlberg, Lawrence. 1973. "The Claim to Moral Adequacy of a Highest Stage of Moral Judgment." *Journal of Philosophy* 70: 630–46.

Kornhaber, Mindy Laura. 1997. "Seeking Strengths: Equitable Identification for Gifted Education and the Theory of Multiple Intelligences." Ed.D. dissertation, Harvard University, Cambridge, MA.

Krajcik, Joe, Charlene M. Czerniak, and Carl F. Berger. 1998. *Teaching Children Science: A Project-Based Approach*. Boston: McGraw-Hill.

Kubota, Ryuko. 2001. "Discursive Constructions of the Images of U.S. Classrooms." *TESOL Quarterly* 35(1): 9–38.

Labov, William, Philip Cohen, Clarence Robins, and John Lewis. 1968. *A Study of the Non-Standard English of Negro and Puerto Rican Speakers in New York City*, vol. 1, *Phonological and Grammatical Analysis*. Cooperative Research Project No. 3288. U.S. Office of Education.

Lacy, William B., and Ernest Middleton. 1981. "Are Educators Racially Prejudiced? A Cross-Occupational Comparison of Attitudes." *Sociological Focus* 14: 87–95.

Ladson-Billings, Gloria. 1994. *The Dreamkeepers: Successful Teachers of African-American Children*. San Francisco: Jossey-Bass.

LaFollette, Marcel C. 1988. "Eyes on the Stars: Images of Women Scientists in Popular Magazines." *Science, Technology and Human Values* 13: 262–75.

Lamont, Michèle. 2000a. *The Dignity of Working Men: Morality and the Boundaries of Race, Class, and Immigration*. New York: Russell Sage Foundation; Cambridge: Harvard University Press.

———. 2000b. "The Rhetoric of Racism and Anti-Racism in France and the United States." In *Rethinking Comparative Cultural Sociology: Repertoires of Evaluation in France and the United States*, ed. Michèle Lamont and Laurent Thévenot, 25–55. London: Cambridge University Press; Paris: Presses de la Maison des Sciences de l'Homme.

Lareau, Annette. 1987. "Social Class Differences in Family-School Relationships: The Importance of Cultural Capital." *Sociology of Education*, 60(2): 73–85.

———. 2000. *Home Advantage: Social Class and Parental Intervention in Elementary Education*. 2nd ed. Lanham, MD: Rowman & Littlefield.

———. 2003. *Unequal Childhoods: Class, Race, and Family Life*. Berkeley: University of California Press.

Lee, Stacey J. 1996. *Unraveling the "Model Minority" Stereotype: Listening to Asian American Youth*. New York: Teachers College Press.

Lee, Valerie E., and Susanna Loeb. 2000. "School Size in Chicago Elementary Schools: Effects on Teachers' Attitudes and Student Achievement." *American Educational Research Journal* 37: 3–32.

Lee, Valerie, and Julia B. Smith. 2001. *High School Restructuring and Student Achievement*. New York: Teachers College Press.

Leggon, Cheryl B. 2001. "African American and Hispanic Women in Science and Engineering." *Making Strides* 3: 7.

Lemann, Nicholas. 1999. *The Big Test: The Secret History of the American Meritocracy*. New York: Farrar, Strauss and Giroux.

Levinson, Meira. 2004. "The Civic Achievement Gap." *Threshold* 2(3): 12–15.

Lewis, Amanda E. 2003. *Race in the Schoolyard: Negotiating the Color Line in Classrooms and Communities*. Piscataway, NJ: Rutgers University Press.

Lindsey, R.B., K.N. Robbins, and R.D. Terrell. 2003. *Cultural Proficiency: A Manual for School Leaders*. 2nd ed. Thousand Oaks, CA: Corwin Press, Inc.

Lipka, Jerry, and Gerald Mohatt, with the Ciulestet Group. 1998. *Transforming the Culture of Schools: Yup'ik Eskimo Examples*. Mahwah, NJ: Lawrence Erlbaum.

Losen, Dan, and Gary Orfield, eds. 2002. *Racial Inequity in Special Education*. Cambridge, MA: Harvard Education Publishing Group.

Louie, Vivian. 2004. *Compelled to Excel: Immigration, Education and Opportunity Among Chinese Americans*. Stanford, CA: Stanford University Press.

———. 2005. "Immigrant Student Populations and the Pipeline to College: Current Considerations and Future Lines of Inquiry." *Review of Research in Education* 29: 69–106.

Lucas, Samuel Roundfield. 1999. *Tracking Inequality: Stratification and Mobility in American High Schools*. New York: Teachers College Press.

———. 2000. "Hope, Anguish, and the Problem of Our Time: An Essay on Publication of *The Black-White Test Score Gap*." *Teachers College Record* 102: 463–75.

———. 2001. "Effectively Maintained Inequality: Education Transitions, Track Mobility, and Social Background Effects." *American Journal of Sociology* 106: 1642–90.

Lucas, Samuel R., and Marcel Paret. 2005. "Law, Race, and Education in the United States." *Annual Review of Law and Social Science* 1: 203–31.

Luttrell, Wendy, James C. Holland, and Janie Ward. 2006. "'Nice Kids', the N-Word, and Signs of Respect: Culturally Relevant Knowledge of Urban Youth." In *Racism as a Barrier to Cultural Competence in Mental Health and Educational Settings*, ed. Madonna G. Constantine and Derald Wing Sue, 145–49. New York: Wiley.

Macdonald, Ian, Reena Bhavnani, Lily Khan, and Gus John. 1989. *Murder in the Playground: The Report of the Macdonald Inquiry into Racism and Racial Violence in Manchester Schools*. London: Longsight.

Macedo, Donaldo. 1994. *Literacies of Power: What Americans Are Not Allowed to Know*. Boulder, CO: Westview.

Mamdani, Mahmood. 2004. *Good Muslim, Bad Muslim: America, the Cold War, and the Roots of Terror*. New York: Pantheon.

Mansbridge, Jane, and Katherine Flaster. 2007. "The Cultural Politics of Everyday Discourse: The Case of 'Male Chauvinist.'" *Critical Sociology* 33(2–3).

Margolis, Jane, and Allan Fisher. 2002. *Unlocking the Clubhouse: Women in Computing.* Cambridge, MA: MIT Press.

Marx, Sherry. 2006. *Revealing the Invisible: Confronting Passive Racism in Teacher Education.* New York: Routledge.

Massey, Douglas S., and Nancy A. Denton. 1993. *American Apartheid.* Cambridge, MA: Harvard University Press.

Massey, Garth C., M. V. Scott, and Sanford M. Dornbusch. 1975. "Racism Without Racists: Institutional Racism in Urban Schools." *Black Scholar*, November, 10–19.

McCarty, Teresa L. 1995. "What's Wrong with *Ten Little Rabbits?*" *The New Advocate* 8 (2): 97–98.

———. 2004. *A Place to be Navajo: Rough Rock and the Struggle for Self-Determination in Indigenous Schooling.* Mahwah, NJ: Lawrence Erlbaum.

McCarty, Teresa L., and Lucille J. Watahomigie. 2004. "Language and Literacy in American Indian and Alaska Native Communities." In *Sociocultural Contexts of Language and Literacy*, ed. Bertha Pérez, 79–110. 2nd ed. Mahwah, NJ: Lawrence Erlbaum.

McCarty, Teresa L., and Ofelia Zepeda. 1999. "Amerindians." In *Handbook of Language and Ethnic Identity*, ed. Joshua A. Fishman, 197–210. New York: Oxford University Press.

McDiarmid, G.W., Paul Ongtooguk, and J. Pingayuq. 2003. Alaskool website: www.alaskool.org.

McFadden, Anna C., George E. Marsh, Barrie J. Price, and Yunhan Hwang. 1992. "A Study of Race and Gender Bias in the Punishment of Handicapped School Children." *Urban Review* 24: 239–51.

McIntyre, Alice. 1997. *Making Meaning of Whiteness: Exploring the Racial Identity of White Teachers.* Albany: State University of New York Press.

———. 2002. "Exploring Whiteness and Multicultural Education with Prospective Teachers." *Curriculum Inquiry* 32(1): 31–50.

McIntyre, Alice, Andrea Bilics, Binta Colley, Sandra Jones, Pipier Smith-Mumford, Barbara Weaver, Monica Weaver, and Clancie Wilson. 1998. "Engaging in Cross-Racial Dialogue: Does/Can Talk Lead to Action?" *Transformations: A Journal of Curriculum Transformation Scholarship and Resources* 9(2): 81–99.

McKenzie, Kathryn Bell, and James Joseph Scheurich. 2003. "Equity Traps: A Useful Construct for Preparing Principals to Lead Schools That Are Successful with Racially Diverse Students." *Educational Administration Quarterly* 48(5): 601–32.

McKown, Clark, and Rhona S. Weinstein. 2003. "The Development and Consequences of Stereotype Consciousness in Middle Childhood." *Child Development* 74(2): 498–515.

McLaughlin, Milbrey, and Shirley Brice Heath, eds. 1999. *Identity and Inner-City Youth: Beyond Ethnicity and Gender.* New York: Teachers College Press.

Mehan, Hugh. 1992. "Understanding Inequality in Schools: The Contribution of Interpretive Studies." *Sociology of Education* 65: 1–20.

Meier, Kenneth J., Joseph Stewart, Jr., and Robert E. England. 1989. *Race, Class and Education.* Madison: University of Wisconsin Press.

Memmi, Albert. 1965. *The Colonizer and the Colonized.* Boston: Beacon.

Mercer, Kobena. 1994. *Welcome to the Jungle: New Positions in Black Cultural Studies.* London: Routledge.

Metropolitan Life. 2001. *The American Teacher*. Washington, DC: Metropolitan Life.

Mickelson, Roslyn Arlin. 2001. "Subverting Swann: First- and Second-Generation Segregation in the Charlotte-Mecklenburg Schools." *American Educational Research Journal* 38(2): 215–52.

———. 2005. "How Tracking Undermines Race Equity in Desegregated Schools." In *Bringing Equity Back*, ed. Janet Petrovich and Amy Stuart Wells, 49–76. New York: Teachers College Press.

Mickelson, Roslyn Arlin, and Anne E. Velasco. 2006. "Bring It On! Diverse Responses to the Charge of 'Acting White.'" In *Beyond Acting White: Reassessments and New Directions in Research on Black Students and School Success*, ed. Erin McNamara Horvat and Carla O'Connor, chapter 1. New York: Teachers College Press.

Milligan, Julie K., and Rebecca S. Bigler. 2007. "Addressing Race and Racism in the Classroom." In *Lessons in Integration: Realizing the Promise of Diversity in America's Schools*, ed. Erica Frankenberg and Gary Orfield. Charlottesville: University of Virginia Press.

Moll, Luis. 1992. "Funds of Knowledge for Teaching: Using a Qualitative Approach to Connect Homes and Classrooms." *Theory into Practice* 31(2): 132–41.

Morrell, Ernest. 2004. *Linking Literacy and Popular Culture: Finding Connections for Lifelong Learning*. Norwood, MA: Christopher Gordon.

Moses, Earl R. 1941. "Indices of Inequality in a Dual System of Education." *Journal of Negro Education* 10: 239–44.

Mukhopadhyay, Carol, Rosemary Henze, and Yolanda T. Moses. 2007. *How Real is Race? A Sourcebook on Race, Culture, and Biology. An Anthropological Source Book for Educators*. 2nd ed. Lanham, MD: Rowman & Littlefield.

Mura, David. 1999. "Explaining Racism to My Daughter." In *Racism Explained to My Daughter*, ed. T. Ben Jelloun. Trans. Carol Volk. 91–137. New York: The New Press.

Naber, Nadine. 2000. "Ambiguous Insiders: An Investigation of Arab American Invisibility." *Journal of Ethnic and Racial Studies* 23(1): 37–61.

Nakanishi, Don T., and Tina Yamano Nishida, eds. 1995. *The Asian American Educational Experience: A Sourcebook for Teachers and Students*. New York: Routledge.

National Association for Bilingual Education (NABE). 2005. "No Child Left Behind Act: Assessing the Impact." *NABE News* 28(3): 3–7.

National Center for Education Statistics (NCES). 2002. *Schools and Staffing Survey, 1999–2000: Overview of the Data for Public, Private, Public Charter, and Bureau of Indian Affairs Elementary and Secondary Schools*. (NCES 2002–313.) Washington, DC: U.S. Department of Education.

———. 2006. *National Assessment of Educational Progress, 2006, Reading Assessments*. Washington, DC: U.S. Department of Education.

National Science Foundation. 2004. *Women, Minorities, and Persons with Disabilities in Science and Engineering: 2004*. NSF 04–317. Arlington, VA.

Native American Rights Fund website: www.narf.org.

Nelson, Donna J. 2006. *A National Analysis of Diversity in Science and Engineering Faculties at Research Universities*. Norman: University of Oklahoma. Accessed January 11, 2006, at http://cheminfo.chem.ou.edu/~djn/diversity/top50.html.

Nelson, Gayle. 1995. "Cultural Differences in Learning Styles." In *Learning Styles in the ESL/EFL Classroom*, ed. Joy M. Reid, 3–18. New York: Heinle and Heinle.

Newberry Library D'Arcy McNickle Center for American Indian History website: www.newberry.org.

Nichols, Roger L. 2003. *American Indians in U. S. History*. Norman: University of Oklahoma Press.

Nieto, Sonia. 1994. "Lessons from Students on Creating a Chance to Dream." *Harvard Educational Review*, 64(4): 392–426.

———. 1999. *The Light in Their Eyes: Creating Multicultural Learning Communities*. New York: Teachers College Press.

———. c2004. *Affirming Diversity: The Sociopolitical Context of Multicultural Education*. 4th ed. Boston: Allyn & Bacon.

Nisbett, Richard E. 1998. "Race, Genetics, and IQ." In *The Black–White Test Score Gap*, ed. Jencks and Phillips, 86–102.

Noddings, Nel. 1992. *The Challenge to Care in Schools: An Alternative Approach to Education*. New York: Teachers College Press.

Oakes, Jeannie. 1985, 2005. *Keeping Track: How Schools Structure Inequality*. New Haven, CT: Yale University Press.

Obidah, Jennifer E., and Karen Manheim Teel. 2001. *Because of the Kids: Facing Racial and Cultural Differences in Schools*. New York: Teachers College Press.

Olsen, Laurie. 1995. "School Restructuring and the Needs of Immigrant Students." In *California's Immigrant Children: Theory, Research, and Implications for Educational Policy*, ed. Ruben G. Rumbaut and Wayne A. Cornelius, 209–33. San Diego: Center for U.S.-Mexican Studies, University of California–San Diego.

———. 1998. *Made in America: Immigrant Students in Our Public Schools*. New York: The New Press.

Omi, Michael, and Howard Winant. 1994. *Racial Formation in the United States: From the 1960s to the 1990s*. 2nd ed. New York: Routledge.

Ong, Maria. 2005. "Body Projects of Young Women of Color in Physics: Intersections of Gender, Race, and Science." *Social Problems* 52(4): 593–617.

Ongtooguk, Paul. 1994. "Listening for a Change: Opening the Discourse of Race in Teacher Education." Paper presented at AERA, New Orleans, LA.

———. 1997. *Modern Alaska Natives—Deal with It*. Barrow, AK: *Arctic Sounder*.

Ortner, Sherry. 1984. Theory in Anthropology Since the Sixties. *Comparative Studies in Society and History* 26(1): 126–66.

Payne, Yasser. 2001. "Black Men and Street Life as a Site of Resiliency." *International Journal of Critical Psychology* 4(1): 109–22.

Perry, Pamela. 2002. *Shades of White: White Kids and Racial Identities in High School*. Durham, NC: Duke University Press.

Phelan, Patricia, Ann Locke Davison, and Hanh Cao Yu. 1997. *Adolescents' Worlds: Negotiating Family, Peers, and School*. New York: Teachers College Press.

Philips, Susan U. 1983. *The Invisible Culture: Communication in Classroom and Community on the Warm Springs Indian Reservation*. New York: Longman.

Phillips, Meredith, Jeanne Brooks-Gunn, Greg J. Duncan, Pamela Klebanov, and Jonathan Crane. 1998. "Family Background, Parenting Practices, and the Black-White Test Score Gap." In *The Black-White Test Score Gap*, ed. Jencks and Phillips, 103–45.

Pizarro, Marcos. 2005. *Chicanas and Chicanos in School: Racial Profiling, Identity Battles, and Empowerment*. Austin: University of Texas Press.

Pollack, William. 1999. "Changing Student Attitudes About Violence." *New York Times*, August 18.

Pollock, Mica. 2001. "How the Question We Ask Most About Race in Education Is the Very Question We Most Suppress." *Educational Researcher* 30(9): 2–12.

———. 2004a. *Colormute: Race Talk Dilemmas in an American School*. Princeton, NJ: Princeton University Press.

———. 2004b. "Race Wrestling: Struggling Strategically with Race in Educational Practice and Research." *American Journal of Education* 111(1): 25–67.

———. 2008. *Because of Race: How Americans Debate Harm and Opportunity in Our Schools*. Princeton, NJ: Princeton University Press.

Powell, John. 2005. "Dreaming of a Self Beyond Whiteness and Isolation." *Washington University Journal of Law and Policy* 18(3): 13–45.

Rampton, Ben. 2004. *Crossing: Language and Ethnicity Among Adolescents*. 2nd ed. Manchester: St Jerome.

Rawls, John. 1971. *A Theory of Justice*. Cambridge, MA: Harvard University Press.

Reddy, Maureen T. 1994. *Crossing the Color Line: Race, Parenting, and Culture*. New Brunswick, NJ: Rutgers University Press.

Resnick, Lauren. 1995. "From Aptitude to Effort: A New Foundation for Our Schools." *Daedalus* 124(4): 55–62.

Riley, Patricia, ed. 1993. *Growing Up Native American: An Anthology*. New York: William Morrow.

Rizvi, Fazal. 1993. "Children and the Grammar of Popular Racism." In *Race, Identity, and Representation in Education*, ed. Cameron McCarthy and Warren Crichlow, 126–39. New York: Routledge.

Roediger, David R. 1991. *The Wages of Whiteness: Race and the Making of the American Working Class*. London, New York: Verso.

Rolón-Dow, Rosalie. 2005. "Critical Care: A Color(full) Analysis of Care Narratives in the Schooling Experiences of Puerto Rican Girls." *American Educational Research Journal* 42(1): 77–111.

Rosaldo, Renato. 1989. *Culture and Truth: The Remaking of Social Analysis*. Boston: Beacon.

Roscigno, Vincent J., and James W. Ainsworth-Darnell. 1999. "Race, Cultural Capital, and Educational Resources: Persistent Inequalities and Achievement Returns." *Sociology of Education* 72: 158–78.

Rose, Tricia. 1994. *Black Noise: Rap Music and Black Culture in Contemporary America*. Middletown, CT: Wesleyan University Press.

Roth, Charles E., Cleti Cervoni, Thomas Wellnitz, and Elizabeth Arms. 1991. *Beyond the Classroom: Exploration of Schoolground and Backyard*. Amherst: University of Massachusetts Press.

Rubin, Beth C. 2003. "Unpacking Detracking: When Progressive Pedagogy Meets Students' Social Worlds." *American Educational Research Journal* 40(2): 539–73.

———. Forthcoming. "Detracking in Context: How Local Constructions of Ability Shape Equity-Geared Reform." *Teachers College Record*.

Said, Edward. 1987. *Orientalism*. London: Penguin.

Samhan, Helen Hatab. 1999. "Not Quite White: Race Classification and the Arab American Experience." In *Arabs in America: Building a New Future*, ed. Michael W. Suleiman, 209–26. Philadelphia: Temple University Press.

Sarroub, Loukia. 2005. *All American Yemeni Girls: Being Muslim in a Public School*. Philadelphia: University of Pennsylvania Press.

Schiele, Jerome H. 1991. "An Epistemological Perspective on Intelligence Assessment Among African American Children." *Journal of Black Psychology* 17(2): 23–36.

Schofield, Janet W. 1995. "Review of Research on School Desegregation's Impact on Elementary and Secondary School Students." In *Handbook on Research on Multicultural Education*, ed. James A. Banks and Cherry A. McGee-Banks, 597–617. New York: Macmillan.

———. 2004. "Fostering Positive Intergroup Relations in Schools." In *Handbook of Research on Multicultural Education*, ed. James A. Banks & Cherry A. McGee-Banks, 799–812. 2nd ed. New York: John Wiley & Sons.

Schultz, Katherine. 2003. *Listening: A Framework for Teaching across Difference*. New York: Teachers College Press.

Segrest, Mab. 1994. *Memoir of a Race Traitor*. Boston: South End.

Seymour, Elaine, and Nancy M. Hewitt. 1997. *Talking About Leaving: Why Under-graduates Leave the Sciences*. Boulder, CO: Westview.

Sharma, Sanjay. 2004. "The Problem with Multiculturalism." In *Institutional Racism in Higher Education*, ed. Ian Law, Deborah Phillips, and Laura Turney. Stoke on Trent: Trentham Books.

———. 2006. *Multicultural Encounters*. London: Palgrave McMillan.

Shores, K. 2003. "Academy Instills Values, Discipline and Structure." *South Florida Sun Sentinel*, January 20.

Singer, Simon L. 1996. *Recriminalizing Delinquency*. Cambridge, UK: Cambridge University Press.

Singleton, Glenn Eric, and Curtis Linton. 2006. *Courageous Conversations about Race: A Field Guide for Achieving Equity in Schools*. Thousand Oaks, CA: Corwin Press.

Slapin, Beverly, Doris Seale, and Rosemary Gonzales. 1992. *How to Tell the Difference: A Checklist for Evaluating Native American Children's Books*. Gabriola Island, BC: New Society Publishers.

Slavin, Robert E. 1993. "Untracking: The 97 Percent Solution." *College Board Review* 168: 27–35.

Sleeter, Carolyn E. 2002. "State Curriculum Standards and the Shaping of Student Consciousness." *Social Justice* 29(4): 8–25.

———. 2005. *Un-standardizing Curriculum: Multicultural Teaching in Standards-Based Classrooms*. New York: Teachers College Press.

Smedley, Audrey. 1999. *Race in North America: Origin and Evolution of a World-view*. 2nd ed. Boulder, CO: Westview.

Smith, David Eugene. 1958. *History of Mathematics*, vol. 2, *Special Topics of Elementary Mathematics*. New York: Dover Publications.

Smith, Lillian. 1994. *Killers of the Dream*. New York: Norton.

Smitherman, Geneva. 1977. *Talkin and Testifyin: The Language of Black America*. Boston: Houghton Mifflin.

———. 2000. *Talkin That Talk: Language, Culture, and Education in African America*. New York: Routledge.

Spillane, James P., Tim Hallett, and John B. Diamond. 2003. "Forms of Capital and the Construction of Leadership: Instructional Leadership in Urban Elementary Schools." *Sociology of Education* 76(1): 1–17.

Stack, Carol. 1996. *Call to Home: African Americans Reclaim the Rural South*. New York: Basic Books.

Stalvey, Lois Mark. 1970. *Education of a WASP*. New York: Morrow.

Steele, Claude M. 1997. "A Threat in the Air: How Stereotypes Shape Intellectual Identity and Performance." *American Psychologist* 52: 613–29.

Steele, Claude M., and Joshua Aronson. 1995. "Stereotype Threat and the Intellectual Test Performance of African-Americans." *Journal of Personality and Social Psychology* 69(5): 797–811.

Stephan, Cookie White, L. Renfro, and Walter G. Stephan. 2004. "The Evaluation of Multicultural Education Programs: Techniques and a Meta-Analysis. In *Education Programs for Improving Intergroup Relations: Theory, Research and Practice*, ed. Walter G. Stephan and W. Paul Vogt, 227–42. New York: Teachers College Press.

Stockman, Ida J. 1996. "Phonological Development and Disorders in African American Children." In *Communication Development and Disorders in*

African American Children: Research, Assessment, and Intervention, ed. Alan G. Kamhi, Karen E. Pollock, and Joyce L. Harris, 117–53. Baltimore: Brookes.

Style, Emily. 1996. "Curriculum as Window and Mirror." The S.E.E.D. Project on Inclusive Curriculum. Accessed November 20, 2003, at http://www.wcwonline.org/seed/curriculum.html.

Suárez-Orozco, Carola, and Marcelo Suárez-Orozco. 1995. *Transformations: Immigration Family Life, and Achievement Motivation among Latino Adolescents.* Stanford: Stanford University Press.

———. 2001. *Children of Immigration.* Cambridge, MA: Harvard University Press.

Sutton-Smith, Brian. 1982. "A Performance Theory of Peer Relations." In *The Social Life of Children in a Changing Society*, ed. Kathryn N. Borman, 65–77. Norwood, NJ: Ablex.

Takaki, Ron. 1990. *Strangers from a Different Shore: A History of Asian Americans.* New York: Penguin.

Tannen, Deborah, and Muriel Saville-Troike, eds. 1985. *Perspectives on Silence.* Norwood, NJ: Ablex.

Tate, William F. 1994. "Race, Retrenchment, and the Reform of School Mathematics." *Phi Delta Kappan*, February.

Tatum, Beverly Daniel. 2003. *Why Are All The Black Kids Sitting Together in the Cafeteria? A Psychologist Explains the Development of Racial Identity.* Rev. ed. New York: Basic Books.

TESOL Board. 1997. Policy Statement of the TESOL Board on African American Vernacular English. Retrieved July 13, 2006, from Center for Applied Linguistics website: http://www.cal.org/ebonics/tesolebo.html.

Thompson, Audrey. 2004. "Anti-Racist Work Zones." In *Philosophy of Education 2003*, ed. Kal Alston, 387–95. Urbana, IL: Philosophy of Education Society. http://www.ed.uiuc.edu/EPS/PES-Yearbook/2003/thompson.pdf.

Thompson, Cooper, Emmett Schaefer, and Harry Brod, eds. 2003. *White Men Challenging Racism: 35 Personal Stories.* Durham, NC: Duke University Press.

Torre, María Elena. 2005. "The Alchemy of Integrated Spaces: Youth Participation in Research Collectives of Difference." In *Beyond Silenced Voices*, ed. Lois Weis and Michelle Fine, 251–66. Albany: State University of New York Press. Available online at http://www.pbs.org/beyondbrown/resources/legacylinks.html.

Torre, María Elena, Michelle Fine, N. Alexander, and E. Genao. Forthcoming. "Moving to the Rhythm of Social Justice: Urban Young Women's Experiences of Research and Action." In *Urban Girls*, ed. Bonnie J. Ross Leadbeater and Niobe Way. 2nd ed. New York: New York University Press.

Torres, Edén E. 2003. *Chicana Without Apology: The New Chicana Cultural Studies.* New York: Routledge.

Tyack, David. 1993. "Constructing Difference: Historical Reflections on Schooling and Social Diversity." *Teachers College Record* 95(1): 8–34.

Tyson, Karolyn, William Darity, Jr., and Domini Castellino. 2005. "It's not 'a Black Thing': Understanding the Burden of Acting White and Other Dilemmas of High Achievement." *American Sociological Review* 70(4): 582–605.

Useem, Elizabeth. 1992. "Middle Schools and Math Groups: Parents' Involvement in Children's Placement." *Sociology of Education* 65: 263–79.

Valdés, Guadalupe. 2001. *Learning and Not Learning English: Latino Students in American Schools.* New York: Teachers College Press.

————. 2003. *Expanding Definitions of Giftedness: The Case of Young Interpreters from Immigrant Communities*. Mahwah, NJ: Lawrence Erlbaum.

Valenzuela, Angela. 1999. *Subtractive Schooling: U.S.-Mexican Youth and the Politics of Caring*. Albany: State University of New York Press.

Van Ausdale, Debra, and Joe R. Feagin. 2002. *The First R: How Children Learn Race and Racism*. Lanham, MD: Rowman & Littlefield.

Verba, Sidney, Kay Lehman Schlozman, and Henry E. Brady. 1995. *Voice and Equality: Civic Voluntarism in American Politics*. Cambridge, MA: Harvard University Press.

Villegas, Anne-Marie, and Tamara Lucas. 2002. *Educating Culturally Responsive Teachers: A Coherent Approach*. Albany: State University of New York Press.

Volpp, L. 2002. "The Citizen and the Terrorist." *UCLA Law Review* 49 (June): 1575.

Walters, Pamela Barnhouse, Holly J. McCammon, and David R. James. 1990. "Schooling or Working? Public Education, Racial Politics, and the Organization of Production in 1910." *Sociology of Education* 63: 1–26.

Walton, G. M., and Geoffrey L. Cohen. 2007. "A Question of Belonging: Race, Social Fit, and Achievement." *Journal of Personality and Social Psychology* 92: 82–96.

Ward, Janie Victoria. 2000. *The Skin We're In: Teaching Our Children to be Emotionally Strong, Socially Smart, Spiritually Connected*. New York: Free Press.

————. 2005. "'I Can't Stay Silent': Moral Dimensions in the Racialized Practices of Black Teachers." Paper presented at the Annual American Moral Education Conference, Cambridge, MA.

Warikoo, Natasha. 2005. "In a Teenage Waistland, Fitting In." *Washington Post*, August 1.

Weinberg, Meyer. 1982. "Notes from the Editor." *Chronicle of Equal Education* 4(3): 7–8.

Weissglass, J. 2003. "Reasons for Hope: You Can Challenge Educational Inequities." *Principal Leadership* 3(8): 24–29.

Wells, Amy Stuart, and Robert L. Crain. 1994. "Perpetuation Theory and the Long-Term Effects of School Desegregation." *Review of Educational Research* 64(4): 531–55.

Welner, Kevin, and Jeannie Oakes. 1996. "(Li)ability Grouping: The New Susceptibility of School Tracking Systems to Legal Challenges." *Harvard Educational Review* 65(3): 451–70.

West, Cornel. 1992. "Black Leadership and the Pitfalls of Racial Reasoning." In *Race-ing Justice, En-Gendering Power: Essays on Anita Hill, Clarence Thomas, and the Construction of Social Reality*, ed. Toni Morrison, 390–401. New York: Pantheon.

————. 1993. *Race Matters*. New York: Vintage.

————. 2001. "Progressive Politics in These Times: From Vision to Action." Mario Savio Memorial Lecture, University of California–Berkeley.

Wheelock, Anne. 1992. "The Case for Untracking." *Educational Leadership* 50(2): 6–10.

Williams, Robert, ed. 1975. *Ebonics: The True Language of Black Folks*. St. Louis: Robert Williams.

Wright, Richard. 1940. *Native Son*. New York: Harper and Row.

Wyatt, Toya. 1995. "Language Development in African American English Child Speech." *Linguistics and Education* 7: 7–22.

Yonezawa, Susan, and Makeba Jones. 2007. "Using Student Voices to Inform and Evaluate Secondary School Reform." In *International Handbook of Student Experience in Elementary and Secondary School*, ed. Alison Cook-Sather and Dennis Thiessen, 681–709. The Netherlands: Kluwer Academic Publishers.

Young, Iris Marion. 1990. *Justice and the Politics of Difference.* Princeton: Princeton University Press.

Zimmerman, Jonathan. 2002. *Whose America? Culture Wars in the Public Schools.* Cambridge, MA: Harvard University Press.

Zweigenhaft, Richard L., and G. William Domhoff. 1991. *Blacks in the White Elite: Will the Progress Continue?* Lanham, MD: Rowman & Littlefield.

Index

ability groups, 318–20
Abu El-Haj, Thea Renda, 179
academic achievement. *See* achievement
"Accessing Strengths and Supporting
    Resistance in Teaching" project,
    275
achievement
    cultural explanations of, 254–56
    group *vs.* individual, 63–64
    high help and high perfectionism and,
        78–81
    investment in educational, 254
    racial disparities in, 62–63
    social-structural analysis and, 257–60
African Americans, 9, 126
    achievement and, 62–64
    cultivating trust of, 310–13
    dehumanization of, 56–60
    nonstandard English and, 102–5
    spotlighting and ignoring of, 230–34
    stereotypes of, 314–17
    tracking and, 318–23
African American Vernacular English
    (AAVE), 71–72, 100, 102–5
Alexander, Natasha, 168–70
Algebra Project, The, 163
Alim, H. Samy, 105
All American Yemeni Girls (Sarroub), 100
American Anthropological Association, 12
Americans, hyphenated, 15
analysis
    of classrooms, student, 212–16
    criminalizing, 157
    of racial incidents, 236–41
    of racial oppression, 156–60, 243–44
    social-structural, 257–60
antiracism
    definition of everyday, xvii–xxii
    impulses of, xviii–xix
Arabs and Arab Americans, 174–79
    hypervisibility of, 176–77
    invisibility of, 175–76
Aronson, Joshua, 69

Asians and Asian Americans, 10, 14,
    257–61
    Pacific (APAs), 115
    South, 186–89
assessment, of racial disparities, 128–29
authenticity, 182
authority, teachers and, 277
Ayers, William, 34
Ayoungman, Vivian, 183

Bailey, Alison, 330
basic skills. *See* skills, basic
Baugh, John, 106
behaviors
    cultural theories on, 127, 222–25
    non-standard, 97–111, 344–45
Bell, Derrick, 246
Bell, Lee Anne, 290
Bell Curve, The (Hernstein and Murray),
    10
Beloved (Morrison), 196
Bend It Like Beckham (BILB) (film),
    186–89
Benham, Maenette, 182
Berlet, Chip, 332
bhangra music, 39–40
biological concept of race, 4–8
Blacks. *See* African Americans
"Black Self/White Self" project, 142
Black-White Test Score Gap, The
    (Jencks and Phillips), 63
blame, 26, 255
Blum, Lawrence, 241
    I'm not a Racist, but . . ., 238
Blumenbach, Johann, 13
Bonilla-Silva, Eduardo, 336
border crossing, 48
Bruchac, Joseph, *Our Stories Remember*,
    182–83

Cajete, Gregory, 182
careers, racially based notions of,
    113–24, 345

caring, institutional failure of, 28–31
Carter, Dorinda J., 234
Carter, Prudence L., 111
"Caucasian," getting rid of, 12–16
Caven, Meghan, 306
Chadwick, Jocelyn A., 198
Chang, Kimberly, 38
change, systemic, 327–42, 348
Charlotte-Mecklenburg (NC) schools,
　　318–22
"Children and Their Cultural Worlds"
　　(course), 35
Chinese and Chinese Americans,
　　257–60
Civil Rights Movement, 12
classrooms, 211–34, 346
　　colorblind, 62–66
　　community in, 288
　　cultural theories on behaviors in,
　　　222–25
　　decorum in, 195–96
　　grouping in detracked, 90–95
　　guests in, 123, 183–84
　　posters in, 191–94, 311
　　predominantly white, 226–34, 279
　　racial spotlighting and ignoring in,
　　　230–34
　　safe spaces and, 226–29
　　silences in, 217–24
　　student analysis of, 212–16
closure, lack of, 21
"cocooning," 44–49
Cohen, Geoffrey, 84
collaboration, xviii, 331–32
collective struggle/action, 158, 331–32
Colombians, 146, 148
colorblind strategies, xviii, 44, 62–66,
　　128, 276–77, 288–89
"colormuteness," 25
communities
　　getting to know, 299–304
　　home, 293–308, 347
　　parents and, 309–23
　　role models from, 48, 120–24, 183–84
　　students researching their, 305–8
　　valuing, 294–98
Compelled to Excel (Louie), 257
Conrad, Rachel, 38
contributions, racially based notions of,
　　113–24, 345

conversations about race, 143, 235–51,
　　343, 346–47
　　children's, 34–38
　　colleagues and, 253–71, 279–82, 347
　　courageous, 18–23
　　race of teachers and, 273–90
　　racial incidents and, 236–41
　　racially charged topics and, 242–45
　　school policy and, 246–51
Cooper, Joanne, 182
Cousins, Linwood H., 323
CREATE-USCD (Center for Research on
　　Educational Equity, Assessment,
　　and Teaching Excellence), 212
cross-racial dialogue, 277–81, 289
cultural deficit perspective, 222, 257, 259
cultural explanations
　　of achievement, 254–56
　　of behavior, 222–25
　　moving beyond, 257–61
cultural imperialism, 178
cultural racism, 107–9, 127
culture
　　dominant, 110
　　language and, 294–98
　　lived, and power, 64–65
　　multiple fluency and, 107–11
　　seen falsely as static set of practices,
　　　176–77, 188–89, 192–93
"culture of poverty," 259
curiosity, 67–68
curriculum
　　counter-stereotypic information and,
　　　151
　　critical hip-hop in, 161–65, 283–84
　　diversity in, 173–98, 346
　　films in, 186–90
　　guests and, 123, 183–84
　　history in, 199–208, 346
　　images in, 180–94
　　opportunity denial and, 155–71, 345
　　participatory inquiry in, 165–71
　　racial identity and, 141–53, 345
　　racially sensitive literature in, 195–98,
　　　232–33
　　"windows" and "mirrors" in, 150–51,
　　　153
Cushman, Kathleen, 308
Cushman, Kathleen et al., Fires in the
　　Bathroom, 305

Dance, Lory Janelle, 60
Dead Prez, 162
debate
    teams, 243–44
    vs. dialogue, 59
Dee, Thomas, 67
dehumanization, 56–60, 181
Delpit, Lisa, 109
desegregation, 62
despair, 337
detracked classrooms, 90–95
Deyhle, Donna, 194
dialogue
    children's conversations and, 34–38
    cross-racial, 277–81, 289
    guidelines for, 18–23
    recording of student, 215
    vs. debate, 59
    See also conversations about race
Diamond, John B., 256
dichos, 46
discipline
    learning and, 134–37
    racial disparities in, 132–34
    safe space and, 228–29
discomfort
    in dialogue, 20–21
    racial-group programming and, 45
diversity, 173–98, 346
    Arab visibility and invisibility and,
        174–79
    classroom posters and, 191–94
    in faculty conversations, 279–82
    in films, 186–90
    literature and, 195–98
    Native American images and, 180–85
    school reform and, 267–71
Dominicans, 260
Duncan-Andrade, Jeffrey, 160
Dybdahl, Claudia S., 208

Ebonics, 102–3
Echoes of Brown (performance), 165–71
educators
    achievement data and, 63–64
    connecting with individual students,
        64–73, 135
    conversations among, 253–71,
        279–82, 347
    in courageous conversations, 18–23
    cultural racism and, 107–10
    ethnicity and, 47–48
    identifying self to students, 283–86
    impact of race of, 67, 273–90, 347
    mindfulness and, 128–29
    multicultural workshops and, 224–25
    precise talk about opportunity and,
        24–27
    responsibility of, for learning, 254–56
    in school reforms, 267–71
    student feedback and, 215–16, 227,
        229, 247–48
    in students' communities, 299–304
    white exceptionalism and, 328–33
Edutainment (album), 162
Embrick, David G., 336
engagement, in dialogue, 19–20
English, nonstandard, 102–6
English-only policies, 52–53
ESL (English as a Second Language),
        98–99
ethics, and discipline, 136
"ethnic absolutism," 40
ethnicity
    Caucasians and lack of, 15
    educators and, 47–48
ethnolinguistic crossing, 40–41
eugenicists, 13
European Americans, 14–15
evolutionary theory, race and, 5
Ewald, Wendy, 142
exceptionalism, white, 329–32, 339
exclusion, 133–34
expectations, 77–89, 344
    basic skills and, 86–89
    high help and high perfectionism and,
        78–81
    supportive feedback and, 82–84
    teachers' beliefs and, 255

faculty. *See* educators
families. *See* communities, home;
    parents
Federal Indian law, 204–6
feedback
    student, 215–16, 227, 229, 247–48
    supportive, 82–84
Ferguson, Ronald, 81
"figurative language journals," 71
films, diversity in, 186–90

Fine, Michelle, 171
Fires in the Bathroom (Cushman et al.), 305
FOBs (Fresh Off the Boat), 147–48
Foley, Douglas, 225
   The Heartland Chronicles, 224
Forty-Cent Tip: Stories of New York City Immigrant Workers, 307
"Four Agreements of Courageous Conversation," 18–22
Freire, Paulo, 158, 334, 337

gaming, Native Americans and, 204–5
Gándara, Patricia, 49
Gandhi, Mahatma, 57
gaps
   data on opportunity, 167–70
   in skills, 85–95, 114–15, 344
García, Eugene, 298
gender patterns, 83, 100, 114, 177
genetic variations, 6
gifted education, 99, 126–31
Gilborn, David, 251
Ginley, Mary, 29
Glass, Ron, 340
gold nuggets, xiv
Gonzales, Rosemary, 182
Goodman, Alan, 8
Gould, Stephen Jay, *The Mismeasure of Man*, 118
Grossman, Virginia and Sylvia Long, *Ten Little Rabbits*, 181
groups
   cross-racial dialogue, 279–81
   in detracked classrooms, 90–95
   faculty study, 268
   integrated inquiry, 165–70
   student inquiry, 212–16
group work practice, 93–94

Haitians, 146, 148
Hall, Stuart, 181
Hamann, Edmund, 101
Haney López, Ian F., 245
Hawley, Willis D., 271
Hays, Cynthia A., 23
Heartland Chronicles, The (Foley), 224
helping practices, 79
Henze, Rosemary, 266

Hernstein, Richard J. and Charles Murray, *The Bell Curve*, 10
heroism, white, 328–33
high help environments, 78–81
high perfectionism environments, 78–81
High School Puente program (CA), 45–46
Hill, Lauryn, 162
hip-hop, in curriculum, 161–65, 283–84
history, 199–208, 346
   local, 200–203
   Native Americans in, 204–8
hooks, bell, 227, 232
hope, revolutionary, 337–40
Horatio Alger myth, 156–57
Horton, Myles, 337
humanity, seeing each other's, 56–60
humiliation, 133–34
Hunter, Madeline, 4
Hunter, Robert, 142
hypervisibility
   of Arabs, 176–77
   of Blacks, 231–34
hyphenated status, 15

identity
   indigenous, 180
   participatory action research and, 166–67, 170
   photography and, 142–45
   racial, 141–53, 345
   reading materials and, 150–53
   strengthening student, 44–49
   writing and, 146–49
ignoring, racial, 230–34
images
   curriculum and, 180–85
   in films, 186–90
   in posters, 191–94
immigrants, 188
   Asian, 257–60
   Mexican, 50–55
   racial identity and, 146–49
Immortal Technique, 162
I'm not a Racist, but . . . (Blum), 238
"imperialist nostalgia," 223
Indian Self-Determination Act, 206
Indigenous peoples, 180
   See also Native Alaskans; Native Americans

individuality, 61–73, 344
    achievement and, 62–66
    knowing students and, 67–69
    sharing teacher's, 70–73
inequality
    subjective, 82–84
    See also racial inequalities
integrated inquiry spaces, 165–70
intellectual ability, race and, 9–11,
    114–15, 117
intelligence
    multiple, 263
    quotient (IQ), 9–10
internalized oppression, 50–55
invisibility
    of Arabs, 175–76
    of Blacks, 231–34
    of whiteness, 283–85
Italians, 9

Jencks, Christopher and Meredith
    Phillips, *The Black-White Test
    Score Gap*, 63
Jews, 9–10
Jim Crow segregation, 9
Johnson, Georgia, 329
Jones, Makeba, 216
justice
    inquiry for social, 165–71
    spaces, 166
    struggle for, 338–40

Kashatok, Grant, 299–300, 304
Klimczak, Susan, 116
knowledge, "standard," 98–101
Kohlberg, Lawrence, 136
KRS One, 161–62

language
    "crossing" and "stylization," 39–41
    cultural roots and, 294–98, 302
    precision of, in racialized society,
        24–27
    racial ideology and, 12–16
Latinos, 45–48
    achievement and, 62–64
    See also Mexicans and Mexican
        Americans
Learning and Not Learning English
    (Valdés), 99

learning style theory, 263–64
Levinson, Meira, 124
Lewis, Monica, 136
Lightfoot, Alexandra, 145
literature
    context for, 196–97
    racially sensitive, 195–98, 232–33
Llano Grande Journal, 306
Long, Sylvia, 181
Louie, Vivian, 261
    Compelled to Excel, 257
Lucas, Samuel R., 66
Luttrell, Wendy, 278

"mamma attitude," 277
Marboe, Elinor, 168–70
Martin Luther King School (MI), 104
McCarty, Teresa L., 185
McIntyre, Alice, 282
mentors, 135
Mesquakis, 222–24
Mexicanidad, 54
Mexicans and Mexican-Americans, 9,
    294–98
    internalized oppression of, 50–55
Mickelson, Roslyn Arlin, 323
Milliken v. Bradley, 62
mindfulness, 128–29
Mismeasure of Man, The (Gould), 118
"model minority" myth, 115, 254,
    257–58
monitoring, of students, 45, 197
Morrell, Ernest, 164
Morrison, Toni, *Beloved*, 196
Mos Def, 162
Mott-Smith, Jennifer A., 149
Moyenda, Sekani, 277
MSEP (Math/Science Equity Project),
    318–22
Mukhopadhyay, Carol Chapnick, 16
multiculturalism
    teaching and, 186–87, 189
    "vanilla," 249
    workshops on, 224–25
"multiracial" *vs.* "of mixed race," 15–16
Murray, Charles, 10
Muslims, Arabs equated with, 175–76

names, linguistic roots and, 294–96
Native Alaskans, 263–64, 299–304

Native Americans, 191–93
  cultural theories about, 222–24
  elders as classroom guests, 183–84
  images of, 180–85
  teaching facts about, 204–8
  See also Native Alaskans
Native Son (Wright), 156–58
Nieto, Sonia, 31
Noguera, Pedro, 137
non-standard behaviors, 97–111, 344–45
"N-Word," responding to, 274–78

Oakland (CA) African American
    Educational Task Force, 103
Obidah, Jennifer, 331–32
objectification, 187
Ong, Maria, 119
Ongtooguk, Paul C., 207–8
opportunity
  "ability" stereotypes and, 114–19
  denial of, 155–71, 345
  discipline and, 132–37
  expectations and, 78–84
  "gifted" programs and, 99, 126–31
  parents and, 309–23
  role models and, 116–18, 120–24
  skill gaps and, 85–95
  standards and, 97–111
  talking precisely about, 24–27
"Opportunity Gap" data, 167–70
oppression. *See* racial oppression
"othermothering," 277
Our Stories Remember (Bruchac),
    182–83
Oyate, 182

pairs, working in, 93
parents, 309–23, 347–48
  cultivating trust of, 310–13
  fighting stereotypes, 314–17
  informing, about opportunities,
    318–23
Parmar, Priya, 284, 286
participation
  cultural theories of, 222–25
  structures, 219–20
  styles, 217–21
Participatory Action Research (PAR),
    165–71
passion, cultivating, 116

peer support, 80
Perry, Pamela, 229
Phillips, Meredith, 63
photography and identity, 142–45
Phyl's Academy, 136
Pleasants, Heather M., 73
political engagement, 120–21
Pollock, Mica, 11, 27
positionality, 283–85
posters in classrooms, 191–94, 311
power
    engagement with, 166
    lived culture and, 64–65
praise, excessive, 83
principles, core, xiv–xv
    four fundamental, xx–xxii
Public Enemy, 162
punishment. *See* discipline

"quiet conversation" strategy, 228

race consciousness, xiii–xiv, 158, 161,
    275, 341
racial categories, xxi, 3–16, 13, 343
  children's conversations and, 34–38
  intellectual ability and, 9–11
  North American system of, 13–14,
    146–49, 187
  as obsolete biological concept, 4–8
  use of "Caucasian" and, 12–16
racial disparities, 125–37, 345
  academic achievement and, 62–63
  assessment of, 128–29
  discipline and, 132–37
  in "gifted" education, 99, 126–31
  imprecise analysis of, 25–26
  in politics, 120–21
  special education and, 310–11
  tracking and, 318–22
racial group experiences, xviii–xix,
    33–60, 150, 343–45
  animosity and, 127
  children's conversations and, 34–38
  curriculum and, 141–53
  dehumanization and, 56–60
  individuality and, 61–73
  internalized oppression and, 50–55
  shared language in, 39–42
  student identity and, 44–49
  teacher's response to, 287–89

racial hierarchies, in school reforms, 262–66
racial identity. *See under* identity
racial inequalities, xxi–xxii
  See also opportunity; racial disparities; racial oppression; racism
racialized society, 17–31
  courageous conversations in, 18–23
  equal opportunity and, 24–27
  failure of caring in, 28–31
  schools within, 334–35
racial labels
  hyphenated, in U.S., 15
  on products, 6
racial oppression
  critical analysis of, 156–60
  internalized, 50–55
racial profiling, 63–64, 239
racism
  Arabs and, 177–78
  definitions of, xvii, 238–39, 246–47
  demographics and, 200–202
  educational policy and, 62–63
  internalized oppression and, 50–55
  intervention and, 239–40
  linguistic dimension of, 99, 102–6
  Native Americans and, 191–92, 224
  parents fighting, 316
  scientific, 12–13
  as shared problem, 228
  structural, 28–31, 156–60, 302–3, 311, 329, 334–35
raíces. See roots *(raíces)*, cultural and linguistic
Rampton, Ben, 42
Real Alternative Program (RAP), 135
"Regarding Race" project, 142–45
representations, racialized, 187–89, 192
  See also images
research projects, 196–97
revolutionary hope, 337–40
Riley, Patricia, 182
Riley, Richard, 103
role models, 116–18, 135
  from the community, 48, 120–24, 183–84
role-playing, 243–44
Rolón-Dow, Rosalie, 30

roots *(raíces)*, cultural and linguistic, 294–98
Rosaldo, Renato, 223
Rubin, Beth C., 95

safe spaces, 58, 166, 214, 264
  cocooning and, 44–49
  in predominantly white classrooms, 226–29
San Antonio v. Rodriguez, 62
Sarroub, Loukia, *All American Yemeni Girls,* 100
scaffolding, grouping and, 92, 94
school experiences
  in classrooms, 211–34
  conversations about race in, 235–51
  faculty conversations about, 253–71
  "race" of teachers and, 273–90
school policy, antiracist, 246–51
school reforms
  effective practices and, 269
  recurring racial hierarchies in, 262–66
  resources and, 269–70
  shared understandings in, 268–69
  spearheading school-wide, 267–71
  sustained effort in, 270
Schultz, Katherine, 221
science, 7, 114–19
scientific racism, 12–13
Seale, Doris, 182
segregation, 62, 264–65
"self-fulfilling prophecy," 87–88
Sharma, Sanjay, 190
silences, 169–70
  in the classroom, 217–24
  in dialogue, 19–21
Singleton, Glenn E., 22–23
skills
  basic, 86–89
  gaps in, 85–95, 114–15, 344
  interpreting, 99
skin color, race theory and, 5–6
Skin We're In, The (Ward), 315–16
Slapin, Beverly, 182
Sleeter, Christine E., 153
Smitherman, Geneva, 104
social classifications, race and, 6

"Social Limitations and Their
     Explosiveness" (unit), 156
social-structural analysis, 257–60
South Asians, 39–41, 186–89
speaking your truth, 21
special education, 310–11
spotlighting, racial, 230–34
Standard English Proficiency Program for
     Speakers of Black Language, 105
standards, 97–111, 344–45
  meeting high, 78–81
  movement, 98, 100
  multicultural fluency and, 107–11
  nonstandard English and, 102–6
  vs. "standard" knowledge, 90–101
  See also tests, standardized
"standards-plus" orientation, 98, 100
State v. John Mann, 242
Steinberg, Shirley R., 283–84, 286
STEM (science, technology,
     engineering and mathematics)
     fields, 114–18
stereotypes
  of African Americans, 314–17
  of Arabs, 174–77
  discussions of, 143
  intellectual ability and, 9–11, 114–15,
     117
  "model minority," 115, 254, 257–58
  of Native Americans, 181–82,
     191–93, 204, 223
  racialized objectification and, 187
  of South Asians, 186–88
stereotyping, 37, 67–68, 92
strategy, general, xiv–xv
students
  changing names of, 294–96
  feedback from, 215–16, 227, 229,
     247–48
  immigrant, 50–55, 146–49
  marginalization of, 133–34, 219
  monitoring of, 45, 197
  researching their communities, 305–8
  See also under conversations about
     race; identity; individuality; school
     experiences
stylistic presentations, 108–11
stylization, 39–41
Suárez-Orozco, Carola and Marcelo, 147
subjective inequality, 82–84

support
  feedback and, 82–84
  peer, 80
suspension, 133–34, 136

Tatum, Beverly Daniel, 313
Taylor, Amanda, 89
teachable moments, 236–41
teachers
  triangle and triangulating, 299–300
  See also educators
teaching
  expanded definitions of "good," 287–90
  multicultural, 186–87, 189
  relevance of race to, 273–90
  See also curriculum
Teel, Karen, 331–32
Ten Little Rabbits (Grossman and Long),
     181
terrorism, as "cultural trait," 176
tests, standardized, 63, 67, 83, 115
textbooks, 150–51
thinking, levels of, xiv
Thompson, Audrey, 333
Tieken, Mara, 203
Time to Kill, A (film), 157–58
Torre, María Elena, 171
tracking, 90, 166
  racial disparities and, 318–22
tribal autonomy, 204–6
Tripod Project for School Improvement,
     78
trust
  cultivating, 310–13
  gap, 82–83
  lack of, 302–3, 310–12
"try tomorrows," xiv–xv
Tyson, Karolyn, 131

Understanding Self, Race, Gender, and
     Class to Leverage Student
     Achievement (course), 278
U.S. Constitution, Native Americans
     and, 204–6

Valdés, Guadalupe, Learning and Not
     Learning English, 99
Valenzuela, Angela, 55
Velasco, Anne, 318
Vietnamese, 147–48

violence, against Arabs, 176
vulnerability
context and, 239
of white teachers, 276–77

Ward, Janie Victoria, 275, 317
The Skin We're In, 315–16
Weinberg, Meyer, 29–30
Welborn, Jennifer, 5
West, Cornel, xxi, 18–19
Whites, 10, 13, 126
"Caucasian" label of, 12–16
classrooms predominantly of, 226–34,
279
exceptionalism and, 329–32, 339
invisibility and, 283–85

responses of, to racism, 249–50
and vulnerability as teachers,
276–77
Williams, Brian, 318
Williams, Robert, 103
Wimberley, Jesse, 332
Wright, Richard, *Native Son,* 156–58
Wyman, Leisy, 299, 304

X-Clan, 162

Yonezawa, Susan, 216
Yoon, Sam, 122
Young, Iris, 178
Yup'ik community, 299–304
Yuuyaraq, 302

ALSO AVAILABLE FROM THE NEW PRESS

Beyond the Bake Sale: The Essential Guide to Family-School Partnerships
Anne T. Henderson, Karen L. Mapp, Vivian R. Johnson, and Don Davies

A practical, hands-on primer on helping schools and families work better together to improve children's education.

978-1-56584-888-7 (pb)

Black Teachers on Teaching
Michele Foster

An oral history of black teachers that gives "valuable insight into a profession that for African Americans was second only to preaching" (Booklist).

978-1-56584-453-7 (pb)

The Case for Make Believe: Saving Play in a Commercialized World
Susan Linn

From the author of *Consuming Kids*, a clarion call for preserving play in our material world—a book every parent will want to read.

978-1-56584-970-9 (hc)

City Kids, City Schools: More Reports from the Front Row
Edited by William Ayers, Gloria Ladson-Billings, Gregory Michie, and Pedro A. Noguera

This new and timely collection has been compiled by four of the country's most prominent urban educators to provide some of the best writing on life in city schools and neighborhoods.

978-1-59558-338-3 (pb)

City Kids, City Teachers: Reports from the Front Row
Edited by William Ayers and Patricia Ford

A classic collection exploding the stereotypes of city schools, reissued as a companion to *City Kids, City Schools*.

978-1-56584-051-5 (pb)

Dismantling Desegregation: The Quiet Reversal of Brown v. Board of Education
Gary Orfield and Susan E. Eaton

"Powerful case studies . . . the authors convincingly argue that the ideal of desegregation is disappearing."—*Kirkus Reviews*

978-1-56584-401-8 (pb)

Fires in the Bathroom: Advice to Teachers from High School Students
Kathleen Cushman

This groundbreaking book offers original insights into teaching teenagers in today's hard-pressed urban high schools from the point of view of the students themselves. It speaks to both new and established teachers, giving them first-hand information about who their students are and what they need to succeed.

978-1-56584-996-9 (pb)

Fires in the Middle School Bathroom: Advice to Teachers from Middle Schoolers
Kathleen Cushman and Laura Rogers

Following on the heels of the bestselling *Fires in the Bathroom*, which brought the insights of high school students to teachers and parents, Kathleen Cushman now turns her attention to the crucial and challenging middle grades, joining forces with adolescent psychologist Laura Rogers.

978-1-59558-111-2 (hc)

Made in America: Immigrant Students in Our Public Schools
Laurie Olsen

With a new introduction by the author, this timely reissue probes the challenges facing teachers and immigrant students in our public schools.

978-1-59558-349-9 (pb)

The New Press Education Reader: Leading Educators Speak Out
Edited by Ellen Gordon Reeves

The New Press Education Reader brings together the work of progressive writers and educators—among them Lisa Delpit, Herbert Kohl, William Ayers, and Maxine Greene—to discuss the most pressing and challenging issues now facing us, including schools and social justice, equity issues, tracking and testing, combating racism and homophobia, and more.

978-1-59558-110-5 (pb)

Other People's Children: Cultural Conflict in the Classroom
Lisa Delpit

In this anniversary edition of a classic, MacArthur Award–winning author Lisa Delpit develops ideas about ways teachers can be better "cultural transmitters" in the classroom, where prejudice, stereotypes, and cultural assumptions breed ineffective education.

978-1-59558-074-0 (pb)

Race: How Blacks and Whites Think and Feel about the American Obsession
Studs Terkel

Based on interviews with over one hundred Americans, this book is a rare and revealing look at how people feel about race in the United States.

978-1-56584-989-1 (pb)

Racism Explained to My Daughter
Tahar Ben Jelloun

The prizewinning book of advice about racism from a bestselling author to his daughter, introduced by Bill Cosby. The paperback version includes responses from William Ayers, Lisa Delpit, and Patricia Williams.

978-1-59558-029-0 (pb)

She Would Not Be Moved: How We Tell the Story of Rosa Parks and the Montgomery Bus Boycott
Herbert Kohl

From a prizewinning educator, a meditation that reveals the misleading way generations of children have been taught the story of Rosa Parks, offering guidance on how to present the Civil Rights movement to young students.

978-1-59558-127-3 (pb)

The Skin That We Speak: Thoughts on Language and Culture in the Classroom
Edited by Lisa Delpit and Joanne Kilgour Dowdy

A collection that gets to the heart of the relationship between language and power in the classroom.

978-1-59558-350-5 (pb)